THE FRENCH NAVY AND AMERICAN INDEPENDENCE

THE FRENCH NAVY

AND

AMERICAN INDEPENDENCE

A Study of Arms and Diplomacy, 1774-1787

Jonathan R. Dull

PRINCETON UNIVERSITY PRESS

PRINCETON, NEW JERSEY

Copyright © 1975 by Princeton University Press
Published by Princeton University Press, Princeton and London

ALL RIGHTS RESERVED

Library of Congress Cataloging in Publication Data will
be found on the last printed page of this book
Publication of this book has been aided by the
Andrew W. Mellon Foundation
This book has been composed in Linotype Janson
Printed in the United States of America
by Princeton University Press, Princeton, New Jersey

Observe good faith and justice toward all nations. Cultivate peace and harmony with all. Religion and morality enjoin this conduct. And can it be that good policy does not equally enjoin it?

George Washington
Farewell Address
17 September 1796

CONTENTS

Contents

Contents

PREFACE

W ARS are too important to be left to military historians. The study of war generally has been restricted to the recounting of battles or at best campaigns. Naval history in particular has been dominated by the descendants of Mahan, sharing all too often his antiquarian interest in battle tactics and his political biases. Although political, social, and economic historians are now beginning to ask their own questions about armies and navies, diplomatic historians have been slow to follow them. This is unfortunate since the conduct of diplomacy, particularly during wartime, is greatly influenced by the instruments of force at its disposal, by the requirements of war strategy, and by the appeal of victory. In the belief that military history is an essential component of diplomatic history I have studied the French navy as the means by which French diplomacy won its greatest (and most costly) victory of the eighteenth century, the achievement of American independence.

This book is not about the French navy as a political pressure group—lacking an instrument like the English Parliament to transmit political pressure, French naval officers as such enjoyed little influence within the French court. Instead, it treats the share of long-range naval requirements in the French decision to aid the American colonists, the part played by naval rivalry in the transition from limited aid to full-scale war, and the ways naval considerations affected French wartime diplomacy, particularly the French direction of the complex alliance system which finally defeated Britain. There is a good deal about shipbuilding, the naval budget, and even naval administration, insofar as they affected France's diplomatic options. The major naval subject missing will be battle tactics, for I am interested in the strategic setting and consequences of battles rather than their mechanics.

Since I believe both the background and the immediate consequences of the French participation in the American war integral to this topic, my work extends from the accession of Louis XVI on 10 May 1774 to the death on 13 February 1787 of the Count de Vergennes, the principal author of the French intervention. It is based on approximately equal amounts of research in the naval collection of the French national archives and in the diplomatic correspondence of the French foreign ministry at the Quai d'Orsay. A final point—the first two-thirds of this book originally was written as a doctoral dissertation,[1] from which I have eliminated a large body of information which I felt was of interest only to those preparing to do research on related subjects. For such readers I recommend reading the two versions in conjunction.

I would like to acknowledge the help of Gerald Cavanaugh (who directed my thesis), the late Raymond J. Sontag, Orville T. Murphy, Svetlana Kluge Harris, Richard Herr, Brian Morton, John Schaar, Charles Berberich, Robert Hamburger, my typists Barbara Zelwer and Penny Ruby, and my editor Sanford Thatcher. My family has been of continual help: my mother Mrs. Earl Dull; my parents-in-law Mr. and Mrs. Robert West; my sister and cartographer Caroline Dull Hamburger; and above all my wife Agnes and elder daughter Veronica. I wish to dedicate this book to my brave and wonderful younger daughter Caroline.

[1] Jonathan R. Dull, "The French Navy and American Independence: Naval Factors in French Diplomacy and War Strategy, 1774–1780" (Ph.D. diss., University of California, Berkeley, 1972). It has been microfilmed by University Microfilms; the order number is 72-24,439. This work will be cited hereafter as Dull: Dissertation.

GLOSSARY

Aʟʟ translations unless otherwise noted are my own. I have attempted when translating or paraphrasing documents to follow the phraseology of the original as closely as good style permits. Foreign Ministry documents from Spanish sources here cited are in French translation.

Allied: "Allied" refers to French, American, Spanish, and Dutch forces at war with Britain. "Britain" and "England" are used interchangeably, and, with no greater accuracy, the United Provinces of the Netherlands has been referred to as both "Holland" and "the Netherlands."

Armaments, Matériel, Munitions: "Armaments" refers to ships having crews and placed in service or to the act of placing them in service. "Matériel" refers to all the equipment necessary to place ships in service—sails, masts, hemp, etc. "Munitions" refers to guns and ammunition.

Battalion: The battalion was the basic infantry unit of the French army during the war. An infantry regiment usually, but not always, contained two of these 650- to 850-man units (French and more often British regiments sometimes contained only a single battalion). The term "battalion" has been used for a regiment of only a single battalion.

Council of State: "Council of state" is my translation for *le Conseil d'Etat du Roi*, the supreme advisory body to the king, whose members, the ministers of state, generally numbering about a half-dozen, functioned much as did the members of the British cabinet—although they lacked the parliamentary responsibility which could also act as a buffer against the king's displeasure.

Fleet and Squadron: "Fleet" refers to all the ships operating from a European port and "squadron" to a detachment, however large.

Military: The adjective "military" includes "naval" unless it is clear from the context that only army affairs are discussed.

Money: The basic unit of currency mentioned is the livre. I have used the following conversion formulas: 23 livres: £ 1 (eighteenth century), as recommended by Robert and Elborg Forster, *European Society in the Eighteenth Century* (New York: Harper Torchbooks, 1969), p. 410; 5 livres: 1 Spanish piastre, the standard conversion figure used in diplomatic correspondence of this period. The Forsters estimate that the livre in 1760 was roughly equivalent in purchasing power to the American dollar in 1968. This rough equivalency would still seem valid for 1774 and the present.

Naval Minister: The translations "Naval Minister" and "Foreign Minister" have been used for the secretaries of state having charge respectively of naval affairs (among others) and foreign affairs. Their "department" refers to all under their charge; "ministry" refers to the central directing body of each department. Note that neither was necessarily a "minister of state" (see Council of State).

Overhaul: Both *le radoub* and *la refonte* have been translated as "overhaul," although the former was less extensive an operation than the latter. The even more extensive *reconstruire* has been translated as "reconstruct."

Ship of the Line: A ship of the line was, in theory, a ship of sufficient strength to fight in the standard line-ahead or column formation of the eighteenth century. French usage of the eighteenth century has been followed in counting 50-gun ships as ships of the line, although they were not always used as such. All English figures have been adjusted to correspond to this usage. A "three-decker" is a ship of the line with at least 90 guns (on 3 decks). Smaller warships, such as the frigate of 22 to 44 guns and the corvette of up to 20 guns, were used for scouting, convoy escort, etc. *La gabare* has been translated as "store ship" and *la flûte* as "transport." These ships did not generally engage in combat, although a warship serving temporarily as an armed auxiliary (*en flûte*) would generally have her guns returned on reaching her destination and revert to her former designation.

Windward and Leeward Islands: Eighteenth century French usage has been followed in referring to those islands east of Porto Rico as the Windward Islands and Porto Rico, Santo Domingo, Cuba, and Jamaica as the Leeward Islands. It should be remembered that sailing ships sail easily to destinations to leeward but must laboriously tack to windward.

MAPS

The Windward Islands

Atlantic Ocean

20°   20°

ST. THOMAS
Danish

PORTO RICO
Spanish

ST. MARTIN
Dutch

ST. EUSTATIUS
Dutch

ST. CHRISTOPHER
British

ANTIGUA
British

GUADELOUPE
French

DOMINICA
British

15°   15°

Caribbean

MARTINIQUE
French
Fort Royal

ST. LUCIA
French

ST. VINCENT
British

BARBADOS
British

GRENADA
British

TOBAGO
British

Porto Cabello
SOUTH AMERICA

TRINIDAD
British   10°

To Cayenne

65°   60° W of G

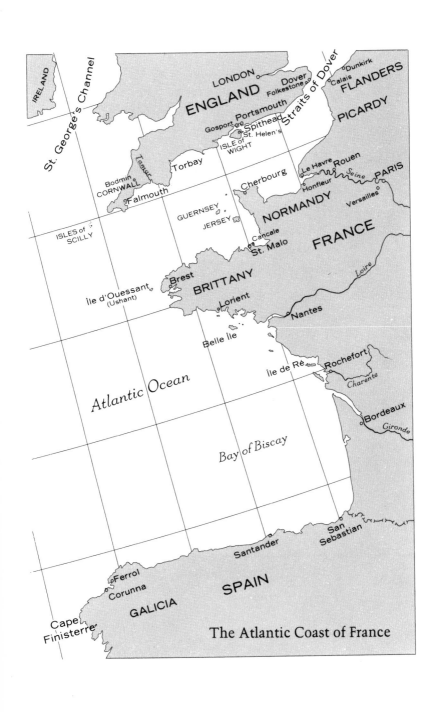

The Atlantic Coast of France

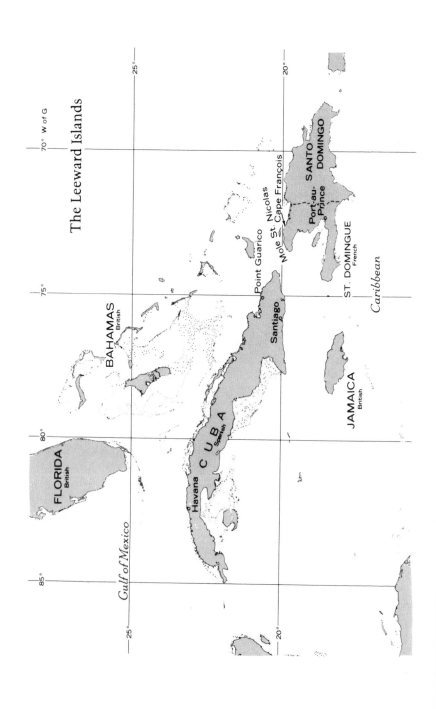

The Leeward Islands

THE FRENCH NAVY AND AMERICAN INDEPENDENCE

CHAPTER ONE

1774—The Inheritance of Louis XVI

1. The Diplomatic Inheritance

NINE days after the death of Louis XV, the royal council of state heard a report prepared by a senior member of the ministry of foreign affairs. This report had been drafted to inform the new king, Louis XVI, of France's diplomatic position. It began:

> Sire, I believe it is my duty to place under the eyes of Your Majesty the state of foreign affairs of your kingdom and its relations with foreign powers. It will be seen that they find themselves in a fortunate calm. No disagreement in fact menaces its [the kingdom's] tranquility and neither the dignity of its crown nor the interest of its people have any blow to carry or to fear.[1]

Peace was always precarious in eighteenth century Europe, whose states were dominated by aristocracies justified by war, but in May 1774 no major crisis seemed near.[2] The six-year-old war between Russia and France's ally, the Ottoman Empire (Turkey, but including the Balkans), had exhausted both combatants; the final campaign, already be-

[1] French foreign ministry archives, Memoirs and Documents collection, France 584: 76, "Tableau succinct de la situation politique de la France vis-à-vis des autres puissances de la Europe," read to the king in council, 19 May 1774 (drawn up by M. Gérard for M. Bertin, interim secretary of state). I will follow a simplified format for footnotes from primary sources, giving the series (by country for documents from the foreign ministry archives, by letter for documents from the naval archives) followed by volume number and page number. The documentary series are described in the first section of the bibliography.

[2] The best introduction to eighteenth century diplomacy is Albert Sorel, *Europe and the French Revolution*, vol. 1, *The Political Traditions of the Old Régime*, trans. Alfred Cobban and J. W. Hunt (Garden City, N.Y.: Doubleday and Co., Anchor Books, 1971).

gun, ended in July 1774 with the Treaty of Kutchuk-Kainardji. The other Eastern powers, Prussia and Austria, were ruled by monarchs grown old and cautious. The situation in Western Europe was even more reassuring. France had fought four major wars in the past eighty-five years against Great Britain. Numerous sources of dispute still remained from the Peace of Paris of 1763: the presence of an English commissioner to prevent the fortification of Dunkirk, English harassment of French fishermen off Newfoundland, unresolved disputes in India. At the moment, however, English attention was concentrated on resolving a worsening series of crises in North America, which had culminated in the Boston Tea Party of 1773 and, at virtually this very moment, Parliament's responding Coercive Acts. Throughout 1774, French diplomatic reports stressed the current British desire for untroubled relations with France. Charles-Jean Garnier, the first secretary of legation (and acting French diplomatic representative)[3] in Britain wrote in a dispatch of July 1774 about contested fishing rights off Newfoundland: "By principle the English ministers in general can hardly be favorable to our fishing which they regard with reason as the nursery of our best sailors and one of the most firm supports of our navy, but they love peace above all things and desire nothing so much as to live with us in the best harmony."[4]

The following month Garnier wrote that England, far from desiring any new conquests, could only regard a foreign war as fatal to its existence. This was because of its current debts, its growing public expenses, and its declining credit, as well as because of the disproportion between the

[3] The French ambassador, the Count de Guines, was in France awaiting a hearing on charges of malfeasance of which he was cleared in July 1775.

[4] French foreign ministry archives, Political Correspondence collection, England 506: 11, Garnier to the French foreign minister, the Count de Vergennes, 1 July 1774. All further diplomatic correspondence cited will be from the Political Correspondence collection unless noted as Memoirs and Documents.

home island and its extended possessions with their universal spirit of revolt. Garnier believed that the only things that could currently determine England to war would be the necessity of repelling a violent insult or the certainty that she was to be attacked.[5]

If no storm seemed likely to intrude on the new reign, neither did it seem likely that the nineteen-year-old king would set about attracting one. The last three years of Louis XV's reign were dominated by domestic affairs. His grandson immediately abandoned the attack on the Parlements upon which Louis XV's domestic policy had hinged, but it quickly appeared evident that Louis XVI would also concentrate on strengthening the domestic position of the monarchy. This likelihood was based not only on Louis' unmartial character and interests but upon the choices for his chief political appointments.

The most critical were not necessarily the secretaries of state who headed the great departments which administered executive policy—the army minister, navy minister, foreign minister, controller general of finances, and minister of the king's household.[6] These positions despite their great importance did not guarantee entry into the body which advised the king twice weekly on the great questions of state, the royal council of state. During 1774 Louis XVI appointed seven men (called ministers of state) to the body; of those, two were holdovers from the preceding reign and two were secretaries of state of short duration. The last three were to contest domination over the young king and thus domination over French domestic and foreign policy, since Louis exercised his theoretically absolute powers through the council (which monitored the departments of state).

The king, inexperienced and insecure, depended for psy-

---

[5] England 506: 155–156. Garnier to Vergennes, 10 August 1774.

[6] Technically there was another secretary of state at Louis XVI's accession, Henri-Léonard-Jean-Baptiste Bertin, having charge of mines, manufactures, etc. His post was abolished in 1780 and had never been important.

chological support and political advice most heavily on Jean-Frédéric Phélypeaux, Count de Maurepas (1701–1781). Maurepas, having been French naval minister for twenty-five years, had been dismissed from public life by Louis XV in 1749. Although Louis XVI wished to be his own chief minister and gave Maurepas neither a department nor title of superiority over his fellow ministers of state, he became in fact equivalent to a prime minister.[7] His political acumen, his intelligence, and his influence with the king gave him great power which he devoted solely to the maintenance of his own position. Lacking interest and experience in foreign affairs, indolent, basically solitary, he had little inclination for risking his own position to the chances of war.

The most active member of the council promised to be Anne-Robert-Jacques Turgot (1727–1781), naval minister for six weeks and then controller-general of finances. With the king's support Turgot soon undertook a program for the regeneration of the monarchy and state. By his character and fate Turgot resembled not a bureaucrat but a tragic hero: no royal servant since Colbert had equaled his genius, his vision, and his energy, but Turgot's arrogance and ambition aided his enemies in undercutting the king's trust and in preparing the destruction of his political life, his program, and finally his king. As a *philosophe* his personal philosophy was opposed to war; his political program was menaced by it; his last political act was to fight courageously and hopelessly against French involvement in Britain's war with her American colonies.

The last of Louis' influential advisors was Charles Gravier, Count de Vergennes (1717–1787), minister of state and the new foreign minister. He too seemed an unlikely advocate of war. During the 1760s French foreign policy had been aggressively anti-English. The French foreign minister, the Duke de Choiseul, had even sent a secret

[7] Maurepas, however, was named in 1776 head of one of Louis' other advisory councils, the Council of Finances.

agent to report on dissatisfaction in British North America. Following Choiseul's fall in December 1770 and the diversion of Louis XV's attention to his domestic opponents, Anglo-French tensions had diminished. Although Louis XV's last foreign minister, the Duke d'Aiguillon, was dismissed by the new king, Choiseul, the archenemy of Louis XVI's deceased father, failed to recover his position. Instead, Louis XVI gave the department to Vergennes, who had served Choiseul as ambassador to the Ottoman Empire and Aiguillon as ambassador to Sweden. Vergennes was a markedly different sort of man than his bitter enemy, the flamboyant and aggressive Choiseul. In many ways Vergennes represented at its best the conservatism of the state servant of Old Regime France. Vergennes had been raised from childhood in the diplomatic corps and had spent his life in indefatigable service to it and its traditions.[8] It is difficult in reading his correspondence not to acquire great respect for this man of deep kindness, urbanity, gravity, and dedication. What perhaps takes longest to fully comprehend is the cohesion and simplicity of the principles which underlay his conduct of diplomacy. For Vergennes the function of diplomacy was to maintain the security of his monarch's possessions, which in turn depended on the maintenance of peace in Europe. Peace in Europe depended on preserving the balance of power from whomever would disturb it—in the last analysis, upon maintaining the status quo. Vergennes' ideal was Cardinal Fleury, foreign minister during his childhood, who through cooperation with Britain had brought France her greatest security in

[8] The best description of Vergennes is Orville T. Murphy, "Charles Gravier de Vergennes: Portrait of an Old Régime Diplomat," *Political Science Quarterly* 83 (1968): 400–418. The traditions I mention include those eulogized in Sir Harold Nicolson, *The Evolution of Diplomatic Method* (London: Constable and Co., 1954)—civility, confidentiality, professionalism. It should be noted that Vergennes had participated in the secret diplomacy pursued by Louis XV without the knowledge of Choiseul and Aiguillon. For Vergennes' admiration of Fleury see Memoirs and Documents, France 446: 352, Vergennes to Louis, c. January 1781.

[7]

the last century. By his ability Vergennes would gradually win from the king considerable independence to implement his system—a system grounded in a contradiction.

Vergennes was a man dedicated to peace who assumed office at a moment of calm and yet ironically he, more than anyone, was to be responsible for bringing France into the American war—a war which so weakened the financial base of the monarchy as to lead to the crisis that finally destroyed all he so faithfully served.

The explanation of Vergennes' tragedy is the perilous disequilibrium of Vergennes' diplomatic universe. The moment of calm at Louis' accession presented to Vergennes not stability, but a brief opportunity to right that universe before disaster struck. The French war for America was a preventive war, fought not to forestall immediate danger, but to reverse the gradual disintegration of the system upon which in the long run French security was based.

French diplomacy, like all Old Regime diplomacy, was based on the concept of the balance of power—the belief that international order was effected through the cooperation of the relatively weak against the threateningly strong. France had two particularly strong reasons for believing her security menaced should another of the great states of Europe threaten the balance of power by disturbing the status quo. First, the security of French borders was protected by a cordon of minor states, from the semiautonomous Austrian Netherlands to the Republic of Genoa, separating her from those who might invade her. No document was more vital to France than the Treaty of Westphalia, dividing Germany into two great states of Prussia and Austria to be played off against each other and hundreds of minor states to be protected. Second was the isolation of France among the great powers of the continent. In theory, Louis of France and Maria Theresa of Austria were allied much as were Frederick of Prussia and Catherine of Russia. In fact, the eighteen-year-old alliance with France's ancient enemy was now directed against Austria itself. It was used solely to gain leverage to restrain any Austrian expansion. The façade would be broken should England end her diplomatic isolation (and break her own nominal links with Prussia) or should the conservative Maria Theresa die. Her son Joseph was already her coregent; his ambition and his unstable character threatened crises the French-Hapsburg alliance could not absorb.

France's other major ally was Spain, linked with France not only by the Family Compact of 1761, but by ties of blood between their two kings, both members of the House of Bourbon.[9] Spain was of great potential use against England, but of almost no weight in continental affairs. The Spanish navy could add enough support to the French to match England's fleet; Spanish trade was a powerful motive for England to keep peace; Spain held an English ally, Portugal, a perpetual hostage. To the powers of the continent, on the other hand, Spain was a poor country without a major army and of no importance. France's real alliance system was in fact an alliance with all the minor powers of Europe against the other great continental powers—Prussia, Austria, and Russia. French subsidies and support bolstered most of the minor courts of Europe—Stockholm, Genoa, Munich, Warsaw, Constantinople, and many more.

This alliance system was utterly dependent on the ability of France to intimidate those who would disturb it and to use the mutual jealousy of the other great powers to find support for any endangered member. In both respects the system had suffered tremendous shocks. By the Treaty of

[9] Under the terms of the Family Compact Spain was obligated to provide 20 ships of the line, six frigates, 10,000 infantry, and 2,000 cavalry to France should France be attacked; France was to provide similar aid (except 6,000 cavalry) if Spain were attacked. Edward Corwin, *French Policy and the American Alliance of 1778* (Princeton, N.J.: Princeton University Press, 1916), 35-36. Louis referred to King Charles III of Spain as his uncle, and I will follow this usage. Actually, Louis' great-grandfather was the brother of Charles' father. "The Bourbons" signifies Louis and Charles only, although another member of the same royal house occupied the throne of the Kingdom of Naples.

Paris England had not only defeated France, but humiliated her. Vergennes wrote: "The consideration and the influence of any power is measured and regulated by the opinion one has of its intrinsic forces."[10] Could one respect the intrinsic force of France when an English commissioner sat in Dunkirk, when English w. ships interfered with French fishermen in the French fishing grounds of Newfoundland, when English ambassadors treated France contemptuously? The English blows to French prestige represented as real a loss to France's diplomatic weight as had the French expulsion from Canada. Even more dangerous for France was the despoiling of Poland in 1772 by Austria, Prussia, and Russia. Vergennes agonized, "If force is right, if convenience is a title, what will henceforth be the security of states?" Heretofore the major states had protected the minor lest a rival gain an advantage; now the major powers had proportioned the spoils of a helpless neighbor. Vergennes looked on this brave new world with horror and sought to restrain its forces.

As he realized, the solution to his problems lay in reconciliation with England. Such a reconciliation would permit diversion of French resources from the navy to the army. Of ever greater importance, Anglo-French cooperation could greatly limit the power of the other continental powers which had great armies but not the finances to engage in major wars. Only from France or England with their numerous colonies and enormous trade could come subsidies. A half-century before, the England and France of Walpole and Fleury had cooperated as equals; France had been se-

[10] The Treaty of Paris (1763) ended the Seven Years War. For the French alliance system and Vergennes' view of the current diplomatic scene see both his instructions to his ambassador in Vienna and his brilliant memoir to Louis XVI (from which the quotations are taken): France, Commission des Archives Diplomatiques, *Recueil des instructions données aux ambassadeurs et ministres de France depuis les traités de Westphalie jusqu'à la Révolution Française*, 1: 454–500 (hereafter cited as *Recueil*), instructions for the Baron de Breteuil, 28 December 1774; French national archives, general holdings, K 164 (papers of Louis XVI) item no. 3, Vergennes to Louis, December 1774.

cure, but now England was the England of Pitt: arrogant, aloof, contemptuous of France. To reduce England to a position of equality, France had to take from her a share of her strength, her monopoly of American trade and markets. This book will tell how Vergennes sought and won a war which finally failed to weaken England, which failed to bring about the rapprochement he sought, and which raised dangers from within the monarchy far greater than those which threatened it from without.

2. The Naval Inheritance

In Old Regime France, naval affairs passed through cycles. A period of concentration on naval construction, repairs, and operations was generally followed by a diplomatic crisis or war, which in turn was often followed by a period of inattention to the navy. The last fifteen years of Louis XV's reign were those of such a cycle. The French navy was almost completely destroyed by the British navy in a series of battles in 1759. In October 1761, Choiseul, the foreign minister, became naval minister as well. For nine years he and his cousin, the Duke de Choiseul-Praslin (naval minister from August 1766 to December 1770) rebuilt the French navy. They added new ships, filled the dockyards with matériel, and reformed naval administration. When the crisis with England for which they had prepared finally occurred (over the possession of the Falkland Islands), Louis XV and his Spanish allies backed down and Choiseul fell from power. During Louis XV's last three years naval affairs were downgraded. Not even enough ships of the line were built to replace those scrapped because of age or lost by accident and repairs were not undertaken to offset the aging of the fleet.[1] Garnier reported in

---

[1] For the definition of "ship of the line" see the Glossary. The theoretical life span of a ship of the line was about a dozen years (although this varied according to the port of construction); ships were frequently rebuilt, but kept their original name. Alexandre Lambert de

1774 that England had 142 ships of the line, of which 72 were in service or ready to be immediately armed;[2] the French naval ministry could report only 64 ships of the line, of which 34 could be readied if needed.[3] In fact the French navy was even less prepared for hostilities than its numbers suggested. To save expenses the French navy had consumed the reserves of masts, wood, hemp and other naval supplies that the Choiseuls had accumulated. Until the dockyards were refilled, the French navy was barely capable of fitting a fleet for the most limited operations.

An even more immediate crisis almost prohibited even the routine movement of ships. Louis XV's last minister, Bourgeois de Boynes, had attempted extensive reforms of naval administration. Although many were excellent in theory, their implemention produced such chaos that the navy could barely send ships from one port of France to another.[4] Four sets of measures were chiefly responsible. First, Boynes attempted to organize France's naval forces like the French army. He divided its ships and officers into eight brigades. The brigades were so autonomous that officers could be promoted only within their own brigade and ships equipped only from the brigades' stores. In practice the system had to be ignored even to outfit a small training squadron.

Members of the naval officer corps were outraged not

Sainte-Croix, *Essai sur l'administration de la marine de France, 1689–1792* (Paris: Calmann-Levy, 1892), 269. During these three years, six new ships of the line were completed, but eight were sold, accidentally destroyed, or demolished.

[2] England 596: 163, Garnier to Vergennes, 10 August 1774. This includes 50-gun ships and ships in construction.

[3] Naval holdings of the French national archives, B⁵9: unpaged, "Etat de la marine, 1774." I have made slight adjustments to the figures, since the source lists two ships of the line already demolished. The ships of the line and frigates of the French navy in August 1774 are listed in Appendixes B and D.

[4] Vincent-Félix Brun, *Guerres maritimes de la France: Port de Toulon, ses armements, son administration depuis son origine jusqu'à nos jours* (Paris: Henri Plon, 1861), 1, 526–529.

only by interference with their chances of promotion but also with the insult of seeing naval traditions violated. A second set of measures also increased the navy's similarity to the army. The navy was given increased responsibility for providing its own infantry and artillery support and regiments of naval troops were assigned to the brigades and naval "colonels" named to command them.

Another set of measures produced still further resentment. The majority of French naval officers had been trained as naval cadets aboard ship.[5] Boynes threatened their status by establishing a competing naval academy at Le Havre with a fixed curriculum supplemented by training cruises.

The most sweeping and disastrous of Boynes' reforms pertained to the administration of the naval ports. The naval ports (Brest, Toulon, Rochefort, Lorient, and some smaller ports) had functioned by a system of competition established a century before by Colbert. Power was divided along clear lines between a civilian official, the intendant, generally devoted to economy, and a military officer, the port commandant, devoted to the fleet's preparedness. The intendant commanded a body of civilian officers (the corps of officers of administration or "officers of the pen"), the port commandant, a body of military officers (the "officers of the sword"), some of whom were "officers of the line," others port officers restricted to service in the ports. Choiseul had given increased power to the military officers but had preserved Colbert's basic system. Boynes sought to replace the competition between "pen" and "sword" by co-operation, but in practice produced only a breakdown of lines of responsibility and a struggle for power between intendant, port commandant, the "colonels" and the head of the port officers. In January 1774 he even tried to com-

---

[5] Of 944 naval officers (1 January 1776), 832 had been naval cadets ("gardes du pavillon" or "gardes de la marine"). Didier Neuville, *Etat sommaire des archives de la Marine antérieures à la Révolution* (Paris: L. Baudoin, 1898), 357.

bine naval engineers, port officers, and officers of administration into a single corps, in effect attempting to solve disputes over power by giving everyone the same uniform.

Louis XVI, though not of a martial temperament, was
extremely concerned with naval affairs, largely because of
his childhood interest in geographical exploration. The brilliant Turgot was placed at the head of the naval department, but since the problem of royal finances was even
more pressing he was soon moved. His replacement was
selected for the purposes of reorganizing naval administration and overcoming the navy's factional struggles. On 22
August 1774, Louis chose as naval minister another proven
administrator with no previous experience of naval matters,
Antoine-Raymond-Gualbert-Gabriel de Sartine (1729–
1801), the lieutenant-general of the Paris police. The son of
a Catalan intendant and long a friend of Diderot, Sartine
had been responsible for the administration of the city of
Paris since 1759. He became one of the most capable naval
ministers in French history: a firm yet tactful leader, a prudent and courageous war minister, an innovative and me-
ticulous administrator, a man who took particular pride in
the health of his ships' crews. He took as an assistant one of
the navigators whose work so interested the king, Charles
Claret, Chevalier de Fleurieu, who himself became naval
minister in August 1790. Sartine had a wide range of responsibilities. In addition to the navy proper, the twelve
bureaus of the navy department handled the administration
of colonies, maritime commerce, fisheries, a number of consulates, commercial establishments in the Levant and even
the Chamber of Commerce of Marseille, which had an official function in Mediterranean commerce.[6] Sartine eventually also headed committees to reform colonial legislation
and to overhaul the French Levantine establishments and

---

[6] In 1775 these bureaus employed ten first secretaries and 105 under-
secretaries and clerks. G. Dagnaud, *L'administration centrale de la
Marine sous l'ancien régime* (Paris: M. Imhaus et R. Chapelot, 1913),
35; Neuville, *Etat sommaire*, xxv–xlii, 313–315, 449–450.

sat on the Council of Dispatches, the Royal Council of Commerce and, after 1778, the Council of Prizes.[7] He brought to these new tasks the same abilities and dedication he had devoted to improving the administration of Paris. His prior lack of knowledge or interest in naval matters was thus irrelevant; Sartine quickly became as much a spokesman for naval interests as if he had been trained from childhood to be naval minister as had Maurepas.

Sartine's first priority was to reestablish order in the administration of ports. In November 1774 he successfully requested from Louis a return to the administrative forms of Choiseul, pending a comprehensive review of the working of the ports.[8] In November 1774 the administration of ports and arsenals was reestablished according to the ordinances of 1765. Two ordinances of 26 December 1774 regulated the service of the navy's infantry and artillery, reducing the former from 144 companies to 100 and returning much of the responsibility for the latter to the army.[9] Finally, on 2 March 1775 Sartine abolished the Royal Academy of the Navy and cut in half the number of naval cadets.[10] As order returned, Sartine turned to a more recalcitrant set of problems—the limits of his department's budget, the lack of naval matériel, and the disrepair of the fleet.

[7] See the *Almanach Royal* (Paris: D'Houry) for 1775–1781.

[8] G 127: 214–221, untitled and undated memoir, identified G 127: 204 as Sartine to Louis, November 1774.

[9] Gabriel Coste, *Les anciennes troupes de la marine (1622–1792)* (Paris: L. Baudoin, 1893), 231.

[10] Abbé (Albert) Anthiaume, *Un ancêtre du Borda au Havre* (Paris: Ernest Dumont, 1920), 11–13. Sartine argued with some justification that the school was poorly situated for training cruises (which were held in the Bay of Biscay) and could not produce enough officers.

CHAPTER TWO

1775—An Empire at Peace, An Empire at War

1. The French Navy and the Defense
of the French Empire

IT is a measure of the lack of immediate danger from Britain that at the beginning of 1775 the French navy needed at sea or fitting for cruises only a single ship of the line, half a dozen frigates, and a small number of corvettes, transports, and storeships. These ships were assigned an area of responsibility from the English Channel and Bay of Biscay to the Caribbean, Eastern Mediterranean, and Indian Ocean. The first responsibility of the French navy naturally was the protection of France's own coasts. During the last war the British had raided French seaports and in 1759 had even captured Belle Île off Brittany. Although the French had a fleet at Brest to protect against a surprise attack on their coast, they in fact relied upon their 170,000-man peacetime army as their chief deterrent. The British with only 10,612 troops in England and Wales[1] kept 20 ships of the line partially manned to act as "guard ships"; the French in 1775 did not even have regular coastal patrols. Only naval supply ships or an occasional warship changing ports joined the merchantmen passing along her coast.[2]

Far more dependent on the French navy were the French possessions in the Caribbean. There were five major French colonies: Saint Domingue (now Haiti), Martinique, Guadeloupe, Saint Lucia, and Cayenne (on the South American

---

[1] French figures are for 1 May 1774. Léon Mention, *Le comte de Saint-Germain et ses reformes* (Paris: L. Baudoin, 1884), 318. British figures are for April 1775. Piers Mackesy, *The War for America, 1775–1783* (Cambridge, Mass.: Harvard University Press, 1964), 524–525.

[2] For example, the ships of the line *Saint-Michel* and *Artésien* were used in early 1775 to transfer 1,100 troops from Brest to Rochefort and remained there for overhaul. B¹80: 39–40, untitled memoir of September 1774; see also B²404: 85.

coast). These islands had a white population of 50,000 to 60,000, roughly comparable to the white population of the English colonies of Jamaica, Antigua, Saint Christopher, Dominica, Saint Vincent, Barbados, Grenada, and Tobago. From these a militia of 24,000 was drawn,[3] but the colonies' chief protection was four colonial regiments (two at Saint Domingue and one each at Martinique and Guadeloupe), under the control of the navy department which had to replace annual losses from disease of up to 10 percent of their 6,000 troops. The militia and troops had the collateral function of protecting the French colonists against revolts by their slaves (outnumbering colonists by five or ten to one, depending on the island); slave labor was the source of the colonies' trade which together accounted for about two-fifths of all French imports and one-tenth of her exports.[4] The less-productive English colonies had far smaller garrisons; until late 1776 there were less than 2,000 British troops in the West Indies.[5] Given the preponderance of French military strength, the French navy maintained only a token force in the Caribbean. At the beginning of 1775 the only French warships in the West Indies were a frigate and a corvette sent from Toulon to visit Martinique, Saint Domingue, and Jamaica.[6] They were relieved by a frigate sent from Brest in June.

[3] There were 13,000 at Saint Domingue, 7,000 at Martinique, and 4,000 at Guadeloupe. J. Saintoyant, *La colonisation française sous l'ancien régime* (Paris: La renaissance du livre, 1929), 2: 318.

[4] This is based on the average of 1764–1776 computed from the figures in Ruggiero Romano, "Documenti e prime considerazioni intorno alla 'balance du commerce' della Francia dal 1716 al 1780," in *Studi in onore di Armando Sapori* (Milan: Instituto Editoriale Cisalpino, 1957), 2: 1274, 1291. These figures do not include reexports of their sugar, coffee, and other colonial products, which may have accounted for another two-fifths of French exports. See also Jean Tarrade, *Le commerce colonial de la France à la fin de l'Ancien Régime* (Paris: Presses Universitaires de France, 1972), 2: 739.

[5] Mackesy, *War for America*, 524; England 509: 49 and England 516: 393–394, Garnier to Vergennes, 6 March 1775 and 21 June 1776.

[6] Brun, *Port de Toulon*, 1: 533. This was below the usual assignment for the Caribbean of a frigate and two corvettes (B⁴81: 46).

The remaining French possessions in the Western Hemisphere, the tiny islands of Saint Pierre and Miquelon off Newfoundland, received no French naval protection because they were indefensible. The Newfoundland fisheries for which they offered a base employed over 250 ships and some 10,000 fishermen, a vital source of crews for the wartime French navy.[7] In 1755 the British had seized without any warning the Newfoundland fishing fleet; given the proximity of the English naval base at Halifax, the only way to prevent a similar catastrophe would be to recall the fishing fleet at the first danger of Britain's reversing her policy of peace toward France.

Almost as indefensible were the French trading posts in India, which by the Peace of Paris of 1763 the French were forbidden to fortify. As late as 1777 their chief post at Pondicherry had only 700 Europeans capable of bearing arms. The French did have a relatively secure point of support in the Mascarene Islands (Île de France and Bourbon, now Mauritius and Réunion) with some 6,500 colonists and a colonial regiment apiece. The French kept a frigate and some auxiliary ships on regular station in the Indian Ocean and occasionally sent out a small ship of the line "en flûte," that is with part of its guns removed so it could carry supplies. The *Flamand* left Toulon in this manner for Île de France via the colonial recruit depot at Île de Ré in mid-April 1775. She carried masts, artillery, munitions, and 300 recruits as troop replacements and did not return to France until June 1776.[8]

The largest French naval commitments were in the Mediterranean, where French commerce still had to be protected from corsairs. An occasional frigate was sufficient to protect the North African trade, but trade with the Levant (eastern Mediterranean) entailed the regular use of at least

---

[7] Charles de la Morandière, *Histoire de la pêche française de la morue dans l'Amérique Septentrionale* (Paris: G. P. Maisonneuve et Larose, 1962), 2: 999.

[8] Brun, *Port de Toulon*, 1: 514.

four frigates or corvettes. They were sent out in pairs at staggered intervals for six to eight-month cruises, convoying each way the trade with the privileged French entrepôts of the Ottoman Empire.[9] With the end of the Russo-Turkish war this trade became more secure.[10]

Finally, France maintained a slaving station at the island of Gorée off Senegambia on the west coast of Africa. This post was not fortified and received only an occasional visit by a warship.

The largest concentration of French naval strength occurred when training squadrons were fitted out, such as the training squadron of a dozen small ships during the summer of 1775. This squadron, which included four frigates and four corvettes, exercised under the command of a newly promoted commodore, the Count de Guichen. The summer of 1775 represented the peak of naval activity during Sartine's first year as minister. In addition to the ship of the line en route to the Indian Ocean, eight frigates or corvettes were off the French coast, five were on cruise in the Mediterranean, one was in the Indian Ocean, and one in the Caribbean.

The real basis of French naval deterrence obviously lay not in the number of ships at sea, but in the presence of 60 unmanned ships of the line resting at Brest, Toulon, and Rochefort (plus, to a certain extent, 50 or so Spanish ships of the line). Some were ready for manning, others were in overhaul or still in construction, and the majority were in various stages of disrepair. Given time for repairs, most could eventually be used in case of war. In the past the

[9] This trade accounted for about ten percent of French exports and imports. Romano, "Documenti," 1275, 1287. See also Paul Masson, *Histoire du commerce français dans le Levant au XVIIIe siècle* (Paris: Hachette et c^ie, 1911), 348.

[10] To aid the Turks, Turgot while naval minister had secretly sent two ships of the line to Constantinople. The Ottoman Empire purchased the *Ferme*; the *Flamand* returned to Toulon. B²405:141–142, Turgot to Bourgeois de Guendreville, intendant at Toulon, 10 August 1774; Brun, *Port de Toulon*, 1: 534.

French navy had not defeated the English navy, but had been formidable enough to cause Parliament to impose such levies on the English taxpayer that Parliament would not lightly count the French navy as an enemy.

Soon after Sartine made his first administrative proposals, he began to urge improving the readiness of the French navy through an increase of its supply of naval matériel and the overhaul of a number of its unrepaired ships. Sartine's motives in urging extra expenditures seem to have been basically bureaucratic empire-building rather than a response to any immediate danger. He seems to have been initially concerned with standardization of the French fleet, which contained ships of varied sizes as well as vastly differing ages. In March 1775 someone within the naval ministry drafted for Sartine's use such a plan. According to this proposal, the navy would still contain 64 ships of the line, but these would consist of eight ships of 80 or more guns, twenty-four 74s, twenty-four 64s and eight 50s. This would necessitate replacing four old 74s, one 70, one 68, one 60, and two 56s by a reconstructed 116 and 74, three new 64s, and four new 50s. Thereafter, the navy would annually replace eight ships of the line and four frigates.[11] Such a program with its symmetry of numbers indicates a greater concern for orderliness than for preparing for a possible war. Were war a current danger no one would consider constructing 64s and 50s, ships of marginal utility in a line of battle, while disposing of 74s.

There is no indication of whether Sartine even presented this proposal to the council of state. Far less ambitious proposals had already been rejected. Sartine's initial budget request for 1775 had included funds for construction or repair of six ships of the line, but only the overhauls to the *Marseillais* and *Triton* and the reconstruction of the *Sphinx* were initially approved.[12] Sartine's budget had requested

[11] B^{5}10: unpaged, "Résumé du tableau ci-joint pour faire connaître ce qu'il y aurait à faire pour completer la marine," 26 March 1775.

[12] B^{5}9: unpaged, untitled memoir, 28 October 1774. Appendix C

over 13,500,000 livres for the variable expenses of the navy, some 4,000,000 above normal. The navy department as a whole was normally assigned 27,900,000 livres, about 7.5 percent of the royal revenue of 362,000,000 livres in 1774.[13] Of this amount, 10,100,000 went for colonies, 8,000,000 for fixed expenses,[14] and 300,000 for secret or extraordinary expenses, leaving only 9,500,000 for the ordinary naval expenses. These included the expenses of the ports, the purchase of matériel, the costs of overhauls and construction, the expenses of preparing, provisioning, and manning of squadrons, and miscellaneous expenses such as hospitals, civil works, and care of convict labor.[15] As long as Turgot remained dominant on the council, however, the reconstruction of the navy had to remain secondary to his program of retrenchment of royal expenditures.

Sartine's failure to obtain additional money also precluded any resupply of naval matériel. As one example, between his initial and final budget requests Sartine was forced to reduce his request for funds for wood for construction from 1,119,000 livres to 800,000 livres.[16]

---

lists all overhauls requiring a month or longer that were undertaken for ships of the line.

[13] J. F. Bosher, *French Finances, 1770–1795* (Cambridge: At the University Press, 1970), 90.

[14] Under this category came such items as pay for officers and naval cadets (1,800,000 livres), the Royal Corps of Infantry (1,400,-000), the employees of the ministry at Versailles (885,000), the officers of administration (865,000), and a variety of other expenses, such as pensions and the cost of consulates. E 205: unpaged, "Les dépenses fixes de la marine au mois du 7bre [September] 1774," 15 April 1784.

[15] B510: unpaged, "Mémoire au roi," 15 July 1777; B181: 327–336, untitled memoir, 23 December 1775; B4214: 85, memoir of Fleurieu, July 1777. The cost of building a 74 was about 850,000 livres. E 205: unpaged, "Dépenses possibles du département de la marine. . . ," November 1780. The navy, moreover, still owed 13,282,298 livres in debts from the partial mobilization of 1770. E 204: unpaged, "Mémoire sur la situation du département de la marine relativement au fonds," August 1774. See Appendix A for the naval budget and debt.

[16] B59: unpaged, untitled memoir of 28 October 1774; B2405: 237–241, "Extrait du projet arrêté par le Roi des dépenses variables à faire dans les differents ports pendant l'année 1775," 16–23 December 1774.

The lack of naval matériel was an ever firmer guarantee than the disrepair of the fleet that the French navy would be used only for normal peacetime operations. In fact the depletion of Choiseul and Choiseul-Praslin's stocks of matériel rendered difficult even these routine movements.[17] The shortages were selective.[18] The navy had sufficient pitch and tar, and the shortages of anchors and sail canvas (under normal usage, two years' supply and one year's supply respectively) could be fairly easily rectified. The most serious deficiencies were masts, hemp, and wood for construction.

The least serious of these deficiencies was that of masts. From a high point of over 4,300 in 1766, the number of large masts had declined to less than 1,800 in August 1774. This, however, still represented a three-year supply under normal peacetime usage, and the navy was able to purchase masts from Scandinavia. The number of large masts on hand rose to about 2,250 by the end of 1774 and 2,650 by the end of 1775. Although France was still dependent on Scandinavian mast imports, which could be interrupted by war, the supply of masts had risen by almost 50 percent in sixteen months.

The problem of hemp was more challenging. At the end of 1768, there had been a four-year supply on hand, 65,305 cwt. (hundredweight). By August 1774 this supply had dropped to 16,000 cwt. The navy was barely able to meet current needs for rigging and line, let alone accumulate greater reserves of the hemp from which they were made. Although the supply rose to 24,000 cwt. by the end of 1774,

[17] B⁵10: unpaged, "Mémoire sur les dépenses variables de la marine pour 1776," no date but toward the end of 1775, complained that ships could not even be rigged without the use of various expedients.
[18] Information following is based on these sources: B⁵10: unpaged, "Tableau des forces navales du roi dans le courant des treize années," no date but end of 1775 or beginning of 1776; B⁵10: unpaged, "Comparison de l'état où se trouvoir la marine du roi au mois d'août 1774 avec son état actuel," no date but end of 1775. Masts include only those above a certain size.

it dropped again to 17,250 cwt. by the end of the following year. The naval ministry pressed the intendants of hemp-producing provinces to increase production,[19] but the provision of hemp continued to be a problem.

The key matériel problem was that of wood for construction. This category included all the wood, generally oak, used in the construction, repair, and overhaul of the navy's ships. The ministry computed the average peacetime need at 750,000 cubic feet (ft.³) per year. Choiseul-Praslin had built a reserve of 1,900,000 ft.³, but by August 1774 the amount on hand had dropped to barely 1,000,000 ft.³. Under Sartine the supply rose with agonizing slowness—1,139,866 ft.³ at the end of 1774; 1,262,104 ft.³ at the end of 1775. The basic reason for Sartine's failure to build up the supply of wood for construction was financial. Since France's domestic supply of timber was inadequate, much of Europe had to be searched for wood. Toulon eventually received wood not only from Dauphiné, Burgundy, Franche Comté and Corsica, but also from Italy and Albania.[20] The Atlantic ports received wood not only from the forests of northern France but from all over Germany as well, including wood from Prussia sent via Hamburg and Amsterdam. Commissioners were sent abroad to visit forests and deal with contractors,[21] but they had to deal in a seller's market. The navy simply did not have the necessary funds to make the purchases, by one estimate 4,500,000 livres worth, needed to create an adequate reserve.[22] These difficulties would naturally be increased by any building program. The great drydock at Toulon, the major project of 1775, de-

[19] Brun, *Port de Toulon*, 1: 543.

[20] *Ibid.*, 542.

[21] See for example B¹80: 34, a memoir dealing with the request for more money by commissioner Charlot de Granville, visiting forests near Cassel, 5 December 1774; B¹81: 127–128, Commissioner Brun de Ste. Catherine at Rome to Sartine, 10 February 1775.

[22] B⁵10: unpaged, "Tableau général de la situation des arsenaux de la marine," no date but apparently late 1775. As a rule of thumb, calculate the cost of wood for construction at 2.75 to 3 livres per ft.³

manded over 2,000 pieces of wood and 258 masts. The navy had to borrow 1,200,000 livres from the Company of Barbary to build the vital 300-foot-long drydock and the lack of funds and wood forced deferment of two more drydocks.[23]

Unless the king appropriated more funds, the most Sartine could do was to maintain naval operations at their current levels, to guarantee prompt payments to contractors, and to begin to pay off existing debts in order to improve credit and lower prices. The changing diplomatic scene, however, gave Sartine reason to urge more attention to the navy and, over the course of 1775, to ask supplementary appropriations.

2. French Precautions after the Revolt of British North America

If no danger of war seemed to justify the expenses of rebuilding the French navy's ships or of refilling its dockyards, relations with Britain apparently at least necessitated prudence. In February 1775 Garnier asked Vergennes if he wished to continue paying 19,760 livres a year for a network of agents to report on the British navy. Sartine urged Vergennes to continue underwriting the expense. Sartine believed that a change from the current ministry of Lord North or an English accommodation with the Americans could lead to a dangerous diversion of the fleet assembled in America. The safety of the French navy and of French commerce demanded that France take precautions to keep informed.[1]

[23] Work began in May 1774, the outer shell was sunk in place in August 1775, and the drydock (which, unlike the Atlantic drydocks, was built to operate without the help of tides) was finished in 1778. There is a model of it at the superb French naval museum at the Palais de Chaillot in Paris. See Brun, *Port de Toulon*, 1: 539; Léon Guérin, *Histoire maritime de France* (Paris: Dufour, Boulanger, et Legrand, 1863), 5: 10–11. The Company of Barbary was repaid by loaning it the use of part of the Toulon dockyard.

[1] England 508: 241–250, Garnier to Vergennes, 10 February 1775; England 508: 281–288, Sartine to Vergennes, 20 February 1775.

There were some grounds for such concern. Garnier reported as of 6 March 1775 there were 12,184 British troops in North America[2] and 16 British ships of the line, 22 frigates, and 32 corvettes at sea.[3] On the other hand, the total number of all categories of British warships was virtually unchanged from the annual report of the previous year,[4] and in March 1775 Parliament voted lower extraordinary naval appropriations and the use of fewer seamen than in March 1774.[5] Sartine, at any rate, moved to ascertain how many ships could be readied should France need them. On 17 March 1775 he wrote the intendants of Brest, Rochefort, and Toulon to ask how many ships at their ports could be readied for sea.[6] Sartine's inquiries produced near panic and he had to assure the intendant at Brest that his questions did not mean war was imminent, that no fleets would have to be dispatched, and that in fact there was nothing to make one suspect the possibility of war.[7]

Although Lord North's ministry was conciliatory toward France, its treatment of the American colonies was less politic. Its reliance on force to solve the political disputes

[2] England 509: 49, "Nombre et répartition des troupes d'Angleterre et d'Ireland le 6 mars 1775." This is an overestimate. Mackesy, *War for America*, 524–525 lists only 6,991 effectives in North America as of April 1775.

[3] England 509: 52–60, Garnier to Vergennes, 6 March 1775.

[4] *Ibid.*; see also above, Chapter One, Section 2, Note 2.

[5] England 509: 90, Garnier to Vergennes, 14 March 1775. Garnier reported a total British naval budget of £2,039,915, which he computed as 48,155,370 livres. Money was voted to pay 18,000 sailors, compared to 20,000 the previous year. Actual expenditures and number of sailors maintained were larger than those appropriated.

[6] For example, B²406: 48, Sartine to Intendant Ruis-Embito of Brest, 17 March 1775.

[7] B²406: 74, Sartine to Ruis-Embito, 9 April 1775. Brest reported that 17 ships of the line, seven frigates, and six smaller ships could be made ready within three months, and another three ships of the line and a frigate could be made ready within a fourth month if overhauls were promptly begun. Rochefort responded that within three to four months it could finish overhaul or construction of three ships of the line. Toulon responded that 13 to 17 ships of the line could be prepared, depending on the supplies provided. B⁴181: 24–25, 94–95, 218–219, Intendant Ruis-Embito, Intendant d'Auberton, and Commissioner-General Dasque to Sartine, 7–14 April 1775.

with the Americans stimulated force in return, and in April 1775 political disagreement degenerated into war.

The French took only comparatively minor steps to guard against the spread of the war to France. In June the king finally approved 4,000,000 livres of supplemental funds for the navy, of which 1,600,000 were for purchases already made in excess of appropriations and 2,400,000 for overhauls and the construction of small ships.[8] The same month it appears he turned down a request for an additional 6,264,000 livres to construct four frigates and eight smaller ships and to overhaul seven ships of the line and twelve frigates.[9] Sartine was now able, however, to inform the ports that the king's intention was to put the largest possible number of ships of the line in condition to be armed, commencing with those which required the least work and could be readied in the least amount of time. A number of minor overhauls were begun in order to accomplish that aim.[10] Sartine personally went to Brest in August to examine the state of the port (and to view the administration of the port prior to his decision on administrative reform). He reported on his return that his first impression of the naval forces of Brest was more satisfactory than he had dared to hope and that the king could count on the prompt arming of twenty ships of the line and sixteen frigates if need be. He warned, though, that such a fleet would almost completely exhaust the available supplies at Brest and that upon its return it would be impossible to provide for its rearmament.[11]

[8] B⁵10: unpaged, "Mémoire sur les dépenses variables de la marine pour 1776," no date but toward the end of 1775; see also B¹81: 273.

[9] B⁵10: unpaged, untitled memoir of 23 June 1775 requesting these funds; there is no direct evidence this was presented to the king, but it seems highly likely.

[10] B²407: 10, Sartine to Ruis-Embito, 15 July 1775. See Appendix C. Light repairs were also made during 1775 and 1776 to a number of ships of the line, including the *Hardi*, *Guerrier*, *Alexandre*, *Tonnant*, *Fier*, and *Duc-de-Bourgogne*.

[11] B⁴124: 350–357, "Mémoire sur l'état de la marine au port de Brest," no date but late 1775; B⁴124: 289–349, "Voyage dans les ports

French naval operations also were not greatly affected by the British military operations in North America. Ambassador Guines, returned to his post in London, agreed with Vergennes that the most dangerous moment for France would be when these troops were recalled. He commented, referring to the surprise British attack of 1755: "We have already had a cruel experience of the manner in which this country commences a war."[12] The French had to recognize the danger that England would attack France to revenge her own losses or to draw on the colonists' hatred of France as a means of reconciliation, particularly should Lord North's government be replaced by one under the hated William Pitt, now Earl of Chatham. The obvious point of danger was the French West Indies and after obtaining the king's approval, the council sent heavy reinforcements to Martinique, Saint Domingue, and Guadeloupe—six battalions of troops, three frigates, and three corvettes. In order to avoid alarming the British, Vergennes punctiliously informed them in advance of the reinforcements.[13] He also informed the Spaniards that the move was purely precautionary and urged them to take similar steps.[14] In December, work was begun to prepare the ship of the line *Indien* for the Indian Ocean, but the need for warships was not yet serious enough to halt the policy of hiring out ships of the line to private contractors.[15] The *Sagittaire* left for

---

de Bretagne," no date; P. Levot, *Histoire de la ville et du port de Brest* (Paris: Bachelin-Deflorenne, 1866), 2: 171. Sartine was gone from Versailles from 9 August to 17 September. His visit became particularly well-known for his orders to Brest that it be attended by neither ceremonies nor unnecessary expenditures.

[12] England 511: 131, Guines to Vergennes, 18 July 1775.

[13] England 511: 394, Guines to Vergennes, 15 September 1775; B²407: 23, Sartine to Ruis-Embito, 4 August 1775, etc. See also Appendix J. Each battalion contained 32 officers and 532 men.

[14] Henri Doniol, *Histoire de la participation de la France à l'établissement des Etats-Unis d'Amérique* (Paris: Imprimerie Nationale, 1885–1892), 1: 125, Vergennes to the Marquis d'Ossun, French ambassador to Spain, 7 August 1775.

[15] The practice of loaning out ships was considered less harmful to

the West Indies with a load of bricks on 21 January 1776, four days after the departure of the *Bordelais* on a trading voyage to India.

The lack of French naval activity confirms that dangers from Britain were as yet only hypothetical. Guines wrote in August: "Nothing until now announces any bad intentions. A war against the House of Bourbon [France and Spain] would be undertaken dangerously and foolishly. The present ministry has neither means nor motives to attempt it, but in this country the scene changes from one day to another."[16]

Louis simultaneously disarmed a source of more immediate danger than the Anglo-American war. Relations between England's ally Portugal and France's ally Spain had deterioriated so badly over border disputes in South America that the localized disturbances threatened to have European repercussions, but at Vergennes' urging the king wrote his great-uncle Charles III, tactfully refusing any French cooperation with Spain.[17]

The rebellion of the American colonists did not produce any deterioration of Britain's relations with France, largely because of the initial moderation of French policy. As long as France made no move to aid the Americans or to increase the difficulties between Spain and Portugal, and as long as she maintained a level of colonial and naval forces sufficient to discourage attack but not to create tension, this condition promised to continue. Guines was an inept diplo-

---

the navy than competing with private shipyards for scarce building materials. B¹80: 234, "Commerce de l'Inde," September 1774. The *Indien* developed a leak and was eventually replaced by the *Brillant*.

[16] England 511: 156, Guines to Vergennes, 7 August 1775.

[17] Memoirs and Documents, France 1897: 44, Louis to Charles, 7 August 1775. Guines seriously exceeded his instructions in trying to arrange mutual Franco-English neutrality in South America for his own political purposes. He was recalled in January 1776. Edgar Faure, *La disgrâce de Turgot, 12 mai 1776* (Paris: Gallimard, 1961), 468–479; Memoirs and Documents, France 1897: 56, 60–62, Vergennes to Louis, 31 January and 23 February 1776.

mat, but he gave Vergennes one excellent piece of advice. He urged Vergennes to keep the colonies and navy in readiness and for the rest he advised Vergennes "to destroy as much as you can, sir, by a just and precise conduct all the points of difficulty which can exist between the two nations."[18] Vergennes' need to place British relations on a new footing was too strong for a disinterested neutrality; one must forever wonder, however, at the awesome differences in history had he attempted and succeeded in using French neutrality to negotiate the changes in Anglo-French relations for which he instead fought so damaging a war.

[18] England 511: 132, Guines to Vergennes, 18 July 1775.

CHAPTER THREE

1776—The Beginning of Limited Intervention

1. The Proposal to Aid the Americans

I RONICALLY, the first proposal for violating France's "just and precise conduct" toward Britain came from Ambassador Guines. Near the end of July 1775, only ten days after giving this advice, he suggested sending an agent named Achard de Bonvouloir to make contact with the Americans. On 7 August, the very day Louis wrote Charles, "Perhaps there has never been an occasion when the likelihood of a war with England seemed less probable . . . ,"[1] Vergennes sent approval for Bonvouloir's mission. He laid down three conditions: that attention be given so that Bonvouloir's correspondence could not be captured as to compromise France; that Bonvouloir make a report on events and the general mood of the American colonists; and that he assure the colonists of France's good will.[2] Bonvouloir left England in early September and met with a secret committee of the American Continental Congress in December 1775.

Chances of a reconciliation between the Americans and Britain steadily decreased during the latter half of 1775. On 23 August the British prohibited all outside commerce with the Americans, on 19 October prohibited the exportation of warlike stores and ammunition to the colonies, and on 22 December prohibited all commerce whatsoever with the colonies as of 1 March 1776. In January 1776 the British signed treaties for 18,000 German troops to be used against

[1] Memoirs and Documents, France 1897: 44, Louis to Charles, 7 August 1775.

[2] England, supplement 18: 50, observations by Guines on Bonvouloir's report of 15 December 1775; Doniol, *La participation de la France*, 1: 128–129.

the colonies[3] and began seizing foreign ships suspected of carrying munitions to the colonists.[4]

The same month Guines was recalled from his post. He brought with him to France a copy of Bonvouloir's report, which he gave to Vergennes on 27 February 1776. Bonvouloir had asked the Americans "unofficially" what they wished from France. They had responded that they wished to know France's dispositions toward them, the use of two experienced engineers, and the right to trade American goods for French arms.[5]

The reception of Bonvouloir's report was the catalyst for a major shift in the French position toward the American war. Two days later Vergennes forwarded to the king a justification for aiding the Americans written by the playwright, propagandist, and amateur diplomat, Caron de Beaumarchais.[6] Vergennes meanwhile prepared a similar memoir. This memoir, labeled "Considerations," was presented on 12 March to a select committee of the council of state formed to advise the king and a copy was sent to the Marquis d'Ossun, the veteran French ambassador to the Spanish court.[7]

The members of the committee were the king, Maurepas, Vergennes, Sartine, Turgot, and Claude-Louis, Count de

[3] Mackesy, *War for America*, 62. The Russians refused a similar treaty.

[4] England 514: 55–59, Guines to Vergennes, 12 January 1776.

[5] England, supplement 18: 39–45, Bonvouloir to Vergennes, 28 December 1775; *Ibid.*, 50–63, observations by Guines on Bonvouloir's report of 15 December 1775.

[6] Brian N. Morton, *Beaumarchais Correspondance* (Paris: A. G. Nizet, 1969–), 2: 174–176, Beaumarchais to Louis, given 29 February 1776. On 22 January Vergennes had sent a memoir of Beaumarchais to the king, probably that of 7 December alluding in general to the need to weaken England. *Ibid.*, 150–155, Beaumarchais to Louis, 7 December 1775; Memoirs and Documents, France 1897: 55, Vergennes to Louis, 22 January 1776.

[7] England, supplement 18: 115–121, "Considerations." The covering letter to the other members of the committee (dated 12 March 1776) is given in Doniol, *La participation de la France*, 1: 279.

Saint-Germain (1707–1787, minister of the army from October 1775 to September 1777). During almost two years from the beginning of the new reign, no one had challenged Maurepas' primacy in the council. Vergennes had particularly profited from his acknowledgement of Maurepas' position, for in exchange Maurepas acted as a shield against any possible rivals and left Vergennes great independence in the direction of foreign affairs (subject of course to Louis' final approval). Sartine, named minister of state in 1775, had as yet little influence in the council, but would prove an unshakable support of Maurepas and Vergennes. Saint-Germain was not named a minister of state until 19 May 1776, but was invited to the committee because his department was necessarily connected with any aid which might be given to the Americans. Only Turgot had the power and motivation to challenge any proposal of Vergennes concerning foreign policy.[8]

Turgot had just won his greatest victory. On 12 March 1776 his most sweeping reforms—the Six Edicts, which included the abolition of the royal *corvée*—were registered over the protests of the Parlement of Paris. The very extent of Turgot's victory, however, menaced his position, for he had made numerous enemies and aroused the jealousy of Maurepas.[9] Nonetheless, Turgot still held the king's ear and any policy involving increased royal expenditures would be contrary to his program of retrenchment of royal expenditures and expansion of royal revenues. Heretofore, Vergennes' program of diplomatic restraint and Turgot's program of budgetary restraint had been mutually reinforcing.

[8] The three remaining members of the council of state were not involved in the decision on aid to the American colonists. These members were Charles de Rohan, Prince de Soubise (1715–1787) and Henri-Léonard-Jean-Baptiste Bertin (1719–1792), holdovers from Louis XV's reign, and Crétien-Guillaume de Lamoignon de Malesherbes (1721–1794), minister of the king's household and an ally of Turgot.

[9] Douglas Dakin, *Turgot and the Ancien Régime in France* (London: Methuen and Co., 1939), 250–251, 255–263.

The avoidance of conflict with Britain meant there was little immediate need for strong armaments; the lack of capacity for a sustained war in turn acted as a moderating force in foreign policy. So interconnected were the two that abandoning diplomatic moderation would automatically endanger the fiscal restraint. The reversal of France's policy of nonintervention in the American war did in fact lead to naval rearmament and the establishment of a new set of mutually reinforcing tendencies—growing involvement in the American struggle and growing rearmament—which eventually led to war.

The probable repugnance of the king to abandoning his program of domestic reform dictated the argument presented by the "Considerations"—an argument not for offensive measures, but for a "circumspect but active foresight." Rather than arguing the advantages to France of American independence, the document instead stressed the dangers to France should the war end suddenly. It contended that it would be to the advantage of France and Spain should the war last at least another year so that the Bourbons could see to their own defense. To this end France and Spain should surreptitiously provide the American colonists with arms while assuring Britain of their own peaceful intentions. The members of the committee were asked to submit their comments on the proposal.

Before examining the responses provoked by the "Considerations," it is necessary to deal with two questions which the document raises. First, were Vergennes' warnings about the dangers of the American war genuine or were they a camouflage for an aggressively anti-British policy? The evidence seems overwhelmingly to support the latter. Garnier, again in charge in London, had just reported that the present English ministry was still not in political or military condition to fight the Bourbons.[10] (He did, how-

---

[10] England 515: 93, Garnier to Vergennes, 8 March 1776. See also Garnier's further comments, England 515: 326 and England 516: 99, Garnier to Vergennes, 12 April and 10 May 1776.

ever, warn that the government did not have full control over its admirals and generals who might provoke a war on their own.) Only two weeks before, Vergennes' Spanish counterpart, the Marquis de Grimaldi, had written the Count d'Aranda, his ambassador in Paris, to remind him that the French held there was no immediate danger from Britain and that it would suffice to take normal precautions and to provision the ports against any threat. Spain planned merely to take the added precaution of posting a few small warships as vessels of observation in the principal approaches to the Caribbean.[11] Certainly Vergennes' probity was no proof against a willingness to resort to duplicity when he believed it necessary—witness his comments to Garnier on the eve of the king's decision to intervene in Britain's war. He then would write that the English should thank Providence that at such a time, when it would be so easy to strike a mortal blow to England's power, France and Spain should be governed by princes who take for the base of all their conduct the most exact and the most scrupulous justice.[12]

These pieces of circumstantial evidence merely reinforce more direct evidence for Vergennes' motives. Revealing is the way in which the decision to aid the Americans was implemented. No reinforcements were sent to the West Indies during the next year despite their supposed danger from Great Britain. In contrast to 1775, the shipyards undertook long-term overhauls rather than preparing a defensive fleet in being. The squadrons which were outfitted were intended for the protection of the arms shipments to North America rather than for the protection of the French empire. These suggest that it was not the menace of war which *dictated* France's fueling of a civil war within the British

[11] Spain 579: 183–184, 185–188, Grimaldi to Aranda, 26 February 1776. Spain was still more concerned about possible British intervention in the Portuguese dispute than about the possible spillover of the North American war. Aranda had sent Grimaldi a description of how Ireland could be attacked.

[12] England 515: 377, Vergennes to Garnier, 20 April 1776.

empire but rather the ease with which France could harm England which *permitted* it. The chief evidence for Vergennes' primary concern with harming England lies, however, in his willingness to reveal his true motives during the argument over intervention. As we shall see, once this argument was joined, Vergennes spoke not of the dangers of the American war but of its opportunities.

The second question is more difficult to answer: how aware was Vergennes of the likelihood that aiding the American colonists would lead to war with England? The North government was so unwilling to add to its enemies that France initially faced little risk in aiding the Americans even though (as Vergennes knew) she did not as yet have either the matériel to fit out more than a single fleet or more than two dozen ships of the line in condition for war. The long-term dangers in such a policy, however, were massive. Even had Britain tacitly permitted such aid without forcing France to become an actual belligerent in the American war, it would have been extremely difficult, if not impossible, for France to maintain her own limits on the nature of her involvement or the extent of her rearmament. One can only guess at Vergennes' expectations since it was in Vergennes' interest not to reveal the likelihood of war to a king still determined on economy and domestic reform.[13] My own feeling is that Vergennes was far too much the realist not to realize the probable consequences of aiding the Americans and that in his desire for righting the balance of power he was willing to accept the probability of war. For the moment he could postpone that final decision. It was conceivable that a limited aid program in itself might enable the Americans to win their independence and thereby weaken Britain (although the "Considerations" mentioned only the *dangers* of America winning its independence,

---

[13] One should note that for the next year-and-a-half Vergennes' mention of the inevitability of war or of the natural animosity between Britain and France was used rhetorically, however much it may have corresponded to his inner expectations.

thereby provoking a British desire for compensation at French expense). It is hard to believe, however, that Vergennes could put much faith in the untrained American army, particularly since the Americans had fought so poorly against the French during the last war.[14] Probably more important, by limiting aid to the provision of arms Vergennes made a virtue of necessity. Given the unreadiness of France for a naval war against Britain, France was necessarily limited to measures short of actual war. By prolonging the American war France would purchase time to rearm after which Vergennes could worry about overcoming any royal scruples about abandoning domestic reform. Vergennes was even able to leave to Sartine the task of circumventing the king's opposition to heavy expenditures for rearmament.[15]

2. The Case for British Dependence on America

After hearing the "Considerations," the members of the committee were given time to draft replies. During these intervening three weeks Vergennes, perhaps encouraged by the reaction of the French nobility against Turgot's Six Edicts, became more sure of his position. Vergennes' second memoir for the committee, prepared by his gifted aide, Joseph-Mathias Gérard de Rayneval, was far more forthright than the "Considerations." These "Reflections"[1] were probably presented to the committee on or shortly after 6 April, the date of Turgot's own "Reflections." Vergennes' memoir, like those of Maurepas and Sartine,[2] stressed the

---

[14] In this I disagree with my friend Orville T. Murphy. For his view see Orville T. Murphy, "The French Professional Soldier's Opinion of the American Militia in the War of the Revolution," *Military Affairs* 32 (1969): 191–198.

[15] See Section 4 of this chapter.

[1] England, supplement 18: 56–63, "Réflexions sur la situation actuelle des colonies anglaises et sur la conduite qu'il convient à la France de tenir à leur égard" (hereafter cited as "Reflections").

[2] Maurepas probably ordered the drafting of "Réflexions sur la nécessité de secourir les Americains et de se preparer à la guerre avec

American Revolution as presenting France not with a danger to be avoided but with an opportunity she had no choice but to seize. It rationalized French intervention by reference to the "natural" animosity between the two countries, resurrected past injuries done by England, warned of the inevitability of war even if France did nothing, and offered to Louis the prospects of a share of American commerce and points of support for the Newfoundland fisheries.

Its central argument, however, was that by depriving Britain of her possession of the American colonies France could so weaken her as to alter the balance of power. The belief in British dependence on America was the fundamental misperception for which the French crown fought a financially ruinous and diplomatically unproductive war.

The "Reflections" stressed three motives for Britain to try to maintain control over the American colonies: to prevent the loss of American trade, to preserve American aid to the remainder of the British Empire, and to maintain the strength of the British navy.[3] Each of these points was an accepted dogma of the mercantilist orthodoxy of Vergennes' day. To understand the persuasiveness of Vergennes' argument, it is necessary to understand the foundations upon which it was constructed.

The belief in British dependence on America hinged not as much on the individual strength of the three points as upon their interconnection and mutual support. First, the dependence of the British economy upon American trade

---

l'Angleterre," United States 2: 26–27. My colleague Svetlana Kluge Harris has identified the handwriting as that of one of Maurepas' secretaries. Sartine's memoir, England, supplement 18: 112–114, was apparently also drafted in response to the "Considerations." The only memoir of Saint-Germain's that I have found is one of 15 March, which advises that France by reason of equity in the first place, but equally by reason of her momentary lack of strength, should evade war with the greatest care (England 515: 179–180). However dubious Saint-Germain may have been about war, he did not possess the political acumen or the political muscle to be of much weight in the debate.

[3] The second and third points are mentioned in the same paragraph of "Reflections."

was significant to French diplomacy because of the presumed connection between wealth and political power.[4] Vergennes sought to deprive England of her monopoly of American trade to weaken her rather than to increase France's own trade. He later would write:

> American commerce seen in its entirety and subject to the monopoly of the mother country is without a doubt a great object of interest to the latter and a powerful vehicle for the growth of her industry and her power. This commerce delivered, however, to the avidity of all the nations can only be a minimal object to France. That which was necessary to determine her and has in fact determined her to join herself to America is the great weakening England would undergo by the subtraction of a third of her empire.[5]

Ending the British monopoly would, according to mercantilist orthodoxy, naturally decrease Britain's share of that trade, and since mercantilism looked on the amount of trade as static, it would cause Britain's trade to decline absolutely as well as relatively.[6] This in turn would cause a decline in British manufactures and hence harm the British economy, reducing Britain's powers to finance war and to grant subsidies—those powers on which her weight in the balance of power ultimately depended.

[4] This connection is persuasively argued by Jacob Viner, "Power versus Plenty as Objectives of Foreign Policy in the Seventeenth and Eighteenth Centuries," *World Politics* 1 (1948): 10–11; see also Gerald Stourzh, *Benjamin Franklin and American Foreign Policy* (Chicago: University of Chicago Press, 1954), 39–40.

[5] Spain 589: 313, Vergennes to the Count de Montmorin, French ambassador to Spain, 20 June 1778.

[6] Eli F. Heckscher, *Mercantilism*, trans. Mendel Shapiro (London: George Allen and Unwin, 1955), 2: 24; "Reflections." Given the relative nature of the balance of power, even a relative decline in Britain's trade as compared to that of France would accrue of course to France's benefit. The "Reflections" also stressed the immediate drop in British tax revenues if duties could no longer be collected on American trade.

It was understandable that Britain with its relatively small population and advanced economy was regarded as particularly subject to economic dislocation from the decline of trade. What is less immediately understandable is why American trade in particular was regarded as so essential to the British economy. The Americans did their best to encourage this belief—Franklin and his fellow American commissioners later claimed the American colonies as "the principal source of the richness and power of Great Britain."[7] Certainly American trade had greatly increased during the eighteenth century. At the beginning of the century about 6 percent of England's exports went to North America and 6 percent of her imports came from these colonies. By the outbreak of the revolution the percentage of British exports to North America had approximately tripled and the percentage of imports had approximately doubled.[8] Vergennes, who received from Garnier British trade statistics[9] (as well as the exaggerated claims of the defenders of America in Parliament),[10] may have placed more weight on them than did the British merchants who had debts to col-

[7] Doniol, *La participation de la France*, 2: 138–139, American commissioners Franklin, Deane, and Lee to Vergennes, 31 December 1776.

[8] Ralph Davis, *The Rise of the English Shipping Industry in the 17th and 18th Centuries* (London: Macmillan and Co., 1962), 200, 243, 266, 298–299; B. R. Mitchell, *Abstract of British Historical Statistics* (Cambridge: At the University Press, 1962), 294, 312. Former figures do not include Scotland, the latter figures do. North America includes all colonies in North America. Approximately 13 percent of British imports at the beginning of the eighteenth century came from the West Indies, approximately 25 percent in 1771–1773. The West Indian share of British exports climbed from 5–7 percent to 8–13 percent, during the same period (in each case the higher figures are from Davis). Total British imports in 1771–1773 were about 82–89 percent of those of France, while British exports were about 105–120 percent of those of France. I have converted the figures of Romano, "Documenti," 1241, to pounds at 23: 1. Higher percentages in each case are from Mitchell.

[9] The 1770–1772 reports are given in England 507: 115–128, Garnier to Vergennes, 2 October 1774.

[10] One example is Lord Camden, who claimed the continuation of the American war would cost the employment of the crews of 6,000 ships. England 508: 207–211, Garnier to Vergennes, 9 February 1775.

lect from their notoriously unreliable American clients.[11] Nevertheless, it hardly seems credible that England's economic strength should be dependent on a monopoly of a trade which provided less than a fifth of her markets. Choiseul had, after all, for his diplomatic purposes loosened the French monopoly of the far richer French West Indian trade in order to increase their trade with British North America.

The logic of British dependence on the American monopoly depended not on the economic relations between Britain and America but upon America's place in the British Empire as a whole. This empire consisted not of isolated units trading separately with Britain, but rather a mutually dependent collection of units connected by a web of trade patterns—African slaves to the West Indies, West Indian sugar and Virginia tobacco to Britain, British-manufactured goods to Africa and America, Newfoundland fish to the West Indies and Britain and for export, provisions of the northern colonies to the American south and the West Indies. The role of the American colonies, particularly the provision colonies from Pennsylvania north, was so great as even to discomfort British merchants, particularly those unsuccessfully competing with American merchants to supply the West Indies.[12] The American Revolution was cata-

[11] J. F. Rees, "Mercantilism and the Colonies," in *The Cambridge History of the British Empire*, eds. J. Holland Rose; A. P. Newton; and E. A. Benians (Cambridge: At the University Press, 1929), 1: 595–596, 602, and Mackesy, *War for America*, 183–184, discuss British disillusionment with North America as a market.

[12] For a summary of the system of trade see Charles M. Andrews, *The Colonial Period in American History* (New Haven: Yale University Press, 1938), 4: 344–347. One opponent of the American merchants later argued that in 1770 about 30 percent of American trade had been with the British or French West Indies. John Baker Holroyd, Lord Sheffield, *Observations on the Commerce of the American States* (London: J. Debrett, 1784), Appendix VII. Of America's ten largest ports, three had more than half their trade in 1768-1772 with the West Indies, and five others had more than a quarter. Francis Huntley, "Trade of the Thirteen Colonies with the Foreign Caribbean Area" (Ph.D. diss., University of California,

strophic for the West Indies. By 1776 the price of salted food had risen by 50 to 100 percent and corn by 400 percent while the price of sugar had dropped by 25 to 40 percent and rum by over 37 percent.[13] Nevertheless, America's military contribution to the empire was more prized than her economic contribution. For operations in the West Indies Britain could use American troops, like those which in past wars had attacked Cartagena in South America and had taken the great fort of Louisbourg at the entrance to the Gulf of St. Lawrence. Above all, the American colonies provided naval bases safe from hurricanes and supplies for refitting the fleets needed to support the West Indies. Well might George III fear that American independence would bring with it the loss of his West Indian colonies[14]—and with them the disintegration of the economy of the entire empire.

The American colonies probably, however, owed their assumed importance above all to their supposed contribution to the strength of the British navy. Apart from their harbors their *direct* contribution was relatively minor. Despite the success of American privateers the Americans were singularly unsuccessful in building a navy.[15] Perhaps 10,000 of

---

Berkeley, 1949), 25–26. During 1751–1752, half of the ships arriving in Kingston, Jamaica were American. Richard Pares, *War and Trade in the West Indies, 1739–1763* (New York: Barnes and Noble, 1936), 19–26.

[13] Sir William Laird Clowes, *The Royal Navy: A History from the Earliest Times to the Present* (Boston: Little, Brown, and Co., 1898), 3: 396.

[14] Sir John William Fortescue, ed., *The Correspondence of King George the Third from 1760 to December 1783* (London: Macmillan and Co., 1928), 4: 350, George to Lord North, 11 June 1778 (no. 2649).

[15] See, however, the predictions of Franklin quoted by Stourzh, *Benjamin Franklin and American Foreign Policy*, 59–60. One need not take too seriously Vergennes' predictions reported to Secretary of State Rochford by ambassador Stormont, 31 October 1775, given by Benjamin Franklin Stevens, ed., *Facsimiles of Manuscripts in European Archives relating to America, 1775–1783* (London: privately printed, 1889–1898), no. 1306.

the 75,000 seamen in the empire were American, but they generally sailed in American waters where impressment by the British navy was forbidden and elsewhere they fought vehemently this enforced service.[16] The American ship-building industry, although it provided three-eighths of the empire's shipping, was only unwanted competition for British shipyards.[17] American naval stores were regarded as inferior to British and were used only in reserve.[18] Only the great masts of New Hampshire were regarded as superior to Baltic products but after the temporary shortage during the American Revolution New Brunswick was developed as an alternate source.[19]

The main contribution of the colonies to the navy was assumed to be the part British-American trade played in the training of the Royal Navy's sailors. In wartime, France found crews for her warships by conscripting fishermen and the crews from coastal shipping. Britain was more dependent on coastal shipping for her economy (particularly to move coal) and could not safely neglect the fisheries. She instead depended on the seizure (impressment) of the crews of ocean-going merchantmen to fill her crews. Foreigners were then hired to replace those crews, while the

[16] Roland G. Usher, "Royal Navy Impressment during the American Revolution," *Mississippi Valley Historical Review* 37 (1951): 673–688; Davis, *Rise of the English Shipping Industry*, 323. Sir Herbert W. Richmond, *Statesmen and Seapower* (Oxford: Clarendon Press, 1947), 145, claims that only 1,800 Americans served in the British navy in the Seven Years' War.

[17] Vincent T. Harlow, *The Founding of the Second British Empire, 1763–1793* (London: Longmans, Green, and Co., 1952), 1: 475n.

[18] Daniel A. Baugh, *British Naval Administration in the Age of Walpole* (Princeton, N.J.: Princeton University Press, 1965), 279–280.

[19] Robert Greenhaugh Albion, *Forests and Sea Power* (Cambridge, Mass.: Harvard University Press, 1926), 274, 281–315. French naval officers had a low opinion of American timber and the risks of transport prevented much use of it by France during the war. Paul Walden Bamford, *Forests and French Sea Power, 1660–1789* (Toronto: University of Toronto Press, 1956), 184–187.

crews of fishing boats, barges and ships in coastal trade were left undisturbed.[20] For this system to work the British needed a large pool of trained merchant seamen from which the navy could draw (the alternative, that of keeping the navy manned during peacetime was, because of its expense, politically unthinkable). To maintain this pool the British depended on the Navigation Acts, which for the last century had regulated the destination, the ownership, and the composition of the crews of ships engaged in colonial shipping. So accepted was the necessity of this regulation to provide naval crews that even Adam Smith's antimercantilist *Wealth of Nations* (which was published in 1776) approved it, and the Americans claimed to endorse it as long as it was not perverted into an instrument of gaining revenue for the crown.[21]

Continued British domination of the colonial trade of North America and the West Indies was almost universally regarded as vital to the British navy, as was the possession of a share of the Newfoundland fisheries to the French. Colonial trade was considered far superior to European trade for training purposes: more skill was necessary, the ships had larger crews per ton and per invested capital, they did not visit foreign ports where the crews might desert, and their crews were more willing to suffer impressment.[22]

[20] Baugh, *British Naval Administration*, 156–157, 239–240. Lawrence A. Harper, *The English Navigation Laws* (New York: Columbia University Press, 1939), 339, estimates that in 1773 only 303,742 tons of the 581,000 tons of shipping (total) were involved in foreign and colonial trade. Another 125,346 tons were colliers, 89,631 tons were other coastal shipping, 38,585 tons were Newfoundland and Greenland fishing boats and 23,646 tons were other fishing boats.

[21] Adam Smith, *An Inquiry into the Nature and Causes of the Wealth of Nations* (1776; reprint ed., New York: Modern Library, 1937), 431; Oliver M. Dickerson, *The Navigation Acts and the American Revolution* (Philadelphia: University of Pennsylvania Press, 1951).

[22] Henry Brougham, *An Inquiry into the Colonial Policy of the European Powers* (Edinburgh: G. Balfour, Manners, and Miller, 1803), 175–191.

Moreover, this trade employed a sizeable proportion of British shipping,[23] which did not have to worry about being undercut by foreign competition, hindered by restrictive duties, or interrupted by the dislocation of war. By ending Britain's monopoly of American trade France mistakenly believed she could seriously disrupt British "navigation" and thereby restrict the British navy's potential for wartime expansion. Ending this monopoly, just as denying Britain the use of American bases and opening American markets to foreign products, was believed by France ultimately to be contingent upon America's absolute independence from Britain. American independence, the stakes for which France was to risk her own empire, was therefore the means by which France intended Britain to be reduced to parity, if not subordination, to France in the balance of power.

3. Turgot's Counterargument and the King's Decision

Vergennes' "Reflections" proposed that France aid the American colonists by providing money, war provisions, and warships disguised as merchantmen (the last idea was quickly dropped, probably because of the risk). Turgot while willing to permit the Americans to buy arms from France argued against the king's providing them himself. The disagreement between Vergennes and Turgot, while technically on these limited grounds, involved in its implications two vastly different views of the French monarchy's position.

Turgot's memoir, presented on 6 April 1776, was entitled "Reflections drafted on the occasion of a memoir submitted by the Count de Vergennes to the king on the manner in

[23] Davis, *Rise of the English Shipping Industry*, 200, estimates that 373,000 tons of British shipping were engaged in overseas trade (cf., note 20 above), and of this shipping 153,000 tons were in colonial trade.

which France and Spain should envisage the consequences of the quarrel between Great Britain and her colonies."[1] It is a complex document. Although written in answer to the "Considerations" it had also to address the issues the "Considerations" had avoided. In other words, Turgot had to respond to the tacit argument that the American Revolution presented an *opportunity* to France, while also having to counter the ostensible argument that strict neutrality would present a *danger* to France. Turgot's "Reflections" attacked each argument in two ways: on the grounds of its relative importance and on the grounds of its merit.

Turgot challenged the relative seriousness of the danger the American war posed to France by arguing that the condition of royal finances presented the most immediate danger to the monarchy. The ramshackle French tax system was not efficient enough to produce the revenue necessary for France to fight a major war.[2] Turgot's reform projects were aimed at reduction of the debts engendered by the shortage of revenue, modernization of the economy to increase the tax base, and rationalization of the tax system. The monarchy's critical internal problems made discussion of external danger academic. Turgot argued:

> Our condition, nevertheless, is not so hopeless that if it were absolutely necessary to sustain a war one could not find the resources, provided there was a decided probability of success which could shorten its duration. It is necessary at least to state that one should evade it as the greatest of evils, since it would render impossible for a long time and

[1] England, supplement 18: 69–108, "Réflexions rédigeés à l'occasion du mémoire remis par M. le comte de Vergennes sur la manière dont la France et l'Espagne doivent envisager les suites de la querelle entre la Grande Bretagne et ses colonies"; also given by Gustave Schelle, ed., *Oeuvres de Turgot et documents le concernant* (Paris: Félix Alcan, 1923), 5: 384–420, which source I will henceforth cite for this memoir.

[2] Bosher, *French Finances*, discusses the backwardness of the French monarchy's finances.

perhaps forever a reform absolutely necessary to the prosperity of the State and the relief of its people. In making a premature usage of our forces, we would risk making permanent our weakness.[3]

Turgot attacked not only the relative importance of the threat to France but also the idea that the French colonies were useful, let alone critical, to French security. He did so on the grounds that the expenses of their protection outweighed the benefits from their monopoly to France. Unfortunately, he did not carry his point further to conclude that since the possession of colonial monopolies was worthless, a major cause of the continuing hostility between Britain and France was without point and much of the supposed British threat to French security was imaginary. Turgot undercut his argument by conceding the necessity in the current circumstances of preparing for a possible war, including drafting a plan of operations, a detailed sample of which he himself proceeded to offer.[4] If England posed a threat only to the worthless monopoly of a few islands, as Turgot claimed, then such planning was unnecessary. In Britain there were no troops to attack France and France herself had no need to fear the large British forces in North America. Free from any immediate danger, the king could devote his attention to domestic reform.

Turgot's treatment of Britain as a possible enemy also weakened his denial of the importance of American independence to France. Turgot claimed that France's greatest opportunity for weakening Britain would come from a British victory. Any British victory would be pyrrhic and a forcibly held America would be a continual drain on British resources.[5] With Turgot having conceded the desirability of weakening Britain, Vergennes was fighting on his own ground. In his "Reflections" Vergennes admitted the per-

[3] Schelle, *Oeuvres de Turgot*, 5: 406.
[4] *Ibid.*, 412–415.   [5] *Ibid.*, 386–390.

petual costs to Britain of holding America by force, but still could argue that a British victory would mean the continuation of the monopoly by which Britain maintained her manufactures and her navy.

Finally Turgot attacked the central argument—British dependence on America. Again his case was weakened by concessions. He argued that colonies did not produce cheaper raw materials or government revenues,[6] but he did not attack the indispensability of an American monopoly to the navigation system or to English manufactures. He even conceded the military usefulness of colonies in certain eventualities.[7]

Turgot's concessions probably represented less a lack of intellectual rigor than a decision not to challenge without hope of success the views of the king. Within a few days of the presentation of the memoirs, the king's confidence in Turgot began to disintegrate as a result of a campaign of innuendo and private accusations. This political destruction was chiefly the work of Maurepas, although Sartine, to his discredit, contributed as well by resurrecting a scandal involving Turgot's brother and the colonial branch of the navy department;[8] Vergennes, as far as can be known, restricted himself to a rebuttal of Turgot's argument.[9]

The king quickly reached a decision on aiding the Americans. A decision favorable to the majority of the committee was guaranteed by the king's orders of 22 April that enough warships be prepared to counter any British reaction to the

[6] Turgot, however, contradicted his own argument in referring to the revenue Britain derived from India. *Ibid.*, 413.

[7] *Ibid.*, 396–397.

[8] Faure, *La disgrâce de Turgot*, 501–503; Douglas Dakin, *Turgot and the Ancien Régime in France* (London: Methuen and Co., 1939), 257. Sartine's animosity toward Turgot stemmed largely from an incident in 1775, an incident for which Turgot's arrogance was partially the fault.

[9] England, supplement 18: 109–111, "Notes sur les réflexions de M. Turgot du 6 Avril 1776," undated.

sending of arms.[10] The formal decision came on 2 May when Louis released 1,000,000 livres of arms to the Americans, to be supplied through a fictitious commercial house named Roderique Hortalez and Company, to be directed by Beaumarchais.[11] The Spaniards, whose actual interest was in prolonging the war until the end of the Portuguese dispute, matched the French subsidy.[12]

Turgot and his friend Malesherbes were forced to resign on 12 May. With their departure, Maurepas, Vergennes, and Sartine became the dominant members of the council. (Indeed, important questions were often not passed to the other members of the council, so references to the council should be understood as generally referring to this committee or inner council of the council.) Their cooperation gave the council a cohesion far greater than the governments of Spain or England—an enormous advantage when war came —but this unity was not conducive to the critical examination of foreign policy. Here Turgot's loss was irreparable. Turgot's defeat doomed France to eventual war—a war which quickly led to the dangers it hoped to forestall, a war fought for a chimera.

Why did Turgot fail in his program and Vergennes succeed in his? No one has as yet fully studied how the conjunction of the desires of unemployed military officers, Anglophobes, intellectuals, and expansionist businessmen reinforced the gradual acceptance of war by the king.[13] The

[10] I will examine these orders in detail in the next section. Vergennes immediately informed Garnier and Ossun of the decision. England 515: 382; Spain 585: 125, both of 22 April 1776.

[11] The choice of Beaumarchais is difficult to explain; Professor Brian Morton is currently investigating this question.

[12] Spain 579: 306–307, Grimaldi to Vergennes, 14 March 1776; Spain 580: 5–10, Ossun to Vergennes, 1 April 1776. It appears the "Considerations" picked the perfect argument to attract Spanish support, however tangential it may have been to Vergennes' real motives.

[13] See Bernard Faÿ, *The Revolutionary Spirit in France and America*, trans. Ramon Guthrie (New York: Harcourt, Brace, and Co., 1927); Frances Dorothy Acomb, *Anglophobia in France, 1763–1789* (Durham, N.C.: Duke University Press, 1950); H. Carré, P. Sagnac,

most penetrating judgment is still that of Albert Sorel, who wrote that Turgot failed because public opinion was divided on his reforms and because the king did not have the strength to steadfastly support him, while Vergennes succeeded because he enjoyed the support of the public and because his program did not make demands on the king.[14] There is an element of irony in Turgot's defeat. The war of which he warned not only achieved a revolution in America to which the council was indifferent save for reasons of state but also helped prepare both financially and psychologically the crisis which destroyed the French monarchy. Turgot with his dreams of a more modern France was, in a sense, the final victor.

4. Sartine's Battle for Increased Funds

While Vergennes conducted his struggle for French involvement in the American rebellion, Sartine, against greater resistance, fought for increased appropriations for his department. The campaigns of the two ministers eventually reinforced each other; initially, however, the two were independent.

At the end of 1775 the naval ministry prepared for Sartine a draft proposal for the following year suggesting a maximum program 11,000,000 livres above normal and a minimum proposal 7,000,000 above normal.[1] Sartine now had enough political experience to restrict himself to asking Louis merely for a supplemental 2,000,000 livres for a train-

---

and E. Lavisse, *Le régne de Louis XVI (1774–1789)*, vol. 9, part 1 of Ernest Lavisse, ed., *Histoire de France depuis les origines jusqu'à la Révolution* (Paris: Hachette et cie, 1910), 105; Claude H. Van Tyne, "French Aid before the Alliance of 1778," *American Historical Review* 31 (1925): 35.

[14] Sorel, *Europe and the French Revolution*, 293.

[1] B⁵10: unpaged, "Mémoire sur les dépenses variables pour 1776. Feuilles remises à Mgr. pour son travail sur le projet de 1776," no date, but probably November or December 1775. Both programs involved at least 5,000,000 livres for wood for construction.

ing squadron and an extra 3,760,000 livres for the West Indian colonies, presumably to pay for the reinforcements sent in 1775.[2]

By March 1776 the political situation had apparently changed, perhaps as a result of the "Considerations." The naval ministry prepared two reports for Sartine's use. There is no evidence that Sartine dared to present them in council, but they do demonstrate the potential a minister had for deceiving a king like Louis, lacking in experience and independence of judgment.

The first of these reports presented a list of naval matériel on hand versus the amounts the navy needed, and the cost of meeting the deficiency.[3] The navy's needs were computed rather generously: 2,305,000 ft.[3] of wood for construction (by earlier computations well over three years' normal use), 7,014 masts (an eight-year supply) and 94,282 cwt. of hemp (a five-and-a-half-year supply).[4] The cost of providing these would be 17,223,992 livres, equivalent to a year's appropriation for the entire expenses of the navy (although the report did propose to spread those expenses over two years). What are most interesting, however, are the figures for the amount of matériel on hand, which show an extraordinary decline from December 1775. Wood for construction had supposedly dropped from 1,262,104 ft.[3] to only 825,372 ft.[3] and large masts from 2,647 to 2,163 (although hemp had risen from 17,234 cwt. to 19,585 cwt.).[5]

[2] B¹81: 323–336, "Mémoire sur les fonds nécessaires pour le service de la marine et des colonies pendant l'année 1776," 23 December 1775.

[3] B⁵10: unpaged, "Tableau général de la situation des arsenaux de la marine," no date, but attached document is dated 22 March 1776 (hereafter cited as "Tableau général").

[4] Yearly needs given by B⁵10: unpaged, "Tableau des forces navales du roi dans le courant des treize années," no date, but probably 1775, are 750,000 ft.[3] of wood, 588 masts (apparently only those above a certain size—add another 50 percent for smaller masts), and 17,500 cwt. of hemp.

[5] December figures are from B⁵10: unpaged, "Comparaison de l'état où se trouvoir la marine du roi au mois d'août 1774 avec son état

What makes these figures particularly suspicious is the difference between the figure for wood at Brest and those given in the Brest intendant's reports. This difference had not appeared in a ministerial report written before the "Considerations"; it was to become even more marked in a report written at the end of April:

Date	*Ministerial Report*	Date	*Intendant's Report*[9]
		1 Jan 1776	558,270 ft.[3]
31 Jan 1776[6]	567,318 ft.[3]		
22 Mar 1776[7]	491,030 ft.[3]		
		1 April 1776	543,000 ft.[3]
30 April 1776[8]	482,480 ft.[3]		
		1 May 1776	580,879 ft.[3]
		1 June 1776	597,763 ft.[3]
		1 Aug 1776	614,000 ft.[3]
		1 Oct 1776	552,510 ft.[3]

This discrepancy does not appear for the other ports[10] and the amount of evidence is not sufficient to prove deceit, but it does provoke suspicion.

The second report, compiled about April, is also suspi-

---

actuel. . . ," no date, but end of 1775. These figures accord with the figures for 1 January 1776 in B¹84: 280, "Situation des magazins des ports cy-après au 1ᵉʳ janvier 1776, comparée avec celle de 1ᵉʳ janvier 1777," no date, but beginning of 1777. These latter figures are 1,275,970 ft.³ of wood, 3,929 masts of all sizes (i.e., 7″–28″—this figure is about 50 percent larger than other figures for masts, which apparently are restricted to masts above a certain size), and 18,814 cwt. of hemp.

[6] B¹82: 38, untitled memoir, 1 March 1776.

[7] "Tableau général."

[8] B¹82: 42–47, untitled memoir, end of April. This did adjust Brest's annual needs from 1,236,000 ft.³ to 1,000,000 ft.³

[9] B³626: 11, 71, 120–121, 202; B³627: 145–146, 313, Ruis-Embito and Commissioner-General Marchais to Sartine, 8 January, 3 April, 3 May, 5 June, 5 August, and 23 October 1776.

[10] The Toulon figures are obviously in error, probably because of a clerk's error; the Lorient and Rochefort figures are reasonable.

cious.[11] It proposed repairs and overhauls for 1776, including those already begun. Among the 20 ships of the line for which repairs were proposed, it listed 10 on which repairs had already commenced. These included the huge *Bretagne* and the *Bourgogne*. The repairs of the former actually began only in September 1776, those of the latter in 1777.[12] These discrepancies, if deliberate, may have been designed to make more acceptable a program to raise from 23 to 48 the number of available ships of the line (including 5 whose construction was to be completed).[13]

Sartine himself revealed the purpose of his proposals for overhauls and replenishment. His answer to the "Considerations"[14] echoed Vergennes' warnings about the dangers to the West Indies, the natural enmity of England, and the need for preparedness. Concretely, it proposed by the end of the summer to prepare reinforcements for the islands and, in the roadstead of Brest, a squadron of 10 to 12 ships of the line for whatever destination Louis wished.

Sartine quickly won his first victory, a victory also foreshadowing the triumph of Vergennes' policy. On 22 April Louis gave the following orders to the naval ministry:

1. That it continue to maintain four frigates and three corvettes as a patrol in the passages to the West Indies.
2. That it order Brest to hold 12 ships of the line and a

[11] B⁵10: unpaged, "Tableau général de la situation des vaisseaux, frégates, et autres bâtiments qui composent la marine du roi dans les différents ports au 31 mars 1776," no date.

[12] See below for *Bretagne*; B⁸632: 144, port commandant St. Aignan at Toulon to Sartine, 29 October 1776, reporting work not yet begun on the *Bourgogne*.

[13] By my own count 25 ships of the line were ready; this counts as ready 5 ships of the line needing only light repairs, but drops 3 others, which were on loan or subsequently needed unexpected repairs. This represents an increase of 1 in 20 months (add *Victoire, Intrépide, Indien*, delete *Sagittaire, Bordelaise*). Frigates in readiness were to be increased from 22 to 34.

[14] England, supplement 18: 112-114, Sartine to Louis, no date.

proportionate number of frigates ready and in condition to be armed at the first order.

3. That since it could be presumed that England would commence any hostile project by blockading Brest, it order Toulon to hold eight ships of the line and some frigates ready to be placed in armament to carry aid where it should be judged necessary.

4. Finally, that it continue the overhauls already begun and all those that would be necessary and that it order the navy's magazines and arsenals filled with all they lacked to construct, equip and arm the navy's ships.[15]

These orders were confirmed ten days later when the king decided to provide arms to the American rebels. Sartine was privately instructed that the 20 ships of the line and the necessary frigates should be ready by October.[16]

The preparation of so many ships required a major exertion since even those ships listed as ready needed some attention and all this work would compete for workers and wood with existing projects.[17] Sartine even had to order some reconstructions and overhauls to be suspended so work could begin on ships of the line and frigates needing less work.[18]

Sartine naturally saw immediately the connection between the work of the ports and his long-standing effort to obtain more funds. On 3 May Sartine wrote Brest for a detailed listing of anticipated expenditures in money and manpower in order to justify his request for the necessary

[15] Spain 580: 120–123, Vergennes to Ossun, 22 April 1776; England 515: 382, Vergennes to Garnier, 22 April 1776.

[16] B⁴214: 51–54, Fleurieu papers, memoir of January 1777.

[17] For the effects of wood shortages on repairs see B³625: 19, port commandant d'Orvilliers at Brest to Sartine, 27 March 1776; B³626: 94–99, Ruis-Embito to Sartine, 19 April 1776.

[18] B²409: 123–124, Sartine to Ruis-Embito, 27 April 1776; B²410: 123, Sartine to intendant Dasque at Toulon, 29 April 1776. In the latter, Sartine ordered that after the current three overhauls were finished, four new overhauls should be commenced in order of least difficulty.

funds.[19] Two weeks later he repeated these instructions and added that the intendant and port commandant should insure that the good weather of June and July were profitably used. Henceforth Sartine requested weekly progress reports.[20] The intendant reported on 22 May that he could have 16 ships of the line ready by September and 6 more the end of the year.[21] The king, however, was not yet ready for such a program so that Sartine had to restrict Brest to preparing 12 ships of the line and as many frigates as possible. Brest therefore dropped 4 ships of the line, 3 of which were almost ready and could be added at any time.[22] Toulon was restricted to preparing 8 ships of the line, 5 frigates and 5 smaller ships (at a cost of 2,300,000 livres), although for an extra 1,000,000 livres 8 more ships of the line and 7 more frigates could be readied.[23]

In July Brest requested an additional 2,174,000 livres for a second group of 8 ships of the line and 5 frigates. Sartine ordered the port authorities to wait until the king had made up his mind.[24]

By August the 20 ships of the line ordered to full readiness in April were almost finished. Their preparation had been extremely expensive. Exclusive of fixed expenses (ap-

[19] B²409: 128, 129, Sartine to d'Orvilliers and Ruis-Embito, 3 May 1776.

[20] B²409: 152, Sartine to d'Orvilliers, 18 May 1776.

[21] B³626: 155, Ruis-Embito to Sartine, 22 May 1776; B²409: 165, Sartine to Ruis-Embito, 31 May 1776. Ruis-Embito died on 29 May 1776. Commissioner-General Marchais sent even more detailed lists on 5 and 7 June. B³626: 208–209, 217–221, Marchais to Sartine, 5 and 7 June 1776.

[22] B²409: 174, 178, Sartine to Orvilliers and Marchais, 9 June 1776; B³626: 237–239, Marchais to Sartine, 17 June 1776. Sartine emphasized that the decision to defer the remaining four ships was the king's and was based on financial reasons.

[23] B²410: 160, 202, Sartine to Dasque, 8 June and 12 July 1776.

[24] B³626: 362, Marchais to Sartine, 8 July 1776 (résumé); B³626: 383–384, Sartine to Marchais, 19 July 1776 (résumé); see also B³627: 19–43. Rochefort and Toulon suffered from the extreme shortage of wood, which slowed work on the *Fendant*, *Réfléchi*, *Artésien*, *Saint-Michel*, and *Flamand*. See also Appendix C.

parently still about 8,000,000 livres) the navy proper had already spent about 16,181,766 livres during 1776; for the same purposes only 11,721,629 livres had been appropriated for the entire year. Sartine therefore requested a supplemental appropriation of 13,506,438 livres—4,460,137 to cover the existing deficit, 3,000,000 for placing the newly repaired ships in commission, 3,300,868 for the expenses of the remainder of the year, and 2,745,433 to cover the costs of preparing the second group of ships at Brest and Toulon.[25] Louis' resistance was now too weakened to reject completely Sartine's demands, particularly without Turgot's aid to bolster his good intentions. Although he did not grant the full 13,500,000 livres, he awarded a supplement of 9,500,000.[26] By so doing he established the precedent that the navy could spend in excess of appropriations with the confidence that a substantial portion of the excess would be met by supplemental awards. On 20 August Sartine wrote the major ports to tell them to begin work on the second group of ships, carrying all expenses except workers' pay on their accounts for 1777.[27] Sartine, apparently anticipating a favorable decision, had already authorized the overhaul of the *Bretagne*, the largest ship in the French navy and not even in the second group to be repaired, at an estimated cost of 479,000 livres and 135,000 ft.³ of wood.[28]

Brest immediately announced lengthy overhauls to the *Bretagne*, *Saint-Esprit*, *Glorieux*, and *Actionnaire*, and reported that the unbudgeted *Indien*, *Amphion*, and *Fier* plus a frigate and two corvettes were also ready.[29] On 9 and 10

[25] B⁵10: unpaged, "Rapport des extraits ci-joints des projets formes pour les différents ports pour l'année 1776," August 1776; see also B⁵10: unpaged, "Mémoire au roi," 15 July 1777.

[26] B⁵10: unpaged, "Mémoire au roi," 15 July 1777.

[27] B³626: 372, Sartine to Marchais, 20 August 1776 (résumé); B²410: 240–241, 252, Sartine to Dasque, 20 August and 26 August 1776; B³630: 275–276, Sartine to intendant d'Aubenton at Rochefort.

[28] B³626: 371, Sartine to Marchais, 16 August 1776 (résumé).

[29] B³625: 73–74/B³626: 375, d'Orvilliers to Sartine, 28 August 1776; B³627: 215; Marchais to Sartine, 30 August 1776.

September Sartine informed Toulon and Brest in confidence that their full projects should be prepared.[30] The four new overhauls at Brest began that month.[31]

5. The Consequences of Rearmament

One of the most striking aspects of Louis' decision to increase appropriations was its lack of relationship to any immediate necessities. Although the expansion of the rearmament program would soon produce a rapid deterioration of relations with Britain, these relations had thus far remained relatively unstrained. The clandestine arms shipments of the French government had not yet begun (although unsanctioned private shipments had been going on since the beginning of the revolution). Parliament had appropriated almost a third more money for the navy than in 1775, but Garnier estimated the numbers of sailors and amount of money would have to be tripled in case of general war.[1] The total number of British ships was almost unchanged but there was a large increase in the number of smaller ships at sea, particularly frigates needed in America.[2] The British army had greatly increased its strength in North America—General Howe's main British army by mid-August had 30,000 troops, including about 23,000 Brit-

---

[30] B⁴134: 52–53, confidential letters of Sartine to d'Orvilliers and Marchais, 9 September 1776 and to St. Aignan and Dasque, 10 September, 1776.

[31] These overhauls were to the *Bretagne, Saint-Esprit, Glorieux,* and *Actionnaire.* B⁸626: 376–377 ff., Sartine to Marchais, 17 September 1776, Marchais to Sartine, 18 September 1776, etc.

[1] England 515: 426; England 516: 398–411, Garnier to Vergennes, 27 April and 21 June 1776. Parliament voted £2,227,000 (51,221,000 livres) exclusive of debt maintenance, and 28,000 sailors. Expenditures were actually higher.

[2] England 516: 372–375, Garnier to Vergennes, 21 June 1776. Frigates at sea had increased from 22 to 61, including 43 in American waters and seven in the Caribbean. The British navy included 132 servicable ships of the line, as compared to 128 the previous year.

ish regulars—but these troops posed no immediate threat to the West Indies.[3] The British army had evacuated Boston and was now facing an American army of comparable size entrenched at Brooklyn and New York.

The British had thus far taken little notice of France except for the secret decision to raise the number of guard ships from 20 to 24 and to place 12 more ships of the line in condition to be armed if needed.[4] The English foreign secretaries mentioned the work in French ports to Garnier in May and again in August, but when Garnier appeared apprehensive over the sending of a 64-gun ship to the West Indies and supplies to Newfoundland, and over the rumored increase of guard ships to 30, Vergennes discounted his fears. Vergennes assured Garnier that he envisaged these measures as an effect of English disquietude about French intentions rather than as the announcement of a secret, distant project. Garnier, although confirming the addition of the three guard ships, conceded that their purpose was probably defensive.[5]

If English actions did not justify the need for increased armaments, neither did French operations. A squadron under Commodore the Count Louis-Charles du Chaffault de Besné, originally intended for training, cruised in the Bay of Biscay until September to keep the English clear of

[3] Mark M. Boatner, *Encyclopedia of the American Revolution* (New York: David McKay, 1966), 798; England 516: 393–394, 409–410, 451–458; England 517: 168, Garnier to Vergennes, 21 June 1776 and following.

[4] G. R. Barnes and J. H. Owen, eds., *The Private Papers of John, Earl of Sandwich, 1771–1782* (London: Naval Records Society, 1932–1938), 1: 212–213, minute of cabinet meeting, 20 June 1776 (hereafter cited as *Sandwich Papers*); *ibid.*, 215–216, Sandwich to North, 21 July 1776. French naval intelligence possessed a copy of a British newspaper of 3 August 1776 reporting 11 ships of the line were to be held ready. B^{r}439: no. 92, extracts from English papers, 1776.

[5] England 516: 147–153; England 517: 226–233, Garnier to Vergennes, 17 May and 2 August 1776; England 517: 269, Vergennes to Garnier, 10 August 1776; England 518: 43, Garnier to Vergennes, 6 September 1776.

the French coast but met with no incidents.[6] The West Indian patrols, conducted in cooperation with the Spanish, made no major demands on the navy;[7] the four frigates sent in June and three corvettes in October were little more than normal rotation. Vergennes rejected in May a Spanish request that France send 10,000 to 12,000 troops to Saint Domingue, maintaining that the climate would inflict pointless losses among these men and that such an action would justly alarm England.[8] The only other operation undertaken was that of sending the ship of the line *Brillant* (accompanied by a frigate, a transport and 200 recruits) to the Indian Ocean to replace the *Flamand*.

Louis' decision to approve additional expenditures was followed by two other critical decisions. The first concerned naval administration. The actions taken in 1774 had been only an interim solution. With the help of Fleurieu, Sartine began to plan the reorganization of naval administration. His first step, on 1 December 1775, foreshadowed the redistribution of power to come. To the delight of the seagoing line officers, Sartine formalized their distinction from port officers, constituting the latter a separate corps.[9] On

[6] B⁴126 is devoted to this squadron. See also Spain 580: 179–180, Vergennes to Ossun, 3 May 1776; B¹83: 111–114, memoir of Louis for du Chaffault, 12 May 1776. The squadron contained three ships of the line, six frigates, and seven smaller ships. On 12 May it received the order to protect any American ship that asked for protection.

[7] The French authorities in the West Indies were instructed to give protection to any American ships that asked it, but not to offer such protection. They were forbidden to promise that American interests would be favored, but on the other hand French warships ceased their customary searches for illegal American trade with the French West Indies. B⁴128: 194–195, "Projet des instructions correspondantes à celles de la cour d'Espagne," 30 May 1776; B⁴127: 140; B⁴134: 88–89, Sartine to Lts. Montreuil and Labadie, respective captains of the corvette *Rossignol*, 28 December 1775 and 30 May 1776; B⁴134: 88–89, Sartine to commandant d'Argout at Martinique, August 1776.

[8] Spain 580: 228–230, Vergennes to Ossun, 14 May 1776; see also Spain 580: 147, Ossun to Vergennes, 25 April 1776. The French did send 1,350 recruits as troop replacements.

[9] Brun, *Port de Toulon*, 1: 549; Neuville, *Etat Sommaire des Archives*, 342. In September 1776 this separation was relaxed, but port officers were permanently restricted to service ashore.

27 September 1776 Sartine promulgated seven new admin-istrative ordinances.[10] Through them the port comman-dants, who were line officers, received new authority over the dockyards at the expense of the intendants. Henceforth the port commandant would be assigned authority over the disposition, direction, and execution of the work of the ports while the intendant would be restricted to the receipt, expenditure, and accountability of money and matériel. The consequences of these reforms should not be overestimated. Policy recommendations continued to be made by the in-tendant, port commandant, and their chief assistants in committee, and every major decision was made at Versailles. Nonetheless, the emphasis in the dockyards was shifted from economical operation to operational efficiency.

Sartine moved also to cut the number of officers of ad-ministration by about 40 percent, as well as stripping them of certain functions such as administering the conscription system, auditing accounts, and monitoring expenses aboard ship. He also proposed letting the number of line captains, lieutenants, and ensigns drop by attrition from 750 to 700, about double the peacetime need of the navy, so that offi-cers could serve in alternate years—an indication that Sar-tine was still more committed to efficiency than to prepar-ing for an impending war.

Nothing was said in the ordinances about officers of higher rank, whose number was actually increased. Fifteen new commodores were named between April 1776 and the end of the year, partly to make up for the attrition since the last set of promotions in 1771, partly to replace older com-modores who were asked to retire.[11] For the moment the

10 Lambert de Sainte-Croix, *L'administration de la marine*, 276 ff.; Brun, *Port de Toulon*, 1: 548 ff.; A. Deschard, *Notice sur l'organisa-tion du corps du commissariat de la marine française depuis l'origine jusqu'à nos jours* (Paris: Berger-Levrault, 1879), 37–39. See also Sar-tine's memoir to Louis proposing the reforms, G 127: 201–213.

11 Of the 22 commodores of 1775, ten had died, been promoted, or retired by the end of 1776, including seven of the eight most senior. Georges Lacour-Gayet, *La marine militaire de la France sous la règne*

number of higher flag officers remained the same: nine lieutenants-general of the fleet, two vice-admirals, and the
admiral of France.[12]

The last piece needed to complete the new administrative
structure was the creation of a central director of ports and
arsenals at Versailles. This new position was established on
1 November and naturally was given to Fleurieu. The new
port ordinances were not put into effect, however, until the
following spring when a special commissioner to oversee
the transition visited each of the major ports.[13]

The royal decision on administrative reforms had less
immediate impact on relations with England than did a second decision taken in September. The summer's naval preparations had been for a squadron to protect the arms shipments for the Americans. Although these shipments were
not yet ready, the return of du Chaffault's training and
observation squadron had stripped the French coast of
warships. The king therefore ordered the mobilization of
his new squadron.

The new squadron was not large: only six ships of the
line and four frigates to be chosen by the intendant and
port commandant at Brest.[14] On 20 September they chose
the *Intrépide, Magnifique, Protée, Eveillé, Roland,* and *Bi-*

---

de Louis XV (Paris: H. Champion, 1910), 538–539; Lambert de Sainte-
Croix, *L'administration de la marine*, 275. Commodores were port
commandants, or commanded large squadrons or sections of a fleet.

[12] Lieutenants-general commanded major fleets. The rank of vice-
admiral was an honor given the two senior lieutenants-general. The
current admiral of France was the heir of an illegitimate son of Louis
XIV. His largely ceremonial role did not require him to leave Versailles. By the seniority system promotions were almost automatic,
although exceptional ability was rewarded by early promotion. It is
important to realize that promotion did not necessarily mean one
would receive anything to command; many flag officers spent the war
at Versailles or at their own châteaux.

[13] See Brun, *Port de Toulon*, 1: 553, for the transition at Toulon in
March 1777.

[14] B³626: 376, Sartine to Marchais, 15 September 1776 (résumé);
see also Spain 581: 411–412, Vergennes to Ossun, 20 September 1776.

zarre and the frigates *Indiscrète, Inconstante, Zéphyr,* and *Oiseau*.[15] Despite all assurances these ships were not actually ready, and it was six weeks before they were moved from the harbor to the roadstead of Brest.[16]

The British reacted sharply to even this small mobilization, in part because of the continuing deterioration of relations between their ally Portugal and France's ally Spain. As early as March 1776 Spain had 17 ships of the line in full commission.[17] She spent the summer preparing an expedition of 8,000–9,000 troops for South America and kept four ships of the line and four frigates off the Canaries to intercept Portuguese reinforcements for Brazil.[18] Grimaldi even wrote Ambassador Aranda that both France and Spain should prepare for war as if it were inevitable.[19] Vergennes replied with a memoir of unrestrained bellicosity toward England, probably to sound out Spanish intentions and to remind them that France was too involved with weakening England to be an auxiliary to an attack on Portugal.[20] Spain backed down immediately but the threat of an extended war persisted. Given the tenseness of the South American

[15] B³625: 85–86, d'Orvilliers to Sartine, 20 September 1776.

[16] They were placed in the roadstead between 9 and 18 November 1776. The delay was due to a temporary shortage of sails and because of the need to assemble the crews. B³625: 98–100, Marchais to Sartine, 20 September 1776; B³626: 389, d'Orvilliers to Sartine, 15 November 1776. Even more shocking was the condition of the eight ships supposedly ready at Toulon. The *Guerrier* was still undergoing repairs, and the *César, Protecteur,* and *Hector* had not finished their overhauls. See B³632: 377–378, Dasque to Sartine, 9 September 1776; B³632: 160–163, St. Aignan to Sartine, 25 November 1776.

[17] Spain 579: 247, Ossun to Vergennes, 4 March 1776. Charles claimed he could arm 30 ships of the line. Spain 580: 152, Ossun to Vergennes, 29 April 1776.

[18] Spain 581: 235–238, 252–255, 286–288; Spain 582: 81, 299, Ossun to Vergennes, 15 August, 19 August, 26 August, 10 October, 21 November 1776. The squadron returned to port in November, having accomplished nothing.

[19] Spain 581: 283–285, Grimaldi to Aranda, 26 August 1776.

[20] Garnier's copy is given in England 517: 385–390, "Considérations sur la partie qu'il convient à la France de prendre vis-à-vis de l'Angleterre dans la circonstance actuelle," read to the king in committee, 31 August 1776.

situation, the size of the Spanish mobilization, Howe's inability to destroy the inexperienced army of General Washington, and the general nervousness of the North government and its constitutents, the mobilization of even a small French squadron was most inopportune, although it must be admitted that English naval intelligence expected from the French preparations an even larger mobilization.[21]

To add to the possibility of misunderstanding, a new French ambassador arrived in London in late October—the Marquis de Noailles, a disciple of Choiseul, who was named to his new post largely by the influence of Queen Marie Antoinette. He was immediately informed by North that Britain was adding 15 guard ships to her original 20 because of the possibility of war between Spain and Portugal.[22] During November the number of guard ships was increased to the new total and impressment was begun so that the guard ships could be manned at full strength rather than at 60 percent of their complement.[23]

This show of concern unnerved the volatile Noailles. Instead of Garnier's precise reports, Vergennes began to receive emotional reports on the English mood and unsubstantiated gossip about English strength. On 8 November, for example, Noailles listed 41 ships of the line which were supposedly to rendezvous off Spithead to form a squadron of observation; three weeks later he raised the total to 43 and told Vergennes he did not share the latter's confidence about English passivity.[24]

Vergennes treated the English actions calmly, reassuring Noailles about English intentions.[25] Part of his confidence

[21] *Sandwich Papers*, 1: 212, 213–214, reports of 10 June 1776, Sandwich to North, 21 July 1776.

[22] England 518: 353, Noailles to Vergennes, 28 October 1776.

[23] *Sandwich Papers*, 1: 201–202, minutes of cabinet meeting of 18 November 1776; see also *Ibid.*, 217. The list in *Ibid.*, 205–206, includes six later substitutions. Impressment was ordered on 28 October. Ira D. Gruber, *The Howe Brothers and the American Revolution* (New York: Atheneum, 1972), 165.

[24] England 518: 359–360; England 519: 51, 232–233, 239–241, Noailles to Vergennes, 29 October, 8 November, and 29 November 1776.

[25] England 519: 99–103; England 520: 27; England 519: 229, Ver-

was probably based on the increased expectation that France could count on Spanish aid if relations deteriorated too rapidly. In response to Vergennes' anti-British memoir the Spaniards had agreed to keep 14 ships of the line ready at Cadiz (and to arm still more) and had decided to admit all American shipping into the ports of the Spanish empire.[26] Their great convoy carrying 9,300 troops, escorted by six ships of the line and seven frigates, left Cadiz for Buenos Aires in November, guaranteeing that the hostilities with Portugal would at least temporarily be restricted to South America.[27]

With the departure of the Spanish fleet the situation eased enough for Grimaldi to announce his coming resignation as Spanish foreign minister. The English reassured Spain of their peaceful intentions, reducing tensions.[28] Finally, at the end of November Ossun learned that the Portuguese king, Joseph I, was in danger of death. His death was expected to lead to the fall of his chief minister, the Marquis de Pombal, the architect of the aggressive Portuguese policy in South America.

Despite the British restraint and the reduced danger of

---

gennes to Noailles, 14 November, 23 November (copy), and 30 November 1776. See also Spain 582: 213–214, 234–235, 271–275, Vergennes to Ossun, 4 November, 8 November, and 18 November 1776.

[26] Spain 581: 396–398, Ossun to Vergennes, 16 September 1776; Spain 581: 404–405, Grimaldi to Aranda, 19 September 1776; Spain 582: 63–68, Grimaldi to Aranda, 9 October 1776.

[27] Spain 581: 431–435, 445; Spain 582: 35–38, 271–275, Ossun to Vergennes, 26 September, 30 September, 3 October, and 18 November 1776. Portugal had five ships of the line in South America to Spain's one, but by October Spain had 28 ships of the line in commission. Spain 582: 69–78, Grimaldi to Aranda, 8 October 1776. In 1783 the Portuguese navy contained only 11 ships of the line. B⁷480: no. 7, "Etat de la marine de Portugal en 1783."

[28] Spain 582: 296, 312, Ossun to Vergennes, 21 and 25 November 1775. Vergennes also reassured the Spaniards about Britain's good intentions. Spain 582: 213–214, 234–235, Vergennes to Ossun, 4 and 8 November 1776. Grimaldi's resignation was due largely to his hopeless political position (because of setbacks connected with his policy toward Algiers). Sir Charles Petrie, *King Charles III of Spain* (London: Constable and Co., 1971), 160–161.

an extension of the Spanish-Portuguese difficulties, France decided to make a countergesture to the British partial mobilization. Presumably, the council wished merely to make a show of strength. They decided against sending the new squadron, commanded by du Chaffault, to the West Indies, probably because Noailles reported Britain frightened by such a possibility.[29] Instead they sent orders to increase du Chaffault's squadron to thirteen ships.[30] For the first time Vergennes now asked Ossun to compile reports on the actual condition of the Spanish navy, army, and reserves of seamen. He did tell Ossun that the purpose of the new armaments was to force the English to be prudent, that the squadron would not be sent to the Western Hemisphere, and that a second squadron would not be prepared at Toulon.[31]

Before the end of the year Lord Stormont, the British ambassador at Versailles, wrote a fellow ambassador that he believed French protestations of peace sincere—the French preparations had caused the English armaments, and the English armaments had then caused the augmentation of those of the French.[32] Nonetheless the situation was becoming ominous.

During December the British sent four guard ships on patrol in the channel and began issuing letters of marque

[29] England 519: 229, Vergennes to Noailles, 30 November 1776; Spain 582: 358-359, Vergennes to Ossun, 8 December 1776. The orders for the squadron were prepared on 15 November 1776, but were never used. They are given B¹82: 17-21, 28-32. Britain intended to counter any such move by sending equal reinforcements. Gruber, *Howe Brothers*, 170.

[30] England 520: 38, Vergennes to Noailles, 7 December 1776 (copy); B¹83: 302, Sartine to Blouin, first secretary of the naval secretariat, 8 December 1776. Ships added were the *Robuste*, *Actif*, *Dauphin-Royal*, *Fendant*, *Réflechi*, *Triton*, and *Bien-Aimé*.

[31] Spain 582: 279-292, 410, 434-447, Ossun to Vergennes, 18 November, 23 December, and 30 December 1776; Spain 582: 358-359, Vergennes to Ossun, 8 December 1776.

[32] England 519: 355, Stormont to Sir Robert Keith, British ambassador to Vienna, 20 December 1776. Either Stormont gave a copy of this letter to Vergennes or it was intercepted.

permitting shipowners to arm their vessels (avowedly for self-defense but actually for privateering).[33] The first of Beaumarchais' arms ships left port although it was forced back by bad weather,[34] and Benjamin Franklin arrived in France in hopes of negotiating a treaty of amity and commerce. The growth of French arms had brought English warships to French waters and would likely bring English privateers as well. The increased dangers to French security in turn would present further need for arms. The cycle of increased armaments and increased diplomatic tensions had begun.

[33] England 520: 193, 388–389, Noailles to Vergennes, 17 December and 27 December 1776 (copies). The British had been reconnoitering Brest since 25 October. Gruber, *Howe Brothers*, 165.

[34] Roger Lafon, *Beaumarchais, le brillant armateur* (Paris: Société d'éditions géographiques, maritimes, et coloniales, 1928), 86–87, 95. This ship, the *Amphritite*, carried 62 pieces of artillery, 6,100 rifles, and 49 French officer volunteers.

CHAPTER FOUR

1777—The Failure of Limited Intervention

1. The Progress of Naval Rearmament

BY the beginning of 1777 French naval rearmament had made significant progress, but the French navy was still far from being prepared for war. Although the amount of hemp had risen by 132 percent during 1776, the number of masts had risen only 18 percent and the amount of wood by only 14 percent.[1] There were 37 ships of the line in condition by 1 January, an increase of 14 over 1 January 1776 and of ten over 1 September 1776.[2] Nevertheless, as early as June 1776 the English had 82 ships of the line at sea or in condition to be immediately armed[3] and since October they had increased their guard fleet to 35 of the line.[4] Brest reported that by April it could arm 23 ships of the line but that this would empty the magazines of all types of matériel, leaving nothing for future armaments and overhauls.[5]

With the new year, or shortly after, came numerous promotions and changes of personnel within the department —new intendants at the three major ports, new commandants at Martinique, Saint Domingue, Pondicherry, Île de France and Bourbon, four new lieutenants-general, and an

---

[1] B¹84: 280, "Situation des magasins des ports cy-après comparée avec celle de 1ᵉʳ janvier 1777," no date. Masts of all sizes totaled 4,640, hemp, 43,722 cwt., wood for construction, 1,457,634 ft.³

[2] This includes the *Sagittaire* (returned from the West Indies), but not the *Flamand* (returned from India in need of an overhaul) or *Bordelais* (still on loan). See also B¹83: 267–269, Sartine to Louis, 23 November 1776; England, supplement 18: 180, memoir read in council, 27 December 1776. See also Appendix C.

[3] England 516: 396–397, Garnier to Vergennes, 21 June 1776.

[4] See Chapter Three, Section 5.

[5] B³632: 8–9, St. Aignan to Sartine, 31 December 1776; B³625: 184–185, d'Orvilliers to Sartine, 30 December 1776.

added vice-admiral.[6] In February 1777 the new administration of ports was instituted despite the protests of both officers of administration and port officers.[7] During 1776 five new frigates had been ordered but had been postponed for lack of wood; in February 1777 five additional frigates were ordered.[8] Although little progress in replenishing the ports was made before April, the beginning of good weather permitted the commencement of a massive program of resupply.[9] The best indication of its success is a negative one: after April discussion of the matériel in the dockyards almost disappears from the ministerial correspondence. In February the *Languedoc* and *Fantasque* were finished at Toulon and work was resumed on the *Caton* and *Destin*. The *Bretagne*, *Glorieux*, *Saint-Esprit*, and *Actionnaire* were replaced in April at Brest by the *Orient*, *Conquérant*, and *Couronne*. Rochefort and Lorient also completed overhauls. The ports became attractions for royalty, receiving visits from Louis' brothers and from his brother-in-law, traveling incognito, Emperor Joseph of Austria. By the end of the year, 8 new frigates had been added to the navy and an-

[6] The new intendants were Arnauld de la Porte at Brest, Prevost de la Croix at Toulon, and Marchais at Rochefort. The new lieutenants-general included d'Orvilliers, the port commandant at Brest, and du Chaffault, commander of the squadron at Brest. The senior lieutenant-general, the Count d'Estaing, received the vice-admiralship.

[7] Brun, *Port de Toulon*, 1: 553–555; Deschard, *Corps du commissariat*, 110–112. Intendant d'Auberton at Rochefort had already resigned in protest of the new regulations.

[8] B¹84: 288–290, "Frégates de 26 canons de 12 à construire," 7 February 1777. Six more frigates were ordered in September 1777, two in October, and one in November, while another frigate was purchased from a private owner.

[9] B¹84: 315, "Etat des principales marchandises et munitions qui existaient dans les magasins des differents ports cy-après à l'époque du 1ᵉʳ avril 1777," no date; B¹83: 232, "Note des bois de construction qui suivant les marchés existant doivent être livrés dans les différents ports cy-après pendant l'année 1777," no date. Projected purchases for 1777 would increase the supply of wood to more than 3,200,000 ft.³, masts of all sizes to about 7,500, and hemp to approximately 100,000 cwt. Projected costs would be 9,966,748 livres.

other 12 ordered; 14 additional ships of the line were placed in readiness with another 3 still in overhaul.[10]

The work of the ports was probably the key element in the transition from peace to war, underlying the more obvious evolution of diplomacy and naval operations. At the beginning of the year Sartine had little difficulty in obtaining the funds he needed, although in 1776 the navy had spent at least 4,500,000 livres above the appropriation of 42,673,000 livres the king had awarded.[11] For 1777 Sartine asked and received over 45,000,000 livres—20,100,000 for the navy, 16,600,000 for the colonies and a supplemental award of 9,223,000.[12]

2. Growing Tension with Britain

Vergennes and the council were forced to move with great caution during the period of French rearmament, balancing the need to sustain the Americans and prepare for war against the need to avoid precipitating a war for which France was not yet prepared. The complexity of French policy makes the first half of 1777 a difficult period to describe. It is possible to see within this period, however, the development of a pattern—the gradual deterioration of relations with Britain, culminating in a great crisis during the summer of 1777.

Vergennes' first problem was dealing with the American commissioners Silas Deane, Arthur Lee, and Benjamin Franklin, who were now together in Paris. The situation of the United States was so desperate that France dared not

[10] Of the 64 ships of the line (including those in construction) at Sartine's entrance into office, 51 were ready by the end of 1777, 3 were in repair, 1 had been sold (*Hippopotame*), and 9 remained to be repaired (*Citoyen, Diligent, Minotaure, Sceptre, Six-Corps, Souverain, Northumberland, Union,* and *Bordelais*). Most of this last group were little better than hulks.

[11] See Appendix A. This appropriation for 1776 included 19,800,000 livres for the navy, 13,373,000 for colonies, and 9,500,000 for extraordinary expenses.

[12] B⁴214: 77, untitled memoir, Fleurieu papers, July 1777.

risk a commitment from which she could not retreat. Washington's army had been repeatedly defeated and when the commissioners wrote Vergennes for assistance, news had not yet arrived in Europe of the amazing victories at Trenton and Princeton. The commissioners asked for a treaty of commerce and for the use of eight ships of the line, either of which would have led France promptly into war. In return all they offered, should France become involved in war, was neutrality or at best a guarantee of the French West Indies.[1] Vergennes immediately refused the Americans, but to maintain their resolution he promised 2,000,000 livres in aid, to be paid quarterly.[2]

The major problem for the moment, however, was keeping relations with Britain under control. As the year began, there suddenly appeared a possibility of reversing the mutual arms buildup. On 3 January the Earl of Suffolk, one of the three British secretaries of state (with Lord Weymouth and Lord Germain), hinted to the Spanish ambassador that a mutual disarmament among the three powers might be worked out.[3] Despite his skepticism Vergennes was interested in feeling out the British. He suggested to the Spaniards that if the British did not follow up the idea they themselves should advance a concrete proposal. (Vergennes claimed that he did not wish France to make an offer as this might be considered a sign of weakness!) He observed that it was unlikely that the arming of 6 ships of

[1] United States 2: 18–19, Franklin, Deane, and Lee to Vergennes, 5 January 1777. See United States 2: 63–75, for draft treaty of January 1777. The following month the commissioners did offer unofficially not to make a separate peace in case of war between France and Britain resulting from a treaty of amity and commerce. Francis Wharton, ed., *The Revolutionary Diplomatic Correspondence of the United States* (Washington: Government Printing Office, 1889), 2: 260, personal pledge of commissioners, 2 February 1777.

[2] Spain 583: 40–42, Vergennes to Ossun, 12 January 1777. Vergennes admitted that to claim the right to trade with America would be a tacit recognition of American independence. England 524: 41, Vergennes to Noailles, 19 July 1777.

[3] Spain 583: 128–130, Grimaldi to Aranda, 27 January 1777.

the line at Brest would of itself have caused the English to increase their guardships from 20 to 43 [sic], "It is not at all our armaments which chagrin the English; it is the works we have undertaken and which we are continuing for the reestablishing of our navy."[4]

The Spaniards were not interested in pursuing the subject. They agreed to go along with a proportional disarmament if France insisted, but they had doubts about Britain's seriousness and felt the proposal particularly dangerous to France.[5] Although Vergennes admitted to Noailles that he doubted the English had the naval superiority or financial strength necessary for an attack on the Bourbons,[6] he ordered his ambassador to reject a proportional disarmament as impractical. He told Aranda that such a disarmament would be advantageous to Britain and damaging to the American colonists.[7]

The arms race quickly accelerated. Du Chaffault initially used only frigates for patrols but the situation changed when Lord Stormont, the British ambassador, announced that the British were extending their patrols into the Bay of Biscay to intercept American commerce. On 9 February du Chaffault was ordered to send a ship of the line and

[4] Spain 583: 35, Vergennes to Ossun, 11 January 1777. The British had actually only increased their guardships to 35.

[5] Spain 583: 128–130, Grimaldi to Aranda, 27 January 1777. The Spaniards were particularly disturbed by the fact that the British told them that France was the cause of the British armaments and told the French that Spain was the cause. See also England 520: 211–212, Noailles to Vergennes, 17 January 1777.

[6] England 521: 121–123, Vergennes to Noailles, 23 January 1777. Noailles continued to send exaggerated warnings and faulty intelligence. England 521: *passim*.

[7] England 521: 161–163, Vergennes to Noailles, 1 February 1777; Spain 583: 204–205, Vergennes to Aranda, 12 February 1777. Vergennes expressed to Noailles bewilderment as to the cause of the British proposal, but said it would not cause France to relax. The Spaniards proceeded to inform the British that it was their responsibility to make any proposals. This ended the discussion. Spain 583: 310–311, Ossun to Vergennes, 3 March 1777.

three frigates into the Bay of Biscay, to offer protection to any ship that asked it (although not to seek out ships to protect), and to increase the size of his patrols if needed in order to preserve superiority of force.[8] To insure that du Chaffault would have sufficient forces, Sartine ordered the arming of six ships of the line and two frigates at Toulon, which would be available to reinforce either Brest or the West Indies.[9]

Du Chaffault's first patrol, under Captain de Grasse of the *Intrépide*, left Brest in mid-February. By the end of the month du Chaffault's other 12 ships of the line were in the roadstead of Brest.[10] De Grasse met only a single English ship of the line and in mid-March returned to port without incident. His relief, Captain La Motte-Picquet of the *Robuste*, was not as obedient to Sartine's orders for circumspection toward the British. He warned the British ship of the line *Exeter* to stay away from the French coast and told the British that he had orders to protect the commerce of all flags. La Motte-Picquet had to be reprimanded for disobeying orders by his directness[11] and Vergennes was reduced to claiming the English must have misunderstood what he had said.[12] At the end of March the council threat-

[8] B⁴129: 8, 10–11/B⁴134: 171–174, instructions for du Chaffault, 9 February 1777.

[9] B²412: 35, Sartine to St. Aignan, 10 February 1777. This squadron entered the roadstead of Toulon between 12 and 16 April. B⁵10: unpaged, "Etat des vaisseaux et autres bâtiments du roi qui ont été armés au port de Toulon depuis l'année 1777 jusqu'en 1781 inclusivement," 21 January 1782.

[10] B³636: 47, 50, d'Orvilliers to Sartine, 26 and 28 February 1777.

[11] B⁴134: 203, 207, Sartine to du Chaffault, 26 March and 5 April 1777.

[12] England 520: 313–314, Noailles to Vergennes, 2 May 1777 (copy); England 520: 103, Vergennes to Noailles, 3 May 1777 (copy); England 523: 53, Vergennes to Noailles, 10 May 1777. Vergennes had already admitted that although the British had intercepted some French merchantmen they had conformed to maritime law and had stayed clear of the coast, so France had no legitimate complaint. England 520: 90–91, Vergennes to Noailles, 5 April 1777.

ened the addition of seven more ships of the line to the Brest and Toulon fleets in order to avert the reported addition of six more of the line to the British guard fleet.[13]

Du Chaffault was faced with increasing challenges. In February and March four of Beaumarchais' munitions ships sailed for America,[14] and La Motte-Picquet's relief, Captain Hector of the *Actif*, reported the presence of an English 80-gun ship off the French coast. On 28 April du Chaffault informed Sartine that he now intended to reinforce his patrols to maintain superiority; this action was immediately approved.[15] De Grasse sailed on 9 May with a patrol of three ships of the line and du Chaffault was ordered henceforth to keep two 74s and a 64 on station.[16] Incidents nevertheless continued—the sailing of the Marquis de Lafayette to join the American army as a volunteer,[17] the embarrassing cruise of the American privateer captain, Gustavus Conyngham, from a French port[18] and the firing of a warning shot by an English ship of the line across the bow of the French merchantman *Aimable Dorothée*.[19] Toulon was now

[13] For this incident see England 522: 158, Noailles to Vergennes, 28 March 1777; England 522: 399, Vergennes to Noailles, 11 April 1777; Spain 589: 65–67, Vergennes to Ossun, 12 April 1777; B[1]84: 319, memoir approved by king, 4 April 1777; B[2]412: 113, 117, Sartine to St. Aignan, 5 and 10 April 1777; B[3]636: 93, d'Orvilliers to Sartine, 16 April 1777; Gruber, *Howe Brothers*, 186. These British ships were probably only replacements for five guardships intended to be detached to America.

[14] These were the *Mercure, Seine, Amélie,* and *Marquis de la Chalotais.* Morton, *Beaumarchais Correspondance,* 2: 60n; England 522: 15–16, listing of Beaumarchais' ships; England 523: 23–24, Beaumarchais to Vergennes, 4 May 1777; B[4]132: 81–106, "Journal de navigation dans l'Amérique Septentrionale," by Frigate-Lieutenant de Soligné of the *Marquis de la Chalotais.*

[15] B[4]129: 31, du Chaffault to Sartine, 28 April 1777; B[4]134: 208–209, Sartine to du Chaffault, 4 May 1777.

[16] B[4]134: 221, Sartine to du Chaffault, 31 May 1777.

[17] Louis Gottschalk, *Lafayette Comes to America* (Chicago: University of Chicago Press, 1935), 83–123; see also B[4]134: 205, Sartine to minister of war Montbarey, 2 April 1777.

[18] See Section 3 of this chapter.

[19] England 523: 146–154, 418–426, Noailles to Vergennes, 30 May and 11 July 1777. Incidents in the West Indies involving the frigates

ordered to send out ships of the line in pairs on patrol, although this was done mostly for training[20] and warships were sent to Bordeaux and to Dunkirk to restrain both American and British interference with trade.[21]

Discussions with Spain placed almost as many demands on Vergennes and the council as did the growing incidents with Britain. Both Grimaldi and the Count de Floridablanca, who succeeded him in February as foreign minister, urged France to send six ships of the line to Point Guarico, Cuba in order to rendezvous with a Spanish naval force and to send an expeditionary corps of 10,000 men to Saint Domingue.[22] The council again refused but it agreed to arm a new squadron at Toulon which could be sent to the West Indies if necessary.[23] No agreement was reached concerning the expeditionary corps and the only immediate naval reinforcement for the Antilles was the frigate which took to his post the new commandant of Martinique, the Marshal de Bouillé.[24] The Spaniards offered to feed and quarter the French troops in Spanish Santo Domingo, and Charles announced that he would raise his squadron of observation at Cadiz from thirteen ships of the line to eighteen so that six could be sent to Guarico.[25] They argued that a combined West Indian fleet would enable the Bourbons to exert pressure on Britain, while the French argued that Britain

---

Tourterelle and *Indiscrète* also occurred during the same month, April 1777.

[20] B²412: 233, Sartine to St. Aignan, 24 June 1777. See also B⁴134: 240–241; Brun, *Port de Toulon*, 2: 4–5.

[21] B⁴134: 268, Sartine to du Chaffault, 5 July 1777; B⁴134: 270, 278, Sartine to Lt. Marsigny of the corvette *Etourdie*, 12 and 19 July 1777.

[22] Spain 583: 142–143, 264, Ossun to Vergennes, 27 January and 24 February 1777.

[23] Spain 583: 210–213, Vergennes to Ossun, 14 February 1777. This was the squadron for reinforcing du Chaffault if needed.

[24] B⁴214: 55, Fleurieu papers, 9 February 1777; B⁴134: 98, Sartine to des Farges, captain of the frigate *Terpsichore*. There were now five frigates and three corvettes assigned to the West Indies.

[25] Spain 583: 304, 380–381, Ossun to Vergennes, 3 March and 13 March 1777.

should not be alarmed so that she would continue the self-destructive war in America. A large troop reinforcement to the West Indies might even frighten the British into a surpise attack on the Newfoundland fishing fleet as in 1755.[26] Vergennes finally promised that if Britain proved unreasonable France would send five more battalions to Saint Domingue and three more to Martinique.[27] This, plus the assurances that France would have adequate naval supplies on hand by the end of the year and was in the process of constructing ten new frigates,[28] temporarily satisfied Floridablanca, who announced that no further detachments would be sent to Havana.[29] The council was also under pressure from the navy department to increase the French naval presence in the West Indies. The annual detailed intelligence report sent by Noailles in April gave the British naval strength in the West Indies as two 50s, five frigates, and twelve smaller vessels.[30] The naval ministry recommended that two additional frigates be added to the forces on station and by June new patrol stations were drawn up.[31] In fact, the growth of British forces in North America necessitated an even larger reinforcement. On 21 June 1777 the ship of the line *Protée* was ordered to stand by and

[26] Spain 584: 35–42, Floridablanca to Aranda, 7 April 1777; Spain 584: 16, Ossun to Vergennes, 3 April 1777; Spain 583: 425–426, Vergennes to Ossun, 22 March 1777.

[27] Spain 584: 115–120, Vergennes to Aranda, 26 April 1777.

[28] Spain 584: 138–141, Vergennes to Ossun, 2 May 1777.

[29] Spain 584: 224–227, 241–244, Ossun to Vergennes, 22 May and 26 May 1777. Two ships of the line had earlier been sent from Cadiz; three more had just left from Ferrol.

[30] England 522: 491–496, Noailles to Vergennes, 25 April 1777; B⁴214: 68–71, Fleurieu papers, May 1777. The reported total number of British ships of the line at sea or ready was 94, which is probably somewhat exaggerated. *Sandwich Papers*, 1: 422 lists only 85 ships of 50 guns or more as at sea or ready for sea (as of 1 January 1778). The number of ships of the line (50-gun ships and larger) in North America grew even more rapidly—four in 1775, nine in 1776, thirteen in 1777.

[31] B⁴214: 73–75, Fleurieu papers, May 1777; B⁴134: 229, "Etat des croisières de l'Amérique au 20 juin 1777."

three weeks later she accompanied the frigates *Amphritite* and *Renommée* to the West Indies.[32]

By this time the deterioration of relations with Britain replaced the Spanish pressure as a catalyst for strategic movements. In June the Bourbons learned of the Spanish capture of the strategic Portuguese-held island of Saint Catherine off southern Brazil. King Joseph I of Portugal had died in March. His daughter and successor, Queen Maria I, quickly brought her Spanish mother's long campaign against the anti-Spanish minister Pombal to a successful conclusion. With the loss of Saint Catherine the Portuguese war effort was doomed. An armistice was signed in June, almost guaranteeing a quick formal peace. Spain now no longer needed to fear attack from Britain and she announced her intention to send no new reinforcements to the Gulf of Mexico.[33] Ironically France was now to become her petitioner.

3. The Privateering Crisis

Of all the sources of tension between France and Britain the most explosive was the use of French ports by American privateers. Whatever sympathy Vergennes might have felt for the privateers, France could not permit such action without violating the terms of the Treaty of Utrecht of 1713.[1] Therefore du Chaffault was instructed to warn privateers away from the French coast and to bring them into port under escort if they ignored his warnings.[2] The Americans

---

[32] B⁴134: 230, 233, Sartine to d'Orvilliers, 21 June 1777; B⁴134: 256–261, instructions for de Cherisey, captain of the *Protée*, 5 July 1777.

[33] England 520: 113–114, Vergennes to Noailles, 7 June 1777; Spain 584: 303–304, 361–362, Ossun to Vergennes, 5 June and 23 June 1777.

[1] Vergennes himself admitted this. England 522: 135, Vergennes to Noailles, 22 March 1777. This was true despite the fact that the ships mentioned below were commanded by officers of the Continental Navy.

[2] B⁴134: 188, Sartine to du Chaffault, 22 February 1777. See also B⁴129: 9, 12. Vergennes also told Noailles that the Americans could not sell prizes in French ports and that it was up to their dexterity and prudence to devise ways to escape the application of the French

did their best to circumvent French control. Despite a French injunction on the practice the Americans continued to sell the prizes which had been brought by the privateer *Reprisal* into Lorient;[3] the French even briefly arrested the American captain Gustavus Conyngham at Dunkirk and released his prizes.[4] The French were forced to take such action by the continual protests of Stormont, the English ambassador. On 8 July 1777 Stormont again presented a formal protest.[5] Between 28 May and 27 June an American squadron, the *Reprisal*, 16, *Lexington*, 16, and *Dolphin*, 10, took 18 prizes in the Saint George's Channel. This squadron, commanded by Captain Lambert Wickes of the *Reprisal*, was then driven into Saint Malo and the neighboring port of Morlaix by a British ship of the line.

Stormont's protests were again successful. The council ordered that Wickes' squadron be sequestered and moreover suggested to Sartine that the French navy purchase a cutter at Dunkirk reported to be fitting out for the American captain, Conyngham.[6] The council also finally decided that the West Indies needed reinforcements and on about 18 July ordered six battalions of infantry, 600 artillerymen and 200 cavalrymen to the Antilles.[7] Their sailing was, how-

---

ruling. Obviously the French were concerned with the letter of the law rather than its spirit, which made control over local officials very difficult.

[3] B⁴134: 189, Sartine to commissioner Gonet at Lorient, 22 February 1777; B⁴134: 202, Sartine to Vergennes, 24 March 1777.

[4] Robert Walden Neeser, ed., *Letters and Papers Relating to the Cruises of Gustavus Conyngham, a Captain of the Continental Navy, 1777-1779* (New York: Naval History Society, 1915), xxx–xxxii (hereafter cited as *Conyngham Papers*); England 523: 54, Vergennes to Noailles, 10 May 1777; *Sandwich Papers*, I: 221-222, Stormont to Weymouth, 16 April 1777.

[5] England 524: 39-44, Vergennes to Noailles, 19 July 1777; William Bell Clark, *Lambert Wickes, Sea Raider and Diplomat* (New Haven: Yale University Press, 1932), 220-239.

[6] England 524: 9-10, Vergennes to Franklin, 16 July 1777; England 524: 39-44, Vergennes to Noailles, 19 July 1777; Clark, *Lambert Wickes*, 260-272.

[7] Spain 585: 77-78, Vergennes to Ossun, 18 July 1777.

ever, to be delayed until France had time to recall her New-foundland fishing fleet and Spain her expeditionary force and fleet from South America. Vergennes took this precaution for fear of precipitating a premature war—a war which the Americans now attempted to provoke.[8]

On the same day that Vergennes informed Spain of the coming reinforcements (now of little interest to Spain) Conyngham escaped from Dunkirk in his new cutter, the *Revenge*, using fictitious purchase papers and clearance papers for Bergen, Norway. Within eight days the British not only knew of his sailing but had evidence to suggest French complicity. On 26 July one of Conyngham's prizes was recaptured en route to a Spanish port. It had 16 Frenchmen among the 21 members of its prize crew.[9] On 1 August Weymouth told Stormont American agents were boasting that Sartine had arranged a delay in the sequestering of Wickes' ships so they could be refitted and sail and that Sartine was responsible for suggesting that Conyngham send his prizes to Spain.[10]

When Vergennes was confronted on 5 August with these accusations against his fellow minister he conducted Stormont to Sartine. In the presence of Louis, Sartine showed the English ambassador the orders to French port officials to permit no repetition of Conyngham's cruise. (Sartine took care also to renew the orders for sequestering Wickes'

[8] Clark, *Lambert Wickes*, 187–189.

[9] England 524: 50, de Guischard, commandant at Dunkirk, to Vergennes, 18 July 1777; England 524: 174–175, Vergennes to Noailles, 9 August 1777; *Sandwich Papers*, 1: 233–234; Clark, Lambert Wickes, 258–259, 272, 296. While I was in France in January 1970, a squadron of Israeli gunboats built in France but forbidden to leave port escaped with the apparent collusion of local authorities. They had fictitious purchase papers and were supposedly bound for Norway.

[10] Stevens, *Facsimiles of Manuscripts*, no. 1593, Weymouth to Stormont, 1 August 1777; England 524: 175–176, Vergennes to Noailles, 9 August 1777. The cabinet was under pressure to do something about American privateers, as they had just learned of the escape of 18 armed colonial vessels from New England ports, and of the capture by the Americans of an English frigate. Gruber, *Howe Brothers*, 217.

squadron.)[11] Vergennes attempted to exonerate the French commissioner at Dunkirk, claiming that he had permitted himself to be deceived by the Americans out of fear that his port would be raided by the English, as had been threatened by the resident British commissioner. Those responsible for the deception had been ordered arrested and the head of the admiralty at Dunkirk, who was responsible for issuing the false registration papers, had been ordered to render an account of his actions.[12]

Although not yet a crisis, the situation was serious enough to call for precautions. Du Chaffault was ordered to keep six ships of the line ready to sail immediately and he was given four extra frigates. He was then ordered to issue six months' provisions to half of his squadron and three months' to the other half. Port Commandant St. Aignan at Toulon was ordered to keep a frigate standing by in case it should be necessary to recall the ships of the line on cruise.[13]

On 19 August Stormont delivered to Vergennes a demand from Weymouth that Wickes' squadron be ordered to leave its French ports.[14] Three days later the situation drastically worsened. Nathaniel Parker Forth, an agent of the North cabinet, arrived to meet with Maurepas. Forth told Maurepas that he had been sent to warn France that British public

[11] Stevens, *Facsimiles of Manuscripts*, no. 1597, Stormont to Weymouth, 6 August 1777; Clark, *Lambert Wickes*, 267, 302–303; *Conyngham Papers*, 81–82.

[12] England 524: 174–179, Vergennes to Noailles, 9 August 1777; Stevens, *Facsimiles of Manuscripts*, no. 1644, Stormont to Weymouth, 9 August 1777; England 524: 90, Lenoir, lieutenant-general of the Paris police, to Vergennes, 11 August 1777; Clark, *Lambert Wickes*, 303. As mentioned above, the British had received in the peace treaty of 1763 the right to keep a commissioner at Dunkirk to prevent its fortification. The French corvette *Etourdie* arrived at Dunkirk the day before the *Revenge* escaped. B³635: 18, commissioner Devilliers to Sartine, 18 July 1777.

[13] B⁴132: 292, Sartine to d'Orvilliers and du Chaffault, 13 August 1777; B³636: 186, d'Orvilliers to Sartine, 18 August 1777; B⁴134: 295, 296, Sartine to St. Aignan and du Chaffault, 16 August 1777.

[14] Stevens, *Facsimiles of Manuscripts*, no. 1599, Weymouth to Stormont, 8 August 1777; *Ibid.*, no. 1652, Stormont to Weymouth, 20 August 1777.

opinion was so agitated that unless it could be reassured as to France's sincerity, war would be certain.[15] Forth suggested that France return the prizes made by American ships and publish her orders forbidding the sale of prizes in French ports. He told Maurepas that he had to have an answer by his return to England on 26 August and arranged a meeting between Vergennes and Stormont for the evening of 23 August. During a meeting of the council that day, the king agreed to give Forth copies of the French orders to the ports in exchange for the English orders that their captains respect the immunity of French and Spanish flags. The council, however, agreed that France could not return any American prizes without labeling the Americans pirates rather than belligerents.[16] As Vergennes awaited his conference with Stormont, he wrote a personal letter to Noailles expressing his belief that Stormont's visit was only a pretext for delivering a declaration of war and that by the time Noailles received his letter war would have already commenced.[17]

Vergennes' panic was unjustified. The meeting with Stormont produced no change in the situation, although Maurepas offered the additional concession of promising to order Wickes' squadron from port without French escort.[18] The council, however, continued to treat war as imminent. On 23 and 24 August orders were sent to du Chaffault to recall his patrols lest they be captured by surprise, to the commandants of the West Indian colonies to permit no ships to leave port, to all French port commandants to institute a similar embargo, and to Newfoundland for the fishing fleet

[15] Spain 585: 329–332, Vergennes to Ossun, 26 August 1777; England 524: 430–433, Vergennes to Noailles, 30 August 1777; Clark, *Lambert Wickes*, 323–324.

[16] United States 2: 228–229, memoir read to the king in council, 23 August 1777.

[17] England 524: 364, Vergennes to Noailles, 23 August 1777. See also England 524: 470–471, Vergennes to Noailles, 6 September 1777.

[18] Stevens, *Facsimiles of Manuscripts*, no. 1654, Stormont to Weymouth, 23 August 1777.

to return immediately, leaving their catch behind if necessary.[19] When Vergennes wrote the Spaniards on 26 August about the crisis of that day he still expected war.[20] On 27 August, rigid new orders were sent to the ports prohibiting the arming of privateers and restricting the entrance of the privateers and their prizes in French ports.[21] It was not until 6 September that Vergennes wrote Noailles that matters had calmed and that the English had become more conciliatory, either because of events in America or because of other considerations.[22] On the same day du Chauffault was ordered to resume his patrols.[23] The English, however, had not yet achieved the final benefits of the crisis. On 27 August Saint Malo and Morlaix had been ordered to demand the sailing of Wickes' squadron. Between 14 and 17 September Wickes' ships finally sailed; the *Lexington* was quickly captured and the *Reprisal* was lost in a storm while returning to America.[24]

Vergennes later wrote that it was only too apparent that the crisis had been an attempt to intimidate France and that its goals had been to compromise France with the Americans and to inhibit France from sending further reinforce-

[19] B⁴134: 307, 308, Sartine to du Chauffault, 23 August 1777; B⁴134: 309, Sartine to d'Argout, Bouillé, and d'Arbaud, commandants at Saint Domingue, Martinique, and Guadeloupe, 24 August 1777; B⁴134: 319, Sartine to Dampierre, captain of the *Protée*, 24 August 1777; B⁴134: 311, Sartine to the Baron l'Espérance, commandant at Saint Pierre, 24 August 1777; B⁴134: 317, Sartine to Le Moyne, commissioner at Bordeaux, 24 August 1777. All leaves for naval officers were cancelled. Adolphe de Bouclon, *Etude historique sur la Marine de Louis XVI* (Paris: Arthur Bertrand, 1866), 192–193.

[20] Spain 585: 329–332, Vergennes to Ossun, 26 August 1777.

[21] England 524: 472–473, Vergennes to Noailles, 6 September 1777; Spain 585: 346–347, Vergennes to Ossun, 28 August 1777; B⁴134: 320, Sartine to Board of Admiralty at Nantes, 27 August 1777.

[22] England 524: 475–477, Vergennes to Noailles, 6 September 1777.

[23] B⁴134: 329, Sartine to du Chauffault, 6 September 1777. Sartine later ordered a second division of three ships of the line to sea for training. B⁴134: 340, Sartine to du Chauffault, 22 September 1777.

[24] Clark, *Lambert Wickes*, 339–361; England 525: 31, Vergennes to Noailles, 27 September 1777; *Sandwich Papers*, 1: 247–248, Vice-Admiral Palliser to Sandwich, 29 September 1777.

ments to the West Indies.[25] In the latter respect at least Britain failed. Despite British objections, three frigates escorted to the West Indies five battalions of infantry with auxiliary companies of cavalry and artillery. The convoys left Saint Malo, Brest and Bordeaux in October.[26] Vergennes did not mention that the council had been forced into near panic and had made a number of concessions to limit American naval operations as a result of what was probably a bluff. (At any rate Noailles reported London quiet and Naval Minister Sandwich's correspondence indicates he did not believe the British navy ready for a European war.)[27]

With the end of good sailing weather contacts between the British and French navy decreased. On 8 October 1777 Sartine broke up his ready force of a half-dozen ships of the line and used them to relieve ships on patrol.[28] Three weeks later he ordered the ships at sea to return at scheduled intervals.[29] Even though the British had increased their fleet of observation (guard ships) to 42 of the line,[30] Sartine ordered the crews of the French fleet reduced and leave given any officer who requested it.[31] Sartine's careful hus-

---

[25] Spain 586: 120–122, Vergennes to Ossun, 19 September 1777.

[26] For Britain's opposition to France's sending these reinforcements see England 524: 361–364, Vergennes to Noailles, 23 August 1777; Spain 586: 33, Vergennes to Ossun, 5 September 1777; England 524: 529–530, Vergennes to Noailles, 20 September 1777; Mackesy, *War for America*, 173–174.

[27] England 524: 453–457, Noailles to Vergennes, 5 September 1777; *Sandwich Papers*, 1: 235–238, Sandwich to North, 3 August 1777; *Ibid.*, 245, memorandum of Vice-Admiral Palliser, 25 August 1777. The British believed themselves outnumbered in available ships of the line (excluding 50s) by 64 to 44. I do not take too seriously Germain's comment of 4 August to Vice-Admiral Howe that the British had almost been forced to declare war on France to prevent her harboring American volunteers. Gruber, *Howe Brothers*, 221. See also Clark, *Lambert Wickes*, 249–250, 297–298.

[28] B⁴134: 344, Sartine to du Chaffault, 6 October 1777.

[29] B⁴134: 366, Sartine to du Chaffault, 29 October 1777.

[30] *Sandwich Papers*, 1: 335, Sandwich to North, 8 December 1777; *Ibid.*, 2: 273, Admiralty paper of 19 November 1777; England 526: 15–16, Noailles to Vergennes, 20 November 1777.

[31] B³626: 291–295, d'Orvilliers to Sartine, 5 November 1777; B⁴134: 397–398, Sartine to du Chaffault, 22 November 1777.

banding of his ships and crews was prudent; he might soon have need of them.

The crisis at least had aided Sartine with the recurrent problem of obtaining royal approval for his excess expenses. The bulk of the increase in naval expenses came from the daily operation of the ports, the provisioning of matériel and cost of the added overhauls, and the arming and manning of the Brest and Toulon squadrons. In July Fleurieu projected for Sartine these costs as follows: [32]

Category	Normal	1776	*1777* (projected)
For normal works	1,500,000 (livres)	3,649,556 (livres)	4,200,000 (livres)
Supplies, overhauls	5,000,000	9,311,988	12,000,000
Armaments	1,500,000	4,879,130	10,650,000

To the king Sartine estimated that the cost of replenishing matériel had already reached 9,000,000 livres and would cost another 9,000,000.[33] Sartine asked the king and Jacques Necker, the director general of finances, for an extra 6,000,000 livres for regular expenses and 2,103,000 for a variety of miscellaneous expenses.[34] (He claimed in the process that the navy's debts were already 21,464,000 livres although both Fleurieu and later reports estimated them at 16,000,000.)[35] He was able to obtain 4,800,000 livres and maintain the tradition of spending beyond appropriations without fear.[36]

[32] B⁴214: 77, Fleurieu papers, untitled memoir of July 1777; B⁵10: unpaged, "Mémoire au roi," 15 July 1777.

[33] *Ibid.* Thus far in the resupply program, 4,000,000 livres had been spent for wood for construction, 2,000,000 on hemp, 1,500,000 on masts, and 1,000,000 on iron.

[34] *Ibid.*; B⁴134: 298–301, Sartine to Necker, 17 August 1777.

[35] B⁴214: 77, Fleurieu papers, untitled memoir of July 1777; B¹87: 260–265, untitled memoir of 1 November 1778; B¹91: 87–91, memoir of 10 April 1779.

[36] Prior appropriations were 45,823,000 livres; appropriations for the entire year were 50,622,599 livres.

Whatever its consequences for American relations and for the rearmament program the crisis was of course chiefly important for its effects on the council itself. For a moment Vergennes had believed that the program of limited cooperation with the Americans would end in sudden war. The genesis of his own decision for war, however, long predated the events of the summer; to understand their real importance it is necessary to study this development.

4. The Decision for War: The Opening Stages

Before the end of 1776 Vergennes had asked Ambassador Ossun for reports on the condition of the Spanish navy, army, and seamen.[1] At the beginning of January 1777 Vergennes requested that the Spaniards submit their plans for combined operations in case of war with Britain and that Ossun send him a ship-by-ship analysis of the Spanish navy.[2] Ossun's report arrived at the end of February. It listed 59 ships of the line, of which 42 were already in condition to be armed, 5 would be ready in June and yet another 5 by the end of the year. All 59 should be ready by the end of 1778 and Spain planned to construct another 10 ships of the line in the coming three years.[3]

At this time the two powers were still in agreement that for the moment their best course was to prolong the American rebellion. The Spaniards were as yet uncertain what action the Americans would take in case of a war between Britain and the Bourbons;[4] the French believed that the

[1] See above, Chapter Three, Section 5.

[2] Spain 583: 16–17, 60–61, Vergennes to Ossun, 4 January and 17 January 1777. The French had earlier submitted their own preliminary proposals.

[3] Spain 583: 268–277, Ossun to Vergennes, 24 February 1777. There were 28 ships of the line in armament—9 at Buenos Aires, 3 at Havana or Vera Cruz, 3 at Lima, and 13 in Europe. These figures include certain minor corrections on my part.

[4] Spain 583: 95–103, "Mémoire de l'Espagne servant de réponse à celui remis par M. le Cte de Vergennes à M. le Cte d'Aranda, le 3

assembling of French naval supplies and the reestablishment of royal finances were not as yet complete enough for France to risk war.[5] Vergennes also feared compromising France with the Americans by a premature move. Part of his opposition to reinforcing the West Indies had been based on the danger that France might revive the old fears and jealousy of France among the American colonists and lead to an Anglo-American reconciliation. Moreover, any interference in the American rebellion which led to a war between the Bourbons and Britain risked a general European war (since the other European powers would not permit Britain to be crushed), in which the weight would fall on France. Vergennes admitted, however, that if France and Spain could be certain that war would not spread to the continent "the opportunity would be seductive and it would be a sublime effort of virtue to refuse it."[6] At the beginning of May he was able to tell the Spaniards that by the end of the year France would have on hand adequate naval supplies for war.[7] Fleurieu even predicted that by the end of the summer France would have 50 of the line in condition—with 30 Spanish ships this would be enough to act offensively.[8] The council eventually would be faced with the decision of how to use its forces. Once the French rearmament was complete the ultimate decision on war or peace could no longer be deferred. It seems in fact likely that the preliminary decision for war was made by the end of July 1777.

For the council's assistance in making this decision, Vergennes' assistant Rayneval prepared an analysis of the French options.[9] To Rayneval the danger of war with Brit-

---

janvier 1777," 17 January 1777. This memoir also gave Spain's operational proposals.

[5] Spain 584: 65–71, Vergennes to Ossun, 12 April 1777.

[6] Spain 584: 115–120, Vergennes to Aranda, 26 April 1777.

[7] Spain 584: 138–141, Vergennes to Ossun, 2 May 1777.

[8] B[4]214: 68–75, untitled memoir, Fleurieu papers, May 1777.

[9] England, supplement 19: 308–310, untitled memoir, no date. From internal evidence this memoir was most probably written in March or April 1777, just before Ambassador Breteuil returned to Vienna to

ain was that it deprived France of the ability to act militarily on the European continent, above all to protect the Turks from the Russians and perhaps even from Austria. Rayneval believed that however important it was to France to prevent the Russians from taking Constantinople, it was more important to weaken England and to open new markets in America. Russian gains would be counterbalanced by the reaction of the other European powers, and if Austria chose to cooperate with Russia, France could turn to Prussia. France should instead aid the Americans, for the present with money and ultimately with a secret treaty recognizing their independence and promising to sustain them openly by force if circumstances required it. In her ports France should make the same preparations as if war with England were going to commence during the following March—by making repairs and constructions and by sending reinforcements to the West Indies and India. Finally, when war was decided upon, a squadron should be prepared in order to blockade and burn Admiral Howe's squadron in America. Diplomatically the French, to secure their goals, must:

1. Assure themselves that the Americans would not make any peace with England without their consent and their participation.

2. Assure themselves the guarantee of the peace.

3. Require a reciprocal guarantee for their islands and all the Spanish possessions.

4. Require some commercial advantages or at least to be put on the base of most favored nation.

---

ascertain Austria's attitude toward an impending Russo-Turkish crisis. Also it seems to have been written before the dockyard work began in earnest with good weather. The gradual dissipation of the threat of a Russo-Turkish war probably was the final factor freeing the council to act against Britain. By January 1778 Vergennes was confident that there would be no war between Russia and Turkey. Spain 588: 83–84, 333, Vergennes to Ambassador Montmorin, 16 January and 5 March 1778.

Rayneval's program would be almost fully realized. By the end of July Louis and his council had decided that France had ultimately to choose whether to aid America openly or to abandon her. After first warning the Spaniards of the likelihood of American-British negotiations at the end of the 1777 campaign,[10] Vergennes, through Louis, asked Charles' advice on the decision facing France[11]—a rhetorical device for presenting the case for open aid and war.

This argument was sent to Spain in the traditional form of a memoir approved by the king in council.[12] It discussed the natural animosity between England and the Bourbon kingdoms, the dangers to their possessions, and the insufficiency of existing aid to the Americans. It warned that direct assistance would be incompatible with peace, so the decision should be made in time for plans to be coordinated and American cooperation assured. After the return of the French fishing fleet nothing would form an obstacle to France's executing whatever policy should be agreed upon. Europe was at peace, Spain's difficulties with Portugal had been removed, and England's only possible ally was Russia, which could give only limited assistance. If Spain and France waited past January or February, the opportunity would be lost.

The Spanish response to this overture was very cautious. They agreed it would not be to the Bourbons' interest to see America return under the English yoke, either directly or indirectly. They also agreed that the present policy was insufficient to prevent this. On the other hand, they were greatly concerned for their treasure fleet from Mexico, which they did not expect before spring, and for their fleet at Buenos Aires, which the English might also intercept. Moreover, preparations for war might drive England to

---

[10] Spain 585: 90–91, Vergennes to Ossun, 22 July 1777.

[11] Spain 585: 112–113, Vergennes to Ossun, 26 July 1777.

[12] Spain 585: 95–102, "Mémoire communiqué au roi le 23 juillet 1777 et approuvé le même jour." It is also given by Doniol, *La participation de la France*, 2: 460–469.

make a compromise peace with the Americans. The Spaniards therefore favored instead a plan of guaranteeing any peace treaty between the colonists and the British in order to ensure American autonomy. This would be a more honorable policy than soliciting an alliance from the American commissioners.[13]

Vergennes responded with the hopeful assurance that since France and Spain would each have 50 ships of the line ready by the end of the year Louis did not fear war.[14] Immediate war proved another matter. Spain responded generously to France's danger during the privateering crisis, promising full aid if France were attacked and announcing her intent to add 4 or 5 extra ships of the line to the 16 at Cadiz (or en route).[15] By the time France learned of the Spanish offer the crisis had already dissipated.[16]

The events of the summer were surely an indication of the limitations of limitation. The policy of limited intervention itself had almost led to war. Furthermore, the crisis demonstrated that events were passing out of the council's control. The British had countered the munitions shipments to America by seizing merchantmen regardless of nationality on suspicion of carrying either munitions to the American colonies or transshipped American goods.[17] In July the British ambassador to Spain told Floridablanca that if the present British campaign in America was unsuccessful, they

[13] Spain 585: 183–184, 185–192, Floridablanca to Vergennes, 8 August 1777. This same information was relayed by Ossun, who said that Charles and his ministers did not fear war, but desired to evade it until the 5,000,000-piastre (25,000,000-livre) shipment of precious metals arrived from Vera Cruz. Spain 585: 128, 211–213, Ossun to Vergennes, 28 July and 9 August 1777.

[14] Spain 585: 162–166, Vergennes to Ossun, 4 August 1777.

[15] Spain also announced she would assemble troops and warn the Indies. Spain 586: 50–51, Ossun to Vergennes, 8 September 1777. I suspect most of the credit for the Spanish generosity should be given Charles himself.

[16] For Vergennes' message of gratitude see Spain 586: 147–149, Vergennes to Ossun, 26 September 1777.

[17] England 524: 41, Vergennes to Noailles, 19 July 1777.

would concentrate all their future efforts on cutting off American trade, even under neutral flags.[18] Although Vergennes had not taken this threat seriously,[19] Britain had enough naval strength to substantially disrupt both French and American trade in addition to carrying out military operations.[20] The council, moreover, was having increasing difficulty in exercising control over its own affairs. Repeated orders were necessary to force local authorities, such as those of Dunkirk and Saint Malo, to obey instructions given reluctantly by the council in response to Stormont's protests.

Except for the clandestine operations of Beaumarchais' ships (which Stormont was able to hinder but not halt) the business of providing arms was in private hands, as was the less favorably viewed business of privateering under the American flag. Both businesses were expanding rapidly. At Nantes, for example, not only did shipments of all sorts to America double from 1776 to 1777, but also over 50 ships were fitted out as privateers.[21] Considerations of honor as well as profit were behind the hostility toward Britain. La Motte-Picquet's challenge to the British was not atypical. During 1777 the naval ministry received a variety of unsolicited plans for attacking England. Among these plans, mostly of aristocratic origin, were plans submitted by Bouillé at Martinique and by the Count de Broglie, who had prepared similar plans for Louis XV.[22] Public support had been at least indirectly an aid to Vergennes' policy of

[18] Spain 585: 84, Ossun to Vergennes, 18 July 1777.

[19] Spain 585: 177, Vergennes to Ossun, 8 August 1777.

[20] By the time hostilities formally began (July 1778) the British had already seized about 130 French ships, worth some 16,000,000 livres, for carrying contraband. This is exclusive of 22 French ships trapped by circumstances in British ports. B⁴130: 229–248, "Etat des bâtiments français pris avant les hostilités," no date.

[21] Gaston Martin, "Commercial Relations between Nantes and the American Colonies," *Journal of Economic and Business History* 4 (1932): 822, 827. See also Ruth Y. Johnston, "American Privateers in French Ports," *Pennsylvania Magazine of History* 53 (1929): 358; Clowes, *Royal Navy*, 3: 396.

[22] These are given in B⁴132.

aid to the Americans. Now the combination of Anglophobia, desire for glory, and hope for profits was leading the former supporters of that policy to oppose or circumvent its restraints.

As naval operations tapered off during the autumn so did discussions with Spain, which now dealt mainly with wooing Portugal from her ally Britain, with further financial aid to the American colonists, and with the return of the treasure fleet and Buenos Aires squadron (expected by February or at the latest July 1778).[23] Matters were so quiet that the aged Ossun was promoted to the council of state (quickly followed by the new war minister, the Prince de Montbarey). His successor as ambassador was the ex-minister to the elector of Trier, the 32-year-old Count de Montmorin-Saint-Hérem.[24] The calm was due to no shift in French plans or policy; rather, activity was suspended to await the results of the supreme British effort to destroy the American Revolution.

5. The Decision for War: The Effect of Saratoga

The campaign of General Howe, which resulted in the hollow victories of Germantown and Brandywine and the strategically meaningless capture of Philadelphia, and the parallel campaign of General Burgoyne, which resulted in the loss of his army at Saratoga, were in two regards critical in the military history of the American war. In a negative sense the campaign of 1777 represented a failure by the British to decisively exploit a heavy superiority of forces. In a positive sense it represented a further step in the American attainment of a decisive moral superiority over the British—a process which began with Bunker Hill, con-

[23] By the 1778 campaigning season Spain expected to have in readiness 32 ships of the line at Cadiz and 8 at Ferrol, presumably including 8 expected back from South America and 3 from the Gulf of Mexico. Spain 586: 319–322, Ossun to Vergennes, 30 October 1777.

[24] This transfer had been deferred since August. Memoirs and Documents, France 1897: 80, Louis to Charles, 14 August 1777.

tinued with Trenton and concluded with Yorktown. In this sense Saratoga (and to a lesser extent Washington's impressive, although unsuccessful battles against Howe) deserves its historical reputation, provided that it is recognized as one link in a chain dependent on all of its links.

Saratoga has been assigned, however, an importance which it does not merit, that of having so demonstrated the capacity of the American army that France was willing to enter the war as America's ally. Certainly a minimal American capability for war was necessary to an alliance since France needed the pressure of the American army on British military reserves in order to fight Britain on fair terms. The French council of state, however, had already faced the necessity of eventually abandoning a policy of limited involvement made obsolete by the almost uncontrollable growth of tension with Britain. In making war practicable it was probably more the work of the dockyards than the decisions of American battlefields which permitted France to cast off the restraints of limited involvement. I suspect that the French decision for open war was reinforced less by Saratoga than by Washington's defeats which demonstrated that although the Americans could destroy large detachments, they were still incapable of destroying the main British army without more direct assistance.

Diplomatically Saratoga served not as a cause for France to abandon her neutrality, but as an excuse. Since their failure at the beginning of 1777, the American commissioners in France had played masterfully a waiting game, offering their commerce in exchange for an alliance while saving their trump card, the formal offer of military cooperation with the British.[1] News arrived in Europe at the beginning of December of the capture at Saratoga of Burgoyne and

[1] I am less impressed by their efforts to compromise the French with the British. Vergennes complained of their leaking of negotiations to the British, while their encouragement of the American privateers could have led to disaster for the French navy, upon which American independence ultimately depended. See Vergennes' complaints to Ossun, Spain 585: 290–294, 22 August 1777.

6,000 troops on 17 October.[2] The commissioners moved immediately to threaten Vergennes with a compromise peace unless France took further steps to aid the colonists. On 8 December they raised again the question of a commercial treaty which would, they claimed, increase American credit abroad, strengthen the resolution of the colonists and offset the bad impression given by the treatment of American vessels and the uncertainty as to French intentions.[3] Giving credence to the veiled threats of alternative action were the reports of Noailles that Lord North was preparing a plan of reconciliation for the reopening of Parliament on 29 January 1778[4] and intelligence reports that both Franklin and Deane had been contacted by the British.[5]

Vergennes almost immediately made use of the threat of a compromise Anglo-American peace which would save Britain from the loss of American commerce and markets. In fact the compromise peace was a boogeyman with which the Americans needlessly attempted to frighten an already convinced Vergennes and with which Vergennes, in turn, unsuccessfully tried to frighten Floridablanca so as to secure Spanish participation in the war. There is a variety of evidence to suggest that Vergennes was not forced into action by the commissioners' threat: the prior memos of Rayneval and the council on the need to change policy (including in the latter the mention of January or February 1778 as a deadline for making use of the opportunity); the char-

---

[2] England 526: 117–124, Noailles to Vergennes, 2 December 1777; Spain 587: 163, Vergennes to Montmorin, 5 December 1777.

[3] United States 2: 289–290, American commissioners to Vergennes, 8 December 1777.

[4] England 526: 323–325, Noailles to Vergennes, 23 December 1777.

[5] England 526: 265–266, 270, Beaumarchais to Vergennes, 15 and 17 December 1777; United States 2: 298, 310, unknown to Vergennes, 15 and 19 December 1777. Vergennes informed Noailles in general terms of these contacts and told him that he did not expect North to wait for the opening of Parliament before submitting his peace plans. Vergennes did *not* inform Noailles of the Franco-American negotiations. See England 526: 318–319, Vergennes to Noailles, 20 December 1777.

acter of Vergennes, who generally responded to crisis by an increase of caution (as shown by his participation in the council's decision to recall the fishing fleet); and the obvious improbability of a successful compromise between the British who had not yet despaired of victory and the Americans who had received the greatest possible reinforcement for the hope of winning eventual independence.[6] The incongruities of Vergennes' supposed fears would defeat his attempts to enlist Spain in the war without the necessity of diplomatic concessions; the similarity of French and American desires, on the other hand, would lead to a quick consummation of their negotiations.

On 11 December Vergennes informed Montmorin, his new ambassador in Spain, that a conference was scheduled for the following day with the Americans. Louis believed the time had come to form connections with the Americans, but he did not wish to act without the concurrence and sanction of Charles, his uncle. Vergennes claimed there were only two alternatives: should these connections be refused, an eventual war with England conducted without allies or, if they were accepted, an alliance with the Americans which entailed an eventual war but a war conducted with the Americans as allies and with the guarantee of commercial advantages when victory was won.[7]

Vergennes elaborated his ideas in a series of dispatches of 13 December. In the first he reported on his conference with the American commissioners. They had offered only a guarantee of French possessions should the commercial treaty lead to war (as it certainly would), an offer far short

[6] For Britain see Gruber, *Howe Brothers*, 273, 277–279. A further suggestion that for France war was a matter of choice rather than inevitability is the fact that in December 1777 the navy department drafted for the coming year a peacetime budget proposal (albeit it requested 61,620,000 livres). Of course it is conceivable that it was drafted between 1 December and 4 or 5 December, when the news of Saratoga reached the court. B¹84: 394–396, untitled memoir, December 1777.

[7] Spain 587: 181–185, Vergennes to Montmorin, 11 December 1777.

of an alliance. Vergennes warned that American public
pressure might force the Continental Congress into a treaty
with Britain and that with the Americans as allies the British would be irresistible enemies.[8] In his second letter Vergennes warned Montmorin of the traditional French bug-
bear, the possibility that Lord Chatham might return to
power, thereby guaranteeing war.[9] In the third letter Vergennes outlined Spain's interest in seeing the two English-
speaking powers separated, advanced the possibility of
Spain's obtaining Florida, and even argued that the Bourbons' interest in American independence was so great that
it would be even worth a slightly disadvantageous war.
Events had moved more rapidly than anticipated. There
was no longer time to lose or there might disappear "the
most interesting conjunction that the heavens could ever
present" and the two crowns would have to bear the re-
proaches of their own and future generations.[10] Vergennes
over the next few days informed Montmorin of the contacts
between the commissioners and the English.[11]

The American resistance was not strong. On 17 December the commissioners agreed in principle that, in exchange
for French recognition and a treaty of commerce, the Americans would agree that American independence would be
a necessary condition of any peace.[12] It was now obvious
that an actual alliance would not be withheld by the commissioners. The frigate *Belle Poule* was now ordered to
stand by to carry the news to America.[13] Formal negotia-

---

[8] Spain 587: 188–192, Vergennes to Montmorin, 13 December 1777.

[9] Spain 587: 193, personal letter of Vergennes to Montmorin, 13
December 1777.

[10] Spain 587: 194–195, personal letter of Vergennes to Montmorin,
13 December 1777.

[11] Spain 587: 197–198, 223–225, 307–309, Vergennes to Montmorin,
15, 19, and 27 December 1777.

[12] Doniol, *La participation de la France*, 2: 452–454, American commissioners to Continental Congress, 18 December 1777.

[13] B⁴134: 423–426, orders for Lt. de Marigny, captain of the *Belle
Poule*, 20 December 1777. The *Belle Poule* sailed on 6 January, but
was forced by storms into Lorient ten days later.

tions with the Americans had to wait, however, until Spain replied to France's suggestion that she, too, join the alliance.

Vergennes received the Spanish response on 31 December 1777. His initial attempt to stampede the Spaniards into the alliance had failed. On 19 and 22 December Charles and his advisers had discussed the French proposal. Floridablanca had challenged the need for haste, arguing that the American deputies were playing all their cards in order to involve the Bourbons in war, that the English would find it difficult to make a peace treaty, and that the safe return of the treasure ships was vital to the Spanish ability to finance the war. Montmorin, after reporting Floridablanca's account of these heated discussions, added that he nevertheless believed that if France acted, Spain would have to follow.[14] Floridablanca himself wrote Vergennes via Montmorin offering nothing beyond financial aid, mediation if it was requested, and any intelligence he might receive from London;[15] he told Aranda that war was premature and Spain must wait until the fleet and army returned from South America. Aranda was ordered to offer another 2,250,000 livres in aid to the Americans.[16] Obviously, Vergennes would need to apply more direct pressure to force the Spaniards to participate in the coming alliance with the Americans.

[14] Spain 587: 262–268, Montmorin to Vergennes, 23 December 1777.
[15] Spain 587: 269–270, Floridablanca to Montmorin, 23 December 1777.
[16] Spain 587: 271–280, Floridablanca to Aranda, 23 December 1777.

CHAPTER FIVE

1778—War without Spain

1. The American Alliance

VERGENNES took no action for a week after receiving the news of the Spanish refusal. He then received news from Montmorin which eliminated any hope that the Spaniards would by themselves reconsider their decision. Not only did Montmorin report that Floridablanca's thinking on the matter was still the same, but he also reported a serious setback to the Spanish plans for a quick return of their treasure fleet. Its commander, Commodore de Ulloa, had been ordered by José de Gálvez, Minister of the Indies, to leave for Europe in October 1777. The Spanish court now learned that Ulloa, not knowing the reason for his change of orders, had decided to disobey them and to return in February as previously planned. New orders were sent, but it was uncertain when the fleet would arrive.[1]

With this delay France no longer could expect to gain anything through waiting for Spain to change her mind. Parliament might at least be forestalled by France's dealing with the Americans before the British could offer terms, and, in accordance with Montmorin's views, the Spaniards might be forced to follow France by being presented with a fait accompli.

Just at the moment of decision on whether to proceed alone with an alliance, a new complication arose. On 5 or 6 January the council learned of the death without immediate heirs of Maximilian Joseph, elector of Bavaria.[2] With the

[1] Spain 587: 315–317, Montmorin to Vergennes, 29 December 1777. Spanish fears for their treasure fleet were not unreasonable. See Fortescue, *Correspondence of King George the Third*, 4: 46, George to North, 3 March 1778 (no. 2204).

[2] Samuel Flagg Bemis, *The Diplomacy of the American Revolution*, 2d ed., rev. (Bloomington, Ind.: Indiana University Press, 1957), 70–71.

possibility of a disputed succession there also arose the possibility of an Austrian takeover of Bavaria, which would upset the balance of power in Germany, endanger France's position as guarantor of the Treaty of Westphalia, and possibly engender a major war. The situation, however, as Vergennes told Montmorin, was still uncertain, and France was now too deeply involved in the American situation to pull back.[3] Incapable of simultaneously fighting two wars, France had to count on Prussia and Russia to maintain the balance of power in Germany.[4] The king and council elected to proceed with the American alliance.

On 8 January Vergennes informed the Spaniards of the French decision. In his covering note to Montmorin,[5] Vergennes admitted that any engagement with the Americans might become a cause of war, but he claimed that to avoid action would be to risk that the Anglo-American negotiations begun informally through the commissioners might lead to a reconciliation. In any case the British attempts to intercept American trade might lead to war. France was sending a squadron to sea to protect her coast.[6]

Vergennes' main letter was in the customary form of a memoir presented and approved in council.[7] It carried the usual recitation of dangers should France wait, but added the bizarre warning that Lord North might abandon the Navigation Acts to make peace with the Americans—the very objective of the French involvement with the Americans, since the Navigation Acts were the foundation of the

[3] Spain 588: 40–44, Vergennes to Montmorin, 8 January 1778. Vergennes said that France would not be deterred from the great object which fixed her attention.

[4] See England 528: 481, Vergennes to Noailles, 28 February 1778, concerning Prussia.

[5] Spain 588: 17–21, Vergennes to Montmorin, 8 January 1778.

[6] A squadron of five ships of the line under La Motte-Picquet sailed in two groups in January and put into Quiberon Bay (near Lorient) in mid-February.

[7] Spain 588: 22–36, memoir labeled "Lu au roi le 7 janvier 1778 et envoyé en Espagne le lendemain." Vergennes sent his own thoughts to Montmorin in a personal letter of 8 January 1778, Spain 588: 37–39.

British monopoly of American trade.[8] It criticized the Spanish offer of further financial aid to the Americans as insufficient, the offer of mediation as causing either war or the enmity of the colonists, and the offer of observation as pointless. Because Parliament's reopening was so near, Louis took it upon himself to initiate negotiations with the Americans, talks that hopefully would lead to treaties of commerce and of alliance. France would, however, delay signing any treaties until Spain had responded. Also the treaties would contain a secret clause reserving for Spain the right to adhere to the treaty when she judged it appropriate.

To understand subsequent French diplomacy and war strategy, it is first indispensable to understand the reasons for Vergennes' desire that Spain share in the war effort. In January 1778 Vergennes was prepared to act alone only because *for the moment* France had achieved *effective* naval parity with Britain. When the overhauls to the *Vengeur* and *Diadème* were completed in the spring, France expected to have 53 ships of the line in condition to fight.[9] More important, since France could conscript coastal sailors and fishermen, Vergennes could be certain that these ships would be manned. Since England could only man her navy by stripping incoming merchantmen of their crews, her mobilization would be a much more time-consuming process. Although Britain had some 80 ships of the line in condition to fight,[10] no more than 66 were actually manned dur-

---

[8] See also England 528: 23–24, Vergennes to Noailles, 3 January 1778.

[9] Of these ships the *Victoire* proved to need a short overhaul, but this did not interfere with her service. The *Bizarre*, of La Motte-Picquet's squadron, was not so lucky. See succeeding section, note 9, and Appendix E.

[10] This number does not include five ships of the line used only for port defense (also called guard ships). *Sandwich Papers*, I: 422, lists 85 ships of the line (among which I count the 50s he lists) in condition to serve, as of 1 January 1778. Three of these were probably for port defense or other uses. Another war damaged in a fire in March 1778, and 3 more needed repairs after returning from overseas. Of

ing 1778, hardly more than the 62 manned in 1777.[11] Since by initiating the war France would have the advantages of surprise, the British numerical advantage would be only marginal.

This condition could not be relied on to last for more than one campaigning season. Once the English navy was fully manned, its superiority in seaworthy ships of the line and ships of the line in construction was so large that even the fast-working French shipyards could not overcome it. Only in January 1778 did wood reserves permit the undertaking of a construction program for ships of the line—3 each at Brest, Toulon, and Rochefort. Unless Britain could be defeated in one campaign, the aid of the Spanish navy, with its 50 ships of the line, would be indispensable to maintain a superiority of numbers.[12] If this superiority were lost it was probable that Britain would gain the initiative and eventually France would in all likelihood suffer a repetition of the disasters of 1759 (and without French arms, money, and munitions America's future would be no more promising). Americans have been as reluctant to recognize Spain's contribution to American independence as they have been generous in recognizing France's. Although the Spanish navy was to win no naval battles nor even to capture a single English ship of the line, it was by its mere presence eventually to make a decisive contribution to the effort against England.

Vergennes had a clear understanding of this situation. On 9 January 1778, Noailles sent a new listing of the British

---

the remaining 78, 66 saw use. See Appendix E. For further details see Dull: Dissertation, 172n., 179n. Noailles on 15 March reported that there were 82 ships of the line in condition to serve and that 81 of these had been ordered armed. B⁴137: 45–46.

[11] In 1777 there had been 35 ships of the line in a partially-manned squadron of observation, seven more added to the squadron in the autumn, 14 in North America, three in the West Indies, and one each in the Indian Ocean, the Mediterranean, and on convoy duty.

[12] See Chapter Six and Appendix F for dispositions in 1779.

navy, giving 56 ships of the line already armed, 16 more in the process of arming but still needing crews, eight in good condition, 29 in construction, and six in repair. He also estimated that to man 80 ships of the line (with their attendant smaller ships) would require 80,000 sailors.[13] In response to this intelligence a report was prepared for Vergennes.[14] This memoir estimated that between 77 and 92 British ships of the line (including 50s) were in condition to be armed. It noted, however, that "it is not at all by the number of ships of the line that the English compute their naval forces, but by the number of sailors." The report added that in the last war England did not use more than 80,000 sailors (or authorize more than 70,000).[15] Vergennes' concern for the manning of the British navy is manifested, however, by more than this one report. He required from Noailles intelligence not only of available ships but also of the current strength of their crews,[16] and he would closely follow the return during the summer of the great convoys to Britain which provided the crews for the expansion of the British navy.

As Vergennes awaited the Spanish response he continued his negotiations with the Americans. Had the French demanded special commercial privileges or had the Americans withheld a military alliance these negotiations might have been difficult. Vergennes did not demand the former

[13] England 528: 58–62, Noailles to Vergennes, 9 January 1778; this is a covering letter for a ship-by-ship listing, which is missing.

[14] England 528: 70–73, "Etat de la marine d'Angleterre, d'après les états comparées de Londres et de Versailles, l'un et l'autre du 9 janvier 1778," no author listed, no date (but probably compiled by navy department).

[15] At its maximum size in 1782 the French navy had only 73 ships of the line (see Appendix I), while the British navy eventually reached almost 100. Even should France have no war losses, Vergennes could not count on the French navy reaching 80 of the line for another three years.

[16] Vergennes also took great interest in Parliament's budgeting for 60,000 sailors in 1778 as compared to 45,000 in 1777. England 526: 178–179, Vergennes to Noailles, 6 December 1777.

in hopes that his moderation would eventually attract neutrals like the Netherlands to the alliance;[17] by 11 January it was obvious from Franklin's and Deane's responses to the French proposals that the Americans would not refuse the latter.[18] The only problem arose in convincing the Americans to accept a delayed alliance (which would give France the option of when to enter the war) rather than an immediate alliance. This difficulty was solved by the end of January.[19]

The Spaniards promised to remain more difficult. Even before Louis' memoir could reach Spain, Floridablanca sent Aranda a list of questions about the proposed Bourbon alliance with the Americans and its potential military and diplomatic consequences.[20] Floridablanca complained that Spain would receive no benefits commensurate with the American commerce and conquests in the West Indies or Newfoundland which might accrue to France. He also pointed out that the fleets from Mexico and South America were now not expected back before July. Vergennes dutifully answered these questions at the end of January. He claimed that France's only interests were American independence and the satisfaction of Spanish desires—the recovery of Gibraltar and Minorca and the expulsion of the English from the Gulf of Mexico.[21]

On 4 February Vergennes finally received a response to his communications of 8 January. According to Montmorin Floridablanca went into such a rage that his body trembled all over and he was initially unable to speak. Floridablanca

[17] Spain 588: 387–391, Vergennes to Montmorin, 17 March 1778.
[18] United States 2: 344, untitled draft of December 1777; United States 3: 8, 18, responses of Franklin and Deane, 8 and 11 January 1778.
[19] Spain 588: 207–210, Vergennes to Montmorin, 30 January 1778.
[20] Spain 588: 64–75, Floridablanca to Aranda, 13 January 1778. This letter was presented to Vergennes on 21 January.
[21] Spain 588: 152–160, "Projet de réponses à faire aux différentes questions de l'Espagne," approved by Louis, 28 January 1778. Hereafter cited as French responses of 28 January.

was a master of such moods; the young ambassador would know more such scenes. Montmorin maintained his composure and Floridablanca finally told him that Spain planned to do nothing until she learned the details of France's projected treaties. Montmorin still believed that in case of war Spain would be unable to resist joining France.[22]

Two days after the reception of Montmorin's letter, France signed a treaty of amity and commerce and a treaty of defensive alliance with the United States.[23]

2. The Breaking of Relations with Britain

The council's first concern was to take precautions against an immediate war should Britain learn of the treaties and elect to begin hostilities.[1] In January Louis had approved the arming of 12 ships of the line at Brest and 10 at Toulon, an increase of only 4 over 1777,[2] although Vergennes promised the Spaniards the Brest squadron would be raised in the spring to 29 of the line.[3] When the treaties were signed, 6 additional ships were ordered to supplement the 12 fitting

[22] Spain 588: 135–151, Montmorin to Vergennes, 28 January 1778. See also Spain 588: 218–220, Montmorin to Vergennes, 2 February 1778.

[23] Gilbert Chinard, ed., *The Treaties of 1778 and Allied Documents* (Baltimore: Johns Hopkins University Press, 1928). The treaty of alliance was defensive in name only; France had the option of choosing when she would be "attacked." On 21 February Vergennes informed the Austrians he would not support them against Prussia, which had mobilized its army in response to the Austrian seizure of Bavaria. Isabel de Madariaga, *Britain, Russia, and the Armed Neutrality of 1780* (New Haven: Yale University Press, 1962), 27.

[1] British intelligence reported the treaties but the British were not ready to act against France. See Fortescue, *Correspondence of King George the Third*, 4: 36, George to North, 9 February 1778 (no. 2190) and following.

[2] B[1]87: 15, memoir approved by Louis, 18 January 1778. The English were informed of the addition of the four of the line. England 528: 161, Vergennes to Noailles, 24 January 1778.

[3] French responses of 28 January, response 5.

at Brest, the fortifications around Brest were ordered readied, and officers' leaves were cancelled.[4] The precautions proved unnecessary; Floridablanca (whom they may in part have been designed to impress) wrote Aranda in puzzlement as to why they had been taken.[5]

Vergennes, before signing the treaties, told Montmorin that he expected their news would break in America at the end of April or beginning of May; it would be necessary to communicate them to Britain by that time.[6] This gave France three months in which to persuade Spain to join the alliance before the crisis broke. France gave up on this help well before the deadline. She had already offered to send 10 ships of the line from Toulon to Cadiz to help protect the incoming Spanish fleets;[7] Spain refused the offer on 16 February. Ten days later Montmorin reported that there was no hope that the Spaniards would change their minds before their fleets returned and that they still believed the treaties to be premature.[8] Once Vergennes received this information there was no longer reason to delay the break with Britain.[9]

On 6 March Vergennes wrote an impassioned letter to Montmorin[10] requesting a definite answer to the offer of the Toulon fleet since the king could no longer ignore the in-

[4] B⁵11: unpaged, untitled memoir of 6 February 1778; B¹87: 21, memoir of 5 February 1778; B⁸650: 66–67, La Prévalye, commissioner-general at Brest, to Sartine, 11 February 1778; Spain 588: 252, Vergennes to Montmorin, 6 February 1778; England 528: 287–288, Vergennes to Noailles, 7 February 1778; Bouclon, *Etude historique de la Marine*, 196; P. Levot, *Histoire de la ville et du port de Brest* (Paris: Bachelin-Deflorenne, 1866), 2: 183–184.

[5] Spain 588: 300, Floridablanca to Aranda, 23 February 1778.

[6] Spain 588: 209, Vergennes to Montmorin, 30 January 1778.

[7] French responses of 28 January, response 6.

[8] Spain 588: 253, 284, 307–315, Montmorin to Vergennes, 9 February, 16 February, and 26 February 1778.

[9] Vergennes, however, was still concerned about La Motte-Picquet's squadron, which finally returned safely to Brest on 18 March and 23 March, although a collision damaged the *Bizarre* so badly she was lost for the campaign.

[10] Spain 588: 338–339, Vergennes to Montmorin, 6 March 1778.

sults of England. This letter was merely a gesture since Vergennes had already acknowledged the Spanish refusal of the offer.[11] Before Spain could send another reply Vergennes sent a copy of the treaty of commerce (dated 7 March) to Noailles, with orders to communicate it to King George.[12] Noailles delivered the treaty on 13 March; Stormont announced on 16 March that he had been recalled to England, and Noailles reciprocated on 19 March.[13] War between France and Britain was now virtually inevitable.

In explaining the break to Spain Vergennes claimed it would be good policy to give maximum publicity to the treaty so as to diminish the possibility of America signing a treaty with Britain.[14] I believe the council acted for a mixture of reasons. Probably the desire to forestall any possible Anglo-American reconciliation played a part, although there is no more cause for Vergennes to be frightened into hasty action than there was in December.[15] The terms presented by North to Parliament at the end of February called for a renunciation of Parliament's right to tax for rev-

[11] Spain 588: 307–315, Vergennes to Montmorin, 23 February 1778.

[12] England 529: 46–47, 59–61, Vergennes to Noailles, 10 March 1778. This was Noailles' first notification. Britain was not told of the treaty of alliance. See also Memoirs and Documents, France 1897: 84, Louis to Charles, 9 March 1778, informing him of Louis' intentions.

[13] England 529: 116–118, Noilles to Vergennes, 15 March 1778; England 529: 132, Stormont to Vergennes, 16 March 1778; England 529: 150, Vergennes to Noailles, 17 March 1778; England 529: 198, Noailles to Weymouth, 19 March 1778; England 529: 199, Weymouth to Noailles, 19 March 1778.

[14] Spain 588: 338–339, Vergennes to Montmorin, 6 March 1778. The French frigate *Nymphe*, which was to carry the treaties to Boston, was delayed by contrary winds, and did not leave port until 27 February, six days after the departure of the British frigate *Andromeda* with the proposed bills of conciliation. Spain 588: 303, Vergennes to Montmorin, 23 February 1778; B⁷650: 92, d'Orvilliers to Sartine, 27 February 1778; England 528: 409–413, Noailles to Vergennes, 24 February 1778. The *Nymphe* finally arrived at Boston at the beginning of May.

[15] Noailles' intelligence system had not informed Vergennes of the nearly disastrous winter of Valley Forge which followed the American victory at Saratoga.

enue, but retained intact both the Navigation Acts and
America's responsibility to contribute to the defense of the
Empire.[16] Both Floridablanca and Franklin saw that these
terms would be unacceptable;[17] they were rejected unanimously by the Continental Congress on 22 April 1778 before Silas Deane's brother arrived at Boston with copies of
the treaty with France.[18] There was some sentiment for
holding discussions with the peace commissioners named
conjointly by the British but this was eliminated by the ratification of the treaties with France on 4 May 1778.[19]

Partly, to be sure, the breaking of relations with Britain
was designed to put more pressure on Spain—a logical continuation of the policy of diplomacy by fait accompli urged
by Montmorin and followed by Vergennes. Vergennes told
Noailles that by presenting the treaty with the Americans
he hoped to distract the English from passing the Conciliatory Bill offering peace terms to the Americans and hoped
to make it more difficult to obtain funds for the government.[20] One may question Vergennes' frankness to Noailles
on the matter. In any case, the conciliation bills had already
just been passed and the break with France helped the government's credit—a government loan floated by North was
fully subscribed.[21] Probably the major reason for the quick
breaking of relations with Britain was psychological. This
act of defiance by Louis' government was a demonstration
to the Americans, to the British, to the Spaniards, to the

[16] England 528: 380–381, Noailles to Vergennes, 19 February 1778.
[17] Spain 588: 342, Floridablanca to Aranda, 9 March 1778; United
States 3: 166, Franklin to Vergennes, 1 April 1778. Franklin said that
the British terms were offered two years too late.
[18] Spain 590: 84–87, Committee for Public Affairs of the Continental Congress to Vergennes, 14 May 1778, copy to Montmorin from
Vergennes, 17 July 1778.
[19] Bemis, *Diplomacy of the American Revolution*, 66–68. The peace
commissioners left England only on 21 April 1778.
[20] England 529: 62, Vergennes to Noailles, 10 March 1778. See also
England 529: 183–186, memoir read in council, 18 March 1778; England 529: 65–72, Noailles to Vergennes, 10 March 1778.
[21] Spain 589: 54, Montmorin to Vergennes, 10 April 1778, relaying
Spanish intelligence from London.

other powers of Europe, and to France herself of the government's resolution to achieve American independence, even at the cost of war.[22]

France was now free to prepare openly for war. If France was to begin the campaign before the returning convoys from the West and East Indies brought the sailors needed to man the British navy to full strength, such preparations could not be delayed. Upon France's notifying Britain of the treaty of commerce, Sartine ordered Toulon to begin preparing a second squadron of seven ships of the line immediately after it had prepared its first squadron of ten of the line.[23] He ordered Brest to begin preparing the huge *Bretagne, Ville-de-Paris,* and *Duc-de-Bourgogne* for service.[24] On 7 March the king approved orders for the *Protée* to convoy back to France the commerce of the West Indies[25] and ten days later domestic commerce was ordered to navigate with caution.[26] The major problem to be resolved by both France and England, however, was that of drafting strategy for the naval war into which the revolt of the American colonies would soon largely be transformed.

3. War Strategies

The approaching entrance of France into the war forced Britain to severely modify her strategy for suppressing the American rebellion. Heretofore the British had tried to

---

[22] Vergennes told Montmorin that England already knew of the French treaty with America and was keeping it quiet to maintain the government's credit and to transform the French silence into an act of weakness before the Americans. If war resulted from the breaking of relations, it would be to the advantage of France, since England was not yet ready. Most important, public commentary would carry news of the treaty to the Americans. Spain 588: 370–374, Vergennes to Montmorin, 10 March 1778.

[23] B¹85: 245–246, Sartine to St. Aignan, 9 March 1778.

[24] B¹85: 37, untitled memoir, no date; B⁸650: 114, d'Orvilliers to Sartine, 13 March 1778.

[25] B¹87: 72, memoir of 7 March 1778; B⁴140: 58, Dampierre to Sartine, 27 May 1778. The orders were actually dated 13 March 1778.

[26] Brun, *Port de Toulon,* 2: 9.

crush the rebellion at its center—a center first defined as the American army, and later defined in geographical terms.[1] This strategy failed. General Washington preserved the nucleus of his army despite repeated defeats by General Howe's main British army. Possessing a force to check the main enemy army, the Americans made use of militia and their own detachments to destroy British detachments at Bennington, Oriskany, and Saratoga. The presence of an American army also prevented the British from substituting their Loyalist supporters for British occupying forces. Since the American colonies were predominantly rural, the British were unable to destroy the rebellion by occupying the chief rebel cities (Boston, New York, Philadelphia, Newport, and later Charleston).

Upon learning of the French alliance George initially considered abandonment of military operations in North America in favor of a naval blockade of the colonies.[2] If Britain did not have the military strength to crush both France and the Americans, neither did she have the naval strength to both fight France and blockade the enormous American coastline. After the initial panic passed, the British cabinet instead decided on a war of attrition against both of the new allies by dividing British forces between the American colonies and the West Indies. By 21 March 1778 the cabinet approved plans to send an expeditionary force of 5,000 men to attack the island of Saint Lucia, which would provide an excellent base for observing Martinique.[3] In North America, the cabinet decided to abandon Philadelphia and to concentrate on New York and on the periph-

---

[1] Gruber, *Howe Brothers*, 188 (and elsewhere).

[2] Fortescue, *Correspondence of King George the Third*, 4: 30–31, 36, George to North, 31 January and 9 February 1778 (no. 2182, no. 2190).

[3] *Sandwich Papers*, 1: 324, 363, 365–367, instructions for Lieutenant-General Sir Henry Clinton (replacing General Howe), 8 March 1778, minutes of cabinet meeting of 18 March 1778; memoir of Lord Amherst (new commander of the British army); Germain to Sandwich, 21 March 1778; secret instructions for Clinton, 21 March 1778.

ery of the American colonies (Canada, Nova Scotia and Florida). They would then be able to wear down the Americans' resistance by detaching mobile forces from New York.

There were serious deficiencies in the British strategy. For a variety of causes Britain did not establish a sufficient superiority of force to make a strategy of attrition viable. New York was very difficult to defend and the size of its garrison seriously reduced the military forces in North America available for detachments against the American colonies. The British were overextended and badly outnumbered in the West Indies. Most important, Sandwich was so afraid of an invasion of England that he hesitated detaching the naval forces from Europe to maintain superiority in American waters.[4] Britain was left little margin of error.

Considered in another manner Britain's strategy was faulty because it failed to exploit the opportunities the changed war presented Britain. The American colonies were absolutely dependent on France for munitions, for markets for their exports (chiefly tobacco), and for the financial backing necessary to hold their army together. Once Britain was at war with France these might be cut off at their source by blockading the French coast. Better still, if the French navy could be decisively defeated, Britain could then devote all her naval forces to destruction of American and French commerce. By concentrating instead on the problem of how to counter any French moves the British forfeited the naval initiative.

Given the initiative by Britain's unwillingness to initiate hostilities, France's essential strategic problem was that of best exploiting her advantage. France unlike Britain possessed a fleet in the Mediterranean. While the Brest fleet menaced Britain the Toulon fleet had two options. If France

---

[4] *Ibid.*, 2: 22–23, opinions delivered by Sandwich, 4 and 6 April 1778; Mackesy, *War for America*, 194–196. For Vergennes' comments about the British fear of invasion see Spain 589: 310, Vergennes to Montmorin, 20 June 1778.

wished to launch an invasion against Britain or Ireland the Toulon fleet could come to Brest;[5] but it might also move against Admiral Howe's scattered fleet and the vulnerable army in New York.

The decision on the use of the squadron of course had to be made by Louis. In practice, however, the king did not have the experience, intelligence, or self-confidence necessary to override the advice of his council. The distribution of power had not altered since the victory of the war party in the spring of 1776.[6] With the dismissal of Turgot, Malesherbes, and (in mid-1777) Saint Germain, power was divided among Maurepas, Vergennes, and Sartine. As already remarked, the three formed a remarkably cohesive unit in comparison to the British cabinet and Spanish council.[7] They were particularly well-suited to conduct the coming naval war. Maurepas, in addition to his political acumen, could contribute from his own experience as a naval minister. The loyal and indefatigable Sartine, aided by his brilliant assistant, the Chevalier de Fleurieu, drafted campaign plans and represented the views of the navy. The dominant member of the triumverate, however, became Vergennes. With his balance of prudence and audacity, his firm common sense, and his perpetual emphasis on the diplomatic consequences of military action, Vergennes would become

---

[5] In February 1778 England and Wales still were garrisoned by only 14,471 troops. Mackesy, *War for America*, 524–525.

[6] Sources for the working of the council (which did not take minutes) are indirect—the correspondence of Vergennes and the diary of a well-placed and reliable observer, the Abbé de Véri. Baron Jehan de Witte, ed., *Journal de l'Abbé de Véri* (Paris: Jules Tallandier, 1928–1930).

[7] The Spanish council was split by the rivalry between Floridablanca and colonial minister Gálvez, the English cabinet by the animosity of Sandwich and Germain. For the latter see Mackesy, *War for America*, 53–54 and elsewhere. Technically, Charles possessed a council only after 1783. In fact, he consulted his chief ministers much the same as did Louis, so the term "council" will be used for the chief advisers of each king. As already mentioned, advice on major questions facing Louis was given chiefly by an inner council rather than by the entire council of state.

one of the great war leaders of his century. Leaving predominance of place to Maurepas and detailed dispositions to Sartine and Fleurieu, Vergennes became the major director of French war strategy.[8]

The council's first decision would require boldness, whichever option it chose. The attempt in 1759 to transfer the Toulon fleet to Brest for an invasion of Britain had resulted in a disastrous defeat. Such a strategy would give the British a chance to use in their own waters warships, such as guard vessels for the ports, too unseaworthy to use abroad. Moreover, France did not possess a port in the English Channel capable of holding ships of the line. These difficulties when added to the enormous technical difficulties of an invasion outweighed the possibilities of winning an immediate decisive victory.

To send the Toulon squadron across the Atlantic Ocean also presented great dangers. Should the British detach a large squadron from home waters, the Toulon squadron might be trapped and its loss would seriously affect future operations. The possible benefits, however, were almost as great as those of a successful invasion of Britain. There were only a dozen of the line scattered in North America, half of them 50s. Should these be taken, the 33,756 British troops in the American colonies, almost entirely dependent on food shipped from abroad, could be blockaded into starvation and surrender, ending the war.[9] This would, of

[8] For the making of war strategy see Spain 597: 108, Vergennes to Montmorin, 13 January 1780; B⁴214 and B⁴215, Fleurieu papers; Witte, *Journal de l'Abbé de Véri*, 2: 283–284, entry of 1 October 1780. Note that Sartine did not act as spokesman for individual admirals, but for the interests of the service at large. War Minister Montbarey participated intermittently in decision making. The remaining members of the council of state proper—Soubise, Bertin, and Ossun—generally did not share in the inner council's major decisions on diplomacy and military strategy (decisions of course for which the king ultimately was personally responsible).

[9] Mackesy, *War for America*, 214n., 65–66, lists for March 1778 the following British forces in the American colonies: 19,530 at Philadelphia, 10,456 at New York, and 3,770 at Rhode Island. These numbers are strength on paper only—27,000 of these were actually fit for duty.

course, depend on skillful execution and good fortune to exploit France's advantage of surprise.

The council apparently made its preliminary decision in January 1778. To Spain it sent a memoir explaining France's plans for the campaign of 1778.[10] It posited that even with the aid of the Cadiz fleet there would not be sufficient forces to undertake offensive operations in European waters. Therefore it envisaged the use of encampments in Brittany, Normandy, and Picardy to disquiet the English and to force them to maintain naval forces off Île d'Ouessant and in the English Channel. France's major effort would be designed to serve her long-range objective of preserving her own possessions in the Western Hemisphere while assisting the American colonies to gain their independence. According to the proposal, the best means of accomplishing this would be to send a squadron (from Toulon so as not to weaken the diversionary fleet at Brest) to crush the scattered British naval forces in North America. After this the squadron could be split between Newfoundland and the West Indies.

The Spanish refusal of the offer of the Toulon squadron freed the Toulon squadron for the American mission. On 21 March two more ships were added to the original ten, and the following day Vice-Admiral d'Estaing, the senior active officer of the navy, left for Toulon to command the squadron.[11] Vergennes received on 27 March the final confirmation that the Toulon squadron was not desired by the Spaniards.[12] Montmorin reported that the Spaniards had

[10] Spain 588: 212–215, "Mémoire sur les operations auxquelles on pourrait employer nos forces navales contre l'Ang.re," January 1778. See Chapter Four, Section 4 for Rayneval's memoir of 1777, which foreshadowed it.

[11] B³657: 81, Saint Aignan to Sartine, 29 March 1778; Spain 588: 418, Aranda to Floridablanca, 23 March 1778. The Brest fleet was ordered expanded to 25 ships of the line and d'Orvilliers was ordered to its command. B³650: 127, d'Orvilliers to Sartine, 25 March 1778; O. Troude, *Batailles navales de la France* (Paris: Challamel ainé, 1867), 2: 3–5, Sartine to d'Orvilliers, 2 April 1778.

[12] Spain 588: 401–408, Montmorin to Vergennes, 20 March 1778.

received the news of Noailles' recall with little emotion. Although hardly pleased, Floridablanca believed the break with England to be the necessary consequence of the treaties. Floridablanca definitely turned down the offer of ten ships of the line and reiterated his promise that Spain would fulfill its engagements toward France. Montmorin had already warned Vergennes that although Floridablanca had promised Spain would fulfill her obligations under the Family Compact, Spain's cooperation would be halfhearted if she were forced to declare herself now.[13] Montmorin now reminded Vergennes that the Spaniards feared the American colonies even more than they did Britain and that they would give their full cooperation only if matters were involved that touched Spain directly, such as Gibraltar and Florida.[14] Vergennes, however, was not ready to substitute a policy of bribe for a policy of bluff with Spain until France had attempted to conclude the war in a single campaign without her aid.

At the end of March Vergennes told the Spaniards of the plans to send d'Estaing's squadron to America.[15] He justified France's decision to strike first by claiming that England was also resolved on war, as evidenced by the intelligence from Noailles that she was placing her largest warships into commission.[16] Vergennes argued that d'Es-

[13] *Ibid.*; Spain 588: 343–352, Montmorin to Vergennes, 9 March 1778.
[14] In a separate letter Montmorin suggested that the Spanish navy might not be in such a brilliant state as one wished France to believe, and that it might be preferable if Spain remained neutral! Aranda meanwhile was downplaying the readiness of the French for war. Spain 588: 397–398, Montmorin to Vergennes, 20 March 1778; Spain 588: 317–318, Aranda to Floridablanca, 7 March 1778.
[15] Spain 588: 430–435, Vergennes to Montmorin, 27 March 1778.
[16] This was in fact a case of mutual suspicion. Of the five ships newly reported by Noailles ordered placed in commission, a crew was found for only one, the *Victory*, 100. (Numbers following ship names refer to cannon carried.) The *Victory* was placed in commission in response to the reported arming of the *Bretagne*, 110, which in fact had not yet been ordered. England 529: 121, Noailles to Vergennes, 15 March 1778; *Sandwich Papers*, 1: 342–343, 349–351,

taing's squadron would strengthen the Americans, draw British forces away from the Gulf of Mexico (thereby facilitating the safe passage of the treasure fleet), and give the Bourbons (Louis and Charles) another force for use in the Gulf of Mexico if needed. Vergennes promised the Spaniards would share any advantages gained by d'Estaing in Newfoundland. He predicted that d'Estaing would be able to sail by 10 April if not retained by unfavorable winds.

Since the Toulon squadron was almost ready when it received its orders this expectation was nearly fulfilled. The last three ships of d'Estaing's squadron entered the roadstead of Toulon between 6 and 10 April. On the evening of 13 April d'Estaing sailed with 12 ships of the line and 5 frigates.[17] Aboard his flagship was Rayneval's brother, Conrad-Alexandre Gérard, the senior foreign minister official who had been in charge of the treaty negotiations with the Americans. He had been named France's minister plenipotentiary to the United States.

4. The Opening of Hostilities

The English had intelligence of d'Estaing's departure from Toulon but not of his destination. They had the opportunity of intercepting him at the Straits of Gibraltar, but Sandwich was opposed to the idea. As yet, only 20 ships of the line were ready for Admiral Augustus Keppel's home fleet and Sandwich feared an invasion.[1] There were other reasons not to intercept the French. The Toulon fleet might be merely bound for Cadiz or Brest and to needlessly at-

---

Sandwich to North, 27 February and 6 March 1778. The *Bretagne* was finally ordered armed on about 9 March 1778.

[17] B⁸657: 97, St. Aignan to Sartine, 13 April 1778. See also Appendix E.

[1] *Sandwich Papers*, 2: 19–23; Mackesy, *War for America*, 195. The French encouraged such fears by sending troops to Normandy and Brittany. All of these were in position by about the beginning of May. Spain 589: 92, Vergennes to Montmorin, 14 April 1778; see also Spain 590: 7, Montmorin to Vergennes, 1 July 1778.

tack it would eliminate the possibility of obtaining Dutch aid under the Anglo-Dutch defensive alliance. Moreover, it would be to Britain's advantage to delay opening hostilities until as many convoys as possible had returned.[2] Thus, Britain waited to act until she had firm information as to d'Estaing's destination.

France had equal reason to avoid opening hostilities—to give d'Estaing a head start, to permit the preparation of the Brest fleet and of another squadron at Toulon for the Mediterranean, to force the British into the position of aggressor,[3] and to placate Spanish fears for their returning fleets.

The Spanish problem promised to grow even more difficult. At least Montmorin was able to report that the Vera Cruz treasure fleet had finally reached Havana and was due to arrive in Spain in late May.[4] Montmorin believed, however, that by the time the Spanish fleets returned it would be too late to undertake combined operations during the summer campaigning season. Floridablanca had directly warned him that if Spain were forced into war solely to fulfill her treaty obligations she would confine herself to auxiliary operations.[5]

The Spaniards carefully avoided compromising their bargaining powers as neutrals. Floridablanca forbade d'Estaing the use of Cadiz unless he were forced there. He also re-

[2] *Sandwich Papers*, 2: 114–115, Sandwich to Keppel, 8 July 1778. The Spanish *chargé d'affaires* in London estimated that the Leeward Islands (what the French called part of the Windward Islands), Jamaican, and Mediterranean convoys were worth £3,000,000 (almost 70,000,000 livres), and would provide 1,800 sailors for the British navy. England 530: 84, Escarano to Floridablanca, 10 July 1778.

[3] The French desired not only to prevent Britain from claiming Dutch help, but also to use Austria's unwillingness to fight Britain (despite her defensive alliance with France) as an excuse for France not to fight Prussia over the Bavarian dispute.

[4] Spain 588: 437–444, Montmorin to Vergennes, 30 March 1778. See also Spain 589: 134, 142–143, Montmorin to Vergennes, 27 April and 30 April 1778, reporting that the Spanish treasure fleet, carrying 20,000,000 piastres (100,000,000 livres) was supposed to have departed with four ships of the line from Havana on 9 April.

[5] Spain 588: 437–444, Montmorin to Vergennes, 30 March 1778.

fused to predict when Spain might enter the war.[6] Then, at the end of April, Montmorin was informed by the Spaniards that Lord Weymouth, one of the English secretaries of state, had made overtures to Escarano, the Spanish *chargé d'affaires* in England, for Spain to mediate the Anglo-French dispute.[7] Although Vergennes believed the mediation to be a Spanish move to buy time for themselves, France had little choice but to accede to the idea of Spanish mediation between England and France, although Vergennes did insist that American independence was non-negotiable.[8]

The mediation was even more dangerous than Vergennes realized. In May, Escarano suggested to the British that the cession of Gibraltar to Spain might prevent war. The suggestion was rejected and the conversations were temporarily suspended,[9] but the Spaniards prepared to appoint a new ambassador, the Marquis d'Almodóvar, to conduct further discussions.[10] France objected that the appointment of a new ambassador would raise English prestige and create an impression of disunity between France and Spain,[11] but her protests were futile. Also disturbing was the fact that Spain had suspended her war preparations, especially bothersome since Montmorin reported only 25 Spanish ships of the line in armament in Europe.[12]

[6] Spain 589: 43–47, Montmorin to Vergennes, 10 April 1778. See also Spain 589: 8–12, Vergennes to Montmorin, 3 April 1778.

[7] Spain 589: 104–110, Montmorin to Vergennes, 27 April 1778. On 19 April Floridablanca ordered Escarano to offer this mediation. Stetson Conn, *Gibraltar in British Diplomacy in the Eighteenth Century* (New Haven: Yale University Press, 1942), 182.

[8] Spain 589: 105–107, 129, Montmorin to Vergennes, 18 April and 27 April 1778; Spain 589: 153–156, Vergennes to Montmorin, 1 May 1778.

[9] Conn, *Gibraltar in British Diplomacy*, 182–183; Manuel Danvila y Collado, *Reinado de Carlos III* (Madrid: El Progreso Editorial, 1896), 5: 8–9. Each cites Escarano to Floridablanca, 11 May and 20 May 1778.

[10] Spain 589: 131–132, Montmorin to Vergennes, 27 April 1778.

[11] Paul del Perugia, *La tentative d'invasion de l'Angleterre de 1779* (Paris: Félix Alcan, Presses Universitaires de France, 1939), 36.

[12] Spain 589: 65–78, 131, Montmorin to Vergennes, 10 April and 27

The council's frustration at Spain's disinclination to join France was compounded by d'Estaing's slow progress. His squadron passed through the Straits of Gibraltar only on the night of 16–17 May, five weeks after leaving Toulon.[13] Britain failed to use this delay. A squadron with 13 of the 31 ships of the line of the home fleet had been ordered to America with Vice-Admiral John Byron, but Sandwich's fear of invasion caused the orders to be suspended until news was received as to which direction d'Estaing took upon leaving the Straits.[14] Only on 2 June did a frigate arrive with this intelligence; a week later Byron's squadron finally sailed for North America in pursuit of d'Estaing.[15] The French council already had a good idea of Byron's strength and destination,[16] but as Maurepas admitted privately,[17] the council did not dare risk French trade by sending a squadron from Brest in pursuit. D'Estaing had been given a head start and now had to take his chances. The question now facing the council was the initiation of hostilities in Europe.

France had thus far been restricted to conducting war by proxy—sanctioning the arming of French privateers, escorting American warships, welcoming American merchantmen.[18] D'Orvilliers, the new fleet commander at Brest, be-

---

April 1778. There were also nine of the line still at Buenos Aires, three at Lima, or eight either at Havana, Vera Cruz, or en route to Spain.

[13] Spain 589: 211, Montmorin to Vergennes, 25 May 1778, enclosure. On 19 May d'Estaing detached a frigate to return to France with messages and the sick of his squadron.

[14] *Sandwich Papers*, 2: 58, Sandwich to Weymouth, 13 May 1778; *Ibid.*, 2: 374–375, abstract of orders for Byron, 13 May 1778. See also Spain 589: 180, 182–183, 255–256, Vergennes to Montmorin, 12 May, 15 May, and 2 June 1778.

[15] *Sandwich Papers*, 2: 8–9, 369–371, 374–375; Mackesy, *War for America*, 197–201.

[16] Spain 589: 209–210, Vergennes to Montmorin, 25 May 1778.

[17] Witte, *Journal de l'Abbé de Véri*, 2: 117–118, entry for 24 May 1778.

[18] Only the shortage of frigates and corvettes prevented France from providing escorts for American merchantmen. England 529: 296, Vergennes to Robecq, commandant in Flanders, 7 April 1778;

gan sending patrols into the Channel at the beginning of May to watch for Keppel's sailing. By the end of May d'Orvilliers had 27 ships of the line ready to sail, with another 4 arming.[19] On 1 June six captains were promoted to commodore, including de Grasse, La Motte-Picquet, the commandant at Guadeloupe, and two of d'Estaing's captains, now far at sea. France now was in an enviable position, as Vergennes told Montmorin on 12 June.[20] As long as Keppel and Byron remained united with their 30–32 ships of the line France would not seek a naval battle, since their combined fleet menaced neither d'Estaing nor the Spanish fleets. In a few days d'Orvilliers would have 32 of the line;[21] should the English squadrons separate he would attack Keppel.

Within a week Vergennes was able to give Montmorin word that not only had Byron sailed (on 9 June) but Keppel had as well. The latter had put to sea on 12 June with 21 of the line.[22] Vergennes favored giving battle to Keppel if he appeared off the French coast, but no action would be taken until it was certain Byron would not join him. Vergennes added that as much as he was opposed to recklessness, he was convinced that one could not be too audacious at the start of a war.

England 529: 355–356, 357, Sartine to Vergennes, 26 April and 27 April 1778; United States 3: 207, American commissioners to Vergennes, 19 April 1778; B⁸654: 122, Commodore de la Touche, port commandant at Rochefort, to Sartine, 5 May 1778; Samuel Eliot Morison, *John Paul Jones* (Boston: Little, Brown, and Co., 1959), 134–163.

[19] B⁸650: 169, 173, 179, 184, 229, 234–237, 247, d'Orvilliers to Sartine, 22 April 1778–3 June 1778; B¹85: 96, untitled memoir of 25 May 1778. The first patrol consisted of two frigates, a corvette, and a lugger.

[20] Spain 589: 272–275, Vergennes to Montmorin, 12 June 1778. Keppel and Byron actually received their thirty-fifth ship of the line on 7 June. *Sandwich Papers*, 2: 371, 374.

[21] The last of these ships, the *Diadème*, was ordered on 6 June to be armed. See B⁸650: 266, d'Orvilliers to Sartine, 15 June 1778.

[22] Spain 589: 296–302, Vergennes to Montmorin, 19 June 1778. See also B⁴137: 62–63, 66, port reports of 9 June and 12 June 1778.

As the council waited for news from the Channel they received news from Spain which provided the final impetus for war. Montmorin was suddenly able to report a chain of encouraging developments. First, the Spanish told Montmorin that the mediation negotiations with Britain had reached an impasse. According to the story given Montmorin, Weymouth had told Escarano that the only basis for British negotiations with France would be a French retraction of her declaration that she had signed a treaty with the American colonists. Escarano had supposedly replied that Spain could not suggest such an indecent proposal to France. Montmorin, nevertheless, again advised not pressing Floridablanca about Spain's entering the war until the Mexican and Buenos Aires fleets had returned.[23]

Montmorin soon had more good news: the Buenos Aires fleet and a treasure ship from Peru should now be at sea and were expected in Spain about the beginning of July.[24] On 8 June Montmorin sent his most crucial dispatch.[25] Floridablanca had apologized if the proposed Spanish mediation had retarded French operations and claimed that he had advised France not to delay her military operations or even her preparations for war because of Spain. The inexperienced Montmorin leaped to the conclusion that Spain was now ready to enter the war. He believed this would occur by the end of July, although Floridablanca had kept silent about what measures he planned to take.

Vergennes received this letter on 20 June, the day after he had reported Byron and Keppel at sea.[26] One may doubt he shared his ambassador's optimism but Floridablanca's declaration was an invitation for France to begin war if she

[23] Spain 589: 227–236, Montmorin to Vergennes, 26 May 1778.
[24] Spain 589: 247–248, Montmorin to Vergennes, 1 June 1778.
[25] Spain 589: 268–271, Montmorin to Vergennes, 8 June 1778.
[26] All incoming correspondence is annotated to indicate date received. Although Vergennes did not acknowledge Montmorin's letter until 23 June, Montmorin's letter was marked received on 20 June. Vergennes' letter of 20 June was obviously composed in response, based on internal evidence.

wished. Vergennes immediately wrote on behalf of Louis to ask Charles' sentiments about France's issuing letters of marque to French privateers, a de facto declaration of war against Britain.[27] Vergennes suggested reasons for immediate war. D'Estaing had been given sealed orders to open hostilities upon his arrival in America,[28] so news of hostilities would probably reach Europe in July. Moreover, July, August, and September were the months in which the greatest number of merchantmen and hence sailors would reach Britain unless intercepted.[29] Indeed, the best time to have struck England was already six weeks or two months past. He then reiterated the reasons France desired an independent America, stressing how this would weaken England while minimizing its potential economic benefits to France. He estimated that France would be able to arm 65 or 66 ships of the line in 1779, of which at least six would be sent to India. Significantly, Vergennes now spoke of possible objectives of Spanish interest: Gibraltar, Florida, and, above all, Jamaica. In a separate letter, he requested from Spain a definite answer about her intentions.[30]

Now only the uncertainty as to Byron's destination prevented sending d'Orvilliers to sea;[31] the only other problem was how to blame Britain for the start of hostilities. Within a day a courtier from Brest had brought a solution to the latter problem.[32] Captain de La Clocheterie of the frigate

[27] Spain 589: 310–317, Vergennes to Montmorin, 20 June 1778.

[28] B⁴143: 9–10, d'Estaing to Gérard, June (?) 1778; Louis-Edouard Chevalier, *Histoire de la marine française* (Paris: Hachette et cᶦᵉ, 1877), 3: 107–108. See also United States, supplement 1: 15–16.

[29] In fact, Keppel had sailed to cover the British shipping lanes at the entrance to the English Channel, through which the incoming convoys would pass.

[30] Spain 589: 321–326, "Réflexions sur la conduite à tenir dans les circonstances presentes relativement à l'Espagne," 20 June 1778.

[31] Vergennes had mentioned this uncertainty on 20 June. Both Aranda and d'Orvilliers still believed Byron to be only a short distance from Keppel. Spain 589: 332, Aranda to Escarano, 21 June 1778; B⁴136: 103–104, d'Orvilliers to Sartine, 22 June 1778.

[32] B³650: 273, d'Orvilliers to Sartine, 18 June 1778. It seems likely that this information reached Versailles late on 20 June or early on

Belle-Poule had met Keppel's fleet and had refused to submit to the custom of presenting his ship to the fleet flagship. When an English frigate attempted to enforce this protocol, fire was exchanged. The *Belle-Poule* escaped despite casualties to 40 percent of her crew but two frigates on patrol with her were quickly captured by Keppel.[33] Since no rational naval officer would attack 20 of the line with three frigates, France had a *causus belli* (in 1780 the *Belle-Poule* would be captured after dueling a British 64 while de La Clocheterie, a national hero, would die in combat two years later).

Vergennes informed Montmorin on 23 June of the *Belle-Poule*'s combat and announced that France, reassured by Montmorin's letter that Spain would not be displeased, would take reprisals.[34] On 26 June he wrote Ambassador Gérard in America that France considered war as currently existing between her and England; by this date Vergennes was fairly certain that Byron had indeed sailed for America.[35] D'Orvilliers was ordered to be ready to sail at any time,[36] and on 28 June legal action was commenced regard-

---

21 June. Aranda relayed the news to Escarano on 21 June. Spain 589: 332, Aranda to Escarano, 21 June 1778. The quickest possible time from Brest to Versailles was about 50 hours. Georges Lacour-Gayet, *La marine militaire de la France sous le règne de Louis XVI* (Paris: H. Champion, 1905), 126.

[33] B⁸650: 269, 273, d'Orvilliers to Sartine, 17 June and 18 June 1778; B⁴136: 10–13, 17–18, 31–32, reports of the three frigate captains; England 530: 47–49, Escarano to Floridablanca, 26 June 1778. *Sandwich Papers*, 2: 94–96, Keppel to Sandwich, 20 June 1778; Clowes, *Royal Navy*, 4: 14–16; Lacour-Gayet, *La marine militaire sous le règne de Louis XVI*, 112–113.

[34] Spain 589: 343–344, Vergennes to Montmorin, 23 June 1778.

[35] United States 3: 382–383, Vergennes to Gérard, 23 June 1778; Spain 589: 348, Vergennes to Montmorin, 26 June 1778. Vergennes' confidence was probably based on Spanish intelligence reports, which figured from Byron's provisions that he was destined for America. England 530: 41–43, Escarano to Floridablanca, 19 June 1778. Copies of Spanish intelligence reports were left at Versailles by couriers returning to Spain from England.

[36] B⁴136: 105–108, d'Orvilliers to Sartine, 29 June 1778, acknowledging orders of 25 June 1778.

ing the English ships which had been embargoed in French ports since March and general orders were secretly given for indiscriminate reprisals against English shipping.[37] The following day d'Orvilliers was sent sailing orders which he received on the morning of 2 July.[38] Unfavorable winds delayed his departure but he finally sailed on 8 July.[39] Two years of preparations lay behind him, four-and-a-half years of war lay ahead.

5. The First Campaign

D'Orvilliers' prey had escaped long before he sailed. From his prizes Keppel had learned that 27 of d'Orvilliers' ships of the line were ready (information already outdated) and prudently he headed immediately for Portsmouth.[1] He arrived with his 21 ships of the line at the road of Saint Helen's on 27 June and awaited reinforcements. By 9 July, he had been brought to 24 of the line and was able to sail to protect the incoming Jamaican convoy. Within about a week he had 29 of the line with another en route. His fleet was now substantially stronger than d'Orvilliers' fleet of 32 of the line since he had 7 great three-decked

---

[37] England 158: 60–61, "Arrêt du Conseil d'Etat," 28 June 1778; B⁴134: 71, general orders of 28 June 1778. On 29 June Vergennes told Montmorin that some letters of marque had already been issued. Spain 589: 354, Vergennes to Montmorin, 29 June 1778. On 10 July Louis formally ordered the Admiral of France to deliver commissions to all ships which requested them, authorizing them to make reprisals against British shipping—the closest equivalent to a declaration of war that France would make. Spain 590: 56–57, Vergennes to Montmorin, 10 July 1778; Lambert de Sainte-Croix, *L'administration de la marine*, 298–299. The English sent similar orders to their fleet commanders on 19 July and made a formal declaration of them on 2 August. *Sandwich Papers*, 2: 373; England 530: 145–155, declaration of 2 August 1778.

[38] B⁴136: 109–110, d'Orvilliers to Sartine, 3 July 1778.

[39] B⁴136: 118–119, d'Orvilliers to Sartine, 7 July 1778.

[1] *Sandwich Papers*, 2: 98, 99–101, Keppel to Sandwich, 21 June and 27 (?) June 1778.

ships of 90 guns or more to d'Orvilliers' 2 (and no 50s while d'Orvilliers had two).[2]

Keppel's reinforcements radically changed the strategic situation in European waters. Both Sartine and d'Orvilliers knew before d'Orvilliers sailed that Keppel had returned to port and then had been reinforced—intelligence received from Escarano, the Spanish diplomat in London, and d'Orvilliers' patrolling frigates.[3] It took considerable courage for the council not to cancel d'Orvilliers' orders. The only French reserve was four ships of the line at Toulon; if d'Orvilliers were beaten decisively France would be as helpless as after 1759. Sartine was advised by both civilians and naval officers not to risk the Brest fleet;[4] yet, as Vergennes argued, to do nothing would be to give the British time to increase their numbers, expose French commerce to attack, and destroy the morale of the French navy.[5] D'Orvilliers' orders were to cruise for a month but not to seek out battle and not to risk taking his ships up the Channel where France did not have ports.[6] The council let these orders stand, although on 12 July a frigate carried to d'Orvilliers permission to return to port if he deemed it prudent.[7]

---

[2] *Sandwich Papers*, 2: 372–373. There is an obvious similarity between the relative strengths of these two fleets and the relative strength of the fleets at Trafalgar in 1805. Nelson had 27 ships of the line including seven "first-rates." Villeneuve 33 of the line, but only four "first-rates," all Spanish.

[3] England 530: 60–61, 64–65, Escarano to Floridablanca, 28 June 1778; B⁴136: 114–116, 118–119, d'Orvilliers to Sartine, 6 July and 7 July 1778. See also England 530: 98, Almodóvar to Aranda, 17 July 1778.

[4] Chevalier, *Histoire de la marine française*, 3: 80–81; Emmanuel-Henri, Vᵗᵉ de Grouchy and Paul Cottin, eds., *Journal inédit du duc de Croÿ, 1718–1784* (Paris: Ernest Flammarion, 1906–1907), 4: 125–127.

[5] Spain 590: 33, Vergennes to Montmorin, 6 July 1778.

[6] B⁴136: 103–104, d'Orvilliers to Sartine, 22 June 1778.

[7] Chevalier, *Histoire de la marine française*, 3: 83–84; Bouclon, *Etude historique sur la marine*, 205–206.

Luckily for France, fleet actions in the eighteenth century were seldom decisive.[8] D'Orvilliers met Keppel 65 miles off Île d'Ouessant and on 27 July the two fleets fought a general engagement which resulted in over 1,000 casualties and considerable damage to both fleets, but not the capture of any ships. Both fleets then returned to port.

Within three weeks d'Orvilliers repaired all his ships except the *Ville-de-Paris* and sailed again. He cruised in the Bay of Biscay, staying well clear of Keppel's fleet, and returned to port without incident.[9] A major purpose of his cruise was to clear the coast of English privateers which had inflicted severe losses on French commerce.[10] D'Orvilliers' fleet, too unwieldy, captured only three prizes. Upon his return he began sending squadrons of two or three ships of the line with attendant frigates which did far better. The institution of convoys, particularly to the West Indies, and an increase of patrolling frigates and corvettes also contributed to reducing shipping losses to manageable proportions. D'Orvilliers now began the preparation of squadrons for overseas detachment.

The vital theater of naval operations was in America.[11] Upon d'Estaing's squadron rested French hopes of a quick victory which would obviate the need for Spanish help.

[8] Vergennes pointed this out to Montmorin. Spain 590: 140–143, Vergennes to Montmorin, 31 July 1778.

[9] B⁴141: 348 ff., "Brest, journal du 14 juillet au 24 septembre 1778," no date; Lacour-Gayet, *La marine militaire sous le règne de Louis XVI*, 135–137.

[10] See Dull: Dissertation, 221–225 for a fuller discussion. See also Lacour-Gayet, *La marine militaire sous le règne de Louis XVI*, 135–137. Keppel also cruised, from 23 August to 26 October, but did not seek combat.

[11] For naval operations in the Western Hemisphere during 1778, see relevant chapters in Mackesy, *War for America*; Gruber, *Howe Brothers*; Clowes, *Royal Navy*; William Milburne James, *The British Navy in Adversity* (London: Longmans, Green, and Co., 1926); William Bradford Willcox, *Portrait of a General: Sir Henry Clinton in the War of Independence* (New York: Alfred A. Knopf, 1964), particularly 238. Clinton and Howe learned only on 29 June that d'Estaing was en route to America.

D'Estaing, however, was unable to exploit the opportunities presented to him. Lieutenant-General Sir Henry Clinton, General Howe's replacement, received on 9 May 1778 the order to attack Saint Lucia. He postponed the expedition until his main army could evacuate Philadelphia and concentrate on New York. Although his army marched overland he sent his artillery and stores via sea. His 400 merchantmen safely reached Sandy Hook off New York on 1 July, only a week before d'Estaing arrived off the Delaware Capes. D'Estaing moved against the nine ships of the line and the irreplaceable garrison at New York but failed to seize Sandy Hook at the southern entrance to the port. Howe was able to place his smaller squadron next to the shallow entrance and prevent d'Estaing's passage. On 22 July d'Estaing shifted his squadron to a less valuable but more vulnerable target, the 5,000-6,000-man British garrison at Newport, Rhode Island. Byron's squadron had encountered a heavy gale and was so delayed that d'Estaing and a 9,000-man American army were able to closely blockade the British garrison. Howe was soon reinforced by one of Byron's ships of the line, two from Halifax, and one from the West Indies. He lured d'Estaing away from Newport, fought an indecisive battle interrupted by a storm and bought enough time that d'Estaing, fearing the arrival of Byron's squadron, abandoned the siege on 22 August.

Luckily for d'Estaing the brilliant Howe was relieved at the end of September by the undistinguished Byron who was unable to exploit his numerical advantage. When Byron attempted to attack d'Estaing at Boston in October, he lost the *Somerset*, 64, by shipwreck and suffered severe storm damage to most of his squadron. Byron, with his squadron needing repair, then sent ten regiments (of one battalion each) to attack Saint Lucia under the weak escort of two 64s and three 50s. D'Estaing left Boston for Martinique on the same day (4 November) and barely missed capturing the entire force. The British captured Saint Lucia and were able to beat off d'Estaing's fleet and a French landing party.[12] On 6 January 1779 Byron's main fleet of ten ships of the line arrived to establish British superiority in the West Indies; eight more of the line under Rear-Admiral Rowley had sailed from Europe for the West Indies in December. In five months of campaigning d'Estaing had destroyed or captured only five frigates and four corvettes, mostly at Newport. The only consolations for France were d'Estaing's success in at least preserving his squadron from loss, and Marshal Bouillé's success in capturing Dominica by surprise.[13]

If d'Estaing's campaign was disappointing, the opening campaign in the Indian Ocean was disastrous. At the beginning of 1778 Sartine sent the *Flamand*, 56, and a frigate to reinforce the Mascarene Islands, but the French position on the sub-continent was virtually indefensible. The French naval commander abandoned Pondicherry after a brief battle with an equal English naval force[14] dooming the resistance of its garrison of 1,000 troops to 5,000 besieging troops. By the spring of 1779 every French post in India had fallen.[15]

[12] The French advantage was 12 ships of the line against seven and 5,500 troops against 5,000, but in the actual assault 2,000 British troops beat off 3,500 French. See B⁴140 and B⁴141.

[13] Bouillé at Martinique had only three frigates, but he was able to surprise and capture the valuable British island of Dominica, despite the presence of two British ships of the line at Barbados. The British captured without resistance Saint Pierre and Miquelon off Newfoundland. The departure of 15 ships of the line left only two of the line in North America—five others returned to England, one had been shipwrecked, and two more had turned back to England during the storm which hit Byron en route to New York.

[14] The French had the *Brillant*, 64, *Pourvoyeuse*, 40, and three smaller ships. The British had the *Rippon*, 60, *Coventry*, 28, and three smaller ships. S. P. Sen, *The French in India, 1763–1816* (Calcutta: K. L. Mukhopadhyay, 1958), 71 ff.

[15] Chadernagore was captured on 10 July 1778, Pondicherry on 18 October 1778, and Mahé (on the west coast of India) on 19 March 1779. The council had sent orders to evacuate Pondicherry as indefensible, but these orders arrived too late. Spain 591: 414, Vergennes to Floridablanca, 24 December 1778.

Even before the campaign in Europe had ended, France began preparing for the next campaign. Initially, the council hoped to send 4,000 men to India, but these plans had to be changed when the council learned in October that d'Estaing had had to retreat to Boston and that the British were planning to send an expedition to the West Indies.[16] The council no longer had a free hand. At the beginning of November it adopted a new plan of operations involving detaching three squadrons from d'Orvilliers' home fleet. Captain the Marquis de Vaudreuil with the *Fendant* and *Sphinx* would attack the English slaving stations in Senegambia on the African coast, using 430 troops from the Legion of "Foreign Volunteers of the Navy" originally raised by the Duke de Lauzun for service in India.[17] Vaudreuil was then to proceed to Martinique where he was to meet another squadron (containing the *Dauphin-Royal*, *Robuste*, *Magnifique*, and *Vengeur*) under Commodore de Grasse which was to bring a battalion of reinforcements to replace the occupation force for Dominica. Commodore the Chevalier de Ternay was to take the *Annibal*, *Diadème*, *Orient*, *Artésien*, *Réflechi*, and *Amphion* and 1,500 troops to the Indian Ocean.[18] Vaudreuil was able to sail on 15 December, but because of crowding and variety of minor delays the other two squadrons were still at Brest at the end of the year.[19]

In one sense France had been extremely fortunate during 1778. Despite England's numerical naval superiority, France had lost not even a frigate since the opening days

[16] Spain 591: 94, 206, Vergennes to Montmorin, 23 October and 20 November 1778; Jean-François Barrière and M. de Lescure, eds., *Bibliothèque des mémoires relatifs à l'histoire de France pendant le 18e siècle*, vol. 25, *Mémoires du duc de Lauzun* (Paris: Firmin-Didot frères, fils, et cie, 1862), 172–176.

[17] B¹87: 268, instructions for Lauzun, 15 November 1778; B⁴149: 85–93, instructions for Vaudreuil, 28 November 1778.

[18] Spain 591: 152–153, Vergennes to Montmorin, 9 November 1778.

[19] Described in Dull: Dissertation, 233.

of the war. On the continent, too, France had had good fortune. Prussia invaded Austria on 5 July, commencing a war of maneuver at which Joseph matched the great Frederick. The Russians, however, were not willing to risk a Prussian defeat which would upset the balance of power in Germany. Joseph was forced at the end of the campaign to accept the mediation of Russia and France, virtually guaranteeing not only an enforced peace but also the preservation of an independent Bavaria.[20]

The next year did not hold the firm promise of safety, let alone the decisive victories d'Estaing had failed to obtain. France expected to enter the coming campaign with about 66 ships of the line compared to her 52 in 1778.[21] With crews now available for the English fleet and the advantages of surprise gone, France's relative position, however, would be worse—in fact, England would man 90 ships of the line during the coming campaign. The only hope for obtaining a favorable balance of forces was securing the participation of the Spanish navy. This in turn would require greater success than hitherto obtained in diplomatic discussions with Spain.

6. The Spanish Alliance Question

Montmorin was quickly disabused of his expectation that Spain was about to enter the war. During a conference on 20 June, only 12 days after Montmorin's optimistic dispatch, Floridablanca complained to him that France did not really wish to see Spain regain Gibraltar and claimed Spain had

[20] Madariaga, *Britain, Russia, and the Armed Neutrality*, 42, 47–48. For Vergennes' comments on the campaign see Spain 590: 77–78, 121, Vergennes to Montmorin, 17 July and 25 July 1778.

[21] Spain 591: 44, Vergennes to Montmorin, 9 October 1778. This projection was based on the addition of nine ships of the line in construction, four in overhaul (the *Bourgogne, Bizarre, Citoyen,* and *Souverain*), and the purchase of a ship (the *Sévère*) to replace the *Bordelais*. Repairs to the *Ville-de-Paris* and *Duc-de-Bourgogne* were also expected to be completed. See also Appendixes C and F.

little interest in Jamaica or in Florida, except for Pensacola and Mobile.[1] The French decision to begin hostilities met with Floridablanca's approval—he even suggested that d'Orvilliers follow Keppel to port and burn his fleet with fireships—but he would explain his plans only when the Spanish fleets returned.[2] His only concession was to add the *Santísima Trinidad*, 114, and an 80-gun ship to the fleet at Cadiz. Montmorin, his optimism gone, now believed Spain desired a joint declaration of war against England, but only at the beginning of 1779.[3]

As Montmorin suspected, the idea of Spanish mediation was not dead.[4] The Marquis d'Almodóvar, the new Spanish ambassador to the British court, held his first interview with Lord Weymouth in mid-July.[5] Montmorin warned that Spain wished to increase her available forces so she could act as an arbiter of peace and that at the moment any help Spain would be forced to give would be worse than none.[6]

As the European campaign proceeded, the various treasures shipments reached Spain, but not until September did the last ship arrive.[7] At the end of August Floridablanca

---

[1] Spain 589: 341-342, Montmorin to Vergennes, 22 July 1778. See also Spain 590: 30-34, 115-119, Vergennes to Montmorin, 6 July and 24 July 1778.

[2] Spain 590: 7-8, Montmorin to Vergennes, 1 July 1778.

[3] Montmorin noted in a personal letter to Vergennes that Spain expected to have 50 ships of the line ready by the coming spring. Spain 590: 3-6, Montmorin to Vergennes, 1 July 1778. Vergennes complained to Montmorin that Spain had been deceptive. Spain 590: 114-115, Vergennes to Montmorin, 24 July 1778.

[4] Spain 589: 341-342, Montmorin to Vergennes, 22 June 1778.

[5] Danvila, *Reinado de Carlos III*, 5: 10-11.

[6] Spain 590: 92-101, Montmorin to Vergennes, 20 July 1778.

[7] These arrivals were: the Vera Cruz treasure fleet with four ships of the line (29 June), part of the South American expedition with four ships of the line (17 July), a ship of the line from Lima, carrying 3,000,000 piastres (21 July), a galleon from Lima, carrying 1,500,000 piastres (16 September), and another two ships of the line from the South American expedition, carrying 1,500,000 piastres (18 September). Three ships of the line remained at Havana, two at Lima, and one at Vera Cruz (which returned to Spain in January 1779, carrying 4,000,000 piastres). A ship of the line which had been captured by the Portuguese returned to Spain in May 1779. Spain 590:

informed Montmorin of Spain's decision.[8] Spain would take no action until she knew the effect of her *démarche* to England offering mediation. She would continue her armaments and planned to prepare at Ferrol a new squadron of ten ships of the line and to send to Havana a reinforcement of 6,000 to 7,000 troops. Floridablanca also suggested to Montmorin as his own personal idea that the Bourbons combine their forces to form a fleet of 60 ships of the line. This fleet could make possible a descent on England and then the conducting of peace negotiations from London. Floridablanca also mentioned that Weymouth had hinted that England would make sacrifices to obtain Spanish neutrality, although Floridablanca promised such gestures would be rejected—a clear hint on Floridablanca's part that France should begin making specific offers concerning war objectives. Montmorin believed it might be necessary to promise Spain that France would not make peace unless Gibraltar and part of British-held Florida were restored to Spain. Montmorin warned that Charles would not make his decision until the end of the year and that he would not recognize the United States until the conclusion of a general peace. Montmorin suggested that it might be a good idea for France to capture Jamaica which could be later exchanged with Spain for the Spanish possession of Santo Domingo.

A week later Montmorin sent the translation of a letter Floridablanca was about to send Almodóvar.[9] This letter in-

---

37, 149–151, 415, Montmorin to Vergennes, 2 July, 3 August, and 21 September 1778; Spain 590: 88–89, 109, 376, vice-consul Poirel at Cadiz to Montmorin, 17 July, 21 July, and 11 September 1778; Spain 593: 47, Cadiz intelligence summary of 9 March 1779.

[8] Spain 590: 240–251, Floridablanca to Montmorin, 11 August 1778, sent by Montmorin to Vergennes, 18 August 1778; Spain 590: 218–239, Montmorin to Vergennes, 17 August 1778; Danvila, *Reinado de Carlos III*, 5: 13–15.

[9] Spain 590: 277–278, 287–288, Montmorin to Vergennes, 24 August 1778, and enclosure, "Traduction de l'extrait de ce que l'on répond a M. le M^ls d'Almodóvar le 25 août 1778 en consequence de sa lettre du 31 juillet."

sisted that it was not Spain's responsibility to mediate between France and England (i.e., it was England's responsibility to respond to the Spanish offer of mediation). It warned England that she should accord satisfaction to Spain for the injuries done to her[10] or otherwise Charles feared he would be forced to take into consideration the interests of his allies. France was not informed that Floridablanca sent a confidential letter to Almodóvar[11] making explicit demands that Britain make specific positive offers to Spain, including the means of guaranteeing them, or otherwise Spain would take what she wanted.

For the moment the next diplomatic move belonged to England. During September discussions between Spain and France pursued familiar lines. Floridablanca continued to urge France to take decisive action—to make war against England as the Romans had made war against the Carthaginians.[12] Spain began to consider an "enterprise worthy of the two powers," which Montmorin felt certainly meant Floridablanca's suggested invasion of England.[13] Vergennes in turn suggested that since an invasion of England would require 70 ships of the line and 70,000 men, Spain should consider instead the possibility of invading Ireland.[14] He also told Montmorin confidentially that Spain would have to furnish half of the troops for any expedition.[15]

At the end of September Floridablanca finally learned that the English had accepted Spanish mediation, although they did so in very vague terms.[16] He did not inform Montmorin that Lord Barrington, the secretary of war, had en-

[10] These injuries were the seizure of Spanish ships and the conducting of illegal logging operations in Central America.
[11] Danvila, *Reinado de Carlos III*, 5: 20–21; Bemis, *Diplomacy of the American Revolution*, 78–79.
[12] Spain 590: 355, Montmorin to Vergennes, 4 September 1778.
[13] Spain 590: 402–405, Montmorin to Vergennes, 17 September 1778.
[14] Spain 590: 418, Vergennes to Montmorin, 21 September 1778.
[15] Spain 590: 440–441, Vergennes to Montmorin, 29 September 1778.
[16] Spain 590: 392–393, Almodóvar to Floridablanca, 14 September 1778, included with Spain 590: 453–459, Montmorin to Vergennes, 29 September 1778.

couraged Almodóvar to believe England would be willing to give up Gibraltar and Minorca.[17]

Spain now began her role as mediator by requesting both France and England to submit their demands, after which she would propose a plan of pacification. Spain also secretly requested France to submit to her a second confidential list of the *minimum* demands she would insist upon.[18] Vergennes accepted the mediation on behalf of France and informed Spain of France's demands.[19] France was willing to negotiate the right to fortify Dunkirk, the possession of exclusive fishing rights in Newfoundland, and the right to fortify the post of Chandernagore in Bengal. She would not compromise on the withdrawal of the British commissioner at Dunkirk or unconditional independence for the United States, with British withdrawal from all occupied territory.

The British for their part were interested neither in the mediation nor in offering territory to Spain. In the middle of October the cabinet met to discuss the Spanish mediation and demands. George was opposed to any compromise. He believed that only from a successful war could Britain win a stable peace and that by the coming spring the British navy would be strong enough to defeat both Bourbon fleets combined. The cabinet did not challenge his calculations (ultimately to be so disastrous), although the cautious Lord Sandwich requested Britain to temporize until he could reinforce Minorca and Jamaica and strengthen the Channel fleet.[20] Britain therefore did not openly reject the Spanish proposal that she submit her terms for peace. Her response, which reached Spain at the beginning of November, de-

[17] Conn, *Gibraltar in British Diplomacy*, 184–185; Danvila, *Reinado de Carlos III*, 5: 23, citing Almodóvar to Floridablanca, 18 September 1778.
[18] Spain 590: 453–459, Montmorin to Vergennes, 29 September 1778.
[19] Spain 591: 38–41, Vergennes to Montmorin, 9 October 1778; Spain 591: 60–63, 64–72, Vergennes to Montmorin, 17 October 1778.
[20] Fortescue, *Correspondence of King George the Third*, 4: 208, George to North, 13 October 1778 (no. 2434); Mackesy, *War for America*, 249–250.

manded, however, that as a preliminary condition for negotiations France withdraw all forces sent to the aid of the colonies and cease all other assistance to them.[21]

In his turn Montmorin demanded as a precondition that England immediately recognize American independence.[22] On 20 November Floridablanca communicated these reciprocal conditions to the interested parties.[23] While mediating, the Spanish were preparing their forces;[24] Floridablanca was now losing patience and was ready to demand for Spain serious negotiations from both England and France.

Again Spain secretly suggested to England that she be ceded Gibraltar and Minorca. Weymouth responded with insulting directness that in exchange Spain would have to fix her friendship for Britain in very solid terms.[25] There could be no clearer sign of the hopelessness of the negotiations with England.

Spain by now had begun to shift the emphasis of her diplomatic negotiations to France. To keep the possibility of mediation alive Spain suggested to France the idea that by a long truce England could de facto recognize the independence of the United States.[26] More important, she be-

[21] Spain 591: 156–161, Montmorin to Vergennes, 9 November 1778.
[22] Spain 591: 181–189, Montmorin to Vergennes, 16 November 1778.
[23] Spain 591: 235–236, Charles to the French court, 20 November 1778.
[24] Two ships of the line and troop reinforcements were supposed to sail for Havana in mid-October, although they did not actually leave until the end of the year. Five ships of the line had been recently armed at Ferrol and another five were expected to be armed by the end of the year. To deceive England about Spanish intentions Floridablanca suddenly ceased all complaints and informed her that Spain intended to disarm three ships of the line (or so Floridablanca told Montmorin). Spain 591: 42–43, 160; Spain 592: 6, Montmorin to Vergennes, 12 October 1778, 9 November 1778, and 4 January 1779.
[25] Bemis, *Diplomacy of the American Revolution*, 79; Danvila, *Reinado de Carlos III*, 33–34, citing Almodóvar to Floridablanca, 29 December 1778.
[26] Spain 591: 229–230, 363, Montmorin to Vergennes, 20 November and 17 December 1778; United States 5: 370–371, Vergennes to Gérard, 25 October 1778. Franklin indicated this would be acceptable.

gan exploring what offers France would make for Spanish participation in the war. On the same day that Spain submitted the English peace proposals to France, Floridablanca requested commitments from France in case Spain's mediation failed. He wished to know: (1) what would be the plan of combined operations if Spain joined the war; and (2) what advantages Spain could expect from war and in what manner France would obligate herself not to entertain any peace propositions until these advantages had been assured.[27] He demanded absolute secrecy of France.

Montmorin warned Vergennes in the most emphatic terms that it was vitally necessary to appear in agreement with Floridablanca.[28] According to Montmorin, Floridablanca feared France would try to achieve her war goals without giving support to those of Spain. Floridablanca wished Gibraltar for Spain but believed that it was too strong to be attacked directly. If England or Ireland could be invaded, Gibraltar could be won at the peace table. Floridablanca told Montmorin that he favored an attack on Florida and diversions both by d'Estaing and against Gibraltar, since these would draw British forces away from Europe, making possible an invasion of England or Ireland. Montmorin warned that France had the alternatives of supporting the war by herself with only token aid from Spain or of engaging herself in a war of changed objectives and uncertain duration.

Vergennes responded on 1 December that there would be some delay in answering Floridablanca's dispatch as he was in ill health.[29] In fact, the delay was probably necessary

---

Doniol, *La participation de la France*, 3: 595, 599, Vergennes to Montmorin, 4 December and 24 December 1778.

[27] Spain 591: 219–220, Floridablanca to Vergennes, 20 November 1778.

[28] Spain 591: 210–218, Montmorin to Vergennes, 20 November 1778.

[29] Spain 591: 286–287, Vergennes to Montmorin, 1 December 1778.

because Louis, distracted by his wife's advanced pregnancy and delivery (19 December 1778), was faced with a decision of great difficulty. In a personal letter to the king, Vergennes appealed for a policy which would enable France to receive more than token Spanish assistance:

If it is a fact that His Majesty cannot struggle long on equal terms with the English and that a prolonged war, which would not be exempt from disadvantages, could entertain the ruin of his navy and even his finances, and finally that His Majesty reduced to his own means would be less able to make his enemies feel the need of peace than if he were acting in concert with a strong ally, then the most natural consequence is that everything invites him to take some risks in order to activate such a desirable alliance. I will not dissimulate, Sire, that the views and pretensions of Spain are gigantic, but it is necessary to consider that the time one uses to countervail against them will be lost for the establishment of combined operations which one cannot hasten too much to prepare.[30]

Louis could make his decision without worry that France might yet become involved in war in Germany. Vergennes told Montmorin that the warring powers had accepted Franco-Russian mediation and that he expected that peace would be signed within three months.[31] Sometime in December the king acceded to Vergennes' wishes. On 24 December Vergennes sent a plan of combined operations, although he left war aims to Spain to propose and claimed the Family Compact contained sufficient guarantee that France would act in concert with Spain.[32] He also sent two covering letters for Montmorin. In one he warned Mont-

[30] Memoirs and Documents, France 1897: 94, Vergennes to Louis, 5 December 1778.
[31] Spain 591: 297-298, 336–337, Vergennes to Montmorin, 4 December and 11 December 1778.
[32] Spain 591: 412–414, 426–427, Vergennes to Montmorin, 24 December 1778.

morin not to trust Floridablanca, who had misled France in June.[33] He also warned that if the worst came about, France would have to request the 12 ships of the line and 5 frigates promised by the Family Compact. In the other letter, Vergennes explained that his plan of operations was that of a man of peace rather than a man of war—he had consulted no professionals in order to maintain secrecy.[34] He believed the plan if not audacious was at least solid. He insisted that it was necessary to reinforce the West Indies, even though Floridablanca had objected to this as a dispersal of effort,[35] and pointed out that since 40,000 of France's 50,000 seamen were already in the navy, France could not man the transports necessary for any demonstration in the Mediterranean.

Vergennes suggested that Spain and France combine their naval forces to hold the main British fleet in the Channel.[36] Since to attack England would require 70,000 infantry and 5,000 cavalry, Vergennes suggested instead to attack Ireland with 27,000 infantry and 3,000 cavalry, half to be provided by each country. Vergennes expected the Irish, particularly the Irish Presbyterians with their passion for democracy, to rise against the English. Vergennes finished by ruling out attacks on Minorca and Jamaica as impractical and by proclaiming that other than Dominica, already taken, the French desired no conquests in the West Indies.

Montmorin received this correspondence on the last day

[33] Spain 591: 428–430, Vergennes to Montmorin, 24 December 1778.

[34] Spain 591: 415–418, Vergennes to Montmorin, 24 December 1778. I suspect strongly that Sartine and perhaps Fleurieu had helped prepare the plans, whatever Vergennes claimed.

[35] Spain 591: 217–218, Montmorin to Vergennes, 20 November 1778. As already mentioned, Floridablanca favored only diversionary efforts in the Western Hemisphere.

[36] Spain 591: 419–425, "Projet de guerre," included with letters of Vergennes to Montmorin, 24 December 1778. Vergennes predicted that in 1779 England would have at most 92 of the line (including 12 50-gun ships), Spain at least 45, and France at least 62 (nine at Île de France, 18 in the West Indies, 32 at Brest, and three at Toulon), although he hoped France would have as many as 67.

of 1778.[37] Whatever action Spain would take in response, the war against England would necessitate all the resources of the French monarchy. Necker in November 1778 was able to secure a loan of 48,366,222 livres;[38] but even such borrowing could not enable the monarchy to match expenditures by allotments. Sartine now estimated that naval expenses for 1778 would reach 100,000,000 livres and the naval debt would rise to 40,000,000 livres.[39] Not only an increased number of ships would have to be manned, but an increased building program would be needed in 1779—3 ships of at least 90 guns to match the terrifying English "three-deckers" met at Ouessant, 4 74s, and 13 new frigates.[40]

During December Vergennes had received a copy of Almodóvar's latest estimates of British troop strength: 42,783 in Britain, 46,237 under Clinton, 9,120 in Ireland, 7,478 in Canada, 4,633 at Gibraltar, 1,880 at Minorca and 1,589 in the West Indies and at Jamaica.[41] To defeat this enemy would indeed require all the aid France and the United States could obtain.

[37] Spain 591: 454, Montmorin to Vergennes, 31 December 1778.

[38] Marcel Marion, *Histoire financière de la France depuis 1715* (Paris: Librairie nouvelle de droit et de jurisprudence, 1914) 1: 298–299.

[39] B^{1}87: 260–265, untitled memoir of 1 November 1778; B^{1}91: 12, untitled memoir of 9 January 1779. The latter memoir estimated that had there been no war French naval expenses for 1778 would have been 70,000,000 livres.

[40] B^{1}87: 297, untitled memoir of 29 November 1778. See also Dull: Dissertation, 244n–245n for further details.

[41] England 530: 388–389, Almodóvar to Floridablanca, 18 December 1778. For actual British figures see Mackesy, *War for America*, 524–525.

CHAPTER SIX

1779—War at the Center

1. The Convention of Aranjuez

VERGENNES hoped to bring Spain to declare her price for entry into the war. He also sought to minimize the dangers and cost of attacking the center of the British Empire by shifting the target from England to Ireland and by forcing Spain to provide half the troops. He was soon frustrated in both aims even though his plan of operations generally met with Spanish approval.

Montmorin reported on 12 January 1779 the Spanish response to Vergennes' communications of the previous month.[1] Floridablanca reiterated Charles' intention that Louis determine the objectives of the war for both parties, although Floridablanca hinted privately to Montmorin what some of these objectives should be. He considered Gibraltar, western Florida, and the expulsion of the English from their illegal settlements on the Gulf of Honduras as necessary objectives, while Jamaica, Minorca, and the revocation of the existing English rights in Central America (to cut timber in Campeche, i.e., the Yucatán Peninsula) would merely be useful. As to the invasion of Ireland, Spain could not furnish half the troops because of the unreliability of her army, but she would furnish a monetary compensation. Spain approved both the plan of operations and the peace terms which France had presented to England. To preserve secrecy Spain would continue her own negotiations with England until her armament was complete, which would probably be about the middle of May.

Montmorin added some reflections of his own.[2] The Spaniards felt France would be more bound to respect Spanish

---

[1] Spain 592: 37–47, Montmorin to Vergennes, 12 January 1779.
[2] Spain 592: 62–68, 69–72, Montmorin to Vergennes, 13 January 1779.

war aims if France proposed them herself. Floridablanca still believed that Gibraltar could be conquered only through attacking Britain or Ireland. The king, who was against war, was being driven to it by England's unreasonableness. Finally, Montmorin admitted that the Spanish navy, for all its probable deficiencies in maneuver and combat, was still capable of fighting. The addition of 50 to 55 ships of the line would at least draw off English forces.[3]

While Spain awaited France's response, she made her compromise proposal for a peace settlement to the belligerents.[4] Its terms were similar to those she had suggested in December to France. Britain was to withdraw her troops from the colonies and one of three types of truce was to be concluded—a 30-year truce, a truce of unlimited duration, or a three-party truce between Britain, France, and the colonies. Britain temporized until March and then rejected these terms.

It was mid-February before Vergennes took up again the negotiations with Spain. Although he sent a draft convention concerning war aims, he left Montmorin at liberty to sign any convention necessary to bring Spain into the war.[5] Vergennes' main concern now was the plan of operations.[6] He maintained that the Spanish refusal to contribute troops for combined operations in Europe ruled out Ireland as a target. So large an operation mounted solely in French ports would demand too many transports; moreover, it would be impossible to maintain surprise as to its objective. Vergennes believed that the combined forces should instead

[3] Floridablanca promised Vergennes that Spain would have 54 or 55 ships of the line ready by the end of May. Spain 592: 51–53, Floridablanca to Vergennes, 13 January 1779.

[4] Spain 592: 101–103, Montmorin to Vergennes, 19 January 1779; Spain 592: 110–111, Floridablanca to Almodóvar, 20 January 1779.

[5] Spain 592: 229–231, Vergennes to Montmorin, 12 February 1779. Floridablanca in fact did raise objections to the proposed convention.

[6] Spain 592: 233–235, 245–246, Vergennes to Montmorin, 12 February 1779; Spain 592: 247–248, Vergennes to Floridablanca, 12 February 1779.

attempt to destroy English commerce and, if possible, the English fleet. He thought this could be accomplished by stationing a fleet off the entrance to the English Channel while landing an expeditionary force on the Isle of Wight.[7] This force could raid Portsmouth, or better still, help trap and destroy the English fleet at the roadstead of Spithead, lying between the Isle of Wight and Portsmouth. To accomplish this project the Bourbons would need precise intelligence about English forces and at least 45 ships of the line, including as many Spanish 80-gun ships as possible. It was only by controlling the seas that they would be able, as Vergennes said, to "attack Carthage in Carthage itself."[8]

Despite this brave rhetoric, Vergennes' proposals were for only a limited operation bearing little resemblance to the grandiose invasion proposals submitted to Louis XV and XVI by amateur strategists like the Count de Broglie.[9] It did, however, owe something to the common belief that the credit structure of the British government was shaky enough for the government to be toppled.[10] Vergennes believed, too, that the British government could be pressured into peace by the British business community. He told Montmorin in a personal letter that intercepting British

[7] Vergennes included detailed plans for this operation prepared by a former English navy captain named Hamilton who now was in the service of the French navy. Hamilton was not told the purpose of the plans. Spain 592: 236–244, Vergennes to Montmorin, 12 February 1779, enclosure.

[8] Spain 592: 247, Vergennes to Floridablanca, 12 February 1779.

[9] See Broglie's memoir of 17 December 1777. B⁴132: 10, 13–59/B⁴135: 4–68. Broglie had drafted his original plans by orders of Louis XV's unofficial secret diplomatic service.

[10] See Schelle, *Oeuvres de Turgot*, 5: 412–415, for Turgot's acceptance of this idea. Choiseul had also explored the idea. Fernand Calmettes, ed., *Mémoires du duc de Choiseul, 1719–1785* (Paris: Plon, Nourrit et cᶦᵉ, 1904), 393; Cornélius-Henri de Witt, *Thomas Jefferson and American Democracy*, trans. R.S.H. Church (London: Longman, Green, Longman, Roberts, and Green, 1862), 373–374. The French may not have completely forgotten their own experience with the "Mississippi bubble" crash of 1720. Heckscher, *Mercantilism*, 2: 231.

commerce would cause as much consternation and discouragement as an invasion.[11]

Spain responded officially at the end of February to Vergennes' altered proposals.[12] Although the new operational plan was generally acceptable to her, Spain refused to commit herself to a specific time for declaring war until the plans were advanced enough to be put into immediate operation. Spain offered to contribute 20 ships of the line to be combined with 30 French ships of the line; should the English have over 36 ships of the line, Spain would contribute enough extra ships for the maintenance of a superiority of four to three. Montmorin reported to Vergennes that Floridablanca believed 18,000 to 20,000 troops would suffice for the Isle of Wight expedition. He urged Vergennes to humor the Spaniards until they were involved in the war, after which they would become more tractable.

Now the time had come to prepare the detailed plans for the expedition. Floridablanca had demanded that the war be ended in one campaign before, as he put it, lassitude and distrust succeeded courage and cooperation.[13] Vergennes had long been opposed to conducting combined operations with the French and Spanish navies[14] and was not anxious to concentrate French forces in Europe—he complained

[11] Spain 592: 252–255, Vergennes to Montmorin, 12 February 1779. Vergennes later claimed that if France could dominate the English Channel, she could force England to choose between peace and a general bankruptcy. Spain 593: 101, Vergennes to Montmorin, 19 March 1779.

[12] Spain 592: 289–293, court of Spain to court of France, 26 February 1779; Spain 592: 308–319, 331–334, Montmorin to Vergennes, 28 February 1779. Vergennes was now given permission by Spain to discuss the operation with d'Orvilliers and the army general commanding the expeditionary force.

[13] Spain 592: 310, Montmorin to Vergennes, 28 February 1779.

[14] Spain 583: 210–213, Vergennes to Ossun, 14 February 1777. Floridablanca was no more enthusiastic about combined operations, but his desire for a quick victory overcame his objections. See Spain 583: 97, "Mémoire de l'Espagne servant de réponse à celui remis par M. le Cte de Vergennes à M. le Cte d'Aranda le 3 janvier 1777," 17 January 1777.

that if France were using only her own forces she would attempt to compensate for her inequality by celerity and that it would not be in Europe that she would establish the theater of operations.[15] He warned that any invasion would be subordinate to gaining sufficient command of the sea to force the English navy into port. Nevertheless, on 10 March the king, Vergennes, Sartine, Maurepas, and War Minister Montbarey met to discuss the operation.[16] Within ten days the detailed plans were ready.[17]

The plans, largely the work of Sartine and Montbarey, provided for 20,000 troops (all infantry except for a few squadrons of light cavalry) to occupy the Isle of Wight and subsequently to land at Gosport from which the Portsmouth naval arsenal and hopefully the English fleet could be destroyed by mortar fire. Diversionary troops would be concentrated in Normandy and Brittany (as in 1778) and at Dunkirk to divert British attention and perhaps to provide troops for small raids. Vergennes insisted the operation would be a *coup de main* rather than a campaign. The ports of debarkation had not yet been chosen, but there was sufficient shipping available; Vergennes hoped the transports and supply ships would be collected by the end of May. Vergennes was more than willing to provide 30 of the 50 ships of the line for the battle fleet, since this would avoid any argument about its having a French commander. He hoped to have these ships ready by the beginning of May. Corunna, as suggested by Spain, would be an acceptable rendezvous for the Allied fleet.[18]

[15] Spain 593: 35–36, Vergennes to Montmorin, 8 March 1779.
[16] Witte, *Journal de l'Abbé de Véri*, 2: 203, entry of 11 March 1779.
[17] Spain 593: 92–94, 95–98, 99, 100–103, 104, 108–109, Vergennes to Montmorin, with various enclosures, 19 March 1779. Vergennes tactfully left to Charles the details of the financial compensation to France for providing all the troops. Further details of the plans are given by A. Temple Patterson, *The Other Armada* (Manchester: Manchester University Press, 1960), 47–50.
[18] The *Destin* and *Caton*, en route from Toulon to Brest, were presently at Corunna; the *Bourgogne* and *Victoire* were subsequently ordered to follow them.

Vergennes also expressed surprise that Floridablanca had been raising difficulties with Montmorin about the proposed convention concerning war aims, since this proposal was more Floridablanca's work than Vergennes'.[19] Nastily, Vergennes mentioned Floridablanca's legal background, which could account for his *esprit fiscal*. Vergennes also informed Montmorin of the opening of the Conference of Teschen (11 March 1779) to conclude peace between Austria and Prussia and settle the Bavarian question.[20]

Floridablanca was satisfied with these plans, but now he threatened yet another delay. Although England had rejected all previous mediation attempts, Floridablanca now proposed a truce—this time, astoundingly, a truce without the evacuation of British-occupied territory in North America.[21] Vergennes believed this proposal a subterfuge rather than a serious offer,[22] but it presented a serious danger to future American cooperation.[23] Vergennes did predict, with full justification, that the British would not be acute enough to seize this opportunity.[24] Floridablanca presented an intricate blueprint of how this final mediation attempt would provide a cover and justification for war. After presenting the new proposal, Ambassador Almodóvar would wait a week and then deliver an ultimatum for England to respond within 48 to 72 hours. Should England refuse, a courier would leave (on or about 25 April) for France and

---

[19] Spain 593: 105–106, Vergennes to Montmorin, 19 March 1779. See above, Note 5.

[20] Spain 593: 107, Vergennes to Montmorin, 19 March 1779.

[21] Spain 593: 142–144, 150–154, Montmorin to Vergennes, 29 March 1779; Spain 593: 147, Floridablanca to Vergennes, 29 March 1779; Spain 593: 195–198, Floridablanca to Aranda, 3 April 1779; Bemis, *Diplomacy of the American Revolution*, 81–82; Danvila, *Reinado de Carlos III*, 5: 48–49, citing Floridablanca to Almodóvar, 3 April 1779.

[22] Spain 593: 226–227, Vergennes to Montmorin, 9 April 1779.

[23] For discussion of this point see the following: Spain 593: 247–249, 343–344, Vergennes to Montmorin, 12 April and 29 April 1779; United States 8: 31–35, Vergennes to Gérard, 22 April 1779; Spain 593: 320–325, Montmorin to Vergennes, no date, but probably about 26 April 1779.

[24] Spain 593: 247–249, Vergennes to Montmorin, 12 April 1779.

Spain. As soon as the two courts received this news, the Brest and Cadiz fleets would sail to Corunna, which they should reach by 20–25 May at the latest. Floridablanca expected the Brest fleet to be ready to sail on 10–15 May.[25]

Montmorin predicted that the Spaniards would not sign the convention on war aims until Almodóvar's courier reached Spain, probably about 6 May.[26] With operational plans agreed upon and Montmorin amenable to their wishes concerning the convention, the Spaniards decided not to delay the signing. On 12 April 1779 the convention on war aims was signed at Charles' summer residence of Aranjuez.[27] Montmorin had reservations about signing since the convention contained no firm declaration as to when war would be declared, but Charles wished to defer this decision until the safe rendezvous of the Allied fleets. Montmorin, fearing further delays, made use of the full powers already sent him and signed on behalf of France.

The Convention of Aranjuez formally activated the articles of the Family Compact relating to mutual assistance in case of war and indicated Spain's intention to go to war provided that England rejected Spain's final attempt at mediation. It contained an article relating to mutual assistance for an invasion of Britain in accordance with the operational plans in preparation. Spain promised not to make a separate peace, recognizing France's obligation to the American colonies not to make peace unless American independence were secured.[28]

[25] Vergennes on 23 April sent his approval of these arrangements. Spain 593: 313, Vergennes to Montmorin, 23 April 1779.

[26] Spain 593: 155–161, Montmorin to Vergennes, 30 March 1779.

[27] Doniol, *La participation de la France*, 3: 803–810, "Convention entre la France et l'Espagne du 12 avril 1779"; Samuel Flagg Bemis, ed., *The American Secretaries of State and their Diplomacy* (New York: Alfred A. Knopf, 1927) 1: 294–299 (for English translation); Spain 593: 250–252, 253–258, Montmorin to Vergennes, 13 April 1779.

[28] Floridablanca objected to the inclusion of American independence as a war aim of either Bourbon, ostensibly because such a declaration was a redundancy. Montmorin forced through this com-

The critical section of the convention related to the war aims of the Bourbons. Spain and France promised not to end the war until the former had obtained the restitution of Gibraltar and the latter the abrogation of the restrictions placed in 1763 upon fortifying Dunkirk. Floridablanca tried unsuccessfully to insert the capture of Minorca and the Atlantic coast of Florida into the category of absolute preconditions for peace. Each power then announced its other war goals. France announced her intention to acquire the expulsion of the British from Newfoundland, freedom of commerce and the right to fortify her trading posts in India, the recovery of Senegal, the retention of Dominica, and the rectification of the Treaty of Utrecht (1713), governing commercial relations with Britain. Spain announced her intention to obtain the reacquisition of East and West Florida, the expulsion of the English from their illegal settlements on the Bay of Honduras, the revocation of English timber rights on the coast of Campeche, and the restitution of Minorca.

Floridablanca immediately sent orders to the various parts of the Spanish Empire for local commanders to commence hostilities two months after receipt of those orders, unless they later received contrary instructions.[29] Louis' decision of December 1778 to pay any price for Spanish participation had finally borne fruit.

2. The Invasion of England: Plans

The news of the Spanish alliance was most opportune for the French navy. On 10 April Sartine presented his request for funds for 1779.[1] He asked for 127,866,000 livres to meet

---

promise. Spain 592: 320–323, Montmorin to Vergennes, 28 February 1779.

[29] Spain 593: 260, Montmorin to Vergennes, 13 April 1779.

[1] B⁵12: unpaged, "Mémoire au roi," 10 April 1779. A similar memoir, probably a rough draft, dated 1 April 1779, is given in E 204: unpaged.

projected expenses for the year and another 20,000,000 livres to reduce the naval debt. Already at least 35,500,000 livres of notes had been issued to meet non-budgeted expenses, almost all by the present and former treasurers-general of the navy. (Intended by Colbert to be purely administrative officials, these office-purchasers had become the financiers of the navy, using both their own funds and those they could raise from other magnates.) To check this dangerous practice, Necker at the end of 1778 forbade the issuing of more notes without his authorization.[2] Obviously financial limitations would restrict the expansion of the French navy.

The navy was pressed by other limitations in addition to funds. The most crucial was the shortage of sailors. During 1779, 76,912 sailors were used by the navy and requirements continued to grow.[3] Sartine was forced to hire a large number of foreign sailors,[4] to reduce standard crew sizes and their proportion of trained seamen, to employ untrained volunteers and even soldiers, and to add 1,500 men from parishes in maritime areas to the conscription lists.[5]

[2] Neuville, *Etat sommaire*, 619; Brun, *Port de Toulon*, 2: 40; Henri Legohérel, *Les trésoriers généraux de la marine (1517-1788)* (Paris: Cujas, 1963), 249, 264-265, 304-305, 337-339. Debt figures are from Neuville, *Etat sommaire*, 519 and Legohérel, *Les trésoriers généraux*, 249. B¹91: 87-91, untitled memoir of 10 April 1779, states that of 39,934,414 livres of debts, up to 35,000,000 livres was in notes issued by the treasurer's general. Many bills from 1778 had not yet been presented.

[3] E 208: unpaged, "Relevé des équipages et garnisons des vaisseaux et autres bâtiments du roi armes dans les 4 années ci-dessous," no date. This number would grow to 82,534 in 1780, 90,054 in 1781, and 90,420 in 1782. The English navy had 89,243 in November 1779, and 99,831 in September 1781. *Sandwich Papers*, 3: 316, 4: 290.

[4] B²415: 11, Sartine to La Prévalye, commissioner-general at Brest, 2 January 1779; Brun, *Port de Toulon*, 2: 13; J. Captier, *Etude historique et économique sur l'inscription maritime* (Paris: Bussière, Giard, et Brière, 1908), 191-192. Choiseul had been forced to do the same thing. Maurice Loir, *La Marine royale en 1789* (Paris: Armand Colin et cⁱᵉ, 1892), 40-41.

[5] Brun, *Port de Toulon*, 2: 20-23; Captier, *L'inscription maritime*, 192; B³662: 138, La Prévalye to Sartine, 26 March 1779; B²415: 128-

Even the old prejudice against auxiliary officers (nonnoble-men restricted to certain ranks) had to be forgotten. D'Estaing was hated by his subordinates because in addition to his being a former soldier, he had insisted that each of his ships carry three auxiliary officers.[6] Now there were insufficient numbers even of auxiliary officers,[7] and only the need for experienced officers in the dockyards kept officers from being reassigned from port duty.

The need for dockyard workers was almost as acute—workers from Malta, for example, were hired to work at Toulon.[8] There were also some persistent matériel short-ages, particularly of wood pieces of certain proportions.[9] These various limitations were of differing importance according to the time and place. Toulon, always well provided with Italian and Albanian wood, had trouble finding workers. Some of the smaller ports found it extremely difficult to obtain crews for their newly constructed ships.[10] The Atlantic ports, although not impoverished in matériel, were hindered by the refusal of the Dutch to convoy Scandinavian and German wood and masts through the North Sea.

None of the difficulties facing the French navy were crippling, at least in the short run, but cumulatively the limits of money, sailors, dockyard workers, and matériel precluded the expansion of the French navy to a point where

---

129, Sartine to La Porte and d'Orvilliers, 30 January 1779; B²415: 11, Sartine to La Prévalye, 2 January 1779. The French conscription or class system, so admired by the British, broke down almost completely in wartime.

[6] Brun, *Port de Toulon*, 2: 10–11, 25.

[7] *Ibid.*, 2: 14.

[8] *Ibid.*, 2: 17. See also B³670: 27, St. Aignan to Sartine, 15 January 1779; B³665: 60, commissioner Thevenard at Lorient to Sartine, 24 May 1779 (for similar complaints).

[9] For example see B³662: 216–217, 307–309, La Prévalye to Sartine, 26 April and 9 June 1779. The only complete wood statistics for 1779 that I've found are those for Rochefort in March: 597,715 ft.³ (or, counting small pieces, 665,954 ft.³). B³667: 68, La Touche to Sartine, 16 March 1779.

[10] For example see the enormous difficulties in finding a crew for the new frigate *Fine* at Nantes. B³666: 295–322.

it could match the British navy, which could draw on more shipyards, more merchant seamen, more accessible matériel and wider credit resources. The French navy had to be reinforced and the Spaniards were the world's only other major naval power.

The first months of 1779 were a time of frustration and embarrassment for the French navy. A dockyard fire destroyed the ship of the line *Roland* and the frigate *Zéphyr*. Three new ships of the line were so top-heavy that they nearly capsized in a calm sea.[11] A raid on the English Channel Islands failed and the raiding force was trapped in Cancale and destroyed by an English squadron.[12] The overhaul of the *Ville-de-Paris* (converted in the process to a 100-gun ship) was delayed and she did not return to the water until 30 April.[13] La Motte-Picquet, with troop reinforcements and 60 merchantmen for the West Indies, was held in Brest by unfavorable winds for almost a month.[14] Worst of all, when d'Orvilliers arrived at Versailles for conferences on 22 April he had to report that his fleet was not ready.[15] Nine ships of the line had not yet reached Brest (three from Rochefort, four from Toulon,[16] and two returning from escorting an outbound Indian convoy). Final work still had to be done on the *Ville-de-Paris* whose 100 guns

[11] See letters of La Touche to Sartine, 4 March–20 May 1779, B³667: 121–126, 155–158, 162–163, 189, 204, 227–228, 259. The *Scipion* and *Hercule* needed to have their masts shortened; extra ballast sufficed for the *Pluton*.

[12] The frigate *Danaé* and two smaller ships were lost there under embarrassing circumstances. Clowes, *Royal Navy*, 4: 25.

[13] B³662: 224–225, La Prévalye to Sartine, 30 April 1779. The British were in the process of converting their 90s to 98s. *Sandwich Papers*, 3: 41n; Spain 593: 335, Vergennes to Montmorin, 29 April 1779.

[14] See below, Section 4.

[15] Spain 593: 335–340, 341–342, Vergennes to Montmorin, 29 April 1779; B⁵12: unpaged, "Vaisseaux"; B³662: 212–213, La Prévalye to Sartine, 23 April 1779.

[16] The Mediterranean fleet had seen virtually no action in 1778. The *Caton* took a new ambassador to Constantinople; the other four ships of the line cruised in the central Mediterranean from 26 July to 28 October 1778. Brun, *Port de Toulon*, 2: 14–16.

were vital to the line of battle, and there were shortages of crews and provisions.

Vergennes now had no choice but to notify the Spaniards that the Brest fleet would be unable to make the 20–25 May rendezvous at Corunna; indeed the fleet would not be ready to leave Brest before the first week of June.[17] This would expose the French fleet to the danger of blockade, but at least the Spaniards could proceed without fear of attack, since the English would not risk leaving a French fleet between their fleet and its ports. Vergennes requested that the Cadiz fleet proceed without awaiting word that the Brest fleet had sailed, since to convey this information from Brest to Cadiz would take an irreplaceable 16 or 17 days. He suggested that the Spanish squadron at Ferrol sail on 20 May and the Cadiz fleet 5 to 10 days later, and that they rendezvous off Cape Finisterre rather than in the cramped harbor of Corunna where they might be blockaded. The French fleet would sail during the first week of June and should reach the rendezvous between 15 and 20 June. Once this had occurred Vergennes believed the two fleets should be intermixed and divided into ten divisions of five ships each (including a light division of the smallest ships). As to the coming operation, he was not frightened by the English, but he was worried about the possibility of adverse winds.[18]

Vergennes' chagrin at the delay[19] was unnecessary. The Spanish plans were posited on a precision of timing impossible to obtain. The British delayed Almodóvar into sending his first courier without a response. His second courier, carrying Weymouth's categorical denial to the final Spanish offer, left Britain only on 4 May, left a copy of Almodóvar's message at Versailles on 7 May, and arrived at the Spanish

[17] Spain 593: 335–340, 341–342, Vergennes to Montmorin, 29 April 1779. Vergennes mentioned only the situation of the *Ville-de-Paris* to explain the delay.

[18] Vergennes also sent the ratification of the Treaty of Aranjuez.

[19] Spain 593: 353–356, personal letter of Vergennes to Montmorin, 29 April 1779.

court on 15 May, already nine days late.[20] Floridablanca informed Vergennes on 17 May that the Ferrol squadron would sail immediately and that the Cadiz fleet would sail as soon as its officers were familiar with the French signal flags and reconnaissance signals which Vergennes had sent (on 19 March). According to Floridablanca this should be by the first week of June.[21] Floridablanca agreed to change the rendezvous point (although to a slightly different position than Vergennes had suggested), to the intermingling of the two fleets, and to a period of combined maneuvers before the combined fleet left for England.[22] He warned, though, that because of the danger of bad weather, Charles had ordered the Spanish fleet to cease operations at the beginning of September.

Now the great operation waited for the winds to bring the component parts of the fleet to the rendezvous. In order to facilitate the collection of transports, it was decided to divide the 20,000-man expeditionary force into two bodies, one at Saint Malo and the other at Le Havre.[23] These forces would necessitate between 27,400 and 29,965 tons of ship-

[20] Spain 594: 27–28, Weymouth to Grantham, English ambassador to Spain, 4 May 1779; Spain 594: 42–43, Vergennes to Montmorin, 8 May 1779; Spain 594: 77–79, Montmorin to Vergennes, 17 May 1779; Danvila, *Reinado de Carlos III*, 5: 52.

[21] Spain 594: 80–81, Floridablanca to Vergennes, 17 May 1779.

[22] Spain 594: 53–58, Floridablanca to Vergennes, 14 May 1779, sent by Montmorin to Vergennes, 17 May 1779. See also Spain 593: 336–340, Vergennes to Floridablanca, 29 April 1779.

[23] There were insufficient escorts to protect the transfer of all the ships to one port. Saint Malo and Le Havre cleared with the same wind (from the east) so the two parts could sail simultaneously. The force at Saint Malo was to consist of 20 battalions of infantry, one of Lauzun's legions, and 46 pieces of artillery. That of Le Havre was to contain 14 battalions of infantry, four battalions of artillery, 400 heavy cavalry (dragoons), and 50 pieces of artillery. Reserves were to consist of 10 battalions of infantry, 16 squadrons of heavy cavalry and a light cavalry regiment (hussars), none of which were to be sent to England. Additionally it was hoped the English would be distracted by 34 infantry battalions in Brittany and 12 infantry battalions and 20 squadrons of cavalry at Dunkirk. Spain 594: 245–246, memoir of Montbarey, sent to Montmorin, 21 June 1779.

ping (115–150 ships) well within the 37,652 tons of shipping available.[24] When the English battle fleet had been crushed or had been driven into port, the two divisions would sail for the Isle of Wight under the escort of the light squadron.

Final preparations for the campaign were made by each of the powers. On 7 and 8 May France ordered all correspondence with England intercepted and the French coast closed to all traffic with England except for diplomats still using the Calais packetboat.[25] By 25 May d'Orvilliers' entire fleet was in the roadstead of Brest, except for two ships still on the way from Toulon, and four days later he was sent sailing orders. He sailed on 3 June.[26] At Cadiz the Spanish fleet of 32 ships of the line was hampered by heavy winds which delayed the placing of gunpowder aboard ship and by difficulties in preparing duplicate signal flags. By 4 June it too was in the road, awaiting a favorable wind to sail.[27] The Ferrol squadron of 8 ships of the line had already been transferred to Corunna from which it could more easily reach the rendezvous point.[28]

It was planned that 12 of the Cadiz fleet and the 8 from Ferrol would serve with the combined fleet. The remaining 20 ships of the line from Cadiz would form a reserve from which 6 would be left at the Azores to intercept English shipping.[29] It was hoped that the combined fleet would be

[24] B⁴159: 296–297, untitled memoir of 24 May 1779; B⁴159: 275–278, untitled memoir, no date; B⁴159: 265, untitled memoir of 16 April 1779; B⁴159: 273, untitled memoir, no date.

[25] England 531: 446, circular letter of 6 May 1779; Spain 594: 39–40, 42–43, Vergennes to Montmorin, 7 May and 8 May 1779. The English halted all packetboat service in July. Spain 594: 394, Vergennes to Montmorin, 9 July 1779.

[26] For sailing orders see Spain 594: 152–170, Louis to d'Orvilliers, 29 May 1779.

[27] Spain 594: 187–188, 209, Montmorin to Vergennes, 31 May and 3 June 1779; Spain 594: 212, Cadiz report, 4 June 1779. Among the other problems the Spaniards did not have the proper dye to duplicate the shade of green used for French signal flags.

[28] Spain 594: 237, Montmorin to Vergennes, 11 June 1779.

[29] Spain 594: 152–170, Louis to d'Orvilliers, 29 May 1779; Spain 594: 237, Montmorin to Vergennes, 11 June 1779.

able to intercept a huge British convoy for America, but it was almost clear of English waters by the time d'Orvilliers left Brest.[30]

The British missed their chance to blockade or intercept d'Orvilliers. Ten ships of the line were absent from 4–10 June to escort the American convoy clear and the remainder of the fleet was hampered by crew shortages. Only on 16 June did their fleet of 31 ships of the line sail. It was under the orders of a new commander, the aged and ineffectual Admiral Sir Charles Hardy.[31]

On 16 June Almodóvar presented a declaration of Spanish grievances which was a virtual declaration of war. Two days later he left England. Orders were already on the way to Admiral Hardy to treat as an enemy any Spanish ships he met.[32]

3. The Invasion of England: Execution

Hardly had d'Orvilliers sailed when the carefully-prepared plans for a limited operation were severely altered. On 11 June Ambassador Aranda presented the French with his own memoir calling for the expeditionary force to be increased from 20,000 effectives to more than 30,000. At a conference the next day Vergennes, Montbarey, Sartine, Marshal de Vaux (the expeditionary commander), and Louis decided to commit the reserve forces and some

[30] See also below, Section 4. Spain 594: 152–170, Louis to d'Orvilliers, 29 May 1779; B⁴155: 43–44, Montmorin to d'Orvilliers, 18 June 1779; Spain 594; 361, Vergennes to Montmorin, 2 July 1779.

[31] *Sandwich Papers*, 3: 4, 36–37, 122; Mackesy, *War for America*, 281; Patterson, *The Other Armada*, 105.

[32] Almodóvar withdrew the Spanish offer of mediation on 27 May, but he had to wait to deliver his declaration until Spanish shipping had a chance to leave England. On 15 June Admiral Hardy was ordered to treat Spain as an enemy. Spain 594: 132–135, Floridablanca to Almodóvar, 28 May 1779; Spain 594: 138–139, Almodóvar to Floridablanca, 28 May 1779; Spain 594: 140–143, Montmorin to Vergennes, 28 May 1779; United States 8: 355, Vergennes to the Chevalier La Luzerne (see below), 26 June 1779; *Sandwich Papers*, 3: 4–5.

additional light cavalry companies from Brittany to the expeditionary force. This would permit the French to occupy Portsmouth rather than merely bombard it. Portsmouth could be kept as a war prize or exchanged for Gibraltar.[1]

This was virtually the only occasion during the war in which the council permitted enthusiasm, overconfidence, and inflated ambition to overcome realism, prudence, and common sense. (It was also one of the few times the council ignored the advice of Sartine and Fleurieu.) For a number of reasons the expansion of the Isle of Wight expedition to include the capture of Portsmouth was a serious strategic mistake:

First, if successful, it would have destroyed Vergennes' diplomatic strategy of portraying the war as a defensive effort to end British preponderance rather than as merely an attempt to improve France's own diplomatic position. Had the expeditionary force established itself on the English mainland, the temptation would have been enormous to adopt the Count de Broglie's plan of marching on London—particularly since the expeditionary force contained as many regular troops as there were in all of England and Wales.[2] Even had this temptation been resisted, an actual landing in England would have had severe diplomatic repercussions. Denmark, Sweden and Russia had announced their decisions to arm fleets to protect their shipping;[3] these gestures were as yet of minor significance and were not spe-

[1] Spain 594: 247–252, memoir of Montbarey, sent to Montmorin, 21 June 1779.

[2] Mackesy, *War for America*, 524–525, lists 23,027 regulars and 33,573 militia in England and Wales in July; Patterson, *The Other Armada*, 108, estimates there were 20,000 regulars. French intelligence estimated 30,500 regulars and a similar number of militia. England 531: 206–213, report of 1 June 1779.

[3] Spain 592: 264–265, Montmorin to Vergennes, 18 February 1779; Spain 592: 288, Vergennes to Montmorin, 26 February 1779; Spain 593: 86, 274, Montmorin to Vergennes, 18 March and 13 April 1779. At this point Denmark planned to arm ten ships of the line, Sweden six, and Russia three or four. The Russians were not yet ready to coordinate operations.

cifically directed against France, but too marked a French success might well have altered their character. More important, such a threat to England's position in the balance of power would have courted counteraction by the Austrians, who had just suffered the humiliation of having to abandon their hopes for Bavaria (by the Treaty of Teschen, signed 13 May)—a humiliation to which France had been a contributor.[4]

Second, the expansion of forces placed a severe strain on French shipping and raised enormously the cost of the operation. Sartine and Fleurieu immediately protested the change of plans. Not only would almost 40,000 personnel (including officers' servants and non-combatants) have to be embarked instead of 23,000, but, even worse, the flotilla would have to carry almost 8,000 cavalry mounts instead of 300 and almost double the previous weight of artillery.[5] There were insufficient ships in the Channel ports for such an expanded flotilla and insufficient crews even had the ships been available. Faced with the fact that the revised plan would require an additional 20,000 tons of shipping, the council substituted as reinforcements four battalions of infantry (about 2,000 men) in place of 2,000 dragoons. The new plan called for 50 battalions of infantry, five battalions of shock troops (grenadiers), 3,400 cavalry and 1,200 artillerymen. Including noncombatants, 37,376 men were to be embarked. The cost of supplies, hiring ships and hospital services was expected to be about 9,700,000 livres in place of the 3,500,000 livres of the initial plan.[6]

Third, the expansion of the plan markedly increased its already severe operational difficulties. The expanded shipping completely swamped the facilities of Le Havre and

[4] See comments of Perugia, *La tentative d'invasion*, 153.

[5] B⁴159: 304, "Etat comparatif," ca. 13 June 1779.

[6] The total number of troop effectives was 30,988. Spain 594: 293–294, Vergennes to Montmorin, 21 June 1779; B⁴159: 30, 33, 275–278, untitled memoirs, no dates; B⁴159: 305, untitled memoir of 26 June 1779; Patterson, *The Other Armada*, 151.

Saint Malo,[7] exposing the flotilla to English raids, making an orderly sailing almost impossible, and increasing the difficulties of the dangerous passage to England. The flotilla now needed not only a favorable wind, but a favorable combination of wind and tides to exit its ports. Marshal de Vaux estimated this would take a week even with the proper conditions.[8]

As a consequence of the change of plans, Vergennes requested the Spaniards to station the reserve of 16 ships of the line (excluding 4 to be sent to the Azores) at the entrance to the English Channel and Saint George's Channel.[9] The Allies had consistently formed their plans on the basis of 35 opposing ships of the line, but the English might well receive enough time to increase their fleet.[10] Vergennes also requested that the peremptory orders to the Spanish fleet to cease operations at the beginning of September be revoked, since a long seige of Portsmouth might be necessary. Floridablanca granted both requests at the beginning of July; the 16 reserve ships were used to form a squadron

[7] As an example of this overcrowding only one wood ship from the transshipment point of Rouen could unload at Le Havre between May and November, so 135,000 ft.³ of wood accumulated at Rouen. B³661: 48, report of 5 February 1779; B³661: 383, commissioner Langerie to Sartine, 6 October 1779; B³691: 377–398, undated report.

[8] Spain 594: 465, Vergennes to Montmorin, 26 July 1779; B³673: 125, de Vaux to Montbarey, 30 September 1779. Of the 116 ships at Le Havre, 76 had to be placed in the city's commercial port. B³661: 293, commissioner Mistral to Sartine, 28 September 1779. Part of the flotilla was moved across the Seine to Honfleur. Patterson, *The Other Armada*, 151.

[9] Spain 594: 293–294, Vergennes to Montmorin, 21 June 1779. The Spaniards had previously planned to use the reserve to help in the blockade of Gibraltar. Spain 594: 335, Montmorin to Vergennes, 26 June 1779.

[10] Almodóvar predicted that the English would raise their fleet from 36 ships of the line to 48 of the line in June. Spain 594: 139, Almodóvar to Floridablanca, 28 May 1779. The estimate of 35 of the line is repeatedly given in Spain 593 and Spain 594 through the end of May.

of observation and to provide replacement ships for d'Orvilliers' main fleet of 50 of the line.[11]

Vergennes soon had reason to wonder whether the siege of Portsmouth would commence before September, if at all. Unfavorable winds prevented the Cadiz fleet from sailing until 22 June and from reaching the rendezvous with the other parts of the combined fleet until 22–23 July.[12] The Brest fleet arrived with a full epidemic of a debilitating (although seldom fatal) disease, which seriously hampered effectiveness.[13] The English fleet, moreover, had been reinforced to a strength of 36 ships of the line.[14] Vergennes admitted privately to Montmorin that if he were the English minister in charge he would have Admiral Hardy attack d'Orvilliers.[15]

By the end of July Vergennes was completely disillusioned with the European-centered strategy his new ally

[11] Spain 594: 293–294, Vergennes to Montmorin, 21 June 1779; Spain 594: 375–378, Montmorin to Vergennes, 5 July 1779. See also Spain 594: 330, 355, Montmorin to Vergennes, 26 June and 1 July 1779.

[12] England 531: 311–312, 368–369, Bessière, Spanish translator for d'Orvilliers, to Vergennes, 4 July and 28 July 1779; Spain 594: 477–479, Montmorin to Vergennes, 29 July 1779. Vergennes did not receive news of the rendezvous until 11 August.

[13] Descriptions of the disease are not sufficient for a diagnosis. From the relatively low mortality rate, I doubt that it was smallpox, typhus, or typhoid fever, which historians have suggested. A more serious epidemic in Brittany killed 20,000 people. Spain 597: 208, Vergennes to Montmorin, 29 January 1779. By the beginning of August the French fleet had 80 dead and 1,500 ill. One of the first dead was d'Orvilliers' son, also a naval officer. England 531: 368–370; England 532: 9–10, Bessière to Vergennes, 28 July and 3 August 1779. A sad irony is that during his tenure as naval minister the conscientious Sartine had taken a great pride in the health of his ships' crews. Witte, *Journal de l'Abbé de Véri*, 2: 139–140, entry of 6 August 1778.

[14] *Sandwich Papers*, 3: 50–51. For French intelligence reports see Spain 594: 372–373, 400, Vergennes to Montmorin, 5 July and 12 July 1779; B⁷441: nos. 219 and 221, reports of 16 July and 23 July 1779; England 531: 332–333, Aranda to Vergennes, 31 July 1779.

[15] Spain 594: 344–345, Vergennes to Montmorin, 28 June 1779. George felt the same way. *Sandwich Papers*, 3: 50–51, George to Sandwich, 28 June 1779. See also Fortescue, *Correspondence of King George the Third*, 4: 398–399, 400–401, 410–411.

had forced upon him. He began feeling out the prospects of shifting the focus of the war back to the Western Hemisphere. Gérard, because of illness, had to be replaced at Philadelphia. Vergennes requested the Chevalier La Luzerne, his new minister plenipotentiary, to inform him of the views and projects of the Continental Congress.[16] He also asked the Marquis de Lafayette, temporarily in France, for his ideas on an expeditionary force for America.[17] Finally Vergennes suggested to Montmorin that the Allies shift the emphasis of their attack from Europe to America.[18] There was no safe French port in the Channel, the British already had 45 ships of the line [sic] and they would have to be decisively beaten before France could risk sending 40,000 troops to sea in defenseless transports. If the operations did not begin before the end of August, the most that could be hoped for would be the capture of the Isle of Wight; during the coming year it would be impossible to accomplish anything more than had been accomplished during the current campaign. Vergennes wished to use at least 40 ships of the line in the Western Hemisphere while concentrating in Europe on capturing convoys, which could be as decisive a blow as capturing London itself. He asked the opinion of the court of Spain on these questions.

Vergennes' letters reached Spain at the same time as the news that the combined fleet had finally been assembled. Floridablanca violently objected to moving the focus of the war. "It is in England itself that it is necessary to attack the English—that is his great principle," reported Montmorin.[19] If the war were shifted away from Europe, Montmorin explained, England would be left free to detach forces

---

[16] United States 9: 148, Vergennes to La Luzerne, 18 July 1779.

[17] Lafayette suggested that 4,300 troops be used. United States 9: 154–161, Lafayette to Vergennes, 18 July 1779.

[18] Spain 594: 456–459, 461–464, Vergennes to Montmorin, 23 July 1779.

[19] Spain 594: 489–493, 500–507, Montmorin to Vergennes, 31 July 1779; Spain 595: 22–31, Floridablanca to the French court, 5 August 1779. Quotation is from Spain 594: 505.

abroad, where she could attack the overextended Spanish Empire. Floridablanca believed there was still time to attack Hardy. If not, he favored keeping 20 Spanish ships of the line at Brest over the winter so as to renew the attack the following year. At most he would agree to diversionary attacks on Jamaica and Minorca.

It was Aranda, however, who prevented the immediate abandonment of the operation. As early as 21 June he had mentioned the possibility of a landing in Cornwall.[20] At the beginning of August he suggested the landing be switched from the Isle of Wight to the area of Falmouth.[21] Vergennes reported the idea to Montmorin on 6 August[22] and on the following day new orders were sent to d'Orvilliers.[23] Aranda's plan did present the advantages that Falmouth would require no long siege to capture and that it was within striking distance of the major port of Plymouth. Most important, once ashore the expeditionary force would be relatively self-sufficient. Cornwall was a natural fortress once a defense line could be established around Bodmin or along the Tamar River, even though Cornwall was not nearly so fertile as Aranda suggested.[24] I am inclined to believe that Aranda's plan represented the only feasible opportunity left to the Allies.

This plan did not remove the necessity of first finding and defeating Hardy's fleet. After a week of maneuvers, the

[20] Spain 594: 287–290, memoir of Aranda, 21 June 1779.

[21] Spain 595: 13–21, Aranda to Vergennes, 4 August 1779. Aranda apparently broached the matter on 1 August 1779.

[22] Spain 595: 51–54, Vergennes to Montmorin, 6 August 1779.

[23] Spain 595: 100–102, Vergennes to Montmorin, 12 August 1779. Spanish approval is given by Spain 595: 175–179, Montmorin to Vergennes, 21 August 1779.

[24] It was planned that d'Orvilliers would cruise between Cape Ouessant and the Isles of Scilly, while Lieutenant-General Córdoba, commanding the Spanish contingent, would cruise between the Isles of Scilly and Cape Clear, Ireland. Spain 595: 259–261, Vergennes to Montmorin, 5 September 1779. For a critique of the plan see Perugia, *La tentative d'invasion*, 149–150.

combined fleet sailed north at the beginning of August.[25]
Again the winds were contrary and it was mid-August before the great fleet reached the area of Plymouth. There it
had its only piece of good fortune, capturing the *Ardent*, 64,
on her way to join Hardy off the Isles of Scilly. Hardy's
orders to stay to the west of the Channel left the south coast
of England vulnerable to surprise attack since an easterly
wind would simultaneously bring the Le Havre-Saint Malo
flotilla to England and blow Hardy *away* from England. On
the other hand, Hardy's position protected British trade,
shielded Ireland and made him difficult to find—the combined fleet had passed Hardy as it went toward the Channel. D'Orvilliers, when he received his new orders, turned
west to find Hardy. D'Orvilliers was beset by fog, foul
winds, lack of supplies (a supply convoy was prevented by
bad weather and fear of capture from reaching him) and
the spread of the mysterious disease which in the last three
weeks had caused 140 dead and 2,400 ill and had begun to
spread to the Spanish ships. One of d'Orvilliers' ships was
even hit by lightning and had to return to Brest to replace
a mast. On 31 August he finally spotted Hardy, now with 39
of the line, but Hardy sailed for Portsmouth and easily out-
distanced him. Recall orders were sent to d'Orvilliers' fleet
on 3 September, conditional on his not having caught
Hardy. D'Orvilliers received them on 8 September, and
during the course of the following week the combined fleet
limped into Brest, ending the campaign.[26]

The English of Queen Elizabeth's time gave primary

[25] For this period see England 532: 42-55, Captain Hamilton to
Vergennes, 16 August 1779.

[26] Disease figures are for 24 July to 16 August 1779. The replenishment convoy was almost captured by Hardy on 29-30 August. The
supplies were needed, since the fleet carried supplies for only four
months rather than six (in order to leave the lower gun decks less
crowded). Spain 597: 207, Vergennes to Montmorin, 29 January 1780.
For a bibliography of d'Orvilliers' campaign see Dull: Dissertation,
278n.

credit for their deliverance in 1588 to God, who sent the winds which scattered the Spanish Armada. He deserves equal credit for sending the winds which retained the Armada of 1779. There is, however, a way of looking at the campaign more in keeping with the traditional view of a Deity well-disposed toward the United States. Although Hardy's fleet had fewer ships, it was, ship for ship, heavier, faster, commanded by more experienced officers, and manned by healthier crews. Had the bizarre weather ever permitted a battle, the result might well have crippled America's allies and doomed the colonies to eventual defeat. The astute Russians, at any rate, conducted a policy examination during the campaign and concluded that there was little danger of an invasion; that Britain would soon recover its maritime ascendancy; and that the British were not in such danger as to affect adversely the balance of power.[27] Only through the prudence and ability of the French council could the Allies prevent Britain's recovery of the maritime ascendancy, as the Russians had predicted.[28]

[27] Madariaga, *Britain, Russia, and the Armed Neutrality*, 108–109.
[28] A postscript should be added to this account of the summer's operations. The lack of frigates had prevented the French from as yet establishing cruises in the North Sea to intercept British trade with the Baltic. During the summer of 1779 the council arranged with the American commissioners for a joint squadron to cruise in the North Sea for six weeks, after which it would sail to the Texel, the Dutch naval base at the entrance to the Zuider Zee, to meet a timber convoy for French ports. The king provided most of the ships, the Americans most of the crews, with profits to be equally divided. This squadron was composed of two French and one American frigate, a French navy cutter, a corvette, and two privateers and was commanded by an American captain, John Paul Jones. In September the frigates and cutter managed to intercept off England a large Baltic timber convoy escorted by the *Serapis*, 44, and a corvette. Jones' squadron was poorly coordinated and the convoy escaped, although both its escorts were captured. Jones' flagship, the *Bon Homme Richard*, 40, had to be abandoned; the remainder of his squadron proceeded to the Texel with its prizes. Except for the escape of the convoy, Jones' cruise had little strategic significance, but, like the cruises of Wickes and Conyngham, it would have important diplomatic repercussions (which will be discussed later). For a bibliography of Jones' cruise see Dull: Dissertation, 279n.

4. The Conclusion of d'Estaing's Cruise

On 22 February 1779 the council received the shocking news of the English landing on Saint Lucia and a desperate appeal from the commandant at Martinique, Marshal de Bouillé.[1] Although Saint Lucia was not of great economic value, it was an excellent supporting base (because of its wood and water). Its loss endangered adjoining Martinique. Reports now indicated that the English had at least 23 ships of the line on station[2]—a sharp reminder of France's insufficiency to fight England without assistance.[3] Although 7 ships of the line were already en route to join d'Estaing's dozen,[4] they obviously would be insufficient.

The council responded to this crisis with speed and flexibility. Only the *Orient* of Ternay's squadron had sailed as yet for India.[5] The remainder of the squadron was delayed because a ship of the line and a transport were still retained by unfavorable winds at Lorient. A special courier sent from Versailles on 25 February to countermand Ternay's orders arrived at Brest just as the last troops for Ternay's squadron were about to be embarked.[6]

---

[1] Witte, *Journal de l'Abbé de Véri*, 2: 199–200, entry of 23 February 1779; Spain 592: 382, Vergennes to Montmorin, 24 February 1779; B⁴140: 234–237, Bouillé to Sartine, 31 December 1778. See also B⁴161: 176, 238, Bouillé to d'Estaing, 9 January and 1 March 1779.

[2] Spain 592: 283–285, Vergennes to Montmorin, 24 February 1779. With the arrival of Rowley, the British actually had 25 ships of the line on station (excluding their ships at Jamaica).

[3] Spain 592: 287–288, Vergennes to Montmorin, 26 February 1779.

[4] En route were Vaudreuil with his two ships of the line (which first captured a string of British bases along the Senegal and Gambia Rivers in Africa), the *Fier* with a convoy for Saint Domingue, and de Grasse with four ships of the line and a battalion of infantry. B⁴145 and B⁴149: *passim.*

[5] Additionally, however, the *Sévère* sailed for India from Brest (27 March 1779). She escorted two transports, which carried one of Lauzun's legions and 200 recruits. B⁴150: 184–193; B³662: 81, 85 ff.

[6] The courier arrived on 26 February. The last of the troops were scheduled to be embarked on 27 and 28 February, although the *Artésien* did not sail from Lorient for Brest with her transport until 4 March. The British weren't so fortunate. They tried unsuccessfully

It was then decided that this squadron would escort reinforcements and a gigantic supply convoy to the West Indies. Ternay asked to be relieved and was replaced by the impetuous but talented La Motte-Picquet.[7] When he arrived and the French islands were safe, d'Estaing should bring back his original 12 ships of the line to refit and to act as a reserve in case Byron returned to Europe.

La Motte-Picquet with his reinforcements (one battalion of infantry and one of Lauzun's legions) and 60 merchantmen were held in Brest by unfavorable winds from 7 April to 1 May.[8] Nevertheless, he reached Martinique on 27 June, in time to be of great use to d'Estaing. D'Estaing now had 24 ships of the line.[9] Byron was temporarily absent, covering the departure of a homeward bound convoy from Saint Christopher, which gave Bouillé the opportunity to surprise and capture the small island of Saint Vincent (17 June 1779).[10] With La Motte-Picquet's arrival, d'Estaing went after a far more important prize, the valuable island of Grenada, which fell to him on 4 July. When Byron returned he had only 21 ships of the line (since two 50s had been detached and a 50 and 64 were with the convoy). The resul-

---

to recall three of their six ships of the line on the way to India. Mackesy, *War for America*, 251, 261–262.

[7] Spain 593: 98, Vergennes to Montmorin, 19 March 1779; B⁴150: 335, Ternay to Sartine, 3 March 1779; B²415: 331, Sartine to d'Orvilliers, 19 March 1779.

[8] B³662: 158, 235, 236–237, La Prévalye to Sartine, 7 April, 1 May, and 2 May 1779; E 205: unpaged, "Etat des corps des troupes et des recrues qui ont été successivement embarqués pour le service des colonies de 1778 à 1783," no date (hereafter cited as "Troops for colonies").

[9] One of d'Estaing's ships of the line was in repair, but he was able to conscript the *Fier Roderique*, formerly the *Hippopotame* of the French navy and now owned by Beaumarchais.

[10] B⁴142: 70–71, d'Estaing to Sartine, 24 June 1779; B⁴163: 367, account in "La Gazette de Martinique," 24 June 1779; England 531: 254, extract of a letter from Saint Eustatius, 18 June 1779; *Sandwich Papers*, 3: 124. The British were forced to provide a close escort for the 250-ship convoy because wind and tides made a close blockade of Martinique impossible.

tant battle, fought on 6 July, was indecisive, although the British fleet was severely damaged and failed to recapture Grenada.[11]

La Motte-Picquet had brought orders for d'Estaing to return to Europe with his original squadron and d'Estaing had written that he would comply.[12] D'Estaing, however, bent his orders in order to honor the requests for assistance he had received from the American Continental Congress and the Governor of South Carolina.[13] The British at the time they captured Saint Lucia had sent reinforcements to Florida as well. These troops managed to capture Georgia and menace Charleston. D'Estaing, with 2,000 troops from Guadeloupe and 1,600 from Saint Domingue, moved against Savannah, Georgia.[14] With the assistance of 2,000 American troops he undertook an unsuccessful and costly siege of the city, although he did capture the *Experiment*, 50. After a month he abandoned the siege and returned to Europe with the *Experiment* and half of the squadron.[15]

[11] B⁴163: 121–129, Byron's battle report, 8 July 1779; *Sandwich Papers*, 3: 124; P. Auphan, "Les communications entre la France et ses colonies d'Amérique pendant la guerre de l'indépendance Américaine," *La revue maritime* 61 (1925): 345–348.

[12] B⁴142: 56, d'Estaing to Sartine, 29 June 1779. D'Estaing did inform Vergennes at this time of his intention to go to North America. Spain 595: 122–123, Vergennes to Montmorin, 16 August 1779. See also Spain 594: 486, Vergennes to Montmorin, 30 July 1779; B⁴142: 65–67, 69, d'Estaing to Sartine, 21 August 1779; United States 9: 343–344, d'Estaing to Vergennes, 21 August 1779; Witte, *Journal de l'Abbé de Véri*, 2: 248–249.

[13] United States 7: 119–123, Gérard to d'Estaing, 26 January 1779; United States, supplement 1: 278–279, Washington to Gérard, 1 May 1779; United States 8: 87–90, 127–130, Gérard to Vergennes, 6 May and 16 May 1779; B⁴168: *passim*.

[14] D'Estaing left behind three ships of the line—the *Protecteur* and *Fier*, which escorted a convoy back to Europe, and the *Amphion*, which had to be left at Saint Domingue for repairs. Alfred Nemours, *Haiti et la guerre de l'indépendance américaine* (Port-au-Prince, Haiti: Henry Deschamps, 1950), 32–36, 45–46; Spain 595: 122–123, 255, 320, Vergennes to Montmorin, 11 August, 5 September, and 13 September 1779; B⁶12: unpaged, ship rosters; B⁴167: 244, 246.

[15] D'Estaing originally hoped to proceed to Newfoundland after disrupting the British at Savannah, but a storm on 2 September which

Until the other half of the squadron returned to the West Indies,[16] the British had virtually a total monopoly of naval strength in the area. This monopoly was meaningless because the storm season was too dangerous for campaigning and because the British lacked the troops and transports for offensive operations.[17]

D'Estaing's attack on Savannah did have valuable side effects. The British at New York had received heavy reinforcements—the five ships of the line and 3,800 troops which d'Orvilliers had hoped to capture—but d'Estaing's attack so frightened them that they delayed sending reinforcements to Georgia until the end of the year and decided to abandon Newport. D'Estaing thus accomplished from 1,000 miles away what he could not achieve by a close siege the year before.[18] Despite this victory in absentia and the capture of Grenada, d'Estaing's second campaign was no more decisive than his first. To accomplish more would require a greater commitment of forces.

---

damaged his squadron forced him instead to decide to undertake a formal siege of Savannah. Upon returning to Europe, one of his squadron, the *Tonnant*, was forced by storms to instead proceed to Saint Domingue. For the campaign see B⁴142: 119–154, d'Estaing to Sartine, 5 December 1779; B⁴167 and B⁴168: *passim*; United States 10: 225–230, Major General Lincoln, commander of the American troops, to the Committee of Correspondence of the Continental Congress, 22 October 1779; United States 10: 272–276, La Luzerne to Vergennes, 11 November 1779.

[16] Seven ships of the line, including the *Amphion*, reached Martinique on 29 November 1779, four others only after the beginning of 1780 (after they had stopped at Saint Domingue). This does not include two ships of the line (the *Fier* and *Tonnant*) forced back to the West Indies by storms. A corvette and two frigates were captured in December while returning troops from Savannah to the West Indies.

[17] Four of Byron's 23 ships of the line returned to Europe. The *Lion* became separated during the Battle of Grenada and went to Jamaica, but she was replaced by the *Vengeance*, which arrived from Europe.

[18] *Sandwich Papers*, 3: 122, 156–157; United States 10: 155, La Luzerne to d'Estaing, 17 September 1779; Mackesy, *War for America*, 276–278; Clowes, *Royal Navy*, 4: 48. See B⁴151: 149 for a recapitulation of the prizes made by d'Estaing.

5. Debating Future Strategy

Another battle vital to the American theater of war was fought during the autumn of 1779; Vergennes and Florida-blanca were the antagonists. Vergennes well realized that in a war of altered strategy Spanish cooperation was dependent on the proper concessions to soothe Spanish anxieties. On the day that d'Orvilliers' fleet was recalled, Vergennes wrote Montmorin that Louis agreed with his uncle that their grand maxim should be to combine their operations so that the British would have to concentrate their forces in Europe.[1] France had already announced her intention to send 3 ships of the line from Toulon to Brest and had offered their use to Spain to escort a supply convoy to Brest for the Spanish fleet.[2] Another ship of the line and frigate, then at Malaga, were ordered to cruise off the Canaries, where they could protect the southern approaches to Spain.[3] The council agreed to retain 20 Spanish ships of the line under Commodore Gastón at Brest over the winter and offered 40 days of supplies to Lieutenant-General Córdoba, the Spanish fleet commander, if he wished to repair his remaining 15 ships before returning to Spain.[4] Finally, the fiction was preserved that the combined fleet might yet resume the current campaign against Britain.[5]

While thus demonstrating that France was not opposed to maintaining pressure on Britain in European waters, Vergennes sought to prove France's inability to increase her

[1] Spain 595: 249, Vergennes to Montmorin, 5 September 1779.

[2] These ships were the *Triomphant, Souverain*, and *Jason*. Spain 595: 230, Sartine to Vergennes, 1 September 1779, copy to Montmorin.

[3] These were the *Héros* and frigate *Precieuse*. Two ships of the line were retained in the Mediterranean to protect the Levantine trade. For Mediterranean operations in 1779 see Brun, *Port de Toulon*, 2: 25–29; B²416: 72; B³670: 240, 249, 266, 319–320; B⁴160: 235, 249–250.

[4] Spain 595: 233, memoir of 1 September 1779, sent to Montmorin, 5 September 1779; Spain 595: 250–251, Vergennes to Montmorin, 5 September 1779. One Spanish ship of the line had been left behind at Cape Finisterre.

[5] Spain 595: 250–252, Vergennes to Montmorin, 5 September 1779; Spain 596: 3–4, Bessière to Vergennes, 1 October 1779.

forces in that theater. He claimed that France would be unable to contribute more than 30 ships of the line for combined operations in the Channel during 1780.[6] The need of d'Estaing's squadron for repairs would offset new construction so France could not plan on more than 66 ships of the line for the 1780 campaign. Of these, 24 would be needed in the Western Hemisphere, 8 in the Indian Ocean, 2 in the Mediterranean, and 1 or 2 in the North Sea to protect incoming shipping from the Baltic. Vergennes placed on Spain the responsibility for finding the ships to counter the expected British increase of forces in European waters.

Floridablanca gave a guarded initial response to the inference about shifting the focus of the war. He had not yet given up hope for renewing the attack on Britain after the expected bad weather period around the autumnal equinox, but he conceded the difficulty of renewing the attack the following year.[7] He claimed Spain would be able to increase her fleet by six ships of the line, including a new 90. Montmorin also reported that Charles had left to his nephew the choice of when Córdoba's ships would return to Cadiz, although Floridablanca hoped it would be before the end of the year.[8]

In fact, the expedition was virtually dead for the current year. Vergennes told the Spaniards that if it were not ready in October, bad weather would make it impossible.[9] At the beginning of October a conference of senior military officials (including Lieutenant-General du Chaffault, who had replaced d'Orvilliers as fleet commander),[10] killed the project. In addition to other difficulties, the epidemic was still

[6] Spain 595: 250–252, Vergennes to Montmorin, 5 September 1779.

[7] Spain 595: 344–347, Montmorin to Vergennes, 15 September 1779.

[8] Spain 595: 307, Montmorin to Vergennes, 13 September 1779.

[9] Spain 595: 250–251, Vergennes to Montmorin, 5 September 1779; Spain 595: 232–234, memoir of 1 September 1779, sent to Montmorin, 5 September 1779; Spain 595: 384–391, Vergennes to Montmorin, 21 September 1779.

[10] D'Orvilliers resigned for personal reasons, largely connected with the death of his son during the cruise.

increasing and had spread to the Spanish ships. Unfortunately as the weather worsened, mortality was increasing.[11]

While Vergennes awaited a definite response to his proposals, he reminded Spain that in humiliating Britain it was important to avoid giving the impression that the Bourbons wished to crush her.[12] Britain occupied for the other powers of Europe too necessary a place in the balance of power —particularly for Austria, which Vergennes described as "our ally in name and our rival in fact."[13] Vergennes also announced France's intention to send reinforcements of one battalion to Grenada and another to Martinique.

At the end of September Floridablanca responded formally through Aranda and Montmorin to the French proposal.[14] He professed agreement with Vergennes' generalizations that the plans for the campaign of 1780 should be based on those of 1779, but he did not accept Vergennes' claims that France lacked the ships to properly implement those plans. Spain would contribute 26 ships of the line for a renewed attack on Britain and expected France to find another 34, plus perhaps some of d'Estaing's returning vessels. Floridablanca recommended that the entire combined fleet be kept armed through the winter. Córdoba was ordered to return to Spain in mid-October.

Montmorin added a warning that if Spain felt France was not determined to execute the attack on Britain, she would lose her confidence in France, and good relations would end.[15] France would be accused of tricking Spain into a war

[11] Spain 596: 5–8, Vergennes to Montmorin, 1 October 1779; Spain 596: 13–16, results of the conference of 4 October 1779, sent to Montmorin, 15 October 1779. The last of the invasion flotilla was not disarmed until virtually the end of the year. B⁷661: 371, Mistral to Sartine, 27 December 1779.

[12] Spain 595: 384–391, Vergennes to Montmorin, 21 September 1779.

[13] *Ibid.*, 388.

[14] Spain 595: 412–420, Floridablanca to Aranda, copy sent by Montmorin to Vergennes, 26 September 1779.

[15] Spain 595: 424–427, Montmorin to Vergennes, 27 September 1779. Montmorin explained the Spanish desire for an invasion of England as a combination of fear for her own possessions, the desire to see

fought solely for French interests. He added the reassurance that the only new commander for the combined fleet who would please the Spaniards more than du Chauffault was d'Estaing.

Although the question of overall strategy thus became deadlocked over the extent of the forces and operations in Europe, each of the Bourbons announced his intention to reinforce his forces in other theaters. Spain intended to send two ships of the line and two battalions of troops to reinforce Havana and to raise the squadron off Gibraltar from six ships of the line to ten ships of the line. France planned to send 4,000 troops to the West Indies.[16]

Vergennes now brought into action his great unused weapon against Spain. He told Montmorin that since Spain had thus far avoided paying her share of the costs of the campaign against Britain, France would agree to another attack on England or Ireland only if Spain agreed in advance and in an unequivocal manner to share its costs.[17] He left to Montmorin the job of presenting tactfully this demand. Vergennes claimed that now that surprise was gone it was doubtful 70,000 men could take Portsmouth. He warned that 18 of the 30 French ships of the line would have to be disarmed to be prepared for the West Indies and Indian Ocean.[18]

France bear the major proportion of the costs of the war, and the *amour-propre* of Floridablanca and Charles, which was now tied up with the plan. Spain 595: 428–439, Montmorin to Vergennes, 27 September 1779.

[16] Spain 596: 39, 60, Montmorin to Vergennes, 7 October and 11 October 1779; Spain 596: 7, Vergennes to Montmorin, 1 October 1779. One Spanish ship of the line had been shipwrecked on 28 August 1779, reducing the squadron off Gibraltar to six of the line; the four additions presumably were the detachment returning from the Azores.

[17] Spain 596: 78–86, Vergennes to Montmorin, 15 October 1779.

[18] Thirteen ships of the line were for the West Indies to replace d'Estaing's returning ships; the other five were for the Indian Ocean. Spain 596: 87–92, "Observations sur l'écrit de la cour d'Espagne du 26 septembre 1779," sent by Vergennes to Montmorin, 15 October 1779.

Vergennes' threat to force Spain to share the costs of a future attack on Britain was successful, although the Spaniards did not openly acknowledge their diplomatic defeat. Discussions of a renewal of the attack gradually died out.[19] When Montmorin received Vergennes' letter, he predicted the descent on Britain would be renounced and both Córdoba and Gastón recalled to protect the blockade of Gibraltar which Spain had initiated upon her entry into the war.[20]

Montmorin's predictions quickly began to be justified. Córdoba's 15 ships of the line left Brest on 9 November, screened by a group of French frigates.[21] The Spaniards announced their intention to reinforce the Gibraltar squadron to 16–18 ships of the line;[22] Montmorin also reported they planned a major attack on Pensacola.[23] The reinforcement of Gibraltar and attack on Pensacola would distract Britain and thereby serve France's altered war strategy.

Now it was up to France to prepare the detachments to carry the war to the periphery of the British Empire. French war planning and ship preparations, however, suffered a variety of delays. First came a dispute over funds. For 1779 Louis had awarded the department 130,000,000 livres plus a supplement of 1,251,000 livres, but now the navy's preliminary estimate was that it had spent 143,000,000 livres.[24] Its initial estimate was that 138,000,000

[19] Spain 596: 200, Montmorin to Vergennes, 14 November 1779; Spain 596: 353–354, 361–364, Vergennes to Montmorin, 10 December and 17 December 1779; Spain 596: 371–374, Aranda to Vergennes, 13 December 1779, sent by Vergennes to Montmorin, 17 December 1779.

[20] Spain 596: 117–123, Montmorin to Vergennes, 25 October 1779. See also Spain 596: 200, Montmorin to Vergennes, 13 November 1779.

[21] Spain 596: 194, Vergennes to Montmorin, 13 November 1779.

[22] Spain 596: 159, 165–168, Montmorin to Vergennes, 1 November and 4 November 1779.

[23] Spain 596: 224–228, Montmorin to Vergennes, 18 November 1779.

[24] B¹91: 217–218, untitled memoir of 23 November 1779. Of this sum, 104,000,000 livres was for naval expenses proper (including 51,000,000 for armaments and 42,000,000 for construction), 26,000,000 for the West Indies, and 13,000,000 for the Mascarene Islands. See

livres would be needed in 1780.[25] Vergennes told Montmorin that all attempts to find the proper balance between projects and the means to accomplish them had failed and that Sartine had asked a delay to reassess expenses.[26] Vergennes added sarcastically, "I am persuaded that economy is better observed in Spain." Again Necker rescued the situation with a loan of 60,000,000 livres which was subscribed within a week.[27] The navy's budget for 1780 was fixed at 10,000,000 livres per month[28] and its building program restricted to five frigates and possibly two ships of the line.[29]

Naval planning was also delayed by the tardy return of d'Estaing's initial squadron, whose ships arrived individually or in pairs at four different ports between 7 and 13 December. The Spaniards further complicated planning by requesting that 11 ships of the line and 2,000 to 3,000 troops aid their attack on Florida, to which France agreed in principle in December.[30] They also asked that the French squadron for the West Indies also provide escort for two Spanish ships of the line and 1,500 troops for Havana (to which France also agreed).[31]

---

also the partial figures given in B¹214: 170–174, untitled memoir of October 1779.

[25] This is exclusive of 11,000,000 livres for a "projected expedition," presumably the invasion of Britain. E 205: unpaged, "Observations sur l'état des dépenses de 1780," 24 November 1779. A later memoir reduced the request to 120,000,000 livres, but this was obviously either wish fulfillment or an evasion. E 204: unpaged, untitled memoir of 18 December 1779. Again there is no direct evidence either memoir was seen by the council.

[26] Spain 596: 273, Vergennes to Montmorin, 26 November 1779.

[27] Spain 596: 406, Vergennes to Montmorin, 17 December 1779.

[28] B³694: 53, Necker to Sartine, 18 January 1780; Witte, *Journal de l'Abbé de Véri*, 2: 374 ff., entries of 10 September 1779 and following.

[29] B¹91: 172–176, "Projet pour 1780," 28 August 1779. Much of the building projected for 1779 (including an additional 74, the *Northumberland*) was not yet complete.

[30] Spain 596: 225–227, Montmorin to Vergennes, 18 November 1779; Spain 596: 407, Vergennes to Montmorin, 17 December 1779.

[31] Spain 596: 167, Montmorin to Vergennes, 2 November 1779; Spain 596: 238, Vergennes to Sartine, 19 November 1779; Spain 596: 315–317, Sartine to Vergennes, 4 December 1779.

Even greater difficulties in readying the fleet for the West Indies were caused by atrocious weather and the shortage of healthy seamen to form crews. The 13 ships of the line planned for Martinique had to be reduced to 11, and the 5 ships of the line for the Indian Ocean to 3. The *Saint-Michel*, 60, ordered in September to proceed ahead to the West Indies with a merchant convoy, had her sailing delayed indefinitely by a collision among her merchantmen and then by a severe storm.[32] It was finally decided that the five ships of the line closest to being ready would sail to the West Indies with 3,000 French reinforcements and the Spanish reinforcements for Havana. A second squadron, proceeding later, would take another 3,000 troops to the West Indies for future joint operations against Florida.[33] Not even the first squadron was ready at the end of the year, although it was hoped it could sail in January.

6. The Relief of Gibraltar

While the Allies were debating war strategy, the British were preparing to seize the military initiative by what was their most audacious and successful move of the war. They prepared their plans on the basis of a sudden rise in their forces in home waters. During the last half of the year they added 10 ships of the line to their forces, all of them in

[32] B²416: 11, abstract of La Prévalye to Sartine, 29 September 1779; B³668: 186–187, 259, 287, 309, La Touche to Sartine, 12 October, 23 November, 2 December, and 10 December 1779. Also, on medical advice, crews were being rested. Spain 597: 208, Vergennes to Montmorin, 29 January 1780. The council also believed that three ships of the line in the Indian Ocean theater would suffice to maintain parity. They had given up the idea of taking the offensive there. Howard Ray Killion, "The Suffren Expedition: French Operations in India during the War of American Independence" (Ph.D. diss., Duke University, 1972), 63–64.

[33] B²416: 16, abstract of Sartine to La Porte, 20 December 1779; Spain 596: 435, Vergennes to Montmorin, 22 December 1779; Spain 596: 436, Bessière to Vergennes, 22 December 1779. For the problems at Brest see B³663: 255, 289, 302, 331, 335–338; B³664: 112–113, 210, 240–242.

Europe. During the same period 8 were captured or dropped for repairs, only one of which was from their European forces.[1] This permitted them a new freedom of action. Some of their new forces would soon be needed in the West Indies, but the most immediate problem was that of reprovisioning and reinforcing the 5,000 British troops at Gibraltar. Since the beginning of the war they had been blockaded by 10,000 Spanish troops and a Spanish squadron.[2] The British therefore decided to send 21 ships of the line under Admiral Sir George Rodney to Gibraltar with a supply convoy. While most of the fleet then returned to England, Rodney would take three of the ships of the line to the West Indies. Plans also envisaged three reinforcements convoys for the West Indies (including Jamaica), the first of which was to accompany Rodney part of the way.[3]

Spanish naval operations by now centered around the blockade of Gibraltar. Their squadron of 10 ships of the line was to have been reinforced by Córdoba's 15 and 2 others left behind at Ferrol, but adverse weather forced 4 of Córdoba's squadron into Corunna, and both they and the Ferrol ships were unable to make their way south.[4] It had been hoped to keep 16 to 18 ships of the line constantly at sea off Gibraltar,[5] but 6 of the remaining 21 ships of the line

[1] Ships added were the *Alcide*, 74; *Edgar*, 74; *Montagu*, 74 (new); *Princess Amelia*, 80 (reclassified); *Sandwich*, 90; *Ocean*, 90; *Barfleur*, 90; *Ajax*, 74; *Dublin*, 74; and *Torbay*, 74 (repaired). Ships dropped were the *Ardent* and *Experiment* (captured), and the *St. Albans, Isis, Prince of Wales, Royal Oak, Monmouth*, and *Nonsuch* (returned from West Indies in need of repairs). See also Dull: Dissertation, 295. Some ships needing repairs were used by Hardy for a month's cruise in the autumn.

[2] Spain 594: 313, Montmorin to Vergennes, 24 June 1779. For British forces at Gibraltar see Mackesy, *War for America*, 524–525; Spain 595: 50, Cadiz report of 8 October 1779.

[3] Mackesy, *War for America*, 307–314; *Sandwich Papers*, 3: 186–188, 204, 210.

[4] Spain 596: 172–173, Cadiz report of 5 November 1779; Spain 596: 248, Montmorin to Vergennes, 22 November 1779; Spain 596: 327, Bessière to Vergennes, 6 December 1779; Spain 596: 468–469, Montmorin to Vergennes, 30 December 1779.

[5] Spain 596: 166, Montmorin to Vergennes, 4 November 1779.

were in repair at Cadiz and only 11 were at sea at the end of December.[6] The Spaniards considered these ships safe, although a constant stream of intelligence reports warned of an impending effort to reinforce Gibraltar. On 22 October Vergennes warned that the British were preparing three squadrons, of which one was for the Channel, one under Rodney for the West Indies, and one to relieve Gibraltar.[7] Floridablanca believed that the British would only use 2 or 3 ships of the line and that the Spanish forces off Gibraltar would be sufficient.[8]

Aranda, a month later, told both foreign ministers that his information predicted that Rodney with 12 ships of the line would escort the Gibraltar convoy part way.[9] Aranda discounted the possibility that the English would use heavy forces to reinforce Gibraltar, since many of the ships would subsequently need repairs before they could be used in the next campaign. Vergennes added his concurrence—16 to 18 Spanish ships of the line off Gibraltar should be sufficient.[10] His correspondence continued to show greater concern about a possible Austrian mediation of the war and about British diplomatic feelers to Spain relayed by Captain Johnstone of the *Romney*, 50, then at Lisbon.[11]

On 17 December Vergennes warned Montmorin of reports of the provisioning of a number of large ships at Portsmouth. Vergennes now believed four or five ships of

---

[6] Spain 596: 466, Cadiz report of 28 December 1779; Spain 597: 45, Floridablanca to Aranda, 9 January 1780.

[7] Spain 596: 110, Vergennes to Montmorin, 22 October 1779.

[8] Spain 596: 166, Montmorin to Vergennes, 4 November 1779. Sandwich had in fact proposed slipping supplies into Gibraltar, using only a small force. On 16 September the cabinet approved using four ships of the line for this purpose, but these plans were later altered. *Sandwich Papers*, 3: 165, 182.

[9] Spain 596: 220–223, Aranda to Vergennes, 17 November 1779.

[10] Spain 596: 236–237, Vergennes to Montmorin, 19 November 1779. He expressed the same view a little more hesitantly a week later. Spain 596: 274, Vergennes to Montmorin, 26 November 1779.

[11] Spain 596: 257–264, 342–343, Montmorin to Vergennes, 25 November and 9 December 1779; Spain 596: 403–404, 444–445, Vergennes to Montmorin, 17 December and 24 December 1779.

the line for the West Indies would be accompanied part way by a squadron for Gibraltar, probably of about a dozen ships of the line.[12] Not knowing as yet of the condition of the Spanish fleet off Gibraltar, he felt it in no great danger. As the Allies returned to the preparation of their forces for Martinique, Havana, and the attack on Florida, Rodney on 26 December sailed for Gibraltar and the victory which would almost knock Spain out of the war and doom the dreams of Vergennes and Franklin.

[12] Spain 596: 408–409, Vergennes to Montmorin, 17 December 1779.

CHAPTER SEVEN

1780—War at the Periphery

1. Rodney's Victory

O N New Year's Day of 1780, Vergennes sent to Spain the most serious piece of intelligence yet.[1] According to this information, Rodney had already sailed from England with 24 ships of the line, of which 22 were for Gibraltar, including 7 which would thereafter proceed to the West Indies. Vergennes claimed that the council in response had suggested that every ship at Brest sortie to intercept Rodney but that Sartine had rejected the proposal as impractical (as indeed it was, although I doubt the proposal was ever seriously made). Instead, Gastón's squadron, reinforced by 4 French ships of the line, would be sent to Gibraltar in the hope that with favorable winds it could outrace the British squadron, slowed by its convoy.[2]

There were other aspects of the situation which Vergennes did not mention to the Spaniards. Although the entire fleet of 30 French ships of the line was not yet provisioned and manned, 10 ships of the line for the West Indies and 2 for the Indian Ocean were virtually ready to sail.[3]

[1] Spain 597: 3–4, Vergennes to Montmorin, 1 January 1780. Vergennes probably had received this information about 29 December 1779. See Witte, *Journal de l'Abbé de Véri*, 2: 286–287. See also Spain 597: 28, Vergennes to Montmorin, 7 January 1780.

[2] Spain 597: 3–4, Vergennes to Montmorin, 1 January 1780; B³677: 9, La Porte to Sartine, 3 January 1780. France offered to replace any ship of Gastón's squadron which still could use repairs, but Spain, fearing further delay, refused the offer. Spain 597: 87, Montmorin to Vergennes, 11 January 1780. Vergennes later complained that the council had wished to send ten ships of the line rather than four with Gastón. Spain 597: 222–223, Vergennes to Montmorin, 29 January 1780. For the difficulties Brest was experiencing in readying ships see B³677: *passim.*

[3] These dozen ships entered the roadstead of Brest between 27 December and 25 January; half were there by 10 January. B⁵12: unpaged, listing of ship movements. The *Saint-Michel* at Rochefort and

These, however, could not be sent to Gibraltar without in-
terfering with planned operations. Not only did the French
decline to strip these forces, but they even added 3 ships to
the squadron for the West Indies, not telling the Spaniards
until ten days later.[4] The French thus took a calculated
gamble on the ability of the Spaniards to withstand the English—Gastón's squadron of 20 Spanish and four French
ships of the line sailed only on 14 January, hopelessly behind the English. Montmorin reported on the 11th that
Córdoba had been ordered to reassemble his forces, which
should total 20 to 22 ships of the line,[5] so France could assume the situation was not critical.

The French council and ports, moreover, had an enormous amount of work to distract them during the hectic
month of January 1780. Of chief importance was the arrival
of a number of merchantmen with naval supplies from Amsterdam. At the end of 1778, France had placed huge orders
for wood for construction with Prussia and other northern
contractors, expecting the wood to pass via Hamburg and
Amsterdam to French ports.[6] France herself could not provide the escorts for these shipments through the North Sea,
and consequently huge quantities of matériel had backed
up at Amsterdam and Hamburg.[7] The attempt to send a
combined Franco-American squadron under John Paul

Ajax at Lorient were also available. The major difficulty in readying
the ships was still crew shortages. B³677: 12, 22, de Guichen to Sartine, 5 and 12 January 1780.

[4] B³667: 9, La Porte to Sartine, 3 January 1780; Spain 597: 107, Vergennes to Montmorin, 13 January 1780.

[5] Spain 597: 93–94, Montmorin to Vergennes, 11 January 1780. The
San Josef was damaged in a collision and returned to Brest. The
French ships were the *Glorieux*, *Bourgogne*, *Zodiaque*, and *Scipion*,
which were not previously intended for detached service.

[6] See B¹88: 192, "Bois de Hambourg," 23 November 1778. The Royal
Administration of Prussia was supposed to have furnished 352,000 ft.³
during 1779.

[7] B¹92: 149, untitled memoir of 3 December 1779. This memoir
advised letting no further contracts with Prussia until negotiations
were completed with Denmark for providing transportation.

Jones to Dutch waters only attracted English forces, although Jones helped poison Anglo-Dutch relations, as Conyngham and Wickes had done to Anglo-French relations.[8] The obvious solution was to pressure the Dutch into escorting these ships themselves.[9] By November 1779 selective economic pressures forced the Dutch to announce they would provide escorts for a Mediterranean and a West Indian convoy, except for timber ships.[10] Sartine realized the Dutch would not prevent timber ships from sailing with the convoy under their own risk. He sent instructions via the French ambassador, the Duke de la Vauguyon, to the Dutch business associations of the French navy department to send their timber ships with the convoy.[11]

The Dutch convoys, including 25 or 30 ships with naval stores and another 18 or 20 with timber, sailed together in late December 1779. The English sent a larger squadron which intercepted the convoy and seized 7 ships for carrying contraband—not only masts and wood for construction but also hemp and other naval stores.[12] The remainder of the convoy scattered and escaped. Eighteen of these ships

[8] See above, Chapter Six, Section 3, Note 28. The English blockaded Jones' squadron after it arrived at the Texel and began applying diplomatic pressure against the Dutch to expel it.

[9] It should be noted that France was only interested in the Netherlands as a middleman. Dutch naval stores themselves were expensive and of poor quality. Holland 539: 59–60, Sartine to French ambassador La Vauguyon, 6 April 1779.

[10] Francis P. Renaut, *Les Provinces-Unies et la guerre d'Amérique (1775–1784): De la neutralité à la belligérance (1775–1780)* (Paris: Graouli, 1936), 228–242; Friedrich Edler, *The Dutch Republic and the American Revolution* (Baltimore: Johns Hopkins University Press, 1911), 95–130; Bemis, *Diplomacy of the American Revolution*, 130–148. The British claimed that not only timber but all naval stores were contraband and hence liable to seizure.

[11] Holland 539: 153–154, 173–176, Sartine to La Vauguyon, 25 November and 2 December 1779; Holland 539: 178, 185–188, 221–226, La Vauguyon to Sartine, 7 December, 10 December, and 31 December 1779; Holland 540: 9–10, La Vauguyon to Vergennes, 4 January 1780.

[12] *Sandwich Papers*, 3: 10–11, 107–108, 113–114; Edler, *The Dutch Republic and the American Revolution*, 129–132; Holland 540: 41–47, La Vauguyon to Vergennes, 14 January 1780.

[175]

reached Brest with their copper, wood for construction, masts, hemp, pitch, and tar.[13] Others arrived at Le Havre, Nantes, Rochefort, and Bordeaux, while Jones' squadron utilized the opportunity to safely run the Channel to Dunkirk and Lorient.[14] The supplies were useful although not as vital as the British imagined.[15] In fact, the British did serious harm to their diplomatic position by overestimating the importance of the Dutch carrying trade to the French war effort. The outraged Estates General of the Netherlands now formally refused English demands for the military assistance against France claimed by the Anglo-Dutch Treaty of 1678. The British responded by declaring the Anglo-Dutch commercial treaties abrogated and began seizing Dutch merchantmen. In April 1780 the Estates General secretly voted for the adoption of unlimited convoys and prepared to fit out a fleet.[16]

[13] B³679: 28–32, La Porte to Sartine, 14 January 1780.

[14] Holland 539: 241–242, Sartine to La Vauguyon, 21 January 1780; B³674: 8, Anglemont, commissioner at Dunkirk, to Sartine, 2 January 1780. For Jones' squadron see also Dull: Dissertation, 305n.

[15] The British believed that France had major shortages of timber and copper. French timber shortages did exist, but they were localized. After a busy summer's work, Brest still had 467,000 ft.³ B³679: 161–162, commissioner Faissoles to Sartine, 4 October 1780. During the 12 months after the resumption of timber shipments from Rouen (in December 1779), 375,000 ft.³ of timber passed through that port. B³676: 5–29, monthly reports. The British, who had adopted the practice of putting copper plates on their ship hulls to kill marine growths and thereby increase ship speed, sought to prevent France from following suit. France's slowness in doing so was less a result of the lack of copper than of technical problems like the lack of sufficient quantities of proper nails, some delay in appreciating the value of the new technique, and maldistribution of matériel. Half the French ships sent to North America in 1780 were copper-bottomed, however. Serious copper shortages did develop later, but they were at least partially artificial, since much of the supply was in private hands. Mackesy, *War for America*, 356; Brun, *Port de Toulon*, 1: 541; 2: 37–38; Loir, *La Marine royale en 1789*, 204–205; B³677: 90–91, 109–110, Commodore Hector, the new port commandant at Brest, to Sartine, 7 February and 16 February 1780.

[16] Bemis, *Diplomacy of the American Revolution*, 147–148; Edler, *The Dutch Republic and the American Revolution*, 135–136.

As welcome to France as was the deterioration of Anglo-Dutch relations, her chief concern remained the coordination of strategy with Spain. The departure of Gastón's squadron simplified this by killing discussion of renewing the attack on Britain.[17] (Floridablanca had raised the topic again, probably for the purpose of treating its abandonment as an undesirable choice forced on her by France, thereby placing responsibility for any future military failures upon France.)[18] Vergennes now informed Spain of the French ideas for the coming campaign.[19] After the Martinique reinforcements had sailed, the council intended to prepare 6 ships of the line and 3,000 to 4,000 troops for North America. Vergennes approved of the corresponding Spanish plans to send 10 or 11 additional ships of the line to Havana,[20] and offered to send 2,000 French troops and some ships of the line from Martinique to Saint Domingue, which would be at Spain's disposal for an attack on Florida or wherever else she wished. Finally, he suggested that the Bourbons use their remaining forces in Europe to keep the English bottled up in the Channel. A combined squadron, formed off Cape Finisterre, could cruise off the entrance of Saint George's Channel to intercept British commerce for Ireland, Wales, and the west coast of England.

On 22 January Montmorin reported the Spaniards had accepted the fact that the departure of Gastón's squadron precluded a renewal of the previous year's campaign.[21] He also indicated that Spain was studying plans drafted 15

[17] See Spain 597: 91–96, Montmorin to Vergennes, 11 January 1780.

[18] Spain 597: 35–50, Floridablanca to Aranda, 9 January 1780; Spain 597: 51–62, Montmorin to Vergennes, 9 January 1780. Spain also sought to evade paying a subsidy promised by Floridablanca to France for helping to attack Florida.

[19] Spain 597: 207–218, Vergennes to Montmorin, 19 January 1780.

[20] *Ibid.* Floridablanca had announced his intention to reinforce the squadron at Havana to 16 ships of the line and the squadron at Gibraltar to 21 ships of the line, if the attack on England were not renewed. Spain 597: 48, Floridablanca to Aranda, 9 January 1780.

[21] Spain 597: 154–156, 159–163, Montmorin to Vergennes, 22 January 1780.

years ago for an attack on Gibraltar and would use them should the blockade fail.[22]

The Spanish court did not yet know that the blockade had suffered a terrible setback. Rodney's squadron achieved an unbroken series of successes.[23] They began on 8 January 1780 with the capture of a ship of the line belonging to the Spanish Company of Caracas and 21 merchantmen from a 32-ship convoy, which was bringing 2,500,000 piastres worth of naval matériel from San Sebastian to Cadiz. Given the shortage of matériel in Spanish ports, this alone would have been a major blow to the Spanish navy. Eight days later Rodney's 21 ships of the line caught by surprise the Spanish blockading squadron of 11 ships of the line, captured 4 of the line, and destroyed two more.[24] Rodney reached Gibraltar on 18 January and sent a detachment to replenish Minorca.[25] The English fleet was not yet safe. Because of battle and storm damage, one-third of Rodney's ships of the line had been dismasted and the remainder were badly scattered,[26] but the Spaniards were unable to take advantage of the situation. By 4 February, 16 of Gastón's ships of the line had joined nine others ready at Cadiz, but this fleet failed to contest Rodney when his squadron and prizes repassed the Straits.[27] Rodney now sailed for the

---

[22] Spain 597: 169, Montmorin to Vergennes, 22 January 1780.

[23] *Sandwich Papers*, 3: 156–157, 191–207; Mackesy, *War for America*, 322–323.

[24] This squadron was commanded by Lieutenant-General Lángara in the absence of Córdoba, whose flagship was at Cadiz.

[25] Spain 597: 131–136, Cadiz report of 18 January 1780. This report was sent with Spain 597: 187–192, Montmorin to Vergennes, 26 January 1780.

[26] Spain 597: 131–136, Cadiz report of 18 January 1780. Two British ships of the line had even been forced to Lisbon.

[27] Gastón's squadron too had been delayed by bad weather. Spain 597: 202–204, Montmorin to Vergennes, 28 January 1780. See also Spain 597: 238–249, 241–242, Cadiz reports of 1 February and 4 February 1780; Spain 597: 264–265, 266–267, Commodore Beausset, commanding the French detachment, to Montmorin, 7 February and 15 February 1780.

West Indies while Rear-Admiral Digby with the remainder of the squadron returned, prize-laden, to England. The British good fortune was not yet exhausted. Digby met a French squadron outbound for India and on 23 February captured the *Protée*, 64 and part of her convoy.[28]

2. Picking Up the Pieces

The news of the disaster reached the Spanish court on 24 January. For almost a month Spanish war planning seemed to come to a halt. There was little France could do. Montmorin offered French help should Spain wish to attack Gibraltar,[1] and the council ordered the *Héros* which had arrived at Cadiz for repairs, to remain there.[2] It was certain that France would continue to need the help of the 50 ships of the line of the Spanish navy; the council estimated British strength for the coming campaign at between 102 and 104 ships of the line[3] and France's at between 68 and 72 ships of the line.[4]

At the end of February Spain finally announced her intentions.[5] Charles planned to send 8,000 to 10,000 troops and 12 to 14 ships of the line to the Western Hemisphere. He accepted the French offer of 2,000 troops and requested

[28] Spain 598: 113, Vergennes to Montmorin, 13 March 1780; *Sandwich Papers*, 3: 202–204, Digby to Sandwich, 2 March 1780. See also Section 3, below.

[1] Spain 597: 188–189, Montmorin to Vergennes, 26 January 1780.

[2] Spain 597: 251–252, Vergennes to Montmorin, 4 February 1780.

[3] B⁵15: unpaged, "Etat général des vaisseaux de force Anglais, tant dans les différents ports d'Angleterre qui au dehors au 4 février 1780"; Spain 596: 354, memoir sent by Vergennes to Montmorin, 10 December 1779; Witte, *Journal de l'Abbé de Véri*, 2: 302, entry of 21 November 1779. B⁴215: 91–92, memoir of March 1780, raised the estimate to 111, including the prizes (which, however, were not used during the 1780 campaign).

[4] Spain 597: 212, Vergennes to Montmorin, 29 January 1780; B⁵13: unpaged, "Distribution actuelle des forces navales du roi," 26 January 1780.

[5] Spain 597: 354–360, Montmorin to Vergennes, 22 February 1780.

that three or four ships of the line accompany them at the
end of June to Saint Domingue.[6] On the other hand, Spain
rejected Vergennes' proposal for combined operations off
the Saint George's Channel. Charles wished to keep 28 ships
of the line at Cadiz and Algeciras (adjoining the Straits of
Gibraltar) to watch Gibraltar. Montmorin believed both
decisions were dictated by the fear of another defeat,
which, according to Floridablanca, neither king nor country
could absorb.

Montmorin added his own extremely critical impressions
of the condition of the Spanish government and Spanish
navy.[7] While praising Floridablanca he felt that Floridablanca's fellow ministers were united only by their desire
to place the responsibility for the naval disaster on him.
(He was already being blamed by the public.) Montmorin
viewed Aranda as the leader of the opposition to Floridablanca. Only the firm support of the king kept Floridablanca in power. The navy deserved no more respect
than the government. The Marquis de Castejon, the naval
minister, was a cipher who was kept in office by Floridablanca as an ally against colonial minister Gálvez, who
wished to add the office to his own. Córdoba, in command
at Cadiz, was senile, the ships of the Spanish navy in terrible condition, its arsenals and magazines empty. Montmorin
doubted that the squadron for the West Indies would leave
before May, meaning it would arrive too late to accomplish
anything before the hurricane season, which began in late

[6] In order that her own possessions be better covered, Spain also
requested that the French expeditionary force planned for America
initially be sent to Georgia rather than Newport. Spain 597: 320,
Floridablanca to Aranda, 18 February 1780; Spain 597: 384, Aranda
to Vergennes, 26 February 1780. Vergennes denied the request because of the lack of a safe port south of the Chesapeake (since
Charleston was endangered by the British), Spain 598: 14-15, Vergennes to Montmorin, 2 March 1780.
[7] Spain 597: 337-345, 346-351, Montmorin to Vergennes, 21 February and 22 February 1780.

summer. Montmorin wondered if Spain would do France more harm or good in the course of the war; she would certainly cause embarrassment at the peace table.

Vergennes could not afford the luxury of such pessimism. His concern had to be the pragmatic one of somehow preserving the Spanish navy as a viable force for maintaining pressure on Britain. The Spanish refusal to participate in combined operations in Europe endangered the continuation of that pressure. Initially Vergennes restricted himself to the comment that the best European strategy for the Bourbons might be the most narrow kind of defense—a threat, perhaps, of French noncooperation in the Spanish campaign against Gibraltar.[8] Vergennes, however, soon deferred to Spanish fears. Although he argued the dangers to French commerce, to the troop convoy for America, and to the returning ships from the West Indies should English forces be free to operate off Île d'Ouessant and in the Bay of Biscay while 28 ships of the line were being used needlessly for a mere blockade of Gibraltar,[9] he was still willing to offer an alternate plan to substitute for Allied operations in English waters.[10]

This plan would forfeit control over the entrances to the English Channel to the British, but it would decrease the danger of a collision with the British fleet. France would send enough ships of the line from Toulon to increase the French squadron at Cadiz to 9 or 10 of the line. Thus reinforced, the Cadiz fleet could cruise during the summer off the Azores, where it could have a chance of intercepting British convoys while still remaining within a reasonable

[8] Spain 598: 12–13, Vergennes to Montmorin, 2 March 1780.
[9] Spain 598: 108–113, Vergennes to Montmorin, 13 March 1780.
[10] Spain 598: 99–104, memoir of 12 March 1780, sent by Vergennes to Montmorin, 13 March 1780. Both plans envisaged that 15 French ships of the line would return from the West Indies at the end of the summer, while the remaining 13 would be used to cover the movement of 2,000 troops from Martinique or Guadeloupe to Saint Domingue.

distance of the Straits of Gibraltar. At the end of the summer, 7 ships of the line from the French Cadiz squadron and 7 or 8 of the line from French ports could sail to the West Indies to replace 15 worn ships of the line. Sartine was sending alternate orders to Commodore Beausset (who had accompanied Gastón) to take his 5 ships of the line to Toulon or to remain at Cadiz. Montmorin was to forward to him whichever set of orders was desired by Spain.

Vergennes' concessions forestalled a crisis, since Charles was willing to send no more than 6 ships of the line to Brest for fear of weakening the Cadiz fleet.[11] Floridablanca quickly accepted the alternate French plan.[12] He suggested that not only all the available ships from Toulon be sent to Spain, but also as many as possible from Brest. He hoped that the ships from Brest and the Spanish ships from Ferrol could reach Cadiz before the English could blockade it. Even if this were not possible, enough ships could be sent from Brest to Ferrol to force the English to divide their blockading forces between the two Spanish ports. The return of the 15 ships of the line from the West Indies in the autumn would then restore naval superiority to the Bourbons. At any rate, Floridablanca believed they would have sufficient ships at Cadiz to cover the vital returning squadron and to undertake a diversion in the Mediterranean. Floridablanca also asked that the returning West Indian ships escort all available Spanish and French shipping from the Caribbean.

Montmorin advised that France accept Floridablanca's suggestions since the Spanish fleet at Cadiz would not be ready until the end of June, and since fleet operations to the south could at least protect the returning West Indian convoy and might even accomplish something offensively. Vergennes accepted the Spanish proposals on 21 April.[13]

[11] Spain 598: 164, Montmorin to Vergennes, 16 March 1780.
[12] Spain 598: 226–230, Floridablanca to Aranda, 23 March 1780; Spain 598: 306–311, Montmorin to Vergennes, 29 March 1780.
[13] Spain 598: 461–462, Vergennes to Montmorin, 21 April 1780.

Vergennes also sent a memoir drafted by the navy department.[14] The navy viewed the function of the combined Cadiz fleet as primarily that of a fleet in being (for potential rather than actual use) to distract the English. There was no diversion it could profitably undertake in the Mediterranean,[15] and until the arrival of the West Indian ships, it would not be strong enough for major operations in the Atlantic. France would therefore only send to Cadiz ships from Toulon, Brest, and the West Indies on the condition that a new combined fleet would cover the return of the French warships and convoy to Brest. (Vergennes asked Montmorin to send out the Spaniards on naming d'Estaing its commander.) The Spanish contingent of the fleet would have the option of returning immediately to Spain or of refitting at Brest and then escorting clear of the French coast a new squadron of 28 to 30 ships of the line for the Caribbean. The navy also requested that Spain release the ships of the line and troops which had been promised her in the West Indies if she did not need them, so they could be sent to North America. These would be matters of future debate but at least a reasonable compromise had been reached for continued cooperation.

Spain presented problems for French diplomacy other than the coordination of strategy. One of these problems was her relationship with France's other ally, the United States. The Continental Congress had decided to send a representative, the gifted but inexperienced John Jay, to the Spanish court. He arrived at Cadiz in company with the re-

[14] Spain 598: 476–491, "Observations sur la lettre du Cᵗᵉ de Florideblanche," sent by Vergennes to Montmorin, 21 April 1780.

[15] An attack on Minorca or Gibraltar would require too much time to prepare and more transports than were readily available in the Mediterranean. Thus, the Spaniards temporarily gave up any idea of actually attacking Gibraltar, although the pretext of preparations were maintained for the sake of Spanish public opinion. (Naturally the blockade was also continued.) Spain 599: 96–99, Montmorin to Vergennes, 12 May 1780; Spain 599: 281, Vergennes to Montmorin, 12 June 1780.

turning French representative Gérard in January 1780.[16] The Spaniards not only refused to recognize Jay as the American representative but even to receive Gérard publicly in his capacity as French minister to the United States.[17] Montmorin warned that Floridablanca wished to see America reduced to a nullity and felt that for this it would be necessary that she remain attached to Britain by some bonds.[18] Gérard convinced Floridablanca not to let the Americans entertain any suspicion of his feelings,[19] while Vergennes professed himself so shocked by Floridablanca's attitude that he would not even communicate it to Louis and the council.[20] Vergennes realized that there were irreconcilable conflicts of interest between his allies and prudently tried to balance between them. He suggested that Spain at least cooperate militarily with the Americans *as if* America were independent—this would involve no actual recognition.[21] Simultaneously he warned Montmorin not to interfere in any negotiations between Floridablanca and Jay.

A second matter demanded more active French intervention. Since her entry into the war, Spain had seized neutral ships passing through the Straits of Gibraltar on the mere suspicion that they were carrying provisions to Gibraltar.[22] Spain's aggressiveness endangered the impression carefully fostered by Vergennes that the Allied war effort was "for the liberty of the seas and the public cause"[23] rather than

[16] Spain 597: 184–185, Cadiz report of 26 January 1780; Spain 597: 293–294, Montmorin to Vergennes, 14 February 1780.

[17] Spain 597: 304–306, Montmorin to Vergennes, 18 February 1780; Spain 598: 18–19, Vergennes to Montmorin, 2 March 1780.

[18] Spain 597: 361–362, Montmorin to Vergennes, 22 February 1780. See also Spain 598: 105–106, Vergennes to Montmorin, 13 March 1780.

[19] Spain 597: 361–363, Montmorin to Vergennes, 22 February 1780.

[20] Spain 598: 13, Vergennes to Montmorin, 2 March 1780.

[21] Spain 598: 105–107, Vergennes to Montmorin, 13 March 1780.

[22] Spain 597: 168, Montmorin to Vergennes, 22 January 1780; Madariaga, *Britain, Russia, and the Armed Neutrality*, 145.

[23] Spain 598: 13, Vergennes to Montmorin, 2 March 1780. The French maritime ordinance of 26 July 1778 recognized virtually all

for their own ends. One can doubt that the neutral powers placed much faith in any of the belligerent powers' altruism, but Vergennes' assertion of the right of neutrals to trade in noncontraband items with powers at war corresponded to the self-interest of both France and the neutral powers. Vergennes was anxious to see the neutral maritime states (Holland, Russia, Denmark, Sweden, Prussia, Austria, and Portugal) assert their rights.[24] Spain's disregard for these rights led to the danger that the neutrals would view Spain as being as opposed to their interests as was England. This danger seemed realized when, ostensibly because of the Spanish seizure of the Russian merchantman *Saint Nicholas*, the Empress Catherine mobilized 15 ships of the line (on 8 February 1780), and then proposed to the other neutral maritime powers that they join Russia to protect an enumerated list of neutral rights (28 February 1780).[25] Despite dire warnings from Prussia about Catherine's anger,[26] Vergennes knew that Catherine's actions were not chiefly directed against Spain.[27] In actuality the Spanish seizure of the Russian ship had merely given Catherine an opportunity to appear impartial in her implementation of a policy serving Russia's own interests in a manner

---

the rights claimed by neutrals. See Bemis, *Diplomacy of the American Revolution*, 130–139.

[24] Vergennes told Floridablanca that France was trying to lead Sweden and Denmark gradually to make reprisals against England for seizure of their ships, although this goal had to be masked since even the prospect of war would frighten them. Spain 593: 80–81, Vergennes to Floridablanca, 18 March 1779.

[25] Madariaga, *Britain, Russia, and the Armed Neutrality*, 140–184, 439–446. The Russians with about 30 ships of the line were the world's fourth largest naval power. For a listing of the Russian navy in 1782 see B⁷481: piece 17.

[26] Spain 598: 152, Frederick II to Baron Goltz, Prussian representative at Versailles, 14 March 1780, copy sent by Vergennes to Montmorin, 27 March 1780. Prussia of course was interested in seeing good relations between a present and a prospective ally against Austria.

[27] France was informed of this by Catherine. Madariaga, *Britain, Russia, and the Armed Neutrality*, 161–162.

far more dangerous to Britain than to Spain.[28] Although France could do nothing herself directly without undermining Catherine's claim to neutrality, she must restrain Spain if she were to encourage the growth of an armed coalition which could provide protection for the movement of goods and matériel to her ports.[29] Over the summer Sweden and Denmark joined Catherine's League of Armed Neutrality.

An even more serious problem now arose. Montmorin on 13 March informed Vergennes that he had strong suspicions that Floridablanca was engaged in secret negotiations with the British.[30] These negotiations had actually been in progress since the beginning of the year, and, as in 1778, the British had refused to make a definite commitment regarding the cession of Gibraltar. In the middle of February Floridablanca received another temporizing answer.[31] It seems likely, given the skepticism of Floridablanca, that thereafter he used the negotiation with Britain solely to put pressure on France. It is not inconceivable that Montmorin's discovery of the negotiations was even arranged by Floridablanca. Only in April was France notified officially; until then she could only cautiously observe the situation.

[28] Russia's policy was designed to improve her stature and reputation, as well as to stimulate her shipping and trade. *Ibid.*, 174–198, 440–444. Vergennes told Montmorin on 31 March that he believed Catherine's *amour-propre* was at stake, and on 5 March that he believed Russia hoped to present herself as a center around which other powers could rally. He continually treated the development as potentially favorable to France. Spain 598: 277–278, 341, 367–370, Vergennes to Montmorin, 27 March, 31 March, and 5 April 1780.

[29] Madariaga, *Britain, Russia, and the Armed Neutrality*, 182; Spain 598: 464–465, Vergennes to Montmorin, 21 July 1780. Vergennes was also concerned with preserving Russian good will in case he would have to ask for Russian mediation to secure peace. Spain 597: *passim*; Madariaga, *Britain, Russia, and the Armed Neutrality*, 222–223, 226–228.

[30] Spain 598: 125–128, Montmorin to Vergennes, 13 March 1780.

[31] Conn, *Gibraltar in British Diplomacy*, 191–194; Samuel Flagg Bemis, *The Hussey-Cumberland Mission and American Independence* (Princeton, N.J.: Princeton University Press, 1931).

3. Britain's Missed Opportunity

The disruption of the Spanish war effort, which presented so critical a danger to French diplomacy, gave the
British their supreme opportunity of the war to seize permanently the initiative. Their best chance lay in intercepting three great convoys which France and Spain sent across
the Atlantic during 1780; by failing to do so they not only
wasted their own opportunity but permitted the Allies to
achieve a major redistribution of the balance of military
power in the Western Hemisphere. This was a failure not
of military intelligence (which could always ascertain the
preparation of large numbers of ships, although not their
exact destination or time of departure) but of the disposition of forces.

The first of these convoys was the reinforcement convoy
for Martinique, which left Brest while Rodney's squadron
lay at Gibraltar. Its escort was reinforced to 17 ships of the
line.[1] It sailed under the command of the highly-regarded
Lieutenant-General the Count de Guichen at the beginning
of February—22 merchantmen, 39 transports, 200 officers
and 4,400 troops. A smaller convoy of 3 ships of the line, 17
or 18 merchantmen and transports, and 2 battalions of
troops which left Lorient for India in February was intercepted by the British with the loss of a ship of the line and
part of the troops.[2] De Guichen was more fortunate. He ar-

[1] This convoy was combined with the *Saint-Michel's* convoy of
merchantmen and its escort received as reinforcements two ships of
the line from Toulon and a third to which the crew of another ship
of the line from Toulon had been transferred. Spain 597: 82, 122,
Bessière to Vergennes, 10 January and 14 January 1780; B⁴215: 27,
untitled memoir of 11 January 1780; B⁸677: 45, Hector to Sartine,
19 January 1780; Spain 597: 157–158, Vergennes to Montmorin, 22
January 1780. Shortly after the convoy sailed, the *Conquérant* from
its escort was forced back to Brest by storm damage. Had Rodney
been off Brest the French would have had to run a heavy risk of
interception to leave the easily observed roadstead.

[2] E 205: unpaged, "Troops for Colonies"; B⁸682: 27, 31, 36–37,
Thevenard, port commandant at Lorient, to Sartine, 25 January, 7

rived safely at Martinique on 22 March, a few days before Rodney arrived to reinforce the British squadron at Saint Lucia. La Motte-Picquet had already left for Saint Domingue with 4 ships of the line to protect the departure of the returning trade,[3] so during the subsequent campaign de Guichen and Rodney each had 23 ships of the line. De Guichen and Bouillé attempted unsuccessfully to attack Barbados and Saint Lucia, but were foiled by Rodney against whom de Guichen fought three inconclusive battles.[4] Perhaps La Motte-Picquet would have given de Guichen the necessary margin of superiority for success, but Rodney was even more hampered. He eventually received ten ships of the line in reinforcement, but none of them arrived in time to be of use against de Guichen.[5]

The vital moment of the campaign and perhaps during the entire war came after de Guichen and Rodney's battles. On 28 April the promised Spanish convoy for the West Indies left Cadiz. It contained 146 merchantmen and transports and 11,000 troops with the weak escort of 12 ships of the line under Commodore José Solano. Had Rodney been able to capture the convoy, the loss of the irreplaceable matériel, ships, and troops and the psychological blow of another defeat would almost surely have knocked Spain from the

---

February, and 16 February 1780; Spain 598: 113, Vergennes to Montmorin, 13 March 1780; B⁴196: 184–186, instructions for Duchilleau, captain of the *Protée*, 31 January 1780. See also Section 1 of this chapter.

[3] La Motte-Picquet took 20 merchantmen with him to Saint Domingue. The *Fier* took another 65 merchantmen from Martinique to France via Saint Domingue and the *Tonnant*, 55–60 merchantmen from Saint Domingue directly to France. B⁴181: 65–66, La Motte-Picquet to Sartine, 13 March 1780; B⁴181: 76, La Motte-Picquet to Castries, 30 October 1780; B⁴145: 208–320, journal of the *Fier*. For other convoys see Dull: Dissertation, 326n.

[4] B⁴215: 39–49, instructions for Lieutenant-General de Guichen, 22 January 1780; B⁴180: 202–207, de Guichen to Sartine, 29 May 1780.

[5] Rodney had been refused another six ships of the line to initially accompany him. James, *British Navy in Adversity*, 194.

war.[6] Despite sickness which swept his fleet, Solano reached the passage between Dominica and Guadeloupe undetected and then was escorted into Guadeloupe by de Guichen (9 June 1780). It was too late for combined operations by the time Solano reassembled his convoy. They sailed north together at the beginning of July, Solano to Havana, de Guichen to Saint Domingue (with 2,000 troops for use by the Spaniards).[7] The campaign had been a stand-off but the troop reinforcements gave the Allies an overwhelming preponderance of troop strength in the West Indies. The British had less than 12,000 effectives in the Caribbean (including Jamaica), even though the acute Captain Charles Middleton, Comptroller of the British navy, had estimated that 15,000 troops would be necessary to defend the British possessions or to attack Martinique.[8] Without adequate troops British security in the Western Hemisphere was henceforth dependent on uninterrupted naval parity, if not superiority.

De Guichen left Saint Domingue in mid-August, leaving behind 9 ships of the line with Commodore the Chevalier de Monteil but accompanied by La Motte-Picquet and 93 merchantmen. At sea de Guichen opened sealed orders directing him to Cadiz.[9] His 18 ships of the line with their massive convoy arrived safely on 22 October.[10] The English

[6] Spain 599: 486, Montmorin to Vergennes, 18 July 1780; Spain 599: 16, Cadiz report of 28 April 1780.

[7] Spain 601: 394-408, Solano-de Guichen correspondence; Spain 600: 204-205, de Guichen to Sartine, 4 July 1780; Spain 599: 389-395, de Guichen to Sartine, 2 July 1780; B⁴180: *passim*; James, *British Navy in Adversity*, 215.

[8] *Sandwich Papers*, 3: 173-174. Middleton became First Lord of the Admiralty (as Lord Barham) in 1805. Between July 1779 and September 1780 British troop strength in the West Indies (including Jamaica) did rise from 8,119 to 11,153. Mackesy, *War for America*, 524-525.

[9] B⁴215: 154-159, new instructions for de Guichen, 4 May 1780; B⁴215: 169-170, Sartine to de Guichen, 8 June 1780; B⁴180: 225, 227-228, de Guichen to Sartine, 20 August and 30 July 1780. La Motte-Picquet's orders had been changed because his ships were expected to need repairs.

[10] Spain 601: 183-184, Bessière to Vergennes, 28 October 1780.

home fleet of 22 ships of the line, which might have intercepted him, was held at anchor by bad weather and sailed from Torbay only on 26 October.[11] With no vulnerable targets in North America and de Guichen's fleet needing repair, France had wisely chosen to regroup its forces to strike later in greater strength.

The British missed a similar opportunity in North America. As soon as de Guichen's squadron had sailed, the French began preparing a squadron and expeditionary force for North America.[12] Command of the expeditionary force was given to a veteran officer, Lieutenant-General the Count de Rochambeau, that of the escort to Commodore Ternay. From its initial 4,000 men it was increased by stages to 8,000, at the insistence of Rochambeau and the army ministry.[13] Unfortunately the shipping for so large a force could not quickly be found since de Guichen had already taken a large share of the available shipping. Thus, it was decided to divide the expeditionary corps into two parts. The initial component, comprising two-thirds of the corps, was ready to sail by mid-April, but was retained by contrary winds until 2 May. Its 5,500 troops (eight battalions of infantry and 500 of Lauzun's volunteers)[14] were escorted by seven ships of the line, two frigates, and two smaller warships.[15]

[11] *Sandwich Papers*, 3: 278.

[12] United States 11: 165–170, Vergennes to La Luzerne, 5 February 1780; Spain 598: 12–13, 14–15, Vergennes to Montmorin, 2 March 1780; B²417: 2, abstract of Sartine to Hector and La Porte, 29 January and 2 February 1780; B³677: 78, La Porte to Sartine, 2 February 1780.

[13] Jean-Baptiste-Donatien de Vimeur, comte de Rochambeau, *Mémoires militaires, historiques, et politiques de Rochambeau, ancien maréchal de France* (Paris: Fain, 1809), 1: 238; B³667: *passim*; Spain 598: 12–13, Vergennes to Montmorin, 2 March 1780; B⁴183: 9–11, 16–17, 32–33, Ternay to Sartine, 3 March, 8 March, and 22 March 1780; United States 11: 346–347, Vergennes to La Luzerne, 23 March 1780.

[14] See B³677: *passim* for its preparation. The second detachment was to contain four battalions of infantry, 300 of Lauzun's troops, and 200 artillerymen. The appearance of the British home fleet off the French coast killed hopes of sending this detachment.

[15] B⁴215: 104–113, instructions for Ternay, 24 March 1780. Ternay's convoy contained 32 transports and cargo ships. B⁴183: 47, La Porte to Sartine, 26 May 1780.

The Americans were desperately in need of such help. At the end of 1779 the British had sent 3,500 reinforcements to Georgia, enabling the British army to move again against Charleston. After a brief siege, Charleston surrendered on 12 May 1780 with ten regiments, 400 cannon, and three of the United States' seven frigates. By mid-August when the French auxiliary corps arrived to serve under General Washington, the Americans were reduced to a 10,500-man northern army under Washington's personal command and an 8,000-man southern army under Major-General Horatio Gates. Opposing them were over 30,000 crack British troops under Lieutenant-General Sir Henry Clinton and Lieutenant-General Charles Cornwallis.[16] On 18 August Gates was badly beaten at Camden, South Carolina by Cornwallis, further weakening the American war capacity.

The British wasted opportunities to intercept Ternay and Rochambeau at either end of their passage. Because of the refitting necessitated by its Gibraltar mission, the English home fleet was unable to leave port to blockade Brest until 8 June, long after Ternay was clear. The British did send six ships of the line under Rear-Admiral Thomas Graves to join Vice-Admiral Arbuthnot's four of the line at New York and cut off Ternay. Graves was delayed, however, by refitting, bad weather, and a dispute in his squadron over back pay and sailed only on 17 May.[17] By the time he reached New York (13 July), Ternay, thanks to his prudence in avoiding combat with a British squadron he met by chance off Bermuda, was already at Newport. The English were then too slow and cautious to attack Newport, giving Ternay time to successfully fortify his position.[18] Rocham-

[16] United States 13: 295–300, La Luzerne to Vergennes, 15 August 1780. Mackesy, *War for America*, 346 gives 33,819 British effectives as of July.

[17] *Sandwich Papers*, 3: 238–239, 269.

[18] United States 13: 128–136, La Luzerne to Vergennes, 23 July 1780; United States 13: 173–174, La Luzerne to Sartine, 27 July 1780; B⁴183: 41–42, Ternay to de Guichen, 3 August 1780. The British squadron was from Jamaica and was escorting a convoy clear of the approaches to the Caribbean.

beau and his auxiliary corps were left to winter peacefully at Newport.

Meanwhile, because of the departure of de Guichen at the beginning of the August to October hurricane season, the British had been left with a pointless preponderance of force in the Caribbean. Rodney brought 11 of his ships of the line to New York on the basis of faulty intelligence that de Guichen was headed to North America. He, too, made a dilatory exploration of attacking Newport, but left again in November without accomplishing anything. The ships he left behind were even less fortunate. Eight of the line were caught in a hurricane off Saint Domingue in October while escorting a convoy clear of Jamaica. Two were sunk, one driven toward England, and the remainder severely damaged. Another half-dozen ships of the line at Antigua and Saint Lucia were also damaged. Of the 33 ships of the line the British had finally assembled in the West Indies, only 13 were of use in 1781 for anything more than escorting returning convoys.[19]

The British also wasted a splendid opportunity in European waters. Their home fleet was now commanded by another ineffectual admiral, Francis Geary. It contained 24 ships of the line, including 11 of at least 90 guns, and was later reinforced by 4 more—sufficient strength to interdict all French coastal shipping as the British had done after 1759.[20] Not only did it fail to inflict major damage on French shipping, but it was even unable to intercept any of the French warships individually running the British gaunt-

[19] *Sandwich Papers*, 3: 161; 4: 126–131; Sir John Knox Laughton, ed., *Letters and Papers of Charles, Lord Barham, Admiral of the Red Squadron, 1758–1813* (London: Naval Records Society, 1907), 1: 69–78.

[20] *Sandwich Papers*, 3: 276–277. Geary's fleet would have been even stronger had not ten ships of the line been detached to the West Indies, six to North America, one to Jamaica, and at least one for convoy duty. Geary did capture three French frigates in July and August.

let to reach Cadiz, although any large scale movement of French ships proved impossible. Eventually, 6 ships of the line from Toulon and 10 from Brest and Rochefort reached Spain. By the end of the summer only seven ships of the line were left at Brest and although they were virtually inactive the port was not. It managed to convert enough old warhips into transports to carry 3,500 troops across the Atlantic.[21] At the beginning of September du Chaffault was ordered to disarm his tiny fleet so that his ships could be rearmed for the West Indies.[22]

For most of the summer it appeared that the large fleet assembled at Cadiz would accomplish no more than the fleet at Brest. Finally, on the last day of July, Lieutenant-General Córdoba sailed with a combined fleet of 33 ships of the line to protect the incoming trans-Atlantic convoys (hopefully including de Guichen's), which were being diverted from the Bay of Biscay to Cadiz.[23] On the night of 8–9 August the combined fleet, while cruising off the Azores, encountered a 67-ship British convoy for Jamaica and Saint Christopher, escorted by only one ship of the line and two frigates.[24] Thanks to British overconfidence in sending this defenseless convoy so close to Cadiz, the Allies captured 61 merchantmen worth £1,500,000. Córdoba reentered Cadiz

[21] Three old ships of the line, three frigates, and two large merchantmen were converted into transports. Du Chaffault's only military operation was the cruise of three ships of the line between 4 August and 15 August. B³678: 43, Hector to Sartine, 21 July 1780; B⁴174: 203, du Chaffault to Sartine, 26 July 1780; B⁴215: 201, untitled memoir of 28 July 1780; B³679: 102–104, La Porte to Sartine, 30 August 1780; B³678: 180, Hector to Sartine, 6 September 1780.

[22] B²419: 63, Sartine to Montlasan, 4 September 1780; B³678: 159–161, Hector to Sartine, 6 September 1780; B⁴215: 216, untitled memoir of 19 August 1780.

[23] For Córdoba's cruise see Spain 600: *passim*. Córdoba had put to sea for a week in mid-July because of false intelligence of a British fleet off Gibraltar. Spain 599: 448–450, 453–454, Montmorin to Vergennes, 12 July and 13 July 1780.

[24] Mackesy, *War for America*, 357; Spain 600: 164–165, Cadiz report of 17 August 1780.

on 29 August, leaving behind a small patrolling squadron.[25] In a month's cruise far from England he had taken a far greater prize than any taken by d'Orvilliers' fleet, which had cruised for three times as long during 1779.

4. The Dismissal of Sartine

Córdoba's victory hastened the end of the pretense that Spain was seriously negotiating with England. In April, Charles had notified the French that he intended to listen to England's terms and in June a British representative, Richard Cumberland, secretary of the board of trade, had arrived in Spain with his wife and two daughters.[1] The negotiations were a ludicrous masquerade—Cumberland was not empowered to offer any concessions and spent his time awaiting further instructions and acting conspicuous. Vergennes guessed, probably correctly, that the English desired the negotiations for reassuring public opinion and influencing the market,[2] and the Spaniards for putting pressure on France.[3] The affair was certainly an insult to the American representatives, who were told that Cumberland, who was fawned over while they were ignored, was in Madrid to arrange a prisoner exchange.[4] Vergennes feared

[25] Spain 600: 164–165, Cadiz report of 17 August 1780; B⁴175: 180, 184, Mongelas, French consul at Cadiz, who compiled the Cadiz reports, to Sartine, 22 August and 29 August 1780.

[1] For these negotiations see Spain 598, Spain 599, Spain 600, and Spain 601: *passim*; Bemis, *Hussey-Cumberland Mission*; Richard Morris, *The Peacemakers* (New York: Harper and Row, Harper Torchbooks, 1965), 43–66; Mackesy, *War for America*, 371–375; Conn, *Gibraltar in British Diplomacy*, 194–197; Madariaga, *Britain, Russia, and the Armed Neutrality*, 222–223, 226–228.

[2] Spain 599: 285, 407–408, Vergennes to Montmorin, 12 June and 6 July 1780.

[3] Spain 599: 474, Vergennes to Montmorin, 18 July 1780; Spain 600: 445–448, Montmorin to Vergennes, 11 September 1780.

[4] Vergennes, fearing the Americans would learn on their own of the negotiations, informed the American commissioners of them in July. Spain 599: 458, Vergennes to Montmorin, 14 July 1780. For the prisoner exchange story see Spain 599: 222–223, Montmorin to Vergennes, 1 June 1780.

that England would learn of Spain's economic and military difficulties through Cumberland,[5] but the fatuous Cumberland did no serious harm and when the British cabinet in October finally rejected Floridablanca's ultimatum to make a serious offer, the negotiations were effectively finished.[6]

At least Floridablanca was cooperative regarding Vergennes' desire to encourage the neutral powers to defend their right to trade with belligerents. Floridablanca quickly treated the Spanish seizure of the Russian ship (which had precipitated Catherine's proclamation) as an accident[7] and on 13 March 1780 issued new regulations governing merchant shipping.[8] Although these regulations were less liberal than France desired, the Spaniards promised henceforth to maintain great circumspection toward Russian, Dutch, and Swedish vessels passing through the Straits.[9] Further to placate Russia these regulations were provisionally suspended on 18 April 1780 except for certain articles.[10]

The French council over the summer continued discussions with Spain on the coordination of war strategy. The principal subjects of debate were whether the Spanish fleet should accompany the French Cadiz fleet back to France after the arrival of the West Indian convoy and whether it should then wait to see a new squadron for the West Indies

[5] Spain 599: 285–286, Vergennes to Montmorin, 12 June 1780.

[6] Mackesy, *War for America*, 371–375; Conn, *Gibraltar in British Diplomacy*, 196. British public opinion was opposed to ceding Gibraltar. Spain was not yet so weakened as to give up hope for Gibraltar (Spain 599: 225–226, Montmorin to Vergennes, 1 June 1780) and this hope was strengthened by the victory in August. Montmorin had long believed no serious negotiations would occur before the end of the campaign. Spain 598: 320, Montmorin to Vergennes, 29 March 1780.

[7] Spain 598: 377, Montmorin to Vergennes, 6 April 1780.

[8] Spain 598: 118, 302–305, 316–318, Montmorin to Vergennes, 13 and 29 March 1780; Spain 598: 185–194, Floridablanca to Castejon, 19 March 1780; Spain 598: 367–370, 371–374, Vergennes to Montmorin, 5 April 1780.

[9] Spain 598: 215, 377–380, Montmorin to Vergennes, 20 March and 6 April 1780.

[10] Spain 598: 425–431, 432–435, Montmorin to Vergennes, 15 April 1780; Madariaga, *Britain, Russia, and the Armed Neutrality*, 185.

clear of the coast. Even though the French named d'Estaing commander of the returning fleet to please the Spaniards and sent him to Spain to argue the French case,[11] the Spanish, afraid that their fleet would have to winter in Brest, successfully resisted.[12] At the end of August Sartine proposed that the French ships in Spain return without Spanish accompaniment, that the Brest fleet meanwhile be rearmed for the West Indies so that immediately upon d'Estaing's return a squadron of 9 to 13 ships of the line could be sent, and that a second squadron then be prepared for a later departure.[13] This proposal was slightly amended and sent shortly afterward to Spain.[14] Within a week the necessary orders had been sent to Brest.[15]

With this problem resolved the council might have expected a period of respite while awaiting de Guichen's return from the West Indies. Instead there exploded a crisis so severe as to cause a change in the composition of the council and threaten France's continued participation in the war.

[11] He would also bring de Guichen's ships. Spain 598: 461–462; Spain 599: 404–405, 420–427, Vergennes to Montmorin, 21 April, 6 July, and 10 July 1780; B⁴215: 244–251, memoir taken to Spain by d'Estaing.

[12] The Spaniards were willing to accompany d'Estaing to the latitude of Brest but not to enter the port. Spain 599: 478–484, Montmorin to Vergennes, 18 July 1780; Spain 600: 337, Floridablanca to Montmorin, 4 September 1780; Spain 601: 4–5, Montmorin to d'Estaing, 22 September 1780.

[13] B⁴215: 236–239, 240–243, untitled memoirs of 22 August 1780. The navy department had originally planned to send ten ships of the line to Martinique by 15 October and another 17 at the beginning of November. Spain 599: 291–293, memoir of navy department of May 1780; Spain 599: 289–290, Vergennes to Montmorin, 2 June 1780.

[14] Spain 600: 248–253, memoir of navy department of 25 August 1780; Spain 600: 313–314, Vergennes to Montmorin, 30 August 1780.

[15] See above, preceding section, Note 22. At some time prior to 24 September the council decided to send 4,500 recruits to the West Indies as well as the 3,000 regular troops previously planned. These recruits are mentioned in Spain 601: 15, memoir of 24 September 1780, sent by Vergennes to Montmorin, 28 September 1780. I have not found the orders to assemble shipping for them, although Brest was ordered to collect 6,000 tons of shipping for carrying supplies (the troops were to be carried on the converted warships). B⁴174: 60–63, Sartine to La Porte, 31 July 1780.

The crisis began on 12 September when Vergennes received from Floridablanca an incredible proposal for the coming campaign.[16] As Montmorin explained in his covering letter,[17] the Spaniards had now come to believe that only through the total commitment of resources to the Western Hemisphere could the stalemate with Britain be broken. Floridablanca now demanded that France send 12,000 troops and at least 20 ships of the line to the West Indies so that the Allies could undertake a massive combined expedition of 20,000 to 24,000 men and 46 to 50 ships of the line against Jamaica. Montmorin warned that Spain, impoverished and burdened by famine, was capable of only one more campaign. If France did not accept her proposals to end the war in one more campaign, she would have no other choice than to take all means possible to procure the least disadvantageous peace.[18] Floridablanca shortly thereafter also complained that the French plan of sending their squadron in two divisions would amount to committing their forces piecemeal.[19]

These unexpected demands created within the council the most serious crisis of the war. Such a proposal was comparable in scope to the attack on England. Not only was there insufficient shipping for so massive an operation,[20] but the costs would be prohibitive, since France's financial sit-

[16] Spain 600: 315–319, court of Spain to court of France, 30 August 1780; Spain 600: 367–379, Floridablanca to Aranda, 5 September 1780. Both were forwarded by Montmorin to Vergennes, 5 September 1780.

[17] Spain 600: 383–386, Montmorin to Vergennes, 5 September 1780. See also Spain 600: 222–224, Montmorin to Vergennes, 24 August 1780.

[18] Spain 600: 383–386, 440–444, Montmorin to Vergennes, 5 September and 11 September 1780.

[19] Spain 600: 453–455, extracts of Floridablanca to Aranda, 12 September 1780, sent by Montmorin to Vergennes, 28 September 1780. Floridablanca also wished the French squadron to accompany the reinforcements of 6,000 men and six ships of the line Spain intended to send from Cadiz to the Caribbean.

[20] The operation would require 60,000 tons of shipping, of which only one-third could be found in the Bay of Biscay. Spain 601: 33, Vergennes to Montmorin, 28 September 1780.

uation was hardly less desperate than that of Spain. On 26 September Sartine estimated that the other naval expenses for 1781 would be 175,000,000 livres.[21]

The council members were divided over whether the war could be continued. Maurepas, who had already been in contact with the British,[22] favored peace but he was probably alone among the king's chief advisers in this view. Nevertheless, only Vergennes' pleading prevented the king from following Maurepas' advice and informing Spain that France would sue for peace.[23] On 28 September France suggested a compromise proposal to Spain.[24] For lack of shipping and money, she could send no additional troops for an attack on Jamaica, but she would promise to send 20 ships of the line to Martinique by the end of December. France could attack Saint Lucia and Saint Christopher as a diversion for whatever operation Spain desired to undertake. Finally, Vergennes proposed sending more troops and 6 more ships of the line to North America by the first of April.[25] Privately the discouraged Vergennes admitted to Montmorin that the council was inclined to accept Russian mediation of the war and complained of Spain's commitment to direct negotiations with Britain.[26]

[21] B⁴215: 292–293, untitled memoir of 26 September 1780.

[22] Fortescue, *Correspondence of King George the Third*, 5: 103–104, North to George, 28 July 1780 (no. 3111).

[23] Memoirs and Documents, France 1897: 103, Vergennes to Louis, 27 September 1780.

[24] Spain 601: 15–19, memoir of 24 September 1780, sent by Vergennes to Montmorin, 28 September 1780; Spain 601: 32–37, 40–41, Vergennes to Montmorin, 28 September 1780.

[25] Vergennes suggested that the squadron for the West Indies rendezvous at Madeira with any forces Spain wished to send. France planned to send a supply convoy ahead to Martinique with one or two ships of the line. France would continue to place a detachment of troops at Spain's disposal for operations in the Gulf of Mexico.

[26] Spain 600: 39, 53–59, Vergennes to Montmorin, 28 September 1780. Count Panin, the Russian chancellor, had already floated a compromise peace proposal by which each of the American states would decide separately on independence. Vergennes wrote his ambassador in Saint Petersburg, ordering him to pursue the idea, but Catherine was not willing to commit herself. Madariaga, *Britain, Russia, and the Armed Neutrality*, 245–248; Morris, *The Peacemakers*, 169–172.

Despite Vergennes' fears the crisis was weathered. Necker was in favor of peace, but he was more interested in his own power and was able in November to secure an additional loan of 36,000,000 livres so the war could continue to be financed.[27] Although Floridablanca ill-naturedly cancelled the Spanish reinforcement to the West Indies planned under the Jamaican operation, he accepted the French plans for their own forces with remarkably mild complaints —indeed I strongly suspect he had deliberately overstated his case, probably to stimulate French naval activity and to score future points in strategy debates.[28] This might have been merely the most dramatic of a series of Franco-Spanish collisions about strategy had it not triggered a major change on the French council.

Before Vergennes received the Spanish reply on 16 October this change had been made. On 13 October Sartine, Vergennes' closest ally, was dismissed as naval minister; the following day he was replaced by a lieutenant-general of the army, the Marquis de Castries (1727–1801),[29] a protégé of Vergennes' enemies, Necker and ex-Foreign Minister Choiseul. By the end of the year Sartine's friend, War Minister Montbarey, was replaced by one of Castries' colleagues, Lieutenant-General the Marquis de Ségur.

Sartine fell for a variety of reasons. Ostensibly he was dismissed for circumventing Necker in obtaining 17,000,000 livres in loans to cover unappropriated expenditures.[30] Al-

---

[27] Witte, *Journal de l'Abbé de Véri*, 2: 303–304; Marion, *Histoire financière*, 1: 300. For Necker's contacts with the British see Fortescue, *Correspondence of King George the Third*, 5: 106, 163–164.

[28] Spain 601: 99–103, Montmorin to Vergennes, 9 October 1780; Spain 601: 104–106, Floridablanca to Aranda, 9 October 1780. Vergennes suspected that Floridablanca desired a French refusal as an excuse for him to make peace with England for both France and Spain. Spain 601: 38, Vergennes to Montmorin, 28 September 1780. See Spain 601: 224–225, 236, Montmorin to Vergennes, 30 October 1780.

[29] René de la Croix, duc de Castries, *Le maréchal de Castries (1727–1800)* (Paris: Flammarion, 1956), 70–77; Witte, *Journal de l'Abbé de Véri*, 2: 327, entry of 18 October 1780.

[30] Légoherel, *Les trésoriers généraux*, 338–340.

though this action of Sartine's was illegal, it was so sanctioned by custom that it could hardly account of itself for Louis' decision to dismiss him. In part Sartine did fall because his dismissal was crucial to Necker, who found in Sartine's action not only a challenge to the spending reforms he had sponsored but also an opportunity to change the composition of the council to his own political gain. Because of the budget crisis facing the court, Necker was able to use the threat of his own resignation to demand the removal of Sartine.[31]

Sartine was vulnerable to such an attack for a variety of reasons. The strategy of carrying the thrust of the war in foreign theaters had led to a long war, now in stalemate, and during the current campaign had contributed to the humiliation of the Brest fleet's open inability to protect the French coast. Public opinion blamed Sartine for France's failure to win a decisive victory and for the massive expenditures the war had required.[32] The addition to the council of Castries, with his wide contacts and excellent military reputation, was a strategic concession to the council's political opponents, particularly at court and among the military.[33] Sartine, moreover, was relatively expendable because of the expertise of Fleurieu at the naval ministry and the considerable experience of Vergennes and Maurepas in directing the war.

The crisis with Spain, however, was in my belief the chief

[31] Witte, *Journal de l'Abbé de Véri*, 2: 374–395, entries of 10 September to 11 October 1780; Spain 601: 222–223, Vergennes to Montmorin, 30 October 1780.

[32] Witte, *Journal de l'Abbé de Véri*, 2: 314–315, 325, 384, entries of 8 March, 3 August, and 1 October 1780. As early as December 1779, the Austrian ambassador in Paris reported Sartine's relations with the king deteriorating. Arneth and Geffroy, *Marie-Antoinette*, 3: 383, the Count de Mercy-Argenteau to Maria Theresa, 17 December 1779.

[33] Castries, *Le maréchal de Castries*, 70–77. Castries' son, the Count de Charlus, was married to the daughter of the Duke de Guines, the ex-ambassador to Britain and enemy of Vergennes. Before his appointment Castries was introduced to Marie-Antoinette, a useful political ally. Most important, however, were Castries' long friendships with both Necker and Choiseul.

reason for Sartine's fall. It split the cohesion of the Maure-
pas-Vergennes-Sartine political alliance which had so long
resisted the attacks of Maurepas' enemy Marie Antoinette,
Vergennes' enemy Choiseul, and the war's opponent, Necker.[34] Of even greater importance was the fact that since
January 1780 the Spaniards had treated Sartine as responsible for the Allied failure at sea.[35] To Spain, above all, was
Sartine sacrificed; her acceptance of the compromise operational plan, which might have acted as a reprieve for him,
arrived three days after his dismissal.

Sartine was misjudged by the Spaniards. The failure of
the French navy to win an immediate victory was the consequence of a strategy that was probably the only one
which could have achieved American independence. Sartine's failure was not in his capacity as naval minister but
in his shared reponsibility as a member of the council. If he
bears some of the responsibility for the consequences of an
ill-conceived war, he deserves, on the other hand, a substantial share of the credit for the successful direction of that
war. Except for Vergennes there was no more important
French architect of American independence.

Sartine was magnificently rewarded upon his dismissal,
even by eighteenth-century standards. He was created
Count d'Alby and given an exceptionally large gratification
and pension.[36] He did not again serve his ruler and died in

[34] Certainly Maurepas failed to support Sartine. Montbarey claimed
there was ill-feeling between the wives of Maurepas and Sartine, but
not between the ministers themselves. Montbarey, *Mémoires*, 3: 267.
Sartine was more moderate toward Necker than were either Maurepas or Vergennes. Witte, *Journal de l'Abbé de Véri*, 2: 374, entry of
27 September 1780. Sartine may have been somewhat deficient in the
cold-bloodedness necessary for survival at the French court.

[35] Montmorin claimed that Aranda was to blame for the Spanish
dislike of Sartine. Montmorin himself criticized Sartine to Vergennes,
however, and Vergennes failed to counter Aranda's criticism. Spain
597: 155; Spain 599: 118, 146; Spain 600: 411, Montmorin to Vergennes, 22 January, 12 May, 20 July, and 11 September 1780.

[36] *La Grande Encyclopédie* (Rennes: H. Lamirault, 1886–1902) 29:
537, states that the gratification was 150,000 livres and the annual
pension 70,000 livres. Loir, *La marine royale en 1789*, 69, claims the
annual pension was 50,000.

exile on 7 September 1801. His son, like his king, was a victim of the guillotine.

As Sartine was being sacrificed to Spain and the domestic opponents of the council, work was proceeding at Brest on the new squadron for the Western Hemisphere. The first of these ships began entering the roadstead of Brest the day before Sartine's dismissal.[37] Although they were not to sail for another five months they, the final legacy of Sartine's administration, were to be part of the squadron which won the campaign of Yorktown.

5. Castries as Naval Minister

The Marquis de Castries had been chosen naval minister much as an American presidential candidate is chosen—for his acceptability to a diverse group of factions. He brought to his office no more experience of naval affairs than had Sartine, but as a distinguished lieutenant-general in the army he found the naval officer corps already favorably disposed toward him. Certainly Castries possessed real merits —dedication, intelligence, decisiveness, a gift for organization, and like Sartine a concern for the individual French sailor. As a member of the council, however, Castries was less impressive than as a naval minister. His dedication to his work was accompanied by an inability to see beyond the needs of the service, his intelligence by arrogance, his gift for organization by inflexibility. Above all, Castries lacked the gift of compromise, the suppleness, the sense of subordinating means to a larger end needed for the conducting of diplomacy. Gradually the coolness between Vergennes and Castries turned to hatred.[1]

---

[37] B³678: 211, Hector to Sartine, 4 October 1780; B³678: 255, Hector to Castries, 29 October 1780; B⁵13: unpaged, "Etat de situation des vaisseaux. . . ," 10 December 1780. Eight ships of the line were in the roadstead by the end of October 1780.

[1] Library of the Ministry of the Navy, Ms. 182, "Journal du Maréchal de Castries" (actually written by the Countess de Blat—hereafter cited as "Castries' journal") 43, entry of 22 October 1780. For

The terrible risks of the European campaign of 1780 had helped to discredit not only Sartine but his ideas of strategy as well. With Sartine gone, the strategy of subordinating the European theater to the American came under reexamination. The French proposal of 24 September had dealt only with the detachments to be sent to the West Indies and North America. Beyond promising 25 ships of the line for the next campaign the proposal had been vague about plans for Europe.[2]

Shortly after his appointment the new naval minister assisted Vergennes, Maurepas, and Aranda at a conference concerning the course of future strategy. It was Aranda who reintroduced the possibility of an enterprise against England, although Vergennes suspected it was not Aranda's own idea. Whatever his past objections, Vergennes now wrote Montmorin that the situation dictated running all hazards to bring the war to a conclusion.[3]

Montmorin, too, was considering ways to end the stalemated war. Before he received this latest dispatch from Vergennes he confided his thoughts to his foreign minister.[4] They represent the first outline of the dispositions which led to Yorktown.

To Montmorin, America represented the major obstacle to peace, since England would abandon it only at the last extremity and since France could expect little help from Spain in the Americans' regard. With the exception of Jamaica no other victory could be decisive; and, moreover, in America the French could find local support. Mont-

---

a sample of the officer corps' feelings see B⁴193: 192, Captain d'Albert Saint-Hippolyte to Castries, 22 March 1781.

[2] Spain 601: 18–19, navy department memoir of 24 September 1780; Spain 601: 40–41, Vergennes to Montmorin, 28 September 1780. See also Spain 601: 105, Floridablanca to Aranda, 9 October 1780.

[3] Spain 601: 193–194, personal letter of Vergennes to Montmorin, 25 October 1780.

[4] Spain 601: 224–233, Montmorin to Vergennes, 30 October 1780. The same day Montmorin wrote another superb analytical memoir, which is given in Spain 601: 234–238.

morin advised sending to North America in May another expeditionary force and 10 to 12 ships of the line from the West Indies in addition to the ships and troops planned from Brest. As for Europe, Montmorin believed Floridablanca really desired an attack on Minorca, the second British base in the Mediterranean, for which he wished the support of at least 4 to 5 French ships of the line. These ships could winter at Cadiz.

It was not until the end of November that Vergennes replied. He mentioned three possibilities for ending the war. First was the attack on England suggested by Aranda, but prudence demanded that France wait until Spain formally made the suggestion.[5] Second was Montmorin's proposal for carrying the theater of war to North America, a proposal which Vergennes promised would receive the most serious attention of the council.[6] Finally, there was the hope still entertained by Vergennes that Russia would act as a mediator, although he realized that this was strongly opposed by Spain, which believed Gibraltar could more easily be extracted from England by direct negotiations.[7] Indeed, the futile Cumberland negotiations still dragged on, although Floridablanca had admitted to Montmorin their function was to make France more tractable toward Spain.[8] Vergennes ordered Montmorin to suggest to Floridablanca as a personal opinion the possibility of sounding out Russia. Vergennes, more confident than during the crisis of September and October, emphasized that France would not recognize the status quo as a basis for American peace unless driven by absolute necessity.

Along with Vergennes' letters came Castries' first memoir,

---

[5] Spain 601: 377–378, Vergennes to Montmorin, 27 November 1780. Floridablanca claimed he favored the idea, but Charles and Naval Minister Castejon were reluctant. Spain 601: 477–482, Montmorin to Vergennes, 26 December 1780.

[6] Spain 601: 382, Vergennes to Montmorin, 27 November 1780.

[7] Spain 601: 382–383, Vergennes to Montmorin, 27 November 1780.

[8] Spain 601: 275–279, Montmorin to Vergennes, 4 November 1780.

drafted for him by Fleurieu.[9] It left Spain to suggest the European operations for the coming campaign, but made one change in the proposal for American operations. The probability that 8 ships would be sent with Rear-Admiral Samuel Hood to the West Indies (as indeed they were) dictated that the French reinforce the 20 ships of the line for the West Indies. The 6 of the line for North America were therefore to be added to the West Indies squadron, which would escort 6,000 reinforcements to the Windward Islands. Part of the squadron would be used in North America during the following hurricane season, and part sent to Saint Domingue to aid the Spaniards. Those ships still seaworthy would rendezvous at Martinique at the end of October 1781 when hopefully they would be joined by still further reinforcements. No date could be fixed for the squadron's departure from Europe until d'Estaing arrived in French waters, but it was hoped that its preparation would take only six weeks. In fact d'Estaing's wind-hampered passage placed planning in suspension for the remainder of 1780. He sailed from Cadiz within a week of de Guichen's arrival but was forced back by bad weather. Sailing again on 7 November, d'Estaing spent nearly two months en route to Brest fighting contrary winds (but luckily neither the British nor disease).[10] The Spaniards sent 8 ships of the line to cover him, but they accompanied him only as far as Cape Saint Vincent, 150 miles from Cadiz.

The Spaniards were equally unwilling to commit themselves to a proposal for European operations. Although Floridablanca favored the British operation, Charles and his naval minister Castejon feared a repetition of the fiasco

[9] Spain 601: 365–372, navy department memoir sent by Vergennes to Montmorin, 27 November 1780. See also G 165: unpaged, Castries to Fleurieu, 14 November 1780; B⁴215: 295–299, 307–308, 317–325, rough drafts of the memoir above.

[10] D'Estaing, moreover, had left Cadiz with only 50 days of provisions. Spain 602: 11, Montmorin to Vergennes, 3 January 1781.

of 1779 and did not wish to leave Gibraltar uncovered.[11] Montmorin warned that France would have to make any proposals—again he pressed for shifting the focus of the war to North America.[12] Strategic planning for 1781 was still in suspension as 1780 ended, but December had brought major developments in other parts of Europe.

6. Developments in the North and East

In early December Versailles learned of the death on 29 November of Maria Theresa of Austria. Her co-regent, her son Joseph, thereby became sole ruler of the Hapsburg lands. Given the radical instability of his character, his undefined but grandiose ambitions, and the injury done him by France in 1778, the maintenance of peace on the Continent promised to prove more difficult, particularly should Joseph break up the Prusso-Russian alliance which had frustrated his ambitions two years before.

Russia was even more involved in the other developments. On 3 December the members of the League of Armed Neutrality officially notified France (along with the other belligerents) of the existence of their convention. Russia at the same time made a private insinuation (*insinuation particulière*) concerning possible mediation.[1] However much France was willing to accept Russian mediation this feeler would accomplish nothing without Spanish and British acquiescence. Vergennes wrote to Spain to coordinate a joint reply but he had little hope for British cooperation in negotiating peace.[2] Britain, however, soon would

---

[11] Spain 601: 522–525, Floridablanca to Aranda, 30 December 1780, copy given by Aranda to Vergennes, 8 January 1781; Spain 601: 477–482, 508–512, 522, Montmorin to Vergennes, 21 December, 27 December, and 30 December 1780.

[12] Spain 601: 510–511, Montmorin to Vergennes, 28 December 1780. The Spaniards did make a noncommittal response to Castries' proposals on 30 December 1780. See also Chapter Eight, Section 2.

[1] Spain 601: 455–456, Vergennes to Montmorin, 15 December 1780.
[2] *Ibid.*

have great need of a conciliatory gesture toward Empress Catherine because of the injury done by Britain to Catherine's diplomatic suitors, the Estates-General of the Netherlands.

The key to the military usefulness of the League of Armed Neutrality was the participation of the Netherlands, through whose ports and adjoining waters passed the trade of the Baltic powers.[3] Although Denmark and Sweden signed conventions with Russia over the summer, the Dutch hesitated to join the league for fear that England would respond to their adherence by seizing the Dutch overseas possessions—the Cape of Good Hope, Ceylon, the Dutch East Indies, and several possessions in the West Indies. Throughout the late summer and autumn the Estates-General tried unsuccessfully to extract from the empress a specific guarantee of their overseas possessions. On 15 October they began debate on acceptance on the Russian terms, already angered by the news that Admiral Rodney had violated the neutrality of the Dutch West Indian island of Saint Martin in order to seize American ships. On 20 November they voted to enter the league without qualification.[4] La Vauguyon, the French ambassador, congratulated himself on a diplomatic triumph and departed on leave for Versailles to discuss the offers of a secret agent who had promised to deliver him important English papers.[5] He grossly underestimated the English fear of the other neu-

---

[3] For France's Dutch policy and Dutch developments see Holland 540, Holland 541, and Holland 542: *passim* (detailed references are given in Dull: Dissertation, 341n.); Renaut, *Les Provinces-Unies et la guerre d'Amérique*, 310–367; Madariaga, *Britain, Russia, and the Armed Neutrality*, 231–232; Mackesy, *War for America*, 378–380.

[4] Holland 542: 340–343, La Vauguyon to Vergennes, 21 November 1780.

[5] In fact this was apparently part of an English plot to deceive France and to discredit the North cabinet's domestic opposition. Vergennes was too prudent to compromise himself. See Spain 599: 328–329, Vergennes to Montmorin, 22 June 1780; Holland 542: 48, Vergennes to La Vauguyon, 11 September 1780; Fortescue, *Correspondence of King George the Third*, 5: 101, 140, 146.

tral powers becoming involved in the Anglo-Dutch dispute over the right of carrying naval supplies. The English considered the importance of cutting the French North Sea artery for timber, masts, and copper so great that they were willing not only to go to war with Holland but also to run the risks of alienating the Russians. They moved immediately to open hostilities against Holland (20 December 1780) before the Dutch adherence to the league could be signed in Saint Petersburg, using as an excuse for war their knowledge of a draft convention from 1778 between the United States and a representative of the city of Amsterdam.[6]

In the long run this British move was probably a mistake. With Russian protection the Dutch might have been able to increase their commerce in naval matériel with France, but Catherine was not prepared to take serious risks and in any case the French had an inland route for their masts and alternate sources for their timber and copper.[7] England complicated her military problems by opening the North

[6] The treaty was among the papers of Henry Laurens, an American diplomat captured in September 1780 by the British while he was en route to negotiate a commercial treaty with the Dutch. The captured draft treaty had been authorized neither by the Estates-General of the Netherlands nor by the Estates of the Province of Holland and moreover was contingent upon Britain's prior recognition of American independence. Holland 542: 201–210, La Vauguyon to Vergennes, 24 October 1780. As early as July 1780 Vergennes feared that Britain would declare war on the Netherlands to forestall her entry into the League of Armed Neutrality. Holland 541: 309–310, Vergennes to La Vauguyon, 11 July 1780. Britain did not issue a formal declaration of war, but merely withdrew her ambassador and authorized reprisals against Dutch shipping and property.

[7] The French had ingeniously devised a system of moving masts by inland waterways and portaging from Amsterdam through the Austrian Netherlands to the Loire. The first masts reached Nantes in November 1780. Holland 539: 277–319, La Vauguyon-navy department correspondence; Holland 541: 30, 483–484, La Vauguyon to Vergennes, 9 May and 22 August 1780; Spain 600: 5, Vergennes to Montmorin, 21 July 1780; B²419: 63, Sartine to La Vauguyon, 16 September 1780.

Sea as a theater of war and her diplomacy by the need to placate Catherine.

In the short run, however, the Netherlands presented more opportunities as an enemy than she did as an ally. Her great empire extending from Surinam to the East Indies lay undefended and England moved to seize as many possessions as she could before the Dutch could protect them. Only seven Dutch ships of the line were able to sail to their aid and two of these were immediately captured.[8] The British shifted plans for a combined military and naval operation against South America to one against the Cape of Good Hope. The cabinet sent orders to Rodney to seize the West Indian island of Saint Eustatius which had been used for the last five years as a transshipment point for American supplies.[9]

When Vergennes wrote Montmorin to tell him of the opening of English hostilities against the Netherlands he admitted he didn't know whether France should be pleased or disturbed by the news. The Dutch, reposing in a false sense of security, had taken no steps for their own defense and Vergennes feared the "secret" English expedition was going to be sent to attack the Cape of Good Hope (thereby threatening French access to the Indian Ocean). However, if the Dutch responded to the English attack with courage,

---

[8] The *Nassau*, 64, and *Rotterdam*, 56, were ordered to Saint Eustatius, the *Nassau-Weilbourg*, 56, and *Princesse Marie-Louise*, 56, to Curaçao, and the *Amsterdam*, 64, *Princesse Caroline*, 56, and *Princesse Louise*, 56, to Spain, Portugal, and the Mediterranean to meet returning merchantmen. (Dutch ship names translated into French.) The *Rotterdam* and *Princesse Caroline* were captured in European waters by the British. The *Mars*, 60, was already at Saint Eustatius. Holland 542: 375–376, La Vauguyon to Vergennes, 28 November 1780, enclosure.

[9] Mackesy, *War for America*, 379–380; J. Franklin Jameson, "St. Eustatius in the American Revolution," *American Historical Review* 8 (1903): 698; Fortescue, *Correspondence of King George the Third*, 5: 173–174, minutes of cabinet meeting of 29 December 1780 (no. 3223).

enterprise, and increased unity, they might yet return blow for blow, above all by cutting off English trade in the North Sea.[10] For the Allies, all still hinged on maintenance of the initiative, on finding the proper spot to apply their thin margin of superiority, and on France's skill in coordinating the efforts of the disparate enemies England might yet scatter.

[10] Spain 601: 502–503, Vergennes to Montmorin, 27 December 1780. For Vergennes' previously expressed desire that France not have the responsibility of protecting the Netherlands see Holland 541: 15–16, 363–364, 468–471, Vergennes to La Vauguyon, 4 May, 27 July, and 19 August 1780.

CHAPTER EIGHT

1781—The "Annus Mirabilis"

1. The Dutch War's Diplomatic Consequences

THE British instigation of hostilities against the Netherlands on 20 December 1780 preceded by two weeks the signature of the Convention of Armed Neutrality by the Dutch plenipotentiaries in Saint Petersburg.[1] To insure, nonetheless, that their action would not be considered grounds for war with the League of Armed Neutrality the British could not merely rely on the technically accurate claim that the Dutch had not entered the league as a genuine neutral. The British resorted to a feat of diplomatic legerdemain which accomplished their goals but enormously complicated their future diplomacy, just as in a similar manner they complicated their military strategy by the Dutch War.

Britain was presented her opportunity by the private Russian insinuation concerning mediation which accompanied the announcement of the league to the belligerent parties in mid-December. Vergennes, as mentioned above, awaited Spain's response in order to coordinate the Bourbons' reply.[2] He considered the private insinuation to represent only an expression of Catherine's desire to contribute to peace and not a direct offer of mediation.[3] The British, however, saw an opportunity for themselves in Russia's declaration. Lord Stormont, now the secretary of state for the northern department, was acute enough to remember that more than a year previously Vienna also had mentioned officially its concern for peace. Russia as mediator would be

[1] Madariaga, *Britain, Russia, and the Armed Neutrality*, 238. The signing was on 5 January 1781, a few days before news of the Anglo-Dutch break reached Saint Petersburg. Holland 543: 145, 210, La Vauguyon to Vergennes, 23 January and 2 February 1781.

[2] Spain 601: 455–456, Vergennes to Montmorin, 15 December 1780.

[3] Spain 602: 96, Vergennes to Montmorin, 22 January 1781.

less likely to come to the aid of her nominal new ally, and the Austrians would temper any inclination of Catherine to impose her maritime principles on the belligerents. The British therefore announced that the king of England wished to return the marks of friendship of Vienna and Saint Petersburg by accepting the mediation of both imperial courts. The British then proposed Vienna as a site for the negotiations.[4]

The other parties involved were naturally surprised by the British action. The ambitious Joseph was flattered and pleased. Catherine, informed by the Austrians, accepted the mediation as a *fait accompli* without exposing her feelings.[5] Vergennes was forced into a difficult position. Either an acceptance or a refusal would have created "much inconvenience," so Vergennes sent a circumspect answer in order to gain some time.[6] Floridablanca, who suspected all of Europe of being opposed to Spain's acquisition of Gibraltar, was even less pleased by the mediation.[7] Floridablanca had, however, a weapon to combat the mediation—an old and battered weapon, but one that could serve a final time before being discarded. He ordered his ambassador in Vienna to inform Austrian Foreign Minister Kaunitz of the current state of the Cumberland negotiations and to explain that his Catholic majesty could not carry on both direct negotiations with England and those mediated by the imperial courts. The

[4] *Ibid.* Vergennes was incensed that Britain claimed that Spain and France had refused all negotiation. The British action was taken on 23 December 1780.

[5] Spain 602: 270, Vergennes to Montmorin, 2 March 1781; Madariaga, *Britain, Russia, and the Armed Neutrality*, 273–283. Madariaga, whose judgment is generally superb, inclines to the view that Catherine was more displeased than pleased at having the Austrians forced on her.

[6] Spain 602: 97–98, Vergennes to Montmorin, 22 January 1781. Vergennes praised Joseph's improved attitude toward France, but voiced suspicion of Prince von Kaunitz, his foreign minister.

[7] See Spain 602: 154, personal letter of Montmorin to Vergennes, 6 February 1781; Spain 603: 12–13, Montmorin to Vergennes, 1 April 1781.

decision on which negotiations to pursue would be left to England.[8] Floridablanca simultaneously made known very adroitly to the mediators that if the mediation took place, Spain would not consent to peace without the cession or exchange of Gibraltar.[9]

The English, thus presented with a countercoup, had no choice but to recall Cumberland. On 15 March Montmorin gave a safe conduct to Cumberland to pass through France and Cumberland took leave of Floridablanca to return to England.[10]

While France awaited the time when acceptance of the mediation could no longer be deferred, the foreign ministry was forced to perform a painful duty. Should the course of the current campaign, strong pressure by the mediators, or the ever-feared exhaustion of financial resources dictate a negotiated peace, France must decide the acceptable limits of such a settlement. Vergennes' first secretary, Rayneval, drafted a plan for such a contingency.[11] The heart of his memoir was the view that the United States could survive the loss of Georgia and the Carolinas but not the British retention of New York.[12] Far from planning to betray America, the Rayneval memoir represented the obstinacy of the French commitment since the British were not likely to surrender New York, the greatest naval base in North America,

---

[8] Spain 602: 144–149, Floridablanca to the Count d'Aquilar, 5 February 1781; Spain 602: 91–93, Floridablanca to Father Thomas Hussey (contact with Cumberland), 20 January 1781. In December 1780 Floridablanca had also used the existence of direct negotiations as an excuse to avoid mediation. Spain 601: 490–491, Floridablanca to Normandez, Spanish *chargé d'affaires* in Saint Petersburg, 23 December 1780.

[9] Spain 602: 301, Montmorin to Vergennes, 11 March 1781.

[10] Spain 602: 327–328, 337, Montmorin to Vergennes, 12 March and 15 March 1781. Cumberland left the Spanish court on 24 March.

[11] England, supplement 19: 216–223, untitled memoir of February 1781 in hand of Rayneval.

[12] Montmorin believed that if the British kept New York, Charleston, and a base in Chesapeake Bay, America would be independent in name only. Spain 602: 312, Montmorin to Vergennes, 12 March 1781.

unless forced to do so by severe military reverses. Vergennes later warned La Luzerne that necessity might force Louis to modify his commitment to the integrity of the thirteen states but that he would do so only in the last extremity. He cited the example of the Netherlands whose southern provinces were retained by Spain.[13] To Montmorin Vergennes admitted: "I do not fear to say in turn that it would perhaps be better to subscribe at present to a peace such as it is, rather than to have to be led to it by result of humiliations or by a total exhaustion."[14]

Simultaneously, Vergennes urged more vigorous conduct and better coordination between the Bourbons to avoid a bad peace. The campaign of 1781 luckily would prevent the need for Rayneval's concessions.

With the Cumberland mission ended the Bourbons were forced to finally accept the imperial mediation.[15] Now the belligerents had to wait while the co-mediators drafted the bases to serve for negotiation, a task requiring more labor than had Kaunitz' sanctimonious original proposal that no party should propose terms which they would not accept in the other's place.[16]

It was almost the end of May before the combined Austro-Russian proposal was sent to the belligerents. It called for parallel negotiations by the British with the Americans and with the other belligerents (both discussions to take place in Vienna) and for a year's general armistice based on the status quo in order to permit negotiations. Vergennes was opposed to the terms and in particular to an armistice which would give the British time to look

---

[13] United States 17: 234, Vergennes to La Luzerne, 30 June 1781.

[14] Spain 603: 47, Vergennes to Montmorin, 12 April 1781. By exhaustion Vergennes meant the exhaustion of financial resources, above all the exhaustion of credit.

[15] Spain 603: 23, Montmorin to Vergennes, 5 April 1781; Spain 603: 46–49, Vergennes to Montmorin, 12 April 1781.

[16] Madariaga, *Britain, Russia, and the Armed Neutrality*, 273. Floridablanca had demanded that firm bases for negotiation be established. Spain 602: 406, Floridablanca to Aranda, 23 March 1781.

for allies and to subvert the Americans.[17] Floridablanca suggested the Allies stall until August to await developments which might make the response easier.[18] By the time the Allies responded their reply was a matter of form, since England had already rejected Kaunitz' terms.[19] The Allies thereupon demanded a clear statement from Britain regarding the official character of the American agents and a set of mutually acceptable preliminary bases for the negotiations.[20] With these impossible demands the mediation reverted to a passivity which satisfied all the parties involved.

Although the mediation dominated the attention of the Allied diplomats, four other sets of Russian negotiations were in progress. Both England and Holland courted the active participation of Russia in their war—England by the clumsy use of Minorca as a bribe, Holland by the appeal of justice. Catherine prudently rejected both suits.[21]

The third negotiation was more successful. Joseph II was able to negotiate a secret defensive alliance (dated 2 June 1781) with Russia, which in fact established the grounds for a mutual attack against the Ottoman Empire. The negotiations were delayed by a question of protocol which served

[17] Spain 603: 222–225, Vergennes to Montmorin, 31 May 1781.

[18] Spain 603: 313–316, Montmorin to Vergennes, 11 June 1781.

[19] Spain 604: 205–207, Montmorin to Vergennes, 7 August 1781.

[20] Spain 604: 35–41, project of response, sent by Vergennes to Montmorin, 6 July 1781; Spain 604: 249–251, Vergennes to Montmorin, 17 August 1781.

[21] Madariaga, *Britain, Russia, and the Armed Neutrality*, 283–312. Vergennes had hoped that Russia would relieve France of the necessity of defending the Dutch. Spain 602: 103, Vergennes to Montmorin, 22 January 1781. Catherine decided at the end of March 1781 to accept the British argument that the hostilities bore no relationship to the League of Armed Neutrality. Only on 19 May were the Dutch told that Catherine would "make efforts" on their behalf before the conclusion of a general peace. Holland 543: 50–51, 103–104, 276–279, 359–362, 393–396, La Vauguyon to Vergennes, 9 January, 15 January, 9 February, 1 March, and 8 March 1781; Holland 544: 214–215, Vergennes to La Vauguyon, 14 May 1781; Holland 544: 365, Berenger, French *chargé d'affaires* in the Netherlands, to Vergennes, 15 June 1781.

as a reason for their ostensible failure. Although Vergennes did not learn of the secret treaty he well suspected the enormous danger to the stability of Eastern Europe and to the territorial integrity of the Ottoman Empire, a valuable French ally.[22] The Russo-Austrian rapprochement of course was even less welcome to Russia's continued nominal ally, Prussia; to reinforce her position she negotiated with Russia a convention regarding her entry into the League of Armed Neutrality (19 May 1781). Vergennes continually admonished that the European situation could only deteriorate while the American war continued.[23] His prediction would take only a year to be confirmed.

2. Planning the Campaign of 1781

At the beginning of 1781 the French council faced three difficult strategic problems: the possible renewal of the invasion of England, the addition of the Dutch Empire to the Allies' sphere of responsibility, and planning the operations of the great squadron fitting for the Western Hemisphere.

On 3 January 1781 d'Estaing's huge fleet finally arrived at Brest, giving the French 47 ships of the line in Atlantic ports for allocation to the various theaters of war.[1] Drafting the campaign plan, however, required six weeks. Planning was slowed by Vergennes' ill-health[2] and by the necessity of reconciling the council's desire for the invasion of England with the lack of sailors and transports for an invading army.[3] Vergennes finally forwarded the campaign plan to Montmorin on 14 February. He defended its caution by

[22] Spain 605: 293, 523–524, Vergennes to Montmorin, 6 November and 20 December 1781.

[23] Examples are Spain 602: 186; Spain 603: 223–224, Vergennes to Montmorin, 14 February and 31 May 1781.

[1] Spain 602: 24, Vergennes to Montmorin, 7 January 1781.

[2] Spain 602: 134, Vergennes to Montmorin, 30 January 1781. Vergennes suffered among other things from rheumatism.

[3] Spain 602: 65, Vergennes to Castries, 12 January 1781, with annotations by Castries.

telling Montmorin that Castries preferred attempting less than the maximum to promising more than could be done.[4] He added a warning that if Spain failed to cooperate in Europe, France would have to withdraw her forces from the Western Hemisphere, which would endanger the Spanish Empire.

Castries' memoir[5] began with a summary of the previous correspondence concerning the coming campaign—the French proposals of the previous September (to send 20 ships of the line to the West Indies and 6 to North America) and November (to first send the ships for North America to the West Indies) and the Spanish reply of 30 December (which agreed in theory to a diversion against Jamaica and to the attack on England but questioned the means to be used). Castries then dealt with the three critical strategy questions.

He made only brief mention of the Dutch problem. The six additional vessels once planned for North America were now to be dropped entirely from the squadron for the Western Hemisphere. Castries hinted that perhaps Louis would find that since the declaration of war by England against Holland there would be a better destination for this squadron.

Castries also dealt only briefly with the squadron for the Western Hemisphere. He feared that it would arrive too late in the West Indies to accomplish anything before the hurricane season, but the 6,000 men and supplies it was to convoy were so important as to leave Castries no choice but to send them. Castries, however, believed:

> that it is appropriate to extend the powers of the commanders, not to limit them at all, and to leave them the masters, if they find nothing useful to attempt in the Antilles, of abandoning them (after having provisioned them)

[4] Spain 602: 185–186, Vergennes to Montmorin, 14 February 1781.
[5] Spain 602: 234–259, navy department memoir of February 1781, sent by Vergennes to Montmorin, 14 February 1781.

. . . in order to take the greatest part of [the squadron] to the waters of North America in order to second the enterprises which the Americans wish to form or to make an attempt on the Gulf of St. Lawrence if it is opportune.[6]

Castries thought that nothing positive could be decided before France learned what projects Spain planned in the Gulf of Mexico to which any French operations would be subordinate. At the end of the campaign the French squadron would return to the West Indies to meet a new squadron coming from Europe.

The bulk of Castries' memoir was devoted to the European campaign. Castries offered the Spaniards the choice of two plans—either the invasion of England or the covering of the Channel until the new squadron left in October for the West Indies. The French, however, could no longer provide the transports for an army of 30,000 men.[7] Unless the Spaniards provided transports for 15,000 men, the largest operation that could be mounted against England would be a set of raids of uncertain advantage using 15,000 troops carried aboard the warships of the combined fleet. The French contingent of the fleet would be ready about the beginning of June but would have to return to port by 15 September for the refitting of the ships for the West Indies. In any case Castries requested the Cadiz fleet be sent to Galicia or to Brest before the English fleet was ready for sea.

It appears that Castries' memoir was largely an acknowledgment that the invasion of England was hopeless—Castries finally was able to convince the council that there was no longer the available shipping for an invasion (al-

[6] *Ibid.*, 239–240.

[7] Castries claimed that part of the transports had been destroyed, part armed as privateers and part dispersed among the Channel ports. Even if ships could be provided, sailors were not available to man them. France hoped that Spain could use as transports the merchantmen Córdoba had captured the previous year in which case France could find 20,000 tons of shipping to carry artillery and supplies. See also Spain 602: 369, Castries to Vergennes, 16 March 1781.

though Vergennes continued for another month to hope the project could somehow be saved). The memoir placed the onus of suppressing the project on the Spaniards and applied pressure on them to send their fleet to the Channel. Much discussion of this proposal still lay ahead.

At least Vergennes quickly succeeded with the Dutch. Other than sending a warning to the Cape of Good Hope and India, Vergennes initially had been unable to help them. The immediate necessity was protection of the Cape of Good Hope, which in English control would virtually close the Indian Ocean to France. Even before the end of 1780 Vergennes guessed that four ships of the line and 3,000 troops would be shifted by Britain from an attack on South America to an attack on the Cape.[8] Nevertheless Vergennes had to tell La Vauguyon that France could do nothing about the Cape until the Estates-General of the Netherlands made its will known.[9] Vergennes did promise to send two frigates to the Azores to conduct to safety an incoming Dutch East India Company convoy. This action contributed to Dutch confidence in France. The East India Company immediately petitioned that the French squadron for India stop en route at the Cape and the matter was also referred to a secret committee of the Estates-General.[10] Without entering into details the Estates-General adopted the instances of the company relative to its establishment at the Cape and expressed to France its hope for further protection.[11]

France was now free to act. On 2 March Vergennes in-

[8] Spain 601: 502, Vergennes to Montmorin, 27 December 1780. The British cabinet in fact decided on the shift two days later. Mackesy, *War for America*, 379–380. See also Spain 602: 105, Vergennes to Montmorin, 22 January 1781.

[9] Holland 543: 265, Vergennes to La Vauguyon, 8 February 1781; Spain 602: 185–186, Vergennes to Montmorin, 14 February 1781.

[10] Holland 543: 302–310, La Vauguyon to Vergennes, 17 February 1781. Five of the six Dutch ships safely reached Cadiz. Holland 544: 408, Vergennes to La Vauguyon, 21 June 1781.

[11] Holland 543: 323–326, La Vauguyon to Vergennes, 20 February 1781.

formed La Vauguyon that four ships of the line and 1,500 men would leave France for the Cape about 20 March, and that orders would be sent to Île de France to send there its squadron and 1,500 more troops. Vergennes did not expect the English squadron for the Cape to sail until the end of March.[12]

The Spanish reply to Castries' memoir arrived on 8 March.[13] They requested that the entire French West Indian squadron stop at Point Guarico or Cape François to ascertain Spain's plans after which, if not needed, they could proceed to North America (even to Halifax). Floridablanca merely requested that the local Spanish commanders be notified when the French squadron returned to the West Indies at the end of October or the beginning of November.

As usual, Spanish accommodation regarding the Western Hemisphere (where Spain needed France) was not matched by similar cooperation regarding Europe (where France needed Spain). As France surely must have expected, Floridablanca reported that Spain, far from being able to provide transports for 15,000 French troops, was using rented foreign transports herself. (Spain, however, did at least offer to share the costs of renting ships.) Floridablanca regarded raids as neither dignified nor useful and a cruise off the English Channel as useless since alternative routes could be used by English shipping. He suggested an enterprise in the Mediterranean and a cruise off the Azores as diversions to occupy the English. He requested a delay of a month to a month and a half before Charles had to decide about sending the Cadiz fleet to Brest or Ferrol.

Montmorin reported that unless the Spaniards wished to attack Jamaica or had lost Vera Cruz or Caracas they

---

[12] Holland 543: 374–376, Vergennes to La Vauguyon, 2 March 1781.

[13] Spain 602: 258–261, Floridablanca to Aranda, 1 March 1781; Spain 602: 296–298, Vergennes to Castries, 10 March 1781. Vergennes had already received Spain 602: 230–233, Montmorin to Vergennes, 28 February 1781, previewing Floridablanca's memoir.

would not need the French West Indian squadron. Reinforcements from Mexico had increased the army at Havana to 15,000–18,000 men. The Spaniards were waiting to decide on European operations until the long-anticipated next attempt by the British to reinforce Gibraltar (off which the Cadiz fleet had been cruising since 6 February).[14] Montmorin expected a decision before the end of April. He believed that Charles wished the invasion but if the operation were canceled Charles promised to occupy part of the English forces. Charles hoped that if the Dutch occupied another part of them, France would have sufficient strength to invade England by herself.

The day that the Spanish dispatches arrived Castries left Versailles to oversee the dispatch of the long-delayed squadrons for the West Indies and the Cape. Their preparation had taken substantially longer than the six weeks originally planned, despite the presence at Brest of Groignard, the chief engineer of the navy.[15] Only on 8 March was the last of the ships of the line conducted into the road.[16]

Another major problem had been the higher command. First, de Guichen turned down command of the port of Brest, leaving the command to Commodore Hector, the port's ex-director general.[17] Commodore La Touche-Tréville, named in 1780 to command the West Indian

---

[14] Spain 602: 166, Montmorin to Vergennes, 11 February 1781.

[15] B³698: 7–15, journal of 17 January 1781 to 5 March 1781, is very probably his. See B³698: 39, Hector to Castries, 12 January 1781; B⁴216: 181–182, Castries to Hector, 10 January 1781. Hector continually complained of the bad weather at Brest, although Vergennes told the Spaniards in February that the work was not being delayed, and that the workmen were working until 10:00 P.M. B³698: *passim*; Spain 602: 189, Vergennes to Montmorin, 14 February 1781.

[16] B⁵18: unpaged, "Etat de situation des vaisseaux actuellement en armement au port de Brest," 13 May 1781.

[17] B⁸14: unpaged, sheets for February 1781. De Guichen was of course entitled to command of the West Indian squadron. The evidence is inconclusive as to whether he was actually offered the command, but it is my guess that he was being promoted out of a sea command and resisted it. Du Chaffault was now probably regarded as either too old for sea command or too rash for it.

squadron, also submitted his resignation (ostensibly for reasons of health, but at least partly under duress because the command was felt by the council to be too large for him).[18] The veteran de Grasse, who had returned from the West Indies because of ill health in 1780, was finally selected.[19] He arrived only on 25 February. De Grasse's second-in-command, the brilliant La Motte-Picquet, had to be replaced because of an attack of gout by the less-experienced Commodore Bougainville.[20] The Chevalier de Suffren, the commander of the Cape squadron whose abilities had been mentioned long before by Vergennes,[21] only reluctantly agreed to serve in the distant theater of the Indian Ocean.[22] Finally, Commodore the Count de Barras had to be sent by frigate to North America to relieve Ternay who was seriously ill.[23]

On 13 March Castries arrived at Brest. He soon received supplementary instructions from the council. First were some changes in de Grasse's orders.[24] Should de Grasse discover no profitable employment in the West Indies he was to send one of his frigates to the Spaniards to find out their plans and needs and then to divide his forces. He was however to leave no more than 12 or 14 of his 29 ships of the

[18] B⁸14: unpaged, sheets for February 1781; "Castries' journal," 56–58, entries of 1 February 1781 and following; B⁴216: 187–188, Castries to La Touche-Tréville, 17 February 1781. La Touche-Tréville was promoted to lieutenant-general and given a decoration in recompense.

[19] De Grasse was promoted to lieutenant-general, effective upon sailing. He was selected partly because he could get along with Bouillé. "Castries' journal," 56–58, February 1781.

[20] B⁴216: 201, Castries to Vergennes, 16 March 1781; "Castries' journal," 61–62, March 1781. Castries was not displeased; La Motte-Picquet did not get along well with de Grasse.

[21] Spain 600: 105, Vergennes to Montmorin, 11 August 1780.

[22] B⁴216: 194–195, Castries to Hector, 4 March 1781.

[23] B⁴216: 190, Castries to Barras, 16 February 1781. In fact, Ternay had died on 15 December 1780. Barras sailed aboard the frigate *Concorde* on 26 March 1781. See below, Section 5.

[24] Spain 602: 296–298, 299, Vergennes to Castries, 10 March 1781 with enclosure; Spain 602: 339–342, Vergennes to Montmorin, 15 March 1781.

line[25] with the Spaniards, as it was vital to disengage the French squadron blockaded at Rhode Island. Vergennes suggested that Castries leave de Grasse as much latitude as possible.[26] Second, Castries received orders for Commandant Hector to prepare a supplementary squadron of 6 of the line to reinforce the Cadiz fleet if the French ships could sail before the English.[27] These orders were sent to circumvent a request of Aranda that the Cape squadron stop at Gibraltar en route. Vergennes soon had more news to send to Castries. About 14 March Vergennes learned that the British home fleet had sailed on 9 March to relieve Gibraltar.[28] Vergennes was forced to stall Aranda who requested the entire de Grasse-Suffren squadron be sent after it. Vergennes also received intelligence about the expeditionary force for the Cape which accompanied the British fleet to sea. The intelligence was planted by the British secret agent who had won over Ambassador La Vauguyon. He attempted to convince the French that this force was going directly to India;[29] instead he unwittingly convinced

[25] De Grasse would bring 20 ships of the line from France, pick up four more at Martinique, and meet Monteil's five at Saint Domingue. In fact, de Grasse found six of the line at Martinique and four at Saint Domingue. See Appendix H.

[26] Castries recommended to de Grasse that he reserve the right to give the squadron for North America the superiority circumstances might render necessary. B⁴216: 199–201, Castries to de Grasse, 17 March 1781; B⁴216: 201, Castries to Vergennes, 16 March 1781. See also B⁴216: 196–198, Castries to Vergennes, 11 March 1781, urging the importance of de Grasse's presence in American waters. En route to Brest Castries met Colonel John Laurens, sent by the Continental Congress to ask more aid of France. Laurens frightened Castries into believing the Americans in danger of collapse—a danger which must have seemed very urgent since the council had received on 4 March the report from La Luzerne of a revolt of Pennsylvania troops in Washington's army. United States 15: 72–75, La Luzerne to Vergennes, 11 January 1781.

[27] Spain 602: 296–298, 300, Vergennes to Castries, 10 March 1781 with second enclosure.

[28] Spain 602: 330–333, Aranda to Vergennes, 14 March 1781. Actually the British fleet sailed only on 13 March.

[29] Holland 543: 400–401, La Vauguyon to Vergennes, 8 March 1781; Holland 543: 428–429, Vergennes to Castries, 12 March 1781. From a

Castries to add a fifth ship of the line to Suffren's squadron.[30]

By 19 March the squadron and convoy was ready to sail. On 22 March the wind was favorable and the huge assembly of ships sailed—156 merchantmen and transports, 26 ships of the line, and 8 smaller warships bound for the West Indies, the Cape and the Indian Ocean, North America (including the *Sagittaire*, 50, as convoy escort), Africa, and South America.[31]

3. The Maintenance of the European Alliances

Military historians are generally so infatuated with the sound of cannon that the development of strategy and the fighting of battles often appear synonymous. Battles not fought are often just as critical, the untouched convoy or escaping fleet often a great defeat for the opposing strategist. By these criteria the British reinforcement of Gibraltar in April 1781 was one of the war's decisive operations. Even without the accompanying 5 small ships of the line for the Cape (commanded by Commodore George Johnstone), Vice-Admiral George Darby's fleet of 28 of the line was overwhelmingly superior in cannon to the combined French squadrons of 26 of the line which sailed from Brest. Had it sailed on 13 March to blockade Brest, it would have had an excellent chance of meeting the French squadrons encumbered by their massive convoys. Instead, Darby was off Ireland awaiting the provisioning ships for Gibraltar from Cork while de Grasse and Suffren were passing safely to the

---

separate source Vergennes received both a list of the ships in the squadron and the intelligence that the Cape was going to be attacked. England 543: 44–46, Portsmouth reports, 9 March 1781.

[30] B⁴216: 205–206, Castries to Souillac and d'Orves, 17 March 1781; B⁴216: 206, Castries to Suffren, 17 March 1781. Suffren was ordered to sail directly to the Cape, but was to remain there only long enough to disembark troops before continuing to the Mascarene Islands.

[31] B⁸14: unpaged, sheets for March 1781.

south.[1] Darby's slowness cost him a second opportunity. A quick passage might have given him a chance to meet the outgunned 30 ships of the line of the Cadiz fleet off Gibraltar and the opportunity to knock the Spanish navy out of the war. The Spanish fleet, however, had orders to return for supplies and repairs during the bad weather period expected around the spring equinox;[2] it entered Cadiz on 30 March,[3] almost two weeks before Darby's unimpeded arrival at Gibraltar.[4] Darby returned to Spithead only on 22 May, dangerously late if his detachments were to affect the vital campaign being fought against the squadron of de Grasse he had failed to intercept.

For such strategic ineptitude the British cabinet could have no excuse. The blockade of Gibraltar was so loose that with a willingness to accept occasional losses it could have been replenished by unescorted merchantmen.[5] The West Indies could have been rendered safe for an entire campaign by merely forcing de Grasse's squadron to wait until the whole Brest fleet was ready to cover his departure (for Darby hardly needed to fear the Spaniards coming so far north alone). Had de Grasse sailed only in May or June, he would have had to sail directly to North America, which could easily have been protected by detachments from Europe as well as the Caribbean. Moreover, even against all the ships in Brest the British could have fought in June at no worse a disadvantage than 35 ships of the line to 45

[1] Mackesy, *War for America*, 388–389.

[2] Spain 602: 403, Montmorin to Vergennes, 23 March 1781.

[3] Spain 602: 425, Cadiz report of 30 March 1781.

[4] Spain 603: 59, Cadiz report of 13 April 1781, sent by Montmorin to Vergennes, 19 April 1781.

[5] Montmorin had reported the arrival of sufficient merchantmen to reprovision Gibraltar. See Spain 601: 484; Spain 602: 286–287, 315, Montmorin to Vergennes, 21 December 1780, 8 March 1781, and 12 March 1781. I strongly suspect that political expediency may have been partially responsible for the cabinet's decision. Public opinion prized Gibraltar far more highly than did the cabinet. For Sandwich's defense see *Sandwich Papers*, 4: 318–319, 347–348, parliamentary inquiries into the state of the navy, 1782.

(as incoming convoy escorts were added to Darby's fleet) and at an even smaller disadvantage in number of cannon.[6] Vergennes described Gibraltar as an excellent ally of England (because it commanded the interests of Spain);[7] at this crucial moment, however, Gibraltar was the best ally of France.

The relief of Gibraltar, even though probably unnecessary and certainly unwise, did, however, produce one result favorable to England. The failure of France to send six ships of the line to the relief of Gibraltar produced another crisis in her touchy relationship with Spain.

Floridablanca, who accused France of wishing the assistance of the Spanish fleet only in order to aid separate French peace negotiations, had demanded the six ships of the line as a display of good will and to strengthen the Spanish fleet for its passage north.[8] The French agreement to send them was gratefully acknowledged at the beginning of April.[9] Castries did make an effort to get the ships to sea. On 18 March he wrote to offer their command to La Motte-Picquet, his health permitting, and promised they would be ready by the first days of April.[10] Upon Castries' return to Versailles he learned, however, that Darby was at sea and had passed the Isles of Scilly on 20 March.[11] By the time the squadron was ready to sail the English had a lead impossible to overcome and the council postponed its departure.[12] Floridablanca had already found an excuse for keeping the Cadiz fleet far to the south of England—the Vera Cruz trea-

[6] Note too that the British would have had the advantage of not having a convoy to protect. Spain 602:306 gives Montmorin's view.

[7] Spain 602: 315, personal letter of Montmorin to Vergennes, 12 March 1781.

[8] Spain 602: 325–328, Montmorin to Vergennes, 12 March 1781. Montmorin naturally denied the accusation. He told Vergennes that he believed Spain actually was only interested in protecting the Cadiz fleet.

[9] Spain 603: 9, Montmorin to Vergennes, 1 April 1781.

[10] B⁴216: 207–208, Castries to La Motte-Picquet, 18 March 1781.

[11] B⁴216: 211, Castries to Hector, 28 March 1781.

[12] Spain 603: 51–52, Vergennes to Montmorin, 12 April 1781.

sure fleet was expected in July or August and he wished the Cadiz fleet to sail to the Azores to meet it.[13] The failure of the French to reinforce the Cadiz fleet doomed all Montmorin's hopes of changing Floridablanca's mind, despite his threat of withdrawing French forces from the Western Hemisphere.[14]

Vergennes now faced a crisis on two fronts. Not only had military cooperation with Spain reached its lowest point yet, but Necker, Vergennes' most dangerous political opponent, was pushing (with Castries' support) for a seat on the council.[15] The situation, however, was less dangerous than it appeared. Necker had overreached himself by appealing to French public opinion and the seat on the council was denied him; this time his threat to resign was called.[16] With Necker's resignation Castries lost much of his political influence as well.

Floridablanca gave Vergennes an exit from his other difficulty. At the same time Floridablanca conveyed to Montmorin Charles' refusal to send the Cadiz fleet north, he spoke of an attack on Jamaica after November.[17] Spain planned to send six more ships of the line and 3,000 to 4,000 more troops to Havana. With another ten ships of the line an attack on Jamaica would be possible. Montmorin warned Vergennes that it would take ten years to change Charles' mind about the Cadiz fleet. Montmorin believed cooperation with Spain in America would be in France's interest.

[13] Spain 602: 425, Cadiz report of 30 March 1781; Spain 603: 7–8, 38, Montmorin to Vergennes, 1 April and 9 April 1781.

[14] Spain 603: 50–51, Vergennes to Montmorin, 12 April 1781; Spain 603: 85–97, Montmorin to Vergennes, 24 April 1781.

[15] "Castries' journal," 68–72, 11 May to 15 May 1781. Castries also acted as an intermediary between Choiseul and the queen. B⁴216: 162, Castries to Marie Antoinette, 6 March 1781.

[16] "Castries' journal," 73–77, 16 May to 19 May 1781.

[17] Spain 603: 92–97, Montmorin to Vergennes, 24 April 1781. It is possible that Floridablanca had been frightened by the French threats of withdrawing their forces from the Western Hemisphere—threats confirmed by Aranda. Spain 603: 111–113, personal letter of Montmorin to Vergennes, 25 April 1781.

Like all successful diplomats Vergennes combined consistency of ends with flexibility of means. As in 1780, France had to concede to Spain's desires to protect the blockade of Gibraltar, but, unlike the previous year, Spain's proposal for an attack on Jamaica was also feasible enough for France's acceptance. On 17 May Vergennes forwarded a memoir of Castries which largely subordinated France's European campaign to the desires of Spain.[18] The Brest fleet would be ordered to join the Cadiz fleet for its Azores cruise while Darby was revictualing. In order for France to support the Spanish attack on Jamaica, however, the warships, convoy, and troops which must leave for the Western Hemisphere (preferably after the autumn equinox) would need Spanish protection. Castries asked how much support they could expect and the dates for the union off the Azores, the reentry into Brest, and the departure for the West Indies. Vergennes added his own reflections. Vergennes reassured Montmorin that Louis did not blame him for the lack of success with Spain. Vergennes feared that 40 English ships of the line would contain 70 Allied ships of the line (22 French, 30 Spanish, 18 Dutch). Rather than submitting to that humiliation the council had sought a way of uniting the Allied forces indirectly and without compromising the Spanish navy. Louis was disposed to help the Spanish Jamaican operation with 15 ships of the line and 4,000 troops. This was dependent on a safe reentry of the Atlantic fleet (since the necessary supplies for the West Indies could not be assembled in a Mediterranean port). Finally, Vergennes stressed the importance of a quick reply.

As Vergennes awaited the Spanish answer he had news to cheer him. While Darby was at Gibraltar the western approaches to England and France were clear. Castries or-

[18] Spain 603: 191–192, navy department memoir of 15 May 1781; Spain 603: 194–197, Vergennes to Montmorin, 17 May 1781; Spain 603: 98–101, draft of navy department memoir, no date. The additional forces offered by France were in response to a recommendation by colonial minister Gálvez.

dered La Motte-Picquet (his gout cured by a chance at independent command) to sea for a month. A courier would be sent from Cadiz to Brest to warn him when Darby left Gibraltar.[19] La Motte-Picquet took 6 ships of the line to sea on 25 April. Barely two weeks later he returned with 23 prizes, including the bulk of a rich convoy bringing the booty of Saint Eustatius, which had been captured with £ 3,000,000 of goods by Rodney on 3 February.[20] The *Actif*, 74, had become separated, but she too arrived safely after fighting one of Darby's ships of the line.

Vergennes also received the encouraging news that Suffren had overtaken Commodore Johnstone's five small ships of the line en route to the Cape. Suffren had attacked Johnstone's squadron at La Praya Bay at the island of Santiago in the Portuguese Cape Verde Islands.[21] The news from India was encouraging as well. Commodore d'Orves had sailed in October 1780 to the aid of Haidar Ali, the ruler of Mysore who had gone to war with the British in July 1780.[22]

The Spaniards were unusually quick to respond to Vergennes' proposals. On 5 June Montmorin forwarded the replies.[23] The Spaniards would cover the return of the French fleet to Brest at the end of August, provided that

[19] B⁴216: 221, Castries to La Motte-Picquet, 22 April 1782. Less pleasing news also came from Brest—the accidental burning of the *Couronne* on 1 April while she was being prepared for service.

[20] *Sandwich Papers*, 128. See Section 5 of this chapter for the capture of Saint Eustatius. Vergennes forwarded the news of La Motte-Picquet's triumph in Spain 603: 175–176, Vergennes to Montmorin, 12 May 1781.

[21] Spain 603: 208, Montmorin to French Ambassador O'Dunne at Lisbon, 26 May 1781. Although Suffren had violated Portuguese neutrality on 16 April by attacking Johnstone, no serious diplomatic consequences resulted.

[22] Spain 603: 162, Montmorin to Vergennes, 10 May 1781. The news of his destruction of a 4,000-man British force in September 1780 reached Europe about this time. Mackesy, *War for America*, 391; Spain 603: 206, Vergennes to Montmorin, 25 May 1781.

[23] Spain 603: 265–273, Montmorin to Vergennes, 5 June 1781; Spain 603: 213–215, Floridablanca to Montmorin, 28 May 1781; Spain 603: 244–249, Floridablanca to Aranda, 4 June 1781.

ten French ships of the line, including the three-deckers, would then accompany them to Cadiz for the winter. The Spanish fleet would not enter Brest, since the Spaniards believed the new squadron for the West Indies could safely sail without their protection. Provided that nothing unforeseen would have happened, Charles had no objection to the new combined fleet looking for the English fleet the following spring, if necessary even to the coast of England. Four or 5 Spanish ships of the line and 15 French ships of the line added to the Spanish fleet already at Havana should suffice for the Jamaican expedition.[24]

The Spanish offer was not completely satisfactory, but it at least meant a safe return for the Brest fleet and a chance to momentarily menace British trade. The council quickly decided that rather than joining the Spanish fleet off the Azores the Brest fleet (under de Guichen's command) would instead sail to Cadiz to which Córdoba had returned after a brief Atlantic cruise (2 May to 8 June).[25] Two or three of the fleet thereupon would be detached to India. In September the combined fleet would return to Brest, at which time a dozen ships of the line would enter Brest to be prepared for the Western Hemisphere, two others would enter Brest to be armed as transports, and the remaining seven or eight (including five of the three-deckers) would return with the Spaniards to Cadiz. The Cadiz fleet would be gradually reinforced as ships returned from the Western Hemisphere (the nine West Indian holdovers

---

[24] The Spaniards also warned that they might have to send reinforcements to Buenos Aires if Johnstone were headed for South America. Indian revolts, which the Spaniards feared had been fomented by the British, had broken out in the districts of Santa Fé (now Colombia) and Peru. The Santa Fé rebels capitulated on 5 June 1781. Spain 603: 259–262.

[25] Spain 603: 327, 329, navy department memoirs of 15 June 1781; Spain 603: 353–356, 361, Vergennes to Montmorin, 18 June 1781; Spain 603: 357–360, navy department memoir, no date; Spain 603: 347–349, Castries to de Guichen, 17 June 1781. The *Majesteux* also was ordered to Cadiz (from Toulon).

from 1780 and three from North America).[26] To avoid dissatisfaction among the French officers the number of ships to enter Brest and the plans to winter at Cadiz were not included in de Guichen's orders. Vergennes hoped that rather than returning immediately to Cadiz the combined fleet would wait at sea or at Ferrol or La Corogne to cover the sailing of the American reinforcements.[27]

On 22 June de Guichen sailed for Cadiz with 18 ships of the line.[28] Darby might have refitted his fleet in time to intercept him but fears for a huge Jamaican convoy caused him to split his fleet (unnecessarily since the convoy had already been successfully diverted around the north of Scotland).[29] The last element in the European campaign was the Dutch fleet, whose performance had thus far been extremely disappointing. The Dutch managed to arm for the summer campaign only half of the 18 ships of the line to be placed in service in Dutch waters and even these entered service only gradually between April and July.[30] Had a good proportion actually entered the North Sea, it could have cut the English trade with the Baltic and intercepted a convoy of German mercenaries which sailed from the Weser. The Dutch navy was so fearful of an English squadron entering the North Sea that the squadron of 1 ship of

[26] The figures anticipate the addition to the combined fleet of the *Brave* and *Argonaute*, launched at Rochefort in June. See B⁴216: 233–234, Castries to de Guichen, 24 May 1781.

[27] Vergennes was also able to provide Montmorin some details of Suffren's battle at La Praya. Johnstone was unable to follow Suffren, who now had at least a 15-day lead in the critical race to the Cape.

[28] The *Illustre* and *Saint-Michel*, destined ultimately for India, sailed from Rochefort for Spain on 21 July.

[29] *Sandwich Papers*, 4: 9–10, Mackesy, *War for America*, 395–396.

[30] See Appendix H. For Dutch estimates see Holland 543: 65–73, 74, La Vauguyon to Vergennes, 12 January 1781, with enclosure. The army was also to be increased to 50,000 or 60,000 men. For La Vauguyon's changing estimates of Dutch naval capabilities see Holland 543: 109–110, 334–335, 452–453; Holland 544: 26–31, 55–60, La Vauguyon to Vergennes, 15 January, 23 February, 16 March, 6 April, and 13 April 1781.

the line and 4 frigates that finally sailed to intercept British trade reentered port after less than three weeks at sea.[31] The Dutch fleet lay paralyzed in port until in June its admirals were summoned to The Hague. At the end of June La Vauguyon was able to report that they had been ordered to sail from the Texel on 12 July to intercept English commerce.[32]

4. The European Campaign

At the beginning of March, Floridablanca had suggested a diversion in the Mediterranean as Spain's contribution to the European campaign. Other than Gibraltar there was only one target in the Mediterranean: Fort Saint Philip on the British-held island of Minorca. Although Minorca did not have Gibraltar's strategic value it served as a center for large-scale privateering (as, in the West Indies, Saint Eustatius did for smuggling). Fort Saint Philip had been captured in 1756 due to the incompetence of its commander (but returned to Britain at the end of the Seven Years War); its present commander was a fine soldier, and the great fortress was manned by over 2,000 troops.[1] Although a landing could easily be made on the island, Montmorin believed 15,000 to 20,000 troops would be necessary to capture the fort.[2] Vergennes believed the capture of the fort impossible unless there were treason;[3] Castries also doubted it could be taken a second time.[4] Discussion about

---

[31] Holland 544: 179, 255, La Vauguyon to Vergennes, 11 May and 29 May 1781. An English squadron finally did sail for the North Sea on 5 June. See Section 4 of this chapter.

[32] Holland 544: 430–440, 451–460, La Vauguyon to Vergennes, 25 June and 29 June 1781.

[1] Mackesy, *War for America*, 524–525.

[2] Spain 602: 307, Montmorin to Vergennes, 11 March 1781. Montmorin noted that the Spaniards couldn't provide that many troops for an attack.

[3] Spain 602: 342, Vergennes to Montmorin, 15 March 1781. Vergennes told Montmorin he wasn't opposed to the attack.

[4] Spain 602: 368–369, Castries to Vergennes, 16 March 1781.

Mediterranean operations ceased until after the two courts reached agreement in June about European operations, but mysterious preparations continued at Cadiz.[5] On 24 May Montmorin reported that transports were being hired to transport 8,000 men for some expedition—Montmorin guessed Minorca but did not press the Spaniards.[6] On 22 June the expeditionary troops were embarked and on 26 June the Duke de Crillon arrived at Cadiz. Three days later Crillon informed Vergennes of his appointment to command a secret expedition.[7] The expedition now awaited the union of the combined fleet to cover its departure.

De Guichen made an exceptionally rapid passage to Cadiz, arriving on 6 July.[8] There were two other important arrivals—a packetboat with reassuring news that Buenos Aires was quiet despite a serious Indian revolt in Peru, and an American merchantman with news of an important Allied victory.[9]

The hurricane of October 1780 had disrupted a Spanish expedition against Pensacola, the major British post in West Florida.[10] Pensacola with its protected harbor provided an access for the British navy and British trade into the Gulf of Mexico and thereby endangered the tight control of Spain over her American empire. On 28 February 1781 a new expedition of 1,300 troops sailed from Havana with a

[5] The Spanish interest in Minorca was heightened by leaks of the British offer of Minorca to Russia. See Madariaga, *Britain, Russia, and the Armed Neutrality*, 301–302.

[6] Spain 603: 204, 325–326, 373, Montmorin to Vergennes, 24 May, 14 June, and 19 June 1781. See also Spain 603: 163, Montmorin to Vergennes, 10 May 1781.

[7] Spain 603: 379, 397, news of Cadiz and Algeciras, 14 June and 26 June 1781; Spain 603: 410–411, Crillon to Vergennes, 29 June 1781. Crillon had been a French lieutenant-general before transferring to the service of Spain.

[8] Spain 604: 91, Montmorin to Vergennes, 12 July 1781. The *Majesteux* arrived from Toulon on 2 July.

[9] Spain 604: 8–9, Montmorin to Vergennes, 2 July 1781; Spain 604: 86, Floridablanca to Aranda, 12 July 1781. See Section 3 of this chapter, Note 24.

[10] B⁴184: 304, extract of a letter from Havana, 28 November 1780.

ship of the line and two frigates.[11] By the end of March the expedition had been reinforced by 900 troops from Mobile (captured by the Spaniards in 1780) and by 1,338 troops from New Orleans and outnumbered the British by over two to one. The Spanish, however, feared that the British would send a naval force to rescue the garrison. In mid-April, the reported sighting of 8 ships of the line to the west of Cuba caused the Spanish to send 11 ships of the line and 1,500 more troops from Havana.[12] This squadron was accompanied by Commodore Monteil's 4 ships of the line, which had come to Havana in January to help protect the arrival of the Vera Cruz treasure fleet. Monteil accompanied the Spaniards even though they had failed to menace Jamaica as promised and even though the English were blockading over 50 French merchantmen at Saint Domingue.[13] Monteil contributed 800 soldiers and sailors from his squadron to the final attack.[14] An explosion destroyed a key redoubt and the British garrison surrendered on 9 May. It remained to be seen if combined operations in Europe would be as successful.

The new combined fleet of 49 of the line sailed from Cadiz on 21 July for the Azores, and then for the Isles of Scilly.[15] Two days later Crillon sailed for Minorca with almost 7,500 troops aboard 85 transports escorted by 2 ships of the line and 6 frigates.[16] Neither encountered major opposition.

[11] Spain 603: 117, Montmorin to Vergennes, 25 April 1781.

[12] N. Orwin Rush, *Spain's Final Triumph over Great Britain in the Gulf of Mexico: The Battle of Pensacola, March 9 to May 8, 1781* (Tallahassee, Fla.: Florida State University Press, 1966), 32–33; B⁴184: 280–283, Solano, commanding the squadron, to Castejon, 18 May 1781; B⁴181: 230–231, Monteil to Castries, 27 April 1781.

[13] Spain 603: 27–28, Montmorin to Vergennes, 5 April 1781; Spain 603: 77–78, Vergennes to Montmorin, 20 April 1781; Spain 603: 161, Malaga report, 7 May 1781; B⁴184: 285–287, operational summary, no date.

[14] B⁴184: 232, Monteil to Castries, 27 April 1781.

[15] Spain 604: 149–151, personal letter of Montmorin to Vergennes, 26 July 1781.

[16] Spain 604: 144–147, bulletin of the island of Minorca, 23 July to 24 August 1781; Danvila, *Reinado de Carlos III*, 5: 180 and facing page.

Darby with 21 of the line had escorted clear 3 ships of the line for North America and then established a cruise off Cape Finisterre. The approach of the combined fleet forced him to retreat to Torbay, where he arrived on 25 August and quickly established a defensive position. For ten days the combined fleet had absolute command of the western approaches to the British Isles; luckily for Britain it made no important prizes.[17] On 3 September the 19 French ships of the line separated for Brest while the Spaniards began their return to Cadiz. For two months Vergennes and Montmorin had attempted to rectify their failure to obtain a commitment from Charles that Córdoba would cover the outbound fleet for Jamaica. Charles was too fearful of seeing January 1780 repeated to permit his fleet to enter Brest; La Corogne was too small to hold the fleet and Ferrol was useless because of the prevailing autumnal winds.[18] Without Spanish protection the council had no choice but to bring into Brest the French contingent for Cadiz. Only when the Jamaican squadron sailed would it proceed to Cadiz.

The Spanish campaign in the Mediterranean was far more productive. Crillon's passage took almost a month, but when he landed on 23 August he achieved almost complete tactical surprise. The Spaniards captured a gigantic amount of matériel, including 180 cannon and 150 ships; nearly half of the island's garrison was almost cut off before it could retreat to Fort Saint Philip.[19] Floridablanca had already

---

[17] *Sandwich Papers*, 4: 9–13. Darby sailed again only on 15 September.

[18] Spain 604: 52–53, 55–56, 91–97, 100–101, 242–246, 291–292, Montmorin to Vergennes, 6 July to 20 August 1781; Spain 603: 357–360, navy department memoir of 18 June 1781; Spain 604: 75–79, Castejon to Córdoba, 9 July 1781; Spain 604: 86–90, 279–284, Floridablanca to Aranda, 12 July and 20 August 1781; Spain 604: 252–259, Montmorin to Floridablanca, 18 August 1781; Spain 604: 227–231, 262–263, 358–361, Vergennes to Montmorin, 10 August, 19 August, and 5 September 1781; B⁴216: 262, Castries to Hector, 1 September 1781.

[19] Spain 604: 353–354, Montmorin to Vergennes, 3 September 1781; Spain 604: 144–147, bulletin of the island of Minorca, 23 July to 24 August 1781; Spain 604: 315–316, second bulletin of the island of Minorca, 25 August to 7 September 1781.

promised to send 4,000 of the Spanish expeditionary force to the West Indies if the French would send troops to Minorca to replace them (with the indirect threat that otherwise the Spaniards would send no reinforcements to Havana).[20] The French council agreed to send the troops to Minorca and committed itself to provide the 15 ships of the line and at least 4,000 troops (hopefully from Saint Domingue) for the Jamaican expedition.[21] At the same time it again attempted unsuccessfully to pressure the Spaniards into protecting the departure of the convoy by exposing the necessary alternative of having de Guichen's entire fleet enter port.

If the failure to win Spanish consent to remain near the Bay of Biscay broke up the combined fleet, at least the future held promise of Allied cooperation in the Caribbean and Mediterranean. The French commitments to the Jamaican expedition were satisfactory to Floridablanca; planning for Jamaica now chiefly awaited information as to de Grasse's intentions after his return from North America.[22] The offer of troops for Minorca was gratefully accepted; the initial success convinced the Spaniards to undertake a formal siege of Fort Saint Philip with 12,000 troops.[23]

Even the Dutch accomplished more than had been expected of them, although the British continued to control

---

[20] Spain 604: 149–151, personal letter of Montmorin to Vergennes, 26 July 1781; Spain 604: 169–172, Floridablanca to Aranda, 27 July 1781. Montmorin believed the 4,000 reinforcements for Havana necessary for the success of the attack on Jamaica. Floridablanca estimated that no more than 6,000 Spanish and 2,000 French troops were still available for the attack (because of losses from disease).

[21] Spain 604: 227–231, Vergennes to Montmorin, 10 August 1781. See also preceding section.

[22] Spain 604: 260, 276–285, Floridablanca to Aranda, 20 August 1781.

[23] Spain 604: 353–354, 384–385, Montmorin to Vergennes, 3 September and 10 September 1781. Initially Floridablanca had spoken only of destroying privateers and blockading the fort. Spain 604: 169, Floridablanca to Aranda, 27 July 1781.

the North Sea. A British squadron of six of the line had entered the North Sea at the beginning of June. The Dutch fleet met it two weeks after it finally sailed from the Texel on 20 July.[24] Their battle has been enthusiastically applauded by subsequent historians for the high proportion of sailors aboard both squadrons killed or maimed. The capitals of Europe including Versailles were impressed that the Dutch had shown a courage hitherto not shown by their admirals[25]—unduly impressed since after the return of the fleet the admirals resumed directing the navy as they had before the battle. When the Dutch fleet attempted to sail again in September to escort their convoy it accomplished nothing beyond the grounding and loss of a newly-repaired 72-gun ship.[26]

The campaign in Europe had not been as barren as Vergennes and Montmorin had feared. It had been of critical importance as news from America would soon demonstrate. Of their three dozen ships of the line in European waters the British had detached only three to America because of the menace of the Spanish, French, and Dutch squadrons to their coasts and trade. Without further reinforcements the British squadron in North America had finally sacrificed the parity in naval strength on which the safety of the scattered British army depended.

[24] Holland 545: 129, La Vauguyon to Vergennes, 24 July 1781; *Sandwich Papers*, 4: 18–21. The Dutch fleet was escorting a convoy, which was forced to turn back after the battle. The day following the battle, the *Hollande*, 64, foundered.

[25] Holland 545: 325, Vergennes to La Vauguyon, 16 August 1781. At this time the Estates of Holland were debating a proposal for common operations with France, but Vergennes temporarily discouraged the idea because of the lateness of the season. Holland 545: 111–112, La Vauguyon to Vergennes, 20 July 1781; Holland 545: 208–211, Vergennes to La Vauguyon, 30 July 1781.

[26] Holland 545: 46–49, 60–68, 135–138, La Vauguyon to Vergennes, 14 September, 18 September, and 28 September 1781. Contrary winds finally forced abandonment of the attempt. The ship lost was the *Prince Guillaume*, 72. With the convoy were seven 50s of the East India Company.

5. De Grasse's Campaign

De Grasse sailed unimpeded from France largely because of the deficiencies of strategic vision and political courage of Sandwich and his colleagues. His safe arrival at Martinique was the result of deficiencies in the character of Admiral George Rodney who commanded the larger opposing British squadron. In response to cabinet orders sent upon the declaration of war with the Netherlands, Rodney captured Saint Eustatius on 3 February 1781. With it came £3,000,000 in booty and Rodney stationed the Martinique blockading force to leeward in order to better cover its dispatch to Britain aboard the convoy later captured by La Motte-Picquet. Since Rodney remained at Saint Eustatius with a detachment, the British squadron, commanded by Rodney's second-in-command, Rear-Admiral Samuel Hood, was missing 4 of its 22 of the line. Then, since de Grasse was not intercepted to windward, de Grasse's 20 ships of the line were reinforced by 4 more from Martinique. With this advantage de Grasse beat off Hood and brought his huge convoy safely to Fort Royal.[1]

Although de Grasse had made a quick passage (22 March to 6 May) he had only six weeks for operations in the Windward Islands. He split his forces in order to simultaneously attack Saint Lucia and Tobago. When Saint Lucia proved too heavily garrisoned to be stormed,[2] de Grasse reunited his forces at Tobago which surrendered on 2 June before Rodney could rescue it. De Grasse returned to Fort Royal and on 5 July sailed for Cape François, Saint Domingue in company with the Martinique trade. When he arrived after an eleven-day passage Monteil's squadron was waiting for him.[3]

---

[1] *Sandwich Papers*, 4: 127–131; Daniel A. Baugh, "Samuel Hood: Superior Subordinate," in George Athon Billias, ed., *George Washington's Opponents* (New York: William Morrow and Co., 1969), 302–304.

[2] Spain 604: 129–130, Vergennes to Montmorin, 20 July 1781.

[3] In accordance with his instructions, de Grasse had sent a frigate to Havana to announce his intentions. Spain 604: 231, Vergennes to

De Grasse's arrival at Saint Domingue began the major phase of the most important and most perfectly executed naval campaign of the age of sail.[4] The campaign might be said to have begun far earlier, only four days after the departure of de Grasse from Brest, when the frigate *Concorde* sailed from Brest for Boston and Newport. Aboard the *Concorde* was Commodore Barras, who was to command the squadron at Newport. The *Concorde*, however, also brought disappointing news for the American Congress. Ever since the second division of Rochambeau's troops had been cancelled because of the British blockade, the Congress had hoped that in 1781 reinforcements would be sent to Rochambeau.[5] After long consideration the council decided not to send reinforcements because of their cost, because of doubt as to their utility, and because of fear the Americans would mistrust a large foreign army in their country.[6] Instead the council offered 6,000,000 livres worth of military supplies and credit as a subsidy for Washington's army and promised to send part of de Grasse's fleet north—the number of ships to depend on the consultation to be held at Saint Domingue with the Spaniards. Rochambeau was now ordered to actually incorporate his corps into Washington's army.

The *Concorde* arrived at Boston on 6 May and continued immediately to Newport. Ambassador La Luzerne had al-

---

Montmorin, 10 August 1781. See also Spain 602: 339, Vergennes to Montmorin, 15 March 1781.

[4] It was perhaps rivaled by the campaign of Nelson which led to Trafalgar, but differed from it in that no single leader can be found whose genius explains its success.

[5] These hopes were unduly encouraged by La Luzerne. Cf. United States 14: 151–153, Vergennes to La Luzerne, 22 October 1780; United States 16: 3–16, La Luzerne to Vergennes, 20 March 1781; United States 16: 35–40, La Luzerne to Congress, 23 March 1781.

[6] United States 15: 154–155, Lafayette to Vergennes, 30 January 1781; Spain 602: 186, Vergennes to Montmorin, 14 February 1781; Spain 602: 314, Montmorin to Vergennes, 12 March 1781; United States 15: 326–330, untitled memoir of 8 March 1781; United States 15: 341–344, Vergennes to La Luzerne, 9 March 1781. Vergennes recommended that *only* Washington be told of French military plans. La Luzerne and Rochambeau were even more cautious, not even informing Washington. See below.

ready written Vergennes of the discouragement caused by the rumors that the second division would proceed first to the West Indies.[7] The Americans had ample grounds for discouragement. The situation of the northern colonies was no longer as dangerous as it had been at the start of the year when part of Washington's army had revolted. The situation in the south, however, remained critical. At the beginning of the year the British had made a lodgment in Chesapeake Bay, and two attempts by detachments from the Newport squadron to destroy it had failed. The American army had detached 800 regulars under Lafayette to join the Virginia militia; they had barely saved Richmond from some 2,500 British.[8] The American position was precarious and was about to become worse since General Cornwallis, abandoning his attempt to reconquer North Carolina, was marching unopposed to Virginia.[9]

The decision not to reinforce Rochambeau's army was, however, to La Luzerne more than recompensed by the promise of naval assistance. In this the ambassador agreed with Washington, who in sending his aide Colonel John Laurens to France to ask further assistance, had emphasized naval superiority more than troop reinforcements.[10] La Luzerne wrote Barras and Rochambeau to urge immediate help for the southern colonies. La Luzerne believed it urgent that French naval forces and appropriate land forces be sent to the Chesapeake in order to counterbalance the discouragement which would be caused by the cancellation of the second division of troops.[11] Before his

[7] United States 16: 219, La Luzerne to Vergennes, 19 April 1781.

[8] Louis Gottschalk, *Lafayette and the Close of the American Revolution* (Chicago: University of Chicago Press, 1942), 222–227.

[9] Cornwallis rendezvoused with the Virginia force on 20 May, and assumed command from Benedict Arnold. He had marched from Wilmington, North Carolina, on 25 April with about 1,500 troops. Mackesy, *War for America*, 406–408.

[10] United States 15: 86–87, Washington to Laurens, 15 January 1781. See also Section 2 of this chapter, Note 26.

[11] United States 16: 314–320, La Luzerne to Barras and Rochambeau, 20 May 1781; B⁴191: 159–160, untitled memoir, no date, Barras

letter could reach them, Washington and Rochambeau held a conference at Wethersfield, Connecticut (21 to 23 May 1781).[12]

For reasons of secrecy Washington was told only that de Grasse was coming to the West Indies, so Washington and Rochambeau discussed combined naval and land operations only as a theoretical possibility. The conference ended with the decision that upon the arrival of the *Sagittaire*'s convoy at Boston, Rochambeau would put his corps at the disposal of Washington in order to probe the defenses of New York.[13]

If Rochambeau evacuated Newport, Barras had been ordered by Castries to move his squadron to Boston where it could be adequately protected. Barras was readying his squadron for departure when he learned (probably from a merchantman) that de Grasse had reached Martinique. At the urging of Rochambeau, Barras called a conference of naval and army officers aboard the *Neptune* on 8 June. They unanimously decided that the squadron should run the risk of remaining at Newport (protected by American militia) where it would be easier to join de Grasse.[14]

Within a week Rochambeau received a critical letter from de Grasse, written at sea on 29 March.[15] The letter

---

papers. The weakness of the American position in 1781 is shown dramatically by the instructions of Congress to their peace commission (selected at France's urging) to undertake no negotiations without French concurrence (15 June 1781) and by their orders to John Jay to offer the relinquishment of American claims to the navigation of the Mississippi River in exchange for a Spanish alliance with the United States (15 February 1781).

[12] The fullest account of the conference is Douglas Southall Freeman, *George Washington* (New York: Charles Scribner's Sons, 1952), 5: 286–290.

[13] *Ibid.*; Rochambeau, *Mémoires*, 1: 273.

[14] United States 15: 329–330, untitled memoir of 8 March 1781; Rochambeau, *Mémoires*, 1: 275–276; B⁴191: 106–109, Barras to Castries, 1 June 1781; United States 17: 78–81, "Séance du conseil tenu à bord du vaisseau du roi *le Neptune*, le 8 juin 1781." Barras and Rochambeau each later claimed credit for calling the conference.

[15] B⁴191: 90–91, de Grasse to Rochambeau, 29 March 1781.

had been entrusted to the ship of the line *Sagittaire* before it separated from de Grasse's command for the passage to Boston with its part of the great convoy. The *Sagittaire* arrived only on 11 June, so stricken with scurvy that it was unusable for the entire campaign, but in time for its information to be of great use. De Grasse informed Rochambeau that he would be at Saint Domingue at the end of June. He requested that Barras be notified so that pilots with knowledge of American waters could be sent to him along with intelligence about the American war theater. He warned that at the earliest he could be on the American coast by approximately 15 July; with so little time it was important that all be ready for him. This message dictated that Washington now be informed of de Grasse's intentions.[16]

On 20 June the *Concorde* sailed for Saint Domingue carrying the coastal pilots so necessary for de Grasse's mission. It also carried the reports of Barras, La Luzerne and Rochambeau on the American situation.[17] The dispatch of La Luzerne informed de Grasse that Cornwallis now commanded a force of 6,000 men in Virginia, that Rochambeau and Washington planned to make a demonstration against New York which would become a full attack if the English defenses were weak, and that Washington had written that he and Rochambeau believed de Grasse should sail directly to Sandy Hook (off New York harbor). The emphasis of La Luzerne's message, however, was on the crisis in Virginia:

[16] Freeman, *George Washington*, 5: 296. La Luzerne had written Vergennes that he believed that Washington (but only Washington) should be told of the impending arrival of de Grasse. United States 17: 49, La Luzerne to Vergennes, 1 June 1781. Still en route to La Luzerne were Vergennes' *orders* that Washington be told that de Grasse would bring north part or all of his forces. United States 16: 275, Vergennes to La Luzerne, 14 May 1781. See also Note 6.

[17] B⁴191: 117, 118, Barras to Castries, 23 June 1781; B⁴191: 91–92, de Grasse to Barras, 28 July 1781; United States 17: 54–61, La Luzerne to de Grasse, 4 June 1781 (quotation is from f. 59; same letter is given B⁴192: 284–287); Rochambeau, *Mémoires*, 1: 277.

"It is you alone who can deliver the invaded states from that crisis which is so alarming that it appears to me there is no time to lose and that for their existence it is necessary to do all you can by your instructions." Rochambeau concurred in the advisability of sailing to Chesapeake Bay, particularly in light of d'Estaing's experience at Sandy Hook (although Rochambeau thereby contradicted the results of the Wethersfield conference).

After reading the dispatches de Grasse elected to sail to the Chesapeake rather than the Hudson: final credit for that decision is his.[18] He also decided to bring virtually his entire force, leaving behind only the *Actionnaire*, 64, to protect the homeward-bound trade from Martinique and Saint Domingue.[19] He must share credit for this decision, however, with two extraordinary young Spaniards, Bernardo de Gálvez and Francisco de Saavedra.

Gálvez (1746–1786) was acting governor of Louisiana and had captured Natchez, Mobile, and Pensacola, for which he was promoted to Lieutenant-General. It was within his power as senior military commander in the theater to request part of de Grasse's fleet. Not only did he release all of de Grasse's ships, but also the corps at Saint Domingue which had been placed in Spanish service. To coordinate plans with de Grasse he sent his principal aide to Cape François aboard Monteil's flagship. This aide, Francisco de Saavedra (1746–1819), was actually a representative of the Colonial Ministry, which was headed by Gálvez' uncle, José de Gálvez. In his extraordinary public career Saavedra would become finance minister of Spain and an organizer of the resistance to Napoleon; for his role in de Grasse's campaign alone he merits serious historical attention. De

[18] B⁴191: 91–92, de Grasse to Barras, 28 July 1781.

[19] De Grasse's risk was successfully run. The *Actionnaire* and several armed transports left Saint Domingüe for France on 24 October 1781 with 126 merchantmen. The convoy arrived largely intact on 7 December. B⁸14: unpaged, sheets for December 1781; Spain 605: 470, Vergennes to Montmorin, 14 December 1781.

Grasse and Saavedra together drew up the operational plans used for the following nine months.[20]

The remaining goals of the campaign were three: to aid the Americans and defeat Rear-Admiral Arbuthnot (temporarily commanding naval forces at New York), to capture the British Windward Islands, and to conquer Jamaica. De Grasse and Saavedra believed this could be done by putting to use the opportune time and "in undertaking each of them with a massed force superior to the resistance of the common enemy." For this purpose de Grasse would take his entire force to North America from the end of July until October while Solano, the commanding Spanish admiral, moved a covering force as soon as possible to Cape François. De Grasse would embark the expeditionary force left at Spanish disposal "because, seeing the distress in which the Anglo-Americans find themselves according to the advice just received from the Count de Rochambeau, it is indispensable to aid that General with the greatest number of troops possible." If some Spanish possession was menaced de Grasse promised to send aid. In November de Grasse would return to the Windward Islands for three months of operations. At the commencement of March 1782 de Grasse would send to Cape François or the Mole Saint Nicholas all the forces he could, including at least eight 74s and 7,000 troops, where they would rendezvous with the Spanish forces to be used in the Jamaican attack; the Spaniards were also to be given a rendezvous point for the Windward Islands' attack if they wished to participate.[21]

While de Grasse began embarkation of troops—he was able to find 3,300, including artillery and cavalry[22]—he sent

[20] Spain 604: 131–133, convention between de Grasse and Don Francisco de Saavedra, officer of the secretary of state and council general of the Indies, 21 July 1781 (hereafter cited as de Grasse-Saavedra convention). For Gálvez' promotion see Spain 604: .101, Montmorin to Vergennes, 13 July 1781.

[21] This plan was in accordance with the wishes of the French council. See Spain 603: 98–101, untitled memoir, no date, but ca. May 1781.

[22] B⁴184: 166, list of troops embarked at Saint Domingue, no date.

the *Concorde* back to Barras. On 11 August the *Concorde* reached Newport with de Grasse's letters to Barras and Rochambeau. Washington's probe of the New York defenses at the beginning of July had been fruitless. When he learned on 14 August that de Grasse was bringing his whole fleet to the Chesapeake (but only until 15 October), he instantly began preparations to send Rochambeau's corps and 2,500 American troops to Virginia.[23] Cornwallis had fortified himself in a peninsula between the James and York rivers; he and Clinton waited in a paralysis of indecision for the coming blow.[24]

De Grasse sailed on 5 August. He stopped for a day at Matanzas, Cuba, on his way to North America. The *Concorde* had also brought in July a request of Rochambeau for 1,200,000 livres to pay his troops. De Grasse sent the frigate *Aigrette* to Havana whose citizens contributed for this purpose 1,000,000 piastres (5,000,000 livres) in a single day.[25] De Grasse picked up this loan at Matanzas and anchored off the entrance to Chesapeake Bay on 30 August. He brought 28 of the line (the *Intrépide* had accidentally burned on 22 July at Cape François). Hood, detached by Rodney to North America, had already reached New York, but by the overconfidence or carelessness of Rodney and

[23] Washington would have greatly preferred to send the troops by sea had Barras been willing to escort them. It seems obvious in retrospect that Barras was prudent, but it is to the great credit of Washington that he was willing to run the risks of marching by land, despite his own reservations. Freeman, *George Washington*, 5: 309; James Thomas Flexner, *George Washington in the American Revolution* (Boston: Little, Brown, and Co., 1967), 437.

[24] For the campaign from the viewpoints of Cornwallis and Clinton compare Franklin Wickwire and Mary Wickwire, *Cornwallis: The American Adventure* (Boston: Houghton Mifflin Co., 1970) and Willcox, *Portrait of a General*.

[25] B⁸14: unpaged, sheets for August 1781; Spain 605: 48, Vergennes to Montmorin, 3 October 1781. Not all this amount was needed. The people of Havana were grateful for shipments of American wheat. Spain 603: 139, La Luzerne to Montmorin, 1 May 1781. I have a vague suspicion that the city of Havana will not play its deserved role in the coming bicentennial celebrations of the American Revolution.

others he had brought only 14 of the line.[26] He placed himself under the command of Rear-Admiral Thomas Graves, from whose command 2 ships of the line and a 50 were missing for refits or convoying. Under Hood's prodding Graves quickly sailed to protect Cornwallis, but when Graves with 19 of the line and a 50-gun ship attempted to enter the Chesapeake, de Grasse had a sufficient margin of superiority, even with 4 of the line left behind in Chesapeake Bay, to prevent him (the Battle of the Virginia Capes, 5 September 1781). As a result of the maneuvering following the battle Barras was able to enter Chesapeake Bay unmolested with 7 of the line and the vital siege artillery and provisions for the Allied army.[27] Because of Clinton's failure to intercept Rochambeau and Washington and because of Graves' failure to intercept Barras or dislodge de Grasse, Cornwallis was doomed. Only de Grasse's rigid adherence to the time deadline of his campaign plan or the arrival of massive British naval reinforcements could have saved him. De Grasse agreed to extend his stay until the end of October and because of the pressure of the Dutch, Spanish, and French fleets only 3 of the line reached New York from England. By the time Graves made another dilatory attempt at relief Cornwallis had surrendered on 19 October. His 7,200 troops were the only British force in the American colonies not needed for the protection of New York and the other garrisons in which the British were imprisoned.[28]

[26] *Sandwich Papers*, 4: 135–138; Mackesy, *War for America*, 419–424. Rodney returned to Europe. See also appendix H.

[27] De Grasse left Barras the choice of joining him or not. At Rochambeau's request Barras gave up his desire for independent operations in order to serve under de Grasse, once his junior. Barras sailed from Newport on 24 August. B⁴191: 91–92, de Grasse to Barras, 28 July 1781; B⁴191: 120–121, Rochambeau to Barras, 15 August 1781; B⁴191: 129–130, Barras to de Grasse, 19 August 1781.

[28] Freeman, *George Washington*, 335, 513–515. Freeman reports 36,445 British troops in the American colonies on 15 September 1781. The effective forces opposing Cornwallis were, by Freeman's esti-

The British called 1759 the "Annus Mirabilis," the year of miracles, for their world-wide victories. After the conquests of Pensacola and Tobago, the successful landing on Minorca and the capture of Cornwallis' army, the Allies might justly call 1781 their "Annus Mirabilis." The greatest of the victories was Yorktown for it was the culmination of a chain of defeats—Bunker Hill, Trenton, Saratoga, Yorktown—which convinced the British of the hopelessness of reconstructing a British America by force of arms. Behind the Allied victory at Yorktown, however, lies an enigma, or, if you wish, a miracle. No ship in the pages of Melville was more symbolically named than the *Concorde*, which had carried so many communications. For one campaign the leaders of three nations acted selflessly in a common goal. For the great victory honor must be paid to many men, including:

Montmorin, who first urged that the Allied effort be shifted to North America.

Vergennes, who, once convinced of this, pressed for decisive efforts in America.

Castries, who drafted de Grasse's orders and left him freedom to operate.

Gálvez, who released the ships and troops which de Grasse took north.

Saavedra, who according to de Grasse could not have contributed more amenity, good will and disposition for conciliation in the drafting of the plan of operations.[29]

---

mate, 9,500 Americans and 7,800 French. For the second attempt to relieve Cornwallis, 27 ships of the line (including two 50s) sailed from New York on the very day of Cornwallis' surrender. *Sandwich Papers*, 4: 144.

[29] Spain 605: 47–48, Vergennes to Montmorin, 3 October 1781.

Rochambeau, who served Washington superbly and who pressed for the attack on Cornwallis.

La Luzerne, who shared in Rochambeau's appeal that de Grasse come to the Chesapeake.

Barras, who had the courage to disobey orders in order to remain at Newport[30] and who sacrificed his desire for independent command to place his ships at de Grasse's command.

Washington, who sacrificed his own desire to attack New York, who undertook an extremely dangerous march on de Grasse's promise to come to the Chesapeake, and finally who commanded the siege of Yorktown.

De Grasse, an indifferent tactician but a commander whose strategic vision made possible the most important naval victory of the 18th century.

De Grasse sailed from the Chesapeake on 4 November, detached four ships to Saint Domingue to escort the remainder of the trade and moored at Fort Royal on 25 November.[31] As he arrived, Bouillé with 1,500 troops and three frigates recaptured Saint Eustatius as he had captured Saint Vincent and Dominica. Commodore Solano finally managed to send four ships of the line from Havana to cruise off Saint Domingue.[32] The year ended with two un-

---

[30] In Rochambeau's belief, had Barras gone to Boston he would have been possibly a month's journey further away from the rendezvous with de Grasse. Barras made a similar statement to Castries. Rochambeau, *Mémoires*, 1: 275; B⁴191: 152, Barras to Castries, 26 September 1781.

[31] B⁴184: 54–120, journal of navigation, 22 March 1781 to 14 May 1782. These ships, the *Victoire*, *Provence*, *Triton*, and *Vaillant*, were later joined by the *Solitaire*.

[32] Spain 606: 19, Montmorin to Vergennes, 7 January 1782; B⁴193: 194, Captain d'Albert Saint-Hippolyte to Castries, 31 December 1781. The French were very disturbed that Solano had failed to put pressure on Jamaica during the campaign. It was fortunate de Grasse did

successful attempts of de Grasse to reach Barbados against contrary winds.

6. The Grand Design

Since the vital campaigns of the war were fought on the periphery of the British Empire, the war's progress can best be seen not by battles but by the movement of ships and troops. During 1780 the safe passage of Ternay's, Solano's, and de Guichen's convoys gave the Allies a superiority which they exploited at Pensacola and Yorktown. During the autumn of 1781 the council learned of the successes resulting from the safe passage of de Grasse's convoy to Martinique and Suffren's to the Cape. Now to bring the war to a conclusion the French council rushed to prepare two new convoys to sail together from Brest—one for the attack on Jamaica and another to attack the British positions in India. (With them would also sail a contingent of ships for Cadiz.) The momentum of the increasingly successful Allied war effort depended on their safe departure and, as they fitted out, France and Spain prepared their grand design for the capture of Jamaica which of itself might drive England to peace.

Final planning for the Jamaican operation began in earnest only with the arrival of the Saavedra-de Grasse agreement (at the beginning of October), and with formal Spanish acceptance of the Jamaican operation (received 4 October).[1] Until then the council chiefly filled in the details of the French contribution to combined operations.

---

not need the diversion. Spain 603: 147, 272, Montmorin to Vergennes, 1 May and 5 June 1781; Spain 604: 95, 288–290, Montmorin to Vergennes, 12 July and 20 August 1781; Spain 604: 131, de Grasse-Saavedra convention; Spain 604: 277–279, Floridablanca to Aranda, 20 August 1781.

[1] Spain 605: 47–48, Vergennes to Montmorin, 3 October 1781; Spain 604: 448–451, Montmorin to Vergennes, 27 September 1781; Spain 604: 452–454, Floridablanca to Aranda, 27 September 1781.

The 4,000 troops to be sent to the West Indies would be, if Spain insisted, in addition to the 2,000-man corps already there (which would probably need 800 to 900 recruits to replace attrition from disease).[2] Regiments were selected for the 4,000-man auxiliary corps to serve at Minorca under Crillon.[3] France agreed to provide, if needed, the amount of artillery requested by Spain for Jamaica—20 breeching cannon, 22 campaign cannon, 10 mortars, and 12 howitzers.[4] Finally at the end of September, Spain agreed to her contribution. Between the end of October and end of December Spain would send 4,000 men and four of the line to either Cape Guarico or Saint Domingue.[5] The total Spanish contribution would be 10,000–11,000 troops.[6] Montmorin forwarded a translation of Minister Gálvez' instructions to his nephew, the expeditionary commander Lieutenant-General Gálvez, ordering him to assemble the necessary forces at Guarico and expressing the belief that the attack could occur in January while the French made a diversion in the Windward Islands.[7]

[2] Spain 604: 252, Montmorin to Floridablanca, 18 August 1781; Spain 604: 345, Vergennes to Aranda, 27 September 1781. See also Spain 604: 362–365, untitled memoir, no date.

[3] These were the regiments of Bretagne (stationed at Metz), Bouillon (from Grenoble), Royal Suedois (from Belfort), and Lyonnais (from Toulon). See Spain 604: 352, War Minister Ségur to Vergennes, 2 September 1781.

[4] Spain 604: 260, Floridablanca to Aranda, 20 August 1781, enclosure; Spain 604: 356–357, Vergennes to Montmorin, 5 September 1781, enclosure. These would cost about 1,000,000 livres to supply.

[5] Spain 604: 448–451, Montmorin to Vergennes, 27 September 1781. By the end of September Córdoba had arrived at Cadiz and the Havana convoy was expected momentarily. Spain 604: 435–436, Cadiz report of 25 September 1781; Spain 605: 17–19, Montmorin to Vergennes, 2 October 1781.

[6] Spain 604: 452–454, Floridablanca to Aranda, 27 September 1781. See also Spain 604: 171, 278, Floridablanca to Aranda, 27 July and 20 August 1781.

[7] Spain 604: 458–461, José de Gálvez to Bernardo de Gálvez, 27 September 1781; Spain 605: 21–24, Montmorin to Vergennes, 2 October 1781. Spanish forces would be drawn from Cuba, Porto Rico, and Santo Domingo. Troops from New Spain (now Mexico) would be sent as replacements to Havana.

Final Spanish acceptance crossed in transit with a series of French memoirs drafted in response to Montmorin's fears that the Spaniards were ready now to abandon the operation.[8] Vergennes therein proposed that the Spaniards place 6,000 men and 11 or 12 ships of the line at French disposal and promised at any event to send the army corps to Minorca and the ships not needed in the Western Hemisphere to Cadiz as soon as possible. He also raised the possibility of combined Franco-Spanish operations against the remaining British positions in North America either in place of or following the Jamaican operation.[9]

Upon receipt of the Spanish acceptance and the Saavedra-de Grasse agreement the council quickly redrafted its proposals.[10] The Spanish plan envisaged an attack on Jamaica about the end of 1781 *followed* if successful by operations in the Windward Islands. Saavedra and de Grasse had agreed to reverse the sequence of operations. The council believed that in order to afford four months to capture Jamaica before the hurricane season, forces should assemble in Saint Domingue no later than March. This would leave de Grasse December, January and February for operations to windward. France proposed the following:

1. De Grasse should return to the Windward Islands in November.
2. Spain would be free to send forces to join him.
3. In November de Grasse would be sent six or seven ships of the line and 5,000–6,000 troops. These would arrive at Martinique between the end of December and mid-January and would subsequently be sent to Mole Saint Nicholas or Point Guarico.

[8] An example of the latter is Spain 604: 397–405, Montmorin to Vergennes, 15 September 1781.

[9] Spain 605: 13–16, personal letter of Vergennes to Montmorin, 2 October 1781; Spain 605: 34–41, Vergennes to Montmorin, 3 October 1781.

[10] Spain 605: 62–68, response to Spanish memoir of 27 September 1781, sent by Vergennes to Montmorin, 8 October 1781.

4. Spain should also send 4,000 troops (from Europe) with a sufficient escort to Martinique.
5. Spain would send another 6,000 troops to Mole Saint Nicholas or Point Guarico. The total Spanish naval contribution would be 15 ships of the line; the combined squadron would be at least 30 of the line.
6. De Grasse would take at least 15 of the line and at least 6,000 French troops in February to the rendezvous point, the number to be determined by the need.
7. The combined forces might reach 40–45 ships of the line and 15,000–20,000 troops instead of 30 of the line and 16,000 troops.

The council also sent a convention to regulate the combined operations. France anticipated that Lieutenant-General Gálvez would command, seconded by Major-Generals Bouillé from Martinique and Bellecombe from Saint Domingue. Conquests would be held in common and prizes divided equally.[11]

Montmorin refrained from using that part of the council's instructions made obsolete by the Spanish acceptance.[12] Charles was adamantly against using Spanish forces for combined operations in the United States (although willing for Spain to serve as an auxiliary for attacks on Halifax, Nova Scotia, or Newfoundland). Charles did agree to the cruise of an Allied fleet in the Channel until a fixed time.[13]

---

[11] Spain 605: 55–58, Ségur to Vergennes, 6 October 1781. *Maréchal de camp* has been translated *major-general*.

[12] Spain 605: 214–221, 222–226, Montmorin to Vergennes, 21 October 1781.

[13] In an amplifying letter Floridablanca indicated that Spain would accept d'Estaing as the commander of the combined fleet while it was in French waters, but Spain wished a Spanish commander while it was in Spanish waters, and thereafter a Spanish commander for a detached light squadron. The combined fleet would sail in April 1782 to Ouessant, where d'Estaing would take command. The Spanish ships would return to Spain at the beginning of September. Operations during the intervening months would be France's decision, but Spain wished maximum destruction of the British navy. Spain 605: 173–175, Floridablanca to Montmorin, 20 October 1781.

He would leave details to Louis. Spain raised several objections to the council's plan of combined operations. One objection was that the convoy from Spain would carry mercury (urgently needed for mining operations) thereby precluding its going first to Martinique. The major problem, however, arose over the question of the composition of the attacking force. Spain objected to sharing the spoils equally unless the two countries contributed an equal attacking force. Spain offered three options: France to contribute 6,000 troops and 15 ships of the line but to serve only as an auxiliary; the two nations to each contribute equally (either by France's increasing or by Spain's reducing its contribution) or Spain to contribute 6,000 troops and 15 of the line and serve as an auxiliary to 10,000–11,000 French troops.[14]

The council accepted the second alternative but rather than have Spain diminish its contribution it volunteered to contribute 10,000 troops and at least 15 ships of the line.[15] Gálvez would remain as land commander; if more naval forces were available France would contribute them. Louis hoped Charles would reciprocate by giving command of the combined naval force to de Grasse. The attack would occur in March; France suggested the Spanish force proceed first to Cape Guarico and then to Mole Saint Nicholas. Operations subsequent to Jamaica would be decided later. Vergennes told Montmorin in his covering letter that he expected the French convoy to sail by the end of November.

Spain readily acceded to all the French propositions.[16] Indeed during the autumn months of 1781 good news followed good news in such degree that Providence must have seemed to have adopted the French court. The greatest good fortune of course was the birth of a dauphin on 22 Oc-

---

[14] Montmorin favored the third alternative because of diplomatic considerations, but he admitted that providing the extra forces would be difficult and that Spain might not cooperate as well for a commander other than Gálvez.

[15] Spain 605: 276–281, memoir of 3 November 1781; Spain 605: 289–292, Vergennes to Montmorin, 6 November 1781.

[16] Spain 605: 340–342, Spanish memoir of 16 November 1781.

tober, but there was also a succession of fortunate military news—Suffren's victory in the race to the Cape,[17] the successful landing on Minorca,[18] the safe arrival of four ships of the line and the treasure convoy from Havana, together worth 25,000,000 piastres,[19] the news of the supposed end of the Indian revolt in Peru,[20] the safe passage of the French expeditionary corps to Minorca and Crillon's optimistic predictions (for what they were worth) of a successful attack on Fort Saint Philip,[21] and finally a chain of encouraging reports from North America culminating in the arrival on 24 November of one of Rochambeau's colonels with the news of Cornwallis' surrender.[22] Amazingly, a revolution seemed also to have occurred in the relations between France and Spain. Montmorin wrote:

> Never has there reigned more goodwill between the two courts than at this moment. All the suspicions have dissipated and everyone, even the naval minister [Castejon] is

[17] B⁴216: 280, Castries to Hector, 22 October 1781. Suffren left 1,200 troops to guard the Cape, garrisoned before chiefly by volunteers. Holland 546: 330, La Vauguyon to Vergennes, 9 November 1781.

[18] This news reached France by 10 September—see Spain 604: 379, Vergennes to Montmorin, 10 September 1781.

[19] The convoy had left Havana on 29 July. Spain 605: 17, 117–118, 147, 324, Montmorin to Vergennes, 2 October, 15 October, 18 October, and 12 November 1781.

[20] Spain 605: 96–103, Montmorin to Vergennes, 8 October 1781. In the same dispatch, Montmorin reported that the four Spanish ships of the line and convoy for Cape Guarico would be ready by the end of October. The convoy waited to sail from Spain until the French convoy sailed from Brest.

[21] Spain 605: 261, Crillon to Vergennes, 29 October 1781. Montmorin believed Crillon very brave and personable, but not made to inspire confidence. Montmorin, however, promised to keep his silence. Vergennes was no more optimistic about him. Spain 605: 180–181, personal letter of Montmorin to Vergennes, 21 October 1781; Spain 605: 40, Vergennes to Montmorin, 3 October 1781.

[22] Howard C. Rice and Anne S. K. Brown, eds., *The American Campaigns of Rochambeau's Army, 1780, 1781, 1782, 1783* (Princeton, N.J. and Providence, R.I.: Princeton University Press and Brown University Press, 1972), 1: 300.

in the best possible spirits. All my conversations with Monsieur de Floridablanca are trusting and amicable. In a word things present themselves in an aspect so favorable that I am a little like the sailors who sometimes regard a perfect calm as the presage of a coming tempest.[23]

Two things marred the enjoyment of such good fortune. On 21 November the Count de Maurepas died. It is far easier to estimate the part he played in the political destruction of Turgot, Sartine, and Necker than to estimate his share in the direction of the war.[24] One can argue justly that he focused his enormous intelligence and political acumen chiefly on his own survival and that he was too indolent for the painstaking attention to detail which underlies successful strategy. Nevertheless, beyond Vergennes' eulogies of his importance[25] there is a more indirect and hence more reliable indication of Maurepas' position in the formulation of policy. At the beginning of October Vergennes had been forced to warn Montmorin to be more circumspect in criticizing Spain in his dispatches.[26] The dispatches had been read in council where they had caused dissension. Vergennes asked Montmorin to save his reflections for a separate letter and warned him that Louis and Maurepas saw all his letters, even his personal letters to Vergennes, unless

[23] Spain 605: 428, personal letter of Montmorin to Vergennes, 27 November 1781. See also Spain 605: 407, Montmorin to Vergennes, 26 November 1781.

[24] Svetlana Kluge Harris, my best critic, began her criticism of my dissertation with the acute comment that Maurepas was missing from its pages—a failing of this book as well, I fear. The only letter of Maurepas on naval affairs that I have found is Spain 602: 285, Maurepas to Vergennes, 8 March 1781, concerning the instructions for de Grasse.

[25] Spain 605: 397–398, personal letter of Vergennes to Montmorin, 23 November 1781. See also Spain 605: 446–448, personal letter of Montmorin to Vergennes, 3 December 1781.

[26] Spain 605: 13–14, personal letter of Vergennes to Montmorin, 2 October 1781. For another view of this incident see "Castries' journal," 87, 25 September 1781. Castries and Ségur unsuccessfully fought against sending troops to Minorca. Spain 604: 466–468, committee report of 27 September 1781.

they contained objects concerning which Vergennes had been requested to observe silence. The roles of Maurepas, the ex-naval minister, and of Louis himself in the winning of American independence were certainly not negligible; the exact extent of their contribution lies locked behind the closed doors of Louis' council room or Maurepas' apartment, where the committee met when Maurepas was ill.

Amidst the military successes lay a disturbing worry. French intelligence reported the arming of an English squadron of seven of the line for an unknown location as well as a second squadron of unknown size for India.[27] To continue to maintain the initiative the council was still dependent on the work of the ports and, that the ships might find favorable winds, on the working of the Almighty as well.

The key port in French operations was still Brest,[28] which far surpassed its rivals in number of workers[29] and the number of trained sailors.[30] Its commandant, Commodore the Count de Hector, occupied so crucial a position that he turned down Fleurieu's post as director of ports and arsenals, in part because Hector believed himself of greater use as commandant.[31] The ports' major problem was no longer

[27] Spain 605: 291, Vergennes to Montmorin, 6 November 1781.

[28] For excellent drawings of Brest in the 1770s see Rice and Brown, *Rochambeau's Army*, 2: sketches and maps, nos. 1 and 2.

[29] During 1781 the number of workers at Brest varied between 6,100 and 7,750, at Rochefort between 2,725 and 4,160, at Toulon between 3,280 and 3,860, and at Lorient between 1,417 and 1,840. E 205: unpaged, "Relevé du nombre d'ouvriers . . . 1781 et 1782," no date.

[30] B³713: 24, untitled memoir, no date, lists sailors by department of origin. Of 56,513 trained sailors, 40,733 were embarked aboard the ships of the French navy, and of these, Brest contributed 13,081, Le Havre 9,136, Toulon 8,690, Bordeaux 4,410, Rochefort 4,048 and Dunkirk 1,368. Of course there were also many untrained sailors serving aboard the ships of the French navy in capacities such as novice. See B³709: 57 for example. For the total number of sailors in the French navy see Chapter Six, Section 2, Note 3.

[31] Also Hector did not find court life at Versailles congenial. Fleurieu, who had been serving as interim director, was reappointed as permanent director in August 1781. For this complicated story see

how to obtain wood,[32] but copper for doubling ships' hulls,[33] which had achieved great importance, particularly for fitting ships for overseas duty.[34]

They had more to prepare than the squadron for the Caribbean. De Guichen had had to sail on 22 June without the *Illustre* and *Saint-Michel* and their supply convoy for India.[35] It was almost a month until the convoy from Lorient joined the escort vessels at the Île de Ré and finally sailed (although the *Argonaute* which was to be added to the es-

---

B^{8}14; B^{4}216; B^{4}219: *passim*. It appears that Fleurieu played a lesser role under Castries than he did under Sartine, particularly since Castries initiated a private correspondence with the port commandants. See B^{4}216: 6–8.

[32] The amount of wood at Le Havre rose from about 532,500 ft.^{8} at the end of December 1780 to almost 695,000 ft.^{8} at the end of December 1781. B^{5}18: unpaged, "Etats de situation . . . 1781," no date. For transshipments through Rouen see B^{3}696: 178–201. On 1 December 1781, Rouen had 105,443 ft.^{8} of wood waiting to be moved. See also B^{3}708: *passim*, for arrival of wood at Rochefort and B^{3}712: 288, for wood at Toulon.

[33] See for example B^{3}699: 24–25, Hector to Castries, 20 July 1781. Masts were also in relatively short supply. The copper shortage had led to doubling with wood, particularly above the waterline. Copper generally came in sheets 5′ x 18″ (French measure).

[34] B^{5}13, unpaged, ship rosters, lists the various ships of the French navy in 1781 and whether or not they had been doubled. Less than half the ships of the line and slightly more than half the frigates had received copper plating. The elimination of the Dutch as neutral carriers was not, however, the cause of the shortage, since Prussia and other neutral states had taken over the carrying trade. Madariaga, *Britain, Russia, and the Armed Neutrality*, 363, 378; Holland 546: 178, La Vauguyon to Vergennes, 5 October 1781. Copper was purchased from private contractors, who sold to the highest bidder. Hector complained that merchant ports received all the copper they needed. B^{3}698: 25, Hector to Castries, 25 July 1781. As in so many areas we need a full study of the relationship of the navy to the French economy at large.

[35] B^{4}189: 110, de Guichen to Castries, 13 June 1781; Spain 603: 347–348, Castries to de Guichen, 17 June 1781. The *Saint-Michel* lacked part of her crew; the *Illustre* was retained by the winds. The *Illustre* entered the roadstead downriver from Rochefort on 8 May, and the *Saint-Michel* on 23 June. B^{3}707: 154, Captain de la Carry to Castries, 7 June 1781; B^{5}19: unpaged, Rochefort reports.

cort was unable to join them).[36] During the summer the Spaniards demonstrated their reluctance to protect the departure of the Jamaican convoy and the council evidently began to consider alternatives to combined operations in the Caribbean. If troops were to be sent to India, the *Illustre* and *Saint-Michel* would be needed to strengthen their escort; the two warships were ordered to escort the supply convoy only as far as the Azores.[37] Rather than running the risk of returning to France, they were ordered to proceed to Ferrol to wait for the troop convoy—in fact, for further safety, the French ships instead sailed to Cadiz. (Before this information arrived, the *Argonaute* left for Ferrol to join them and had to be recalled.)[38]

In mid-August the council decided on the allocation of troops to be sent from France: 2,106 to Saint Domingue, 1,830 to Martinique, 180 to Guadeloupe, 600 to India, and 830 to Rhode Island.[39] During August, Hector was at Versailles for conferences with Castries. Soon after he returned to Brest to meet de Guichen, he had bad news for the naval minister—he believed the departure of the new convoys could not take place before 1 December because of the

---

[36] This third escort was added on the basis of intelligence from England that three ships of the line would be sent to India. The *Argonaute* entered the roadstead on 23 July, two days after the sailing of the *Illustre*, *Saint-Michel*, and their convoy. The intelligence from England was an underestimate—the *Monarca* sailed from England in mid-April, and the *Magnanime* and *Sultan* in June, two more ships of the line were planned for October, and a 50 was sent to Saint Helena in the South Atlantic. B⁴216: 240–241, Castries to de Guichen, 15 June 1781; Mackesy, *War for America*, 391–393.

[37] I do not have the reference for the original orders for the *Illustre* and *Saint-Michel*. Killion, "Suffren Expedition," 356 indicates that Castries on 21 July wrote the governor of Île de France that a troop convoy would sail in November.

[38] Spain 604: 332, Montmorin to Vergennes, 29 August 1781; B⁴216: 270, Castries to Captains d'Aymar and de Lacqueray, 16 September 1781.

[39] B⁴189: 335, untitled memoir of 15 October 1781. B²420: 172, Castries to commissioner Grandville at Lorient, 26 August 1781, also indicates that 1,100 recruits would be sent to Île de France as replacements for losses.

shortage of sailors and transports.[40] Castries, who had just
written de Grasse that a convoy and six to seven of the line
would sail at the end of October,[41] urged haste on Hector.[42]
The council then made a dangerous decision. In spite of
Hector's warnings about the shortage of transports the
council decided on 21 September to add three battalions of
infantry (2,330 men) to the force for India.[43] On 15 October the council postponed plans to send reinforcements to
Rhode Island, but raised the total force to be embarked to
over 10,000 men, of which about 4,500 were for India.[44]

By the end of October the ships had been selected for the
different components of the great fleet which would escort
convoys "1 M" (for Martinique) and "2 A" (for Asia) clear
of French waters.[45] With the Martinique convoy would go
the *Triomphant, Pégase, Magnifique, Actif, Zodiaque, Robuste,* and *Brave* under the command of Commodore Vaudreuil, who had served under d'Estaing in 1779. To Asia
would go the *Fendant* and *Argonaute* plus the *Hardi* and
Alexandre, temporarily armed as transports. De Guichen,
the overall commander, would take the *Royal-Louis, Bretagne, Terrible, Invincible, Majesteaux, Bien-Aimé, Indien,*
and *Lion* to Cadiz. The *Couronne* and *Dauphin-Royal*
would return to Brest and form the nucleus of a new squadron for La Motte-Picquet.

The last part of the design was the naming as commander

[40] B⁴219: 155, Hector to Castries, 14 September 1781.
[41] B⁴216: 267–268, Castries to de Grasse, 10 September 1781.
[42] B⁴216: 270–271, Castries to Hector, 17 September 1781.
[43] B⁴189: 335, untitled memoir of 15 October 1781. On 12 September, 250 artillerymen had been added.
[44] B⁴216: 276, Castries to Hector, 3 October 1781; B⁴189: 335, 336,
untitled memoirs of 15 October 1781. See also B⁴189: 342–343, untitled
memoir of 19 November 1781. Of these troops, about 1,200 for Île
de France were to be embarked at Lorient and were sometimes not
counted as part of convoy "2 A." Only one-third of the troops from
Lorient actually sailed.
[45] B³699: 234, Hector to Castries, 2 November 1781; B⁴216: 278,
Castries to Hector, 14 October 1781; B⁴219: 169, Hector to Castries,
1 October 1781, listing ships suitable for foreign service.

for the corps of troops for India Major-General the Marquis de Bussy, who had been one of the French commanders in India during the Seven Years War. To preserve secrecy Bussy would travel by land in cognito to Cadiz. The *Saint-Michel* and *Illustre* would leave from there to join the Indian convoy off the Azores.[46] Bussy had argued for an expeditionary corps of 8,000–9,000 troops;[47] he, Castriés, and Ségur probably bear most responsibility for the expansion of the operation and subsequent delays.

Hector's prediction was accurate. The last of the 17 ships from Brest entered the road on 29 November; on the following day the *Brave* and *Argonaute* arrived from Rochefort.[48] There were two final changes to the plans. The *Pégase* was shifted to the Asian expedition and the *Couronne* and *Dauphin-Royal* were ordered detached at sea to meet the incoming Saint Domingue convoy.[49] Because of contrary winds the great fleet and its convoys could not sail until 10 December.

The English were expecting them. From the news of Yorktown there had finally come the energy and direction their efforts had lacked. Their own fleets for the Caribbean and India were not yet ready but less than a month after Darby had brought the home fleet back in, they had prepared a squadron to intercept de Guichen. On 2 December Rear-Admiral Richard Kempenfelt, perhaps the most promising

[46] See B⁴196: 45–47, 233–234, drafts of letters of Castries to Captain d'Aymour of the *Saint-Michel* and to d'Orves, 11 November 1781. Bussy was promoted to lieutenant-general on 14 October 1781.

[47] Killion, "Suffren Expedition," 351–357. Interestingly, "Castries' journal," 83, 18 July 1781, indicates Castries' approval of the entire force asked by Bussy. Castries obviously failed to convince the remainder of the council on this point.

[48] B⁵18: unpaged, roster of ships.

[49] B⁴216: 132–133, Castries to Captain Soulanges of the *Pégase*; B⁴216: 111–114, orders for La Motte-Picquet to command the detachment, 29 November 1781; B⁴189: 132, de Guichen to Castries, 3 December 1781. In B⁴189: 55, instructions for La Motte-Picquet, 18 November 1781, La Motte-Picquet was ordered detached at the entrance of Cadiz in order to sail to Corunna.

officer in the Royal Navy, took 12 ships of the line to sea and ten days later he surprised de Guichen 400 miles south of Cape Clear.[50] De Guichen was to leeward of his convoys and Kempenfelt took about 20 ships before de Guichen chased him off. Although Kempenfelt had not been strong enough to turn back or destroy the convoy, the winds turned westerly and became strong.[51] By 25 December the great convoy had made no progress. It was struck that evening by a great storm[52]—a storm which may have saved Jamaica.

[50] Mackesy, *War for America*, 439–443; *Sandwich Papers*, 4: 15–16; Fortescue, *Correspondence of King George the Third*, 5: 290, cabinet minutes of 20 October 1781 (no. 3427).

[51] Spain 606: 5, Vergennes to Montmorin, 3 January 1782.

[52] The attack occurred at 46° 29′ N, 11° 24′ W, the storm while the convoy was at 47° 43′ N, 11° 01′ W. For descriptions of both see B⁴189: *passim*.

CHAPTER NINE

1782—Disintegration and Reprieve

1. The Allies' Last Victories

WITHIN the first few days of 1782 the council learned the extent of the damage to de Guichen's convoy.[1] Kempenfelt had captured over 1,000 soldiers and about 20 ships,[2] but ever greater disruption had been done by the storm. Most of the damaged ships could be repaired in 15 days, although the *Bretagne* and *Invincible* were forced to enter drydock for repairs. It was of greater importance that virtually all the convoy and its escort had been forced to turn back. Only the *Triomphant* and *Brave* and 18–20 of the convoy continued with Vaudreuil to the Antilles (he could have taken the *Pégase* as well, had her orders not been changed).[3] Vergennes complained to Montmorin that it was the first December for many years without winds from the east and northeast (which would have propelled the convoy clear), and he consoled himself that human power could not have prevented the misfortune.[4] This of course was partially true but had the council deferred all other objectives until the West Indian convoy was safely gone, it could probably have sailed as soon as Darby reentered port at the beginning of November.[5]

[1] Spain 606: 5, 60–61, Vergennes to Montmorin, 3 January and 11 January 1782; B³699: 370–372, Hector to Castries, 31 December 1781.
[2] B⁴189: 341, untitled memoir of 19 January 1782; B⁸14: unpaged, various sheets; B⁸721: 323, untitled memoir of 20 March 1782. See also R. Beatson, *Naval and Military Memoirs of Great Britain from the Year 1727 to 1783* (London: J. Strachan, 1790), 6: 319–320. A merchant convoy from Bordeaux, which was supposed to rendezvous at sea with de Guichen, also had five ships captured and then was hit by the storm.
[3] B⁴192: 91, Vaudreuil to Castries, 30 December 1781.
[4] Spain 606: 5, Vergennes to Montmorin, 3 January 1782.
[5] His reentry was reported in Spain 605: 329, Vergennes to Montmorin, 12 November 1781.

In the making of strategy, timing is critical. The meaningless superiority Sandwich repeatedly obtained in autumn in Europe and in summer in the Caribbean is an indictment of him as a strategist. Finally, however, the British had obtained a meaningful advantage. On 8 January Rodney sailed with 12 of the line for the West Indies and within four weeks 6 of the line had sailed for India and 5 more to join Rodney.[6]

At least the Spanish convoy for the operation with its four ships of the line sailed safely[7] as did the *Illustre* and *Saint-Michel*, which after waiting until 16 January at the Azores proceeded to India.[8] As for de Guichen's setback the council could only follow Aranda's advice, "It is not in man's power to contradict the weather; the sole recourse is to think of how best to repair the misfortune."[9]

Adjustments had to be made. Castries believed the Indian theater to be more vital than the Caribbean.[10] He managed to preserve the 3,300 regulars for India originally intended to be sent from Brest by reducing the contingent for the West Indies from an original 4,500 to 3,000.[11] Because of the storm damage the warships had to be redistributed as well. Now only the *Couronne*, *Magnifique* and *Dauphin-Royal* would sail to Martinique while de Guichen would take to Cadiz only the *Majesteux*, *Royal-Louis*, *Terrible*, *Lion*, and *Indien*. The *Fendant*, *Argonaute*, *Alexandre* and *Hardi* would escort the Indian convoy. The *Robuste*,

---

[6] Mackesy, *War for America*, 450.

[7] They sailed on 4 January and were briefly accompanied by Córdoba's fleet. B⁴205: 202, Castries to de Grasse, 30 January 1781.

[8] *Ibid.*; B⁸14: unpaged, sheets for January 1782.

[9] Spain 606: 6, Aranda to Vergennes, 5 January 1782.

[10] B⁴217: 22–23, Castries to Hector, 9 January 1782. Tarrade, *Le commerce colonial de la France*, 1: 484–485, astutely points out that Castries, unlike his immediate predecessors at the navy department, was oriented by his background toward India rather than the West Indies.

[11] B⁴189: 341, untitled memoir of 19 January 1781; B⁴217: 70, untitled memoir of 15 January 1781.

Zodiaque, Pégase and hopefully the *Actif* would cover the convoy's departure and then would return to Brest.[12]

On 28 January Hector wrote: "The bad weather continues perpetually; there are few examples of a wind as violent and as long lasting. It continually is causing topside damage in the roadstead."[13] Nevertheless on the first of February Hector was able to commence the reembarkation of troops.[14]

As important as was the Jamaican expedition, Vergennes was faced with an equally pressing problem concerning the coming European campaign. Just before the end of the year he sent Montmorin a memoir of Castries strongly protesting the Spanish demands for the campaign (that a Spaniard command the combined fleet while in Spanish waters, that there be a separate light squadron under Spanish command, and that the Spanish contingent depart at the beginning of September).[15] Vergennes elaborated on the memoir, chiefly on the council's fears that the combined fleet would be hampered by time restrictions. With the interval needed for passage to Brest and for the embarkation and disembarkation of troops there would remain only six weeks for operations against England.

Vergennes did not explain the precise operations the council was considering, but Castries later explained to

[12] Also two months provisions instead of four months provisions would be sent to de Grasse. B⁴217: 31–38, Castries to Hector, 26 January 1782; B⁴205: 200–202, Castries to de Grasse, 30 January 1782.

[13] B³719: 31–32, Hector to Castries, 28 January 1782. So bad had been the winds that the *Bien-Aimé*, originally for Cadiz, was dismasted while in the roadstead. Spain 606: 92, Vergennes to Montmorin, 18 January 1782.

[14] B³719: 37–38, Hector to Castries, 1 February 1782.

[15] Spain 605: 476–486, navy department memoir of 15 December 1781; Spain 605: 515–520, Vergennes to Montmorin, 20 December 1781. For the Spanish proposals see Chapter Eight, Section 6, Note 13. The navy department memoir promised that if Spain cooperated, France would provide the shipping, artillery, and troops for an attack on the coasts of England or Ireland.

Hector his own ideas, which were probably close to the council's consensus.[16] With Spanish assistance the Allied naval superiority would be unquestionable, so that the English fleet could be blockaded in Portsmouth. With only 8,000–10,000 infantry in England and Ireland the British Isles would be open to invasion. France could attack Cork, Bristol, or perhaps Plymouth with 15,000 troops. Castries believed such an operation would be even more likely than successes in the Western Hemisphere to force the English to demand peace (although Castries, with his lack of comprehension of diplomatic realities, was disappointed that 50,000 troops were not available to completely conquer England). Castries expected all to be ready by 15 or 20 May.

The adoption of a sufficiently extensive Franco-Spanish operational plan was also important to the success of France's Dutch policy. This policy had changed greatly since the beginning of 1781, when the Dutch had been seen as a military liability and diplomatically as more useful tied to Russia than connected with France. This change in part mirrored France's gradual disillusionment with the League of Armed Neutrality. In March 1781 the Dutch accepted Russian mediation of their dispute with Britain while Britain refused. By August 1781 when the Dutch accepted the meaningless joint imperial mediation, Vergennes was pleased that their fortunes were to be linked with those of France and the other belligerents.[17] At the end of August, however, the members of the league made a joint démarche on Holland's behalf to Britain. The cabinet, led by Secretary of State Stormont, was frightened enough to now accept sole

[16] B⁴217: 48–50, Castries to Hector, 8 March 1782. Castries far underestimated British strength. In March 1782 there were more than 20,000 infantry in England and Wales (exclusive of militia). Mackesy, *War for America*, 524–525. Against 25 British ships of the line in the English Channel and eight or ten in the North Sea, Castries predicted the Allies could commit 47 or 48 of the line. He posited total British strength for the 1782 campaign at 90 to 95 of the line.

[17] Holland 545: 208–211, Vergennes to La Vauguyon, 27 July 1781.

Russian mediation of the Anglo-Dutch war to forestall any possible joint action by the league.[18]

Vergennes by then had military reasons to combat the renewed Russian attempts to bring about a separate peace between Holland and Britain. The Dutch fleet had finally proven itself capable not only of diverting British forces, but also of conducting military operations. Perhaps even more important than the 20 ships of the line Vergennes expected the Dutch to contribute to the 1782 campaign[19] were 8 50-gun ships of the Dutch East India Company which La Vauguyon hoped would sail for the Indian Ocean as soon as the Dutch ports were clear of ice.[20] To preserve these forces for Allied use La Vauguyon supported the efforts of the pro-French faction in the Estates-General to now refuse Russian mediation while accepting an agreement for concerted operations with France for the coming campaign.[21] Vergennes also explained to Montmorin in his letter concerning combined operations that he hoped the Dutch would make a landing in the north of Britain or would at least divert British forces.[22] He did not have to add that meaningful cooperation by Spain was a prerequisite to cooperation by the even more cautious Dutch. Instead he stated that if the Bourbons gratified the interests of Holland they would serve their own interests—of which the most pressing was to multiply the embarrassments of their enemy so as to lead him to demand peace.

Montmorin was able to obtain some modifications in the Spanish position on European operations.[23] Charles, for rea-

---

[18] Madariaga, *Britain, Russia, and the Armed Neutrality,* 337–338.

[19] Spain 605: 518, Vergennes to Montmorin, 20 December 1781.

[20] *Ibid.*; Holland 546: 289–290, 321, Vergennes to La Vauguyon, 1 November and 8 November 1781; Holland 546: 276, 328, 369, 380, La Vauguyon to Vergennes, 26 October, 9 November, 20 November and 23 November 1781.

[21] Holland 546: 121–122, 412–415, Vergennes to La Vauguyon, 27 September and 29 November 1781; Holland 546: 438–441, La Vauguyon to Vergennes, 4 December 1781; Holland 547: *passim.*

[22] Spain 605: 518–519, Vergennes to Montmorin, 20 December 1781.

[23] Spain 606: 38–43, 21–24, Montmorin to Vergennes, 11 January 1781, with enclosure.

sons of pride and of affection for the aged Córdoba, was so inflexible in demanding a Spanish commander in Spanish waters that Montmorin conceded the point. In turn the Spaniards, in effect, agreed to a unified command (with no detached light squadron under Spanish command) in French waters. Moreover, Charles agreed that if an operation were in progress he would not insist on an immediate return of the Spanish contingent. Spain promised that if France provided eight to ten of the line the fleet would contain forty of the line provisioned for six months and ready to sail in the first days of April. Montmorin, however, became increasingly concerned by reports reaching Spain of the severity of the revolts in South America—reports so serious that they were kept from Charles.[24]

On 11 February de Guichen and his long-delayed convoy sailed unopposed from Brest. Hector immediately began preparations to replace de Grasse's missing troops and to provide additional troops for Rochambeau and Bussy.[25] As de Guichen was passing to Cadiz, extraordinary news was passing from Spain to Versailles. Almost simultaneously with de Guichen's arrival at Cadiz on 24 February, there arrived at Versailles the son of the Duke de Crillon.[26] He reported the capitulation of Fort Saint Philip on 4 February. Although the siege had barely begun, the garrison had already been defeated by scurvy. The nature of the victory actually enhanced its value to the kindly Charles, who delighted in the smallness of the casualty list as much as in the return of Minorca to Spain.[27]

[24] Spain 606: 45–47, Montmorin to Vergennes, 11 January 1782; Spain 606: 19–20, 116–117, personal letters of Montmorin to Vergennes, 7 January and 25 January 1782. One bad aspect of the situation was its apparent effect on Gálvez, who wrote his uncle to express doubts about the Jamaican expedition. Spain 606: 109–113, Montmorin to Vergennes, 24 January 1782.

[25] B³719: 54 ff., Hector to Castries, 11 February 1782 and following.

[26] Spain 606: 219–220, Vergennes to Montmorin, 25 February 1782.

[27] Spain 606: 186–188, Montmorin to Vergennes, 17 February 1782. More than 10,000 Spanish troops and about 4,500 French troops were assembled for the attack. After its capture Fort Saint Philip was

Good news was en route to France from the West Indies as well.[28] After the beginning of the year de Grasse turned to attack Saint Christopher, a prize less important than Antigua, Saint Lucia, or Barbados, but still sufficiently valuable to prompt a brilliant defense by Hood. Hood, badly outnumbered, had pursued de Grasse from North America; his squadron was almost trapped at Saint Christopher but escaped to Antigua after the fall of the island (12 February 1782). The French quickly took the small neighboring islands of Nevis and Montserrat, but shortly thereafter Rodney arrived at Barbados and de Grasse retreated to Martinique.[29] There were a variety of other encouraging developments during the opening months of 1782: the recapture of the Dutch settlements in South America by a small French squadron,[30] the arrival of Vaudreuil's two ships of the line and the remnants of his convoy at Martinique,[31] the arrival of the four Spanish ships of the line with their convoy at Saint Domingue,[32] and at the end of March the safe arrival of the West Indian trade at La Corogne and Ferrol with the five of the line detached by de Grasse.

With the apparent revival of the Allies' good fortune a measure of optimism reappeared. As of 16 February Vergennes still doubted the attack on Jamaica could begin before mid-April, which might necessitate postponing it until

---

demolished. Spain 605: 307–308, Babelon (a French engineer at Minorca) to Vergennes, 7 November 1781.

[28] Spain 606: 361, Vergennes to Montmorin, 28 March 1781, reported the capture of Saint Christopher.

[29] *Sandwich Papers* 4: 215–219; Alfred Thayer Mahan, *The Influence of Sea Power upon History* (1890; reprint ed., New York: Sagamore Press, 1957), 418–427.

[30] B⁴195: 66–67, untitled memoir, no date.

[31] Vaudreuil arrived at Martinique at the beginning of February. Spain 606: 361, Vergennes to Montmorin, 28 March 1782.

[32] French colonial archives, C⁹ᴬ152: unpaged, Bellecombe to Castries, 14 February 1782.

the autumn, but he believed the decision should be left to the local commanders.[33] Castries wrote de Grasse the same day to warn him that Spanish forces might have to be withdrawn to be sent to the South American continent to suppress the rebellions.[34] The news received soon thereafter of the capture of Fort Saint Philip encouraged him to predict to de Grasse that any troops needed by Spain could now be taken from the Minorcan forces.[35] With the news of the capture of Saint Christopher he wrote both de Grasse and Bouillé that the available forces should suffice for the attack on Jamaica.[36]

As welcome as was the news from Minorca, its capture in fact served to complicate rather than to simplify combined planning. The success at Fort Saint Philip immediately stimulated Spanish enthusiasm for an attack on Gibraltar. France was partially responsible for the Spanish optimism that the great fortress could be captured. During the previous summer a French engineer, the Chevalier d'Arcon, had carried to Spain a project for its capture, which greatly impressed the Spanish council.[37] With the

[37] Spain 604: 196, Arcon to Montmorin, 6 August 1781.

Minorcan victory, Spain immediately began consideration of Arcon's plans—Montmorin encouraged Vergennes to keep the auxiliary corps at Spanish disposal, despite

[33] Spain 606: 183, Vergennes to Montmorin, 16 February 1782. The Spaniards believed that the attack should go ahead, provided there was sufficient artillery, even if it had to be made with only 15,000 or 16,000 troops. Spain 606: 105–107, 109, Montmorin to Vergennes, 24 January 1782.

[34] G 165: unpaged, Castries to de Grasse, 16 February 1782.

[35] G 165: unpaged, Castries to de Grasse, 25 February 1782.

[36] G 165: unpaged, Castries to de Grasse, 11 March 1782; G 165: unpaged, Castries to Bouillé, 11 March 1782. Castries also asked the Spaniards to order their forces to remain combined with the French forces in the West Indies, whether the Jamaican operation were undertaken now or postponed until October. Spain 606: 296–299, navy department memoir of 14 March 1782, sent by Vergennes to Montmorin, 16 March 1782.

Charles' protests that it would not be needed.[38] Unfortunately the Gibraltar operation quickly took on less favorable ramifications. Charles ordered Córdoba to send 12 Spanish and 5 French ships of the line to cruise an indefinite time under de Guichen's command off Madeira, the Azores, or the Canaries to intercept English commerce.[39] This meant that the departure of the main fleet would be postponed, perhaps well into June. Charles therefore proposed its cruise be postponed until after the capture of Gibraltar. D'Arcon and his engineers believed this would take only 12 to 15 days once preparations were completed in mid-June, but Spanish planners assumed six weeks.

Montmorin wrote a personal letter to Vergennes warning him that de Guichen's cruise was only a pretext to keep the combined fleet at Cadiz until the end of July.[40] He warned Vergennes that once Gibraltar was taken Spain would have all she wanted from the war since she was not interested in American independence. On 12 March de Guichen's squadron sailed from Cadiz.

In response to the Spaniards, Castries argued that if the combined fleet waited until late July or early August to leave Cadiz any operations in English waters would be im-

---

[38] Louis promptly did offer the auxiliary corps for the Gibraltar operation. Spain 606: 186–188, Montmorin to Vergennes, 17 February 1782; Memoirs and Documents, France 1897: 111, Vergennes to Louis, 9 March 1782; Spain 606: 316, Vergennes to Montmorin, 16 March 1782.

[39] Spain 606: 241–244, 227–229, 233–235, Montmorin to Vergennes, 1 March 1782, with enclosures. For ships used see Spain 606: 293.

[40] Spain 606: 248–250, personal letter of Montmorin to Vergennes, 3 March 1782. Ironically, the initial suggestion for such a cruise came from a letter of de Guichen, forwarded by Vergennes to Montmorin. Spain 606: 150, de Guichen to Castries, 5 February 1782; Spain 606: 179–180, Vergennes to Montmorin, 16 February 1782. The difference was that the French intended the cruise to last only until the beginning of April, so as not to delay the departure of the combined fleet. Montmorin failed to put up the resistance he might have, but at least de Guichen did announce upon his departure that he would return no later than 20 April. Spain 606: 329, Montmorin to Vergennes, 18 March 1782.

practical.[41] The Dutch fleet and the 15 of the line to be prepared at Brest would be useless. Castries questioned whether 45 ships of the line would be needed to cover the attack
on Gibraltar. Instead he believed 24 Spanish and 5 French
ships of the line could come to Brest to at least prevent the
English from exercising complete control of the sea. Vergennes in his covering letter[42] argued against exposing the
Dutch to a separate peace—however mediocre their efforts
they diverted in some proportion the efforts of the enemy
and diminished by that much the mass of forces with which
he could oppose France and Spain.

Spain's threatened abandonment of combined operations
in the Channel was extraordinarily ill-timed. On 4 March
the Estates General accepted the good offices of the Empress but with severe restrictions on the terms to which
they would listen. On the same day they proposed a concert
of operations for the coming campaign with France and on
25 March promised not to listen to any peace overtures during the duration of the agreement.[43] This success would be
meaningless if the Dutch fleet was imprisoned in its bases.

If Vergennes' European diplomacy was threatened by
these new developments, his American policy might well be
endangered by the unpredictable consequences of English
political developments. On 27 February the House of Commons voted to no longer wage offensive war against the
Americans.[44] An attempt by the North ministry to open separate negotiations with the various belligerents failed,[45] and
on 20 March North and his cabinet left office.

[41] Spain 606: 300–307, navy department memoir of 14 March 1782,
sent by Vergennes to Montmorin, 16 March 1782.

[42] Spain 606: 313–314, Vergennes to Montmorin, 16 March 1782.

[43] Holland 547: 347–349; Holland 548: 79–83, Vergennes to La
Vauguyon, 23 February and 13 March 1782; Holland 548: 21–28, 175–
177, La Vauguyon to Vergennes, 5 March and 26 March 1782.

[44] It was reported to Montmorin by Spain 606: 294–295, Vergennes
to Montmorin, 14 March 1782.

[45] Spain 606: 316–317, 338, Vergennes to Montmorin, 16 March and
22 March 1782; Morris, *The Peacemakers*, 254–257. See also Holland
548: 181–182, La Vauguyon to Vergennes, 27 March 1782.

2. The European Crisis

News of the changed English political situation reached each of the Bourbon courts by the end of March. Floridablanca had not hidden from Montmorin his distrust for the Americans, who, he believed, remained English at heart. Rather than according further aid to the Americans lest they drop out of the war, the Spanish council sent orders to redouble the preparations for the attack on Gibraltar—indeed Floridablanca even refused to rescue Jay and his mission in Spain from the humiliation of threatened bankruptcy arising from Congress' false anticipation of Spanish financial aid.[1] Gibraltar presented enormous dangers for French diplomacy. Montmorin wondered in what manner, once Gibraltar was taken, Spain would regard a war continued for the independence of the United States: "I swear to you, sir [Vergennes], that that idea torments me." Since Charles was resolved on attacking Gibraltar, Montmorin did not see what could be done. Discouraged at his failure to obtain the 24 Spanish ships of the line needed for operations off the Channel, Montmorin proposed to Vergennes that France cede in good graces and agree that the combined fleet would instead be used for the siege. If France cooperated fully, she would at least acquire a basis for Charles' personal gratitude.

Montmorin's pessimism about future combined operations unfortunately was justified. On 9 April Floridablanca informed Aranda that Charles intended that the greatest part of the Spanish fleet participate in the siege of Gibraltar.[2] To mollify the French, Floridablanca suggested the remainder of the Brest fleet rendezvous off Lisbon for a short cruise, take station off Cadiz during the reduction of Gibraltar, and *then* go to the Channel. He postponed any

---

[1] Spain 606: 369–376, Montmorin to Vergennes, 30 March 1782. France continued to subsidize the Americans and Franklin was eventually able to rescue his colleague.

[2] Spain 606: 435–437, Floridablanca to Aranda, 9 April 1782.

final decision on the distribution of forces until after de Guichen's return.

France's war aims dictated cooperation with the United States, but Vergennes trusted the Americans little more than did Floridablanca. His feelings were well expressed in a letter to Montmorin at the end of 1781, explaining why France could not participate in negotiations without the Americans.[3] The English would present separate negotiations as a certain symptom of a French abandonment and would thereby feed the pacifism of the American people, who would listen to any peace propositions which explicitly or implicitly recognized American independence. Not only would America cease to absorb British naval and military forces, but perhaps the English might even suggest a coalition against the Bourbons "and who will respond that it will not be accorded?" Vergennes admitted this speculation carried things to an extreme but he cited the history of popular governments as evidence of their inconstancy, lack of seriousness, and dependence on the moods of the public. For this reason Vergennes insisted on simultaneous negotiations with Britain by the Bourbons and by the Americans.

Vergennes' fears of being abandoned also explain in large part the campaigns of Gérard and La Luzerne to influence the American peace terms, culminating in Congress' instructions of June 1781, which placed the American commissioners under Vergennes' direction.[4] Vergennes also encouraged La Luzerne to discreetly attempt to moderate America's sweeping western border claims.[5] La Luzerne won concessions on this point as well. In February 1781 Jay

[3] Spain 605: 508–514, Vergennes to Montmorin, 20 December 1781.

[4] William C. Stinchcombe, *The American Revolution and the French Alliance* (Syracuse, N.Y.: Syracuse University Press, 1969) deals with French influence in Congress. Congress' actions are understandable only in the context of the uncertain military and diplomatic situation of the moment. See Chapter Eight, Section 5, Note 11.

[5] United States 21: 341, Vergennes to La Luzerne, 28 June 1782. See also United States 14: 159; United States 15: 254–255, Vergennes to La Luzerne, 22 October 1780 and 19 February 1781.

was authorized to concede American navigation of the Mississippi, although Jay's attempts to secure an alliance and financial aid from Spain in exchange were rejected by Floridablanca, while the pretense of negotiation continued.[6] That the French alliance functioned as well as it did is an indication of the extraordinary tact and political realism of Benjamin Franklin.[7] Franklin's abrasive colleague John Adams, presently in the Netherlands, was so mistrusted by Vergennes that he even suspected Adams of collaboration with the British opposition party.[8] The opposition had used reconciliation with the Americans as part of a platform to defeat North. Upon assuming office Lord Shelburne, the new secretary of state for home and colonial affairs, immediately contacted both Adams and Franklin. Shelburne expected negotiations to be established through Adams, reported ready to make a separate peace, but Adams rejected separate negotiations as he had with North's emissaries.[9] Richard Oswald, a merchant and diplomatic dabbler (like Beaumarchais), was sent to Franklin almost as an afterthought,[10] but it was through Oswald that negotiations were established. On 17 April Franklin brought Oswald to meet Vergennes and to determine France's disposition toward a

[6] Spain 604: 420–425, projected treaty presented by Jay, 22 September 1781; Spain 604: 8–12, Montmorin to Vergennes, 2 October 1781; Spain 606: 47–48, Montmorin to Vergennes, 11 January 1782.

[7] For Vergennes' opinion of Franklin see United States 15: 257, Vergennes to La Luzerne, 19 February 1781.

[8] Holland 547: 55, Vergennes to La Vauguyon, 7 March 1782. Fear of Adams also contributed to the French desire to modify Congress' peace instructions. Instead of Adams acting as sole peace negotiator, Congress named a commission of five members, including Franklin. See United States 15: 257–258, 346, Vergennes to La Luzerne, 19 February and 9 March 1781.

[9] Holland 548: 181–182, 336–345, La Vauguyon to Vergennes, 27 March and 19 April 1782; Spain 606: 397–398, Vergennes to Montmorin, 1 April 1782.

[10] John M. Norris, *Shelburne and Reform* (London: Macmillan and Co., 1963), 165. Oswald was a former trading partner of the captured American peace commissioner Henry Laurens, released on parole to make contact with Adams.

general peace.[11] Vergennes warned him that France could not treat of peace without the concurrence of Spain and wished that the United Provinces of the Netherlands, although not an ally, be admitted to any negotiations. The ingenuous Oswald told Vergennes that orders had been sent to British forces in America to commit no further hostilities against the Americans and suggested to Vergennes' horror that the Americans take reciprocal measures. Vergennes quickly insisted in Franklin's presence that any armistice must be general and based on solid foundations. Vergennes concluded by giving Oswald a passport to return to England for further instructions.

Vergennes, already in terror that the Americans would cease military operations in order to save money,[12] would have been still more horrified had he known that Oswald brought back with him to England not only Franklin's peace terms but also a proposal for Anglo-American reconciliation based on the cession of Canada to the United States.[13] Luckily for Franklin, Shelburne kept this proposal secret (although it was inconceivable that it could be granted); furthermore, he honored Franklin's request that the amateur diplomat Oswald be retained.

Shelburne was not the only dangerous member of the new cabinet, which was headed loosely by the Marquis of Rockingham. Its single secretary of state for foreign affairs (formerly divided between two secretaries) was Charles James Fox, as mercurial, egocentric, and impractical as the

[11] Spain 606: 467–468, Vergennes to Montmorin, 18 April 1782.

[12] Spain 606: 294–295, Vergennes to Montmorin, 14 March 1782; United States 20: 469–470, Vergennes to La Luzerne, 23 March 1782. For this reason the council decided to lend the United States 6,000,000 livres during 1782. The council had loaned, directly or indirectly, over 20,000,000 livres to the United States from 1778 through 1781. United States 20: 461, Vergennes to La Luzerne, 23 March 1782. This is exclusive of the 6,000,000 livre gift of 1781. See Bemis, *Diplomacy of the American Revolution*, 93.

[13] For Franklin's motivation see Stourzh, *Benjamin Franklin*, 208–213.

Emperor Joseph II. Fox's program as a whole was insanely out-of-touch with diplomatic realities: he desired the construction of a triple alliance between Britain, Russia, and Prussia. Its corollaries, however, included a separate peace with America and reconciliation with Holland, so that England could better attack the Bourbons. Fox almost immediately communicated his terms to both Russia and the United Provinces. In exchange for a suspension of arms he was willing to offer a renewal of the liberal commercial treaty of 1674, a major concession to both the Dutch and the Russians.[14]

For the moment the danger of Holland's making a separate peace outweighed even the danger of the Americans doing the same. The Dutch proposal for combined operations, submitted when the Estates General voted to concert operations with France, was dependent on a force off the Channel. (This proposal, although vague in detail, was based on a Dutch squadron of observation of 14–15 of the line in the North Sea in order to cover departing squadrons for the West and East Indies, to open up Dutch trade with the Baltic, and to do whatever harm it could.)[15] As Spain delayed making such a commitment, Vergennes' letters to Montmorin became increasingly demanding.

On 12 April Vergennes complained of the continuing uncertainty.[16] France had been reduced to silence with the

---

[14] Madariaga, *Britain, Russia, and the Armed Neutrality*, 387–392; Holland 548: 227–235, La Vauguyon to Vergennes, 5 April 1782, with various enclosures; Fortescue, *Correspondence of King George the Third*, 5: 247, minutes of cabinet meeting of 29 March 1782 (no. 3603).

[15] This proposal was sent as an enclosure, now missing, to Holland 548: 175–177, La Vauguyon to Vergennes, 26 March 1782, and then to Spain 606: 397–399, Vergennes to Montmorin, 1 April 1782. It can be largely reconstructed from Spain 606: 462–464, Spanish note of 17 April 1782.

[16] Spain 606: 445–447, personal letter of Vergennes to Montmorin, 12 April 1782. La Vauguyon did convey to the Dutch that Louis had received the plan with satisfaction, but this was only a delaying move by La Vauguyon. Holland 548: 245–247, La Vauguyon to Vergennes, 9 April 1782.

Dutch after the overture they had made for concerting operations. Vergennes feared they would make a separate peace and although their cooperation had not hitherto been very effective, they had occupied a small part of the enemy's forces and this year probably would occupy a more considerable portion.

When he wrote again on 23 April, Vergennes had become more desperate.[17] Floridablanca's letter to Aranda of 9 April (that the greatest part of the fleet would be used at Gibraltar) gave little hope that Spain would provide reinforcements at the approaches to the Channel at an opportune time; apparently Spain even wished the few remaining ships at Brest to be sent to Gibraltar. The Dutch were balancing between peace with England and combined operations with France. The 24 extra Spanish ships of the line would be useless for the Gibraltar operation and could help produce a squadron to stand up to the English, encourage a reaffirmation of the Dutch principle of cooperation, and make the new English ministry feel more deeply the need for reasonable sacrifices for peace. Vergennes would try to gain another two or three weeks with the Dutch; he asked Floridablanca to give him an answer within three days.

Montmorin's next letters, received on 30 April, left Vergennes still less hope.[18] Floridablanca refused anything beyond vague assurances to Holland until after France and Spain had reached agreement and this was impossible before

[17] Spain 606: 508–509, Vergennes to Montmorin, 23 April 1782. Vergennes included a letter of La Vauguyon which is not given, but which was probably Holland 548: 318–323, La Vauguyon to Vergennes, 18 April 1782, an extremely peremptory Dutch demand for more detailed information about French plans before the Dutch fleet would sail from the Texel. The Estates General of the Netherlands did indicate their indifference to reconciliation with Britain by admitting John Adams in his capacity as representative of the United States. Holland 548: 346, extract of register of resolutions, 19 April 1782.

[18] Spain 606: 462–464, Spanish note of 17 April 1782; Spain 606: 478–480, 487–491, Montmorin to Vergennes, 18 April and 19 April 1782.

de Guichen's return from his cruise. Montmorin had tried for two weeks to win Arcon's support but the engineer insisted the entire fleet would be necessary for the success of his plan. Arcon believed the siege would not start before September. Although Montmorin feared a cruise off Lisbon would be useless and perhaps even ridiculous, he advised that it might be the sole thing that could be done under the circumstances. The only favorable aspect of the situation was that de Guichen had sent dispatches reporting his impending return to Cadiz. (He arrived 25 April.)

The council now was faced with its most serious crisis since September 1780. It was also faced with new evidence of the probable consequences of a division of forces. After the dispatch of the convoys of February, Hector prepared a new set of convoys at Brest to carry 1,200 troops to Asia, 1,300 troops to the West Indies, and 1,000 to North America.[19] Because of delays in assembling merchantmen and provisions, Castries decided to send each convoy as soon as it was ready.[20] Although a British squadron was reported at sea, the council decided the Indian convoy should sail, taking all possible precautions. On 19 April the *Protecteur*, *Pégase*, *Actionnaire* (serving as a transport), two frigates, and 15 transports began their journey.[21] Two days later they met Vice-Admiral Barrington's squadron of 12 ships of the line, which took the *Pégase*, *Actionnaire*, a dozen transports, and over 1,000 troops.[22] Perhaps most disturbing was the manner in which the escorts abandoned the convoy and particularly the feeble resistance of the new *Pégase* to the *Foudroyant*, 80. The captain of the *Pégase* was subse-

---

[19] B³734: 120, untitled memoir of 4 April 1782.

[20] B⁴217: 49, 52–53, 55, 131–132, Castries to Hector, 13 March to 20 April 1782.

[21] B⁴200: 16–18, 98–100, council of war concerning loss of *Pégase* and *Actionnaire*, decision and summary of events.

[22] B⁸14: unpaged, sheets for April 1782; Mackesy, *War for America*, 477–478; Fortescue, *Correspondence of King George the Third*, 5: 436.

quently cashiered from the service, but the court martial board pointed out that his ship was poorly manned both in officers and crew, citing a 19-year-old ensign in command of the ship's first battery.[23]

There was certainly collaborating evidence that the navy had reached the limits to which it could expand. The captain of one of La Motte-Picquet's squadron complained to Hector that his crew was very bad; Hector in relaying his complaints admitted many other captains had similar complaints and that there were few means of remedying them.[24] This human shortage was far less tractable than the matériel shortages and maldistributions which plagued the ports,[25] yet the navy's most immediate problem was financial. For 1781 the navy and army departments had not increased their budget requests, but for the present year the navy demanded (and received) a major appropriations increase.[26] Necker's replacement, Joly de Fleury (titled minister of state and of finances) had already planned to use perhaps 135,000,000 livres in anticipations on the revenues of 1783 to pay part of the expected 400,000,000-livre deficit for

[23] B^{4}200: 16–18, council of war concerning loss of *Pégase* and *Actionnaire*, decision.

[24] B^{3}719: 52, 93–94, Hector to Castries, 11 February and 6 March 1782. See also Chapter Six, Section 2, Note 3.

[25] Rochefort had so much wood that it could not be stored; Brest complained of shortages, although by 1 May 526,000 ft.^{3} was on hand. On 15 March Hector complained that he had more copper nails than he could use, but had received no sheets of copper. For 1782 the navy ordered 117,265 sheets of copper, of which 29,493 were delivered by August. It must be emphasized that copper, despite its importance, was not as vital as were wood for construction, hemp, and masts. B^{3}719: 58–59, 105, Hector to Castries, 13 February and 15 March 1782; B^{3}722: 134–135, Guillot, intendant at Brest, to Castries, 8 May 1782; B^{1}96: 122, untitled memoir of August 1782; B^{3}719 and B^{3}720: *passim*.

[26] French national archives, M^{1v}663: piece 13, "Dépenses des départements de la marine et de la guerre depuis 1778 jusqu'en et compris 1782," March 1782. These appropriations include the following: 1780—army 108,325,848 livres, navy 143,988,500 livres; 1781—army 111,823,478 livres, navy 147,500,000 livres; 1782—army 113,747,874 livres, navy 183,675,000 livres. See also Appendix A.

1782.[27] Now he faced 35,000,000 livres of supplementary naval expenses.

With the shortages of personnel and money the maintenance of the initiative became even more important. The new English ministry, which was crying for peace, could not be permitted to change its mind.[28] With the possibility of a delay of the Jamaican operation, pressure would have to be brought against England in the Western Approaches and North Sea and this depended on overcoming Charles' resistance to the detachment of the Cadiz fleet from the waters washing Gibraltar.

Incredibly, the council did find a solution. First, it suggested a revised operational plan.[29] La Motte-Picquet would escort the North American and West Indian colonies clear and then reinforce de Guichen. De Guichen would return to French waters with as many Spanish ships as Charles believed appropriate. This combined fleet would cover the departure of new convoys for India and the West Indies, cruise near England, and then return to Gibraltar. The council's hopes, however, rested on another communication carried by Vergennes' courier. The Count d'Artois, Louis' brother and Charles' nephew, wrote personally to his uncle asking if he could participate by his presence at the successful conclusion of the siege of Gibraltar. Montmorin took the letter to Floridablanca who gave it to the king.

When Montmorin was summoned, the king had tears in his eyes. Overcome that he would finally see one of his nephews, Charles was easily convinced by Montmorin that Louis would never do anything to jeopardize the success of

[27] Bosher, *French Finances*, 175. During his two years in office Joly de Fleury went more in debt than Necker had in four years. For statistics see George V. Taylor, "The Paris Bourse on the Eve of the Revolution, 1781–1789," *American Historical Review* 67 (1962): 963.

[28] Spain 606: 470, 509, Vergennes to Montmorin, 18 April and 23 April 1782. See also B⁴217: 131–132, Vergennes to Hector, 20 April 1782.

[29] Spain 607: 35–37, Vergennes to Montmorin, 4 May 1782.

the Gibraltar operation.[30] Within two days Charles decided
to send 27 of his own ships, 5 of de Guichen's and 4 of La
Motte-Picquet's (expected from France) to cruise off the
entrance to the Channel until the beginning of August;[31]
within a week a courier was en route to Cadiz with sailing
orders for Córdoba.[32]

It seems highly probable that d'Artois' gesture was the idea
of Vergennes.[33] When Aranda found out the secret, he
wrote Vergennes: "He [d'Artois] shall have rendered a great
service to the two crowns by his thought of going to Gibraltar. Without flattery I believe you, Monsieur the Count, a
great man. I am confirmed in my opinion by the part, or the
invention perhaps, that you have had in the charming, re-
fined and interesting idea."[34]

I will leave to the reader any comment on the Ancien Régime. Vergennes must, at any rate, be accounted a diplomat
of consummate skill in the use of its weapons including the
exploitation of the family loyalty and personal tenderness
of the kindest of all its kings.[35]

As Vergennes awaited the resolution of the crisis, Oswald
reappeared with Franklin to announce unofficially that
George was disposed to treat of a general peace, that he
preferred negotiations be established in Paris, that the independence of the United States would not be an obstacle to
peace, and that Fox's emissary would soon arrive to confirm

---

[30] Spain 607: 91–92, 93, personal letters of Montmorin to Vergennes,
12 May 1782. For Charles and Louis' family relationship see Chapter
One, Section 1, Note 9.

[31] Spain 607: 103–104, "Résolution . . . ," 15 May 1782; Spain 607:
109–110, Montmorin to Vergennes, 15 May 1782.

[32] Spain 607: 151–152, Montmorin to Vergennes, 20 May 1782.

[33] Montmorin was terrified that the irresponsible d'Artois would do
something to shock the pious Charles, but d'Artois (later King Charles
X of France) behaved with reasonable decorum.

[34] Spain 607: 153, Aranda to Vergennes, 20 May 1782.

[35] Montmorin believed no other tactic would have succeeded with
Charles. Spain 607: 107, Montmorin to Vergennes, 15 May 1782.

all Oswald had said.[36] On 9 May Vergennes was introduced by Franklin to Thomas Grenville, sent by Fox. Grenville did confirm what Shelburne's representative had said, but the young Grenville quickly admitted that he was not authorized to speak with Spain or Holland. Vergennes warned Grenville that France could make neither overtures nor propositions. When Grenville fell silent, Vergennes reassured him that although his mouth was closed his ears remained open. Grenville responded that since American independence was France's war aim, there remained no need for war. Vergennes in turn argued that American independence was only the indirect cause of war and that a variety of objects must be treated. After a second meeting, attended as well by Aranda, both parties agreed to request further instruction from their courts. Vergennes had at least been impressed by Grenville's *esprit*, sagacity, honesty, and modesty and believed that the interest of the current ministry was very certainly to make peace if it could obtain it under proper conditions. Moreover, George had agreed to Paris as a site for the negotiations and to exclude the mediators.

The European crisis now began to lift. The Dutch decided on the basis of La Vauguyon's vague assurances that their fleet would be safe, and on 3 May six ships of the line sailed from the Texel.[37] On 22 May there arrived Montmorin's courier reporting Montmorin's meeting with Charles, but another crisis already had arisen. On the preceding day the first reports had reached the council of potential disaster in the West Indies.[38]

---

[36] Spain 607: 84–87, Vergennes to Montmorin, 11 May 1782; England 537: 27–28, report on conference with Grenville, 9 May 1782; Holland 549: 70–71, Vergennes to La Vauguyon, 12 May 1782. Oswald spoke unofficially because as Shelburne's representative he could negotiate only with the Americans. Note that Britain wished to avoid mediation because she, too, distrusted Austria.

[37] Holland 549: 36–47, 48, La Vauguyon to Vergennes, 7 May 1782, with enclosures.

[38] Spain 607: 180, Vergennes to Montmorin, 24 May 1782.

3. The West Indian Setback

After the successful operations of February, de Grasse had retreated to Fort Royal, Martinique. As in each year since 1779, France's spring campaign awaited the arrival of provisions and reinforcements. For the third consecutive year, Rodney with his superior forces had the opportunity to intercept a vital convoy and immediately win the campaign. Again Rodney failed. After waiting only three weeks (26 February–20 March) de Grasse was reinforced by the last three ships of the line and the critical convoy needed for the Jamaican expedition.[1]

On 8 April de Grasse and his troop convoy sailed for Saint Domingue to rendezvous with the Spaniards and to collect the remainder of the troops. Despite being far behind schedule Gálvez intended to carry out the attack even if the rendezvous was not made until the last days of April.[2] The French, however, had failed to collect sufficient forces to leave any margin for error. One of Rodney's 37 ships of the line was missing, but 3 of de Grasse's 36 were not with him —the *Saint-Esprit*, left for repair at Martinique, and his two 50s, used to cover the convoy. De Grasse might still have outrun Rodney had not collisions deprived him of three more of the line and delayed him until combat was unavoidable. The battle occurred on 12 April off the Îles des Saintes, just south of Guadeloupe. Rodney, fighting with a decisive edge in ships and cannon, captured 5 of the line including de Grasse's flagship, the *Ville-de-Paris*. Rodney's squadron, however, was also badly damaged and the convoy and the scattered remnants of de Grasse's squadron safely reached Saint Domingue (except for 2 damaged ships of the line left behind before the battle, which were

[1] This was the convoy escorted out by de Guichen on 11 February. A chronology of de Grasse's squadron's movements is given by B⁴184: 54–119.

[2] Spain 607: 156–157, Montmorin to Vergennes, 20 May 1782. De Grasse's convoy and fleet carried 4,000 troops. England 537: 321, untitled memoir of 9 July 1782.

captured while attempting to rejoin).[3] By the middle of May, 28 French ships of the line, 11 or 12 Spanish ships of the line, and the entire expeditionary force of 20,000 troops were assembled at Saint Domingue.[4] Their commanders, Gálvez, Solano, and Commodore Vaudreuil (replacing the captured de Grasse) now were forced to decide what to do with this gigantic force before all the provisions of the colony were consumed. They decided to divide the troops among the Spanish and French Leeward Islands, to send Solano's squadron back to Havana, the worst of Vaudreuil's ships back to France as convoy escorts, and the pick of Vaudreuil's squadron to North America to obtain provisions and matériel.[5]

The news of the battle left Vergennes a network of problems to solve.[6] First, Vaudreuil's fleet had to be resupplied with munitions and provisions.[7] The council had unsuccessfully tried to send out a convoy with the *Protecteur* under the protection of La Motte-Picquet's four ships of the line, which were then to have proceeded to Cadiz.[8] The British domination of the French coast which forced La Motte-Picquet back to Brest meant that another resupply attempt would have to await the arrival of Córdoba's combined

[3] The best account of the battle is John Creswell, *British Admirals of the Eighteenth Century* (Hamden, Conn.: Archon Books, 1972), 163–177. See also Mahan, *Influence of Sea Power*, 428–451.

[4] French colonial archives, C⁰ᴬ152: unpaged, Major-General Bellecombe to Castries, 18 May 1782; B⁴205: 179–180, Vaudreuil to Castries, 19 May 1782. The *Zélé* remained at Martinique for repairs.

[5] B⁴206: 181–182, 188–189, Vaudreuil to Castries, 19 May and 18 June 1782; B⁴195: 57–58, 59, projected operations, May 1782. At the beginning of July, Bouillé arrived at Versailles to report on the agreement reached in May. Spain 608: 15, Vergennes to Montmorin, 6 July 1782.

[6] Spain 607: 172–174, 180, Vergennes to Montmorin, 24 May 1782.

[7] According to intelligence reaching Lorient, Vaudreuil's squadron was reduced to 15 minutes worth of munitions. B⁸719: 353–354, port commandant Thevenard to Castries, 17 June 1782.

[8] Spain 607: 88–89, Vergennes to Montmorin, 11 May 1782. Luckily the convoy which had left Saint Domingue in January arrived safely in France at the end of April (after it had stopped in Galicia).

fleet. Vergennes asked that La Motte-Picquet's four ships be replaced by four Spanish ships so as to maintain the combined fleet at 36 of the line.[9]

Vergennes' second problem was to strengthen the Dutch in their resolution. They had been shaken by the appearance of a strong British fleet in the North Sea, which forced the Dutch fleet back to their base at the Texel.[10] Moreover, Fox had followed his offer of renewing the Treaty of 1674 by an offer on 4 May to accept the principles of the League of Armed Neutrality as a basis for a separate peace with the Estates General.[11] Vergennes was dependent on the combined fleet to free the Dutch fleet but he immediately moved to forestall any danger that the Dutch would be receptive to Fox's initiatives.[12] After informing La Vauguyon that the combined fleet was ready to sail, he ordered him to inform the leaders of the republic that Louis' invariable intention was not to make peace without the republic, but that this was on the condition that they observed reciprocity. This should indicate his dispositions toward the Dutch colonies France had recaptured from England; by his engaging the Dutch to take part in a general pacification, the Dutch could assume his intention was not to keep those possessions. Louis, however, refused to take any formal engagement to return them since "they should serve to facilitate first peace between the king [Louis] and England and then between that power and the United Provinces." With

[9] B⁴185: 152, Castries to Vergennes, 24 May 1782; Spain 607: 183, personal letter of Vergennes to Montmorin, 24 May 1782.

[10] Holland 549: 100, La Vauguyon to Vergennes, 17 May 1782; Mackesy, *War for America*, 478.

[11] Madariaga, *Britain, Russia, and the Armed Neutrality*, 395. On 26 June the cabinet voted that its general recognition of these principles must be contingent on a treaty of alliance with Russia. *Ibid.*, 407.

[12] Holland 549: 175–180, Vergennes to La Vauguyon, 25 May 1782 (quotation is from f. 179). Vergennes told Montmorin that if the Dutch abandoned the other Allies, it would add 15 ships of the line to the British forces opposing the Bourbons. Spain 607: 198–199, Vergennes to Montmorin, 28 May 1782.

French troops holding Saint Eustatius and protecting the Cape, the Netherlands were effectively a French satellite. On 1 July they rejected separate negotiations.[13]

The immediate problems of Vaudreuil's squadron and of the fleet at the Texel were merely aspects of the general strategic problem, the preservation of momentum. The critical theme of French strategic thinking in 1782 was that if the Allies could maintain the initiative for another campaign, the British cabinet would be driven by exhaustion to peace.[14] (It was vital to this purpose, too, that the cabinet not be given any hope that the United States or Netherlands would make a separate peace.)[15] The corollary, however, was that if the British were permitted a success, they could regain their strength and, as in previous wars, outlast the Bourbon powers. The battle of the Saintes had not been decisive, but the Allies had to move quickly to reestablish the initiative.[16]

France's first step in restoring the initiative was more important psychologically than for any practical benefits. Louis announced that ten new ships of the line would be started in the dockyards.[17] Vergennes hoped they would be ready by the end of the year, but in fact, only one of them was launched by then (plus two ships of the line already begun in April at Toulon); because of the shortage of sailors, new construction actually was pointless except to replace any battered ships kept too long overseas. The English, faced with the same problem, had to strip their col-

---

[13] Holland 550: 14–17, resolutions of the Estates General, 1 July 1782 (to be communicated to the French court). In return, Louis promised to watch over Dutch interests.

[14] See Spain 606: 296–298, observations of Castries, 14 March 1782; Spain 606: 315, 470–471, Vergennes to Montmorin, 16 March and 18 April 1782.

[15] Spain 607: 88, Vergennes to Montmorin, 11 May 1782.

[16] See the reflections of Vergennes in Spain 607: 200, Vergennes to Montmorin, 28 May 1782; Memoirs and Documents, France 1897: 112–113, Vergennes to Louis, 17 May 1782.

[17] Spain 607: 231–232, Vergennes to Montmorin, 1 June 1782; Holland 549: 247–248, Vergennes to La Vauguyon, 6 June 1782.

liers of crews to increase the fleet to almost 100 of the line.[18] The most important aspect of the French reconstruction program was the enthusiastic support it received. Led by the Estates of Burgundy, various members of the court, cities, and organizations volunteered the funds to replace the battle losses; eventually over 6,000,000 livres were received with which two 118s, one 80, and three 74s were built.[19] Since "victory" and "defeat" are in large part an expression of psychological effects, it became quickly obvious that the Saintes was not a defeat on the order of Yorktown. Nevertheless, it was a serious check, which necessitated, above all, a plan for renewing the attack on Jamaica.

The council had the best possible assistance in drafting such a plan. The brilliant Saavedra was in the French islands after bringing money from Vera Cruz for the expedition; after the battle he was sent to France.[20] Saavedra aided in the deliberations and then carried a copy of the completed plan to Spain.[21] The plan called for an operation

---

[18] Spain 607: 128, Vergennes to Montmorin, 18 May 1782; B⁴186: 152, Castries to Vergennes, 24 May 1782. According to French intelligence the British on 10 May 1782 had 104 ships of the line (including 16 50s) in service. B⁴288: unpaged, untitled memoir, 10 May 1782. By my calculations the British navy reached its maximum size in September 1782—98 ships of the line. Vergennes' expectation that France could man 75 ships of the line in 1783 appears to be highly unrealistic.

[19] B¹100: 72, decision of 21 January 1786 on the use of the funds. See also B¹101: 10. The example for this public action was set at the end of the Seven Years War, when a similar effort was made. Some arm-twisting was applied in both cases. Sartine had turned down in 1778 an offer to raise money to build a ship of the line. B¹87: 315, untitled memoir of 18 December 1778.

[20] Spain 607: 55, 230, Aranda to Vergennes, 5 May and 1 June 1782; B⁴192: 81, Santo Domingo, captain of the frigate *Courageous*, to Castries, 21 October 1781; C⁰ᴬ152: unpaged, Bellecombe to Castries, 26 March 1782.

[21] Spain 607: 329, Vergennes to Montmorin, 14 June 1782. See also Spain 607: 333–335, personal letter of Vergennes to Montmorin, 14 June 1782, in which Vergennes called Saavedra a man of true merit and told Montmorin that he would be as sensible of Montmorin's friendship for Saavedra as if it were direct and personal for him, Vergennes—extraordinary praise, indeed!

massive enough to compare to the combined operations of the Second World War.[22] The European component of its forces would sail from Cadiz under command of Vice-Admiral d'Estaing as soon as the attack on Gibraltar was completed (probably about October) and would comprise 24 ships of the line each from the French and Spanish navies. This gigantic force would escort a convoy of troops to replace those lost during the summer from disease. When the entire force was reassembled for the attack, it would comprise 75 of the line and 25,000 troops. Once Jamaica was captured, all of the Allied naval forces would be returned to Europe to crush the British, if it were still necessary.

As the council awaited the Spanish response, it turned to an equally vital task, the establishment of meaningful diplomatic negotiations with Britain. Oswald's discussions with Franklin were stalled over the American demand for prior recognition of independence, largely because the rivalry between Shelburne and Fox prevented a clear British line of negotiation.[23] Grenville's parallel discussions with Vergennes had not made progress because of two obstacles. The first of these, Grenville's lack of powers to treat with Spain and the Netherlands, was finally overcome when he received new powers in mid-June.[24] The second obstacle was Grenville's insistence that the Treaty of 1763 form the basis of peace between the Bourbons and Britain. Grenville hinted at a way out of the impasse. When Vergennes remarked that mention of the Treaty of Paris caused him to

---

[22] Spain 607: 308–322, "Situation présumée des forces de sa majesté dans les colonies de l'Amérique," 12 June 1782 (hereafter cited as "Situation"); Spain 607: 329–333, Vergennes to Montmorin, 14 June 1782. Castries admitted that a 25 percent superiority of force was necessary just to maintain genuine equality against an English squadron.

[23] Norris, *Shelburne and Reform*, 164–170. The Anglo-American negotiations will be discussed only in their connection with French diplomacy, thereby supplementing the thorough account of these negotiations in Morris, *The Peacemakers*, 248–410, an account which is extremely unreliable when dealing with French motivation.

[24] England 537: 171–172, summary of fifth conference, 15 June 1782. Grenville was authorized to treat with France and "any other princes or states." See Morris, *The Peacemakers*, 278.

shudder, Grenville observed that he did not pretend to say that the treaty should be renewed and confirmed in all its points. He only intended it to serve as a base and that if the proposition was not agreeable to Louis, the king of England invited him to suggest another.[25]

Vergennes was acute enough to see the great advantages to France in Grenville's suggestion.[26] The most important advantage was time. If the Treaty of Paris were accepted as the base, the negotiations would be so well launched the mediators would be unable to intervene—the selling point Vergennes used with Floridablanca, who was even more opposed to the mediators than was Vergennes. Moreover, by confirming the treaty except for certain particulars, whole areas of discussion could be avoided, such as the Protestant succession, the separation of the Bourbon thrones, and the volumes of diplomatic history of the last century confirmed by the treaty.

With the council's advice, Louis therefore accepted the Treaty of Paris as a base for negotiation without necessarily confirming all that was in it. Any discussion of restitutions and compensations (for the conquests of the various parties) would be deferred to the negotiations themselves and the acceptance specified:

> His Majesty expressly reserves to himself to demand of the King of England . . . different exceptions and changes, among others,
>
> 1. new arrangements concerning the East Indies,
> 2. new stipulations relative to Africa,
> 3. an equitable and mutually beneficial regulation in regard to the so-called Newfoundland fishery,
> 4. an arrangement of commerce for the convenience of the two nations in Europe[27]

[25] England 537: 171–172, summary of fifth conference, 15 June 1782.
[26] Spain 607: 367–368, 378–379, Vergennes to Montmorin, 22 June 1782.
[27] Spain 607: 362–368, "Observations relatives à la pacification," 20 June 1782; England 537: 197–198, conference of 21 June 1782. Grenville informed the French that George planned to recognize Ameri-

The next move in the negotiations was returned to Britain. For most of the summer the council's attention was largely centered on the working out of the military, strategic, and diplomatic initiatives undertaken at the summer's beginning—the progress of Córdoba's fleet and its effect on English and Dutch military operations, the conducting of strategic discussions with Spain for the renewal of the Jamaican attack, and the slow development of peace negotiations with Britain.

Córdoba's fleet sailed on 4 June, 32 ships of the line strong.[28] It arrived off Île d'Ouessant at the beginning of July[29] and was soon joined by La Motte-Picquet with the *Invincible, Bretagne, Actif, Bien-Aimé, Guerrier, Protecteur, Robuste,* and *Zodiaque.* Córdoba's cruise was not particularly productive. En route to France he had captured 19 ships from a Newfoundland convoy, but he was subsequently able neither to bring Admiral Howe's Channel fleet of 25 of the line to battle nor to intercept a major convoy. The provisions convoy for Vaudreuil which was to have been sent in May was retained at the Île d'Aix off Rochefort by contrary winds and by storm damage until the beginning of September. At least convoys returning from Saint Domingue arrived safely at the end of July and the end of August (each escorted by 4 of the line).[30] Córdoba's returning fleet arrived off Cadiz on 5 September and proceeded immediately to Algeciras where the remainder of the Spanish fleet and two new ships of the line from Toulon were

---

can independence prior to the peace, an intention applauded by Vergennes. In fact, Oswald, acting under Shelburne's instructions, held the opposite position, which eventually prevailed. Recognition finally accompanied the Anglo-American agreement on peace terms. Norris, *Shelburne and Reform,* 168–169, 258.

[28] Spain 607: 291, 286, Montmorin to Vergennes, 8 June 1782, with enclosure. Vergennes's request that the number of ships be augmented arrived at the Spanish court on the evening of 1 June, too late to be implemented.

[29] Holland 550: 45, Vergennes to La Vauguyon, 5 July 1782.

[30] See Mackesy, *War for America,* 478–479 and Spain 608; B⁴194; and B³728: *passim.*

awaiting it.[31] The summer cruise did accomplish its goal of freeing the Texel fleet and, more importantly, the East Indian convoy with its 8 50s, so vital to the council's hopes for that theater. These sailed together on 7 July.[32] The Dutch dominated the North Sea for the next six weeks, even finding the courage to send a force to Trondheim, Norway to bring back 3 merchantmen.

The Jamaican discussions also proceeded in a reasonably satisfactory manner. By coincidence, on the very day that Vergennes sent the council's proposals to Montmorin, the latter reported Floridablanca's desire that 7,000–8,000 troops and 16–18 ships of the line (about half of each to be Spanish) be sent to the Antilles at the end of September. Floridablanca even hoped that French forces could be sent directly from Gibraltar.[33] As might be expected, Montimorin had slight difficulty in obtaining Spanish agreement to the French plan, although the court had little time for anything except preparing the attack on Gibraltar. The Spanish, however, restricted their contribution to be sent from Europe to the 20 ships of the line in the best condition for overseas service.[34] Spain had only one copper-bottomed ship in their entire navy, and their European fleet had seen much service; even providing a 20-ship detachment promised to be a challenge. Saavedra would be sent ahead to the West Indies at the end of August or beginning of Septem-

[31] Embarrassingly, Hector's dispatch ships were unable to locate the fleet for several weeks, so Córdoba acted until mid-August on his own. Castries intended to bring some ships into Brest for doubling (see Spain 608: 215–216), but was unable to do so. The *Protecteur* and two new ships of the line from Rochefort were detached to escort the convoy as far as Madeira; the *Amphion* accompanied it to Fort Royal, where it finally arrived in November.

[32] Holland 550: 59–61, La Vauguyon to Vergennes, 8 July 1782. The East India Company ships are listed in Holland 550: 38. For subsequent movements of the Dutch fleet see Holland 550: *passim*. The Dutch fleet reentered its base at the Texel on 16 August. About 17 ships of the line had participated in the campaign.

[33] Spain 607: 337–339, Montmorin to Vergennes, 14 June 1782.

[34] Spain 608: 31–34, Spanish memoir of 8 July 1782; Spain 608: 35–38, 61, Montmorin to Vergennes, 9 July and 15 July 1782.

ber; d'Estaing was requested to come to the palace of Saint Ildefonse for further discussions. Until d'Estaing left and the Gibraltar attack was finished, more discussion had little point. By then the French perspective on the operation was greatly altered.

The diplomatic negotiations promised to be far more difficult. The Dutch apparently believed the extent of one's terms of peace should be inversely proportional to the means at hand to obtain them, a belief surprisingly common in diplomatic history. They demanded the acceptance of the principles of the League of Armed Neutrality, a renewal of the commercial Treaty of 1674, restitution of their possessions, and compensation for their damages.[35] Spain was reluctant to engage in any negotiation until the expected successful conclusion of the Gibraltar attack. Aranda was ordered by Floridablanca to conclude nothing, whatever turn the negotiations took—indeed, not even to advance anything positively without first demanding new orders from his court.[36] Moreover, there were already indications that the Anglo-Spanish negotiations once begun would not be easy and that if the Spanish did not capture Gibraltar it would be difficult to negotiate an exchange. Floridablanca rejected exchanging the rich island of Porto Rico and was even dubious about offering to exchange Oran, a Mediterranean port, but a feeble substitute for the great fortress.[37]

France's negotiations with England also did not go smoothly. On 1 July Lord Rockingham died. He was succeeded by Shelbourne. Fox resigned rather than serve under his rival and was replaced by Baron Grantham, former ambassador to Madrid. Thomas Townshend, one of Shelburne's followers, received Shelburne's old position as secretary of state for home and colonial affairs. Grenville

---

[35] Holland 549: 355–356, La Vauguyon to Vergennes, 22 June 1782; Holland 550: 62–63, La Vauguyon to Vergennes, 8 July 1782, enclosure; Holland 550: 353, La Vauguyon to Vergennes, 20 August 1782.
[36] Spain 607: 391–392, Montmorin to Vergennes, 24 June 1782.
[37] *Ibid.*; Spain 608: 22–23, Montmorin to Vergennes, 8 July 1782.

was replaced by a young diplomat, Alleyne Fitzherbert, transferred from Brussels, where he had been minister plenipotentiary. Only on 2 August did Fitzherbert arrive for the resumption of negotiations.[38] His first communication was merely a demand for a more detailed explanation of the changes the French court wished made to the Treaty of Paris.[39] The stalled negotiations, however, were about to explode into activity. After his capture, de Grasse had been taken to London, where until he was exchanged he was treated with the gallantry which, however restricted by social position, was one of the redeeming qualities of the eighteenth century. On 17 August de Grasse's nephew, also a naval officer and ex-prisoner of war, arrived at Versailles. He brought the extraordinary news that Shelburne had asked Lieutenant-General de Grasse to convey to France Shelburne's own terms of peace.[40]

4. Rayneval's First Mission

Shelburne's message began the five months of negotiations which brought to a conclusion hostilities between Britain and her enemies. One of the most striking aspects of the negotiations is the degree of their divorce from public opinion—from the large number of Englishmen anxious to avenge the loss of America, Spaniards anxious to restore Gibraltar to their possession, Frenchmen anxious to recapture France's position in India. Still, the relative degree of freedom enjoyed by the negotiators can be overestimated. Sir Harold Nicolson, a twentieth-century diplomat and diplomatic commentator, so strongly made the point of

[38] England 538: 9, Fitzherbert to Vergennes, 2 August 1782.
[39] England 538: 11–12, "Réponse à la contre-proposition de la cour de France du 21 juin 1782," 4 August 1782. Vergennes was not surprised by Britain's concern at the vagueness of the proposals he had made in order to get the negotiations started. Spain 608: 172, Vergennes to Montmorin, 10 August 1782.
[40] England 538: 56, Lieutenant-General de Grasse to Vergennes, 17 August 1782. De Grasse himself came to Versailles on 18 August.

abhorring the increased effect of public opinion on contemporary diplomacy that his opinion has become a cliché. To a substantial degree, however, the presence of influential opposition to peace could create a real problem even for eighteenth-century negotiators. Vergennes faced the opposition of an important group interested in India, a group which had an entry into the council in Castries (who argued that favorable terms, particularly concerning India, were worth continued war).[1] Shelburne was driven from office for his failure to obtain more favorable peace terms. Finally, the Count d'Aranda had to defy his own court in order to sign terms which did not include the acquisition of Gibraltar. Before understanding the negotiations themselves one must understand what drove the negotiators to run such risks for the sake of peace.

To a large degree the conclusion of peace was dependent on the trust that was finally established between Shelburne and Vergennes. As we shall see, this trust was in part the direct result of the efforts of Vergennes' aide Rayneval, the intermediary between the two men. It was also the reflection of an intense mutual need for peace, a mutual need which alone could overcome the enormous ideological, political, and personal differences between the two leaders.

Vergennes and Shelburne differed both by character and by their relationship to the period in which they lived. Vergennes seems majestic in the simplicity and harmony of his character. Vergennes' world was dangerous and disorderly, but his relationship to it was absolutely stable. Vergennes' genius lay in the dexterity and imagination with which he

---

[1] As do other aspects of public opinion, particularly French public opinion, this area needs serious historical attention before we can escape generalizations. Vergennes at one point of the negotiations reminded Shelburne that the French ministers were obligated no less than their English counterparts to consider public opinion. England 539: 59, Vergennes to Rayneval, 27 November 1782. See also England 540: 262–265, Vergennes to Rayneval, 24 January 1783; England 540: 323–324, Rayneval to Vergennes, 2 February 1783. For Castries' side of the argument see "Castries' journal," 123 ff.

dealt with challenges to his world, while his limitations were in the restrictions that received ideas such as British dependence on America placed on his vision. By the end of his career he was able, to a degree, to transcend those limitations, but two quotations still seem to epitomize his character. One is the warning he once gave La Vauguyon: "Innovations are rarely without inconvenience."[2] A second is his usual way of indicating to Montmorin his trust: "You are prudent and sage"[3] Vergennes conferred no higher compliment.

Shelburne was a complex man, who in many regards was in serious disharmony with his time.[4] Like the ideas of other radical reformers, his recalled a purer past and sought a wiser future. As in the case of other visionaries, his fragmented personality and almost inevitable arrogance produced in his contemporaries deep mistrust and led to his political destruction. His genius lay in the sweep of his vision, while his limitations were in the maladroitness of his political actions (limitations which luckily did not apply to his true calling, the conducting of diplomacy).

Vergennes always had enormous difficulty understanding British politics. He believed Fox sincerely interested in American independence and in peace with France.[5] Shelburne he believed too subservient to George to grant American independence; at best he might use American inde-

[2] Holland 548: 225, Vergennes to La Vauguyon, 4 April 1782. This was in reference to the request of the Stadtholder of the Netherlands to use his title of Prince of Orange on the draft agreement for combined operations.

[3] One example is Spain 607: 139, Vergennes to Montmorin, 18 May 1782. On this occasion Vergennes wrote, "You are prudent and sage; I do not fear explaining myself openly with you."

[4] For Shelburne see Norris, *Shelburne and Reform*, which is excellent although it somewhat stints his diplomacy; Harlow, *Founding of the Second British Empire*; and the adulatory Lord Edmond Fitzmaurice, *Life of William, Earl of Shelburne*, 2 vols. (London: Macmillan and Co., 1912). In writing of Shelburne I am often reminded of another politician who has moved me greatly, Eugene McCarthy.

[5] Holland 550: 88–89, Vergennes to La Vauguyon, 11 July 1782; Spain 608: 49, Vergennes to Montmorin, 13 July 1782.

pendence as a device for splitting the Allies.[6] In reality Fox, no less than Shelburne, was hopeful of using American independence to divide the Americans from the Bourbons and, unlike Shelburne, saw France as a perpetual British enemy. Fox belonged to that class of statesmen who view the present as the simple extension of the past; his courting of a Prussian alliance and his Francophobia made sterile his foreign policy both in 1782 and in 1783 (during his return to office after Shelburne's fall). Shelburne as a diplomat at least had the merit of living in the existing world, which permitted him to understand his adversary's desires. What best differentiated the traditional Fox from the radical Shelburne, however, was not their differing appraisals of the diplomatic constellation of Europe, but rather their views of diplomacy itself. For all his realism, Shelburne's aims were not merely the traditional ones of gaining allies, securing territory, and increasing state security. Instead Shelburne's diplomacy was directed, above all, at peace for its own sake, and like Vergennes he sought in the peace terms not only advantage but also permanency.[7]

On a number of levels war was profoundly disfunctional for Shelburne. Most immediately, Shelburne needed peace to survive politically. His government could not risk the continuation of war and to avoid that danger he was willing to run the opposite risk of negotiating a generous peace—and a generous peace it was, which by a narrow margin in the House of Commons, finally sank his government. On a number of other levels, war was opposed to the things in which he believed: the expansion of trade, the limitation of

[6] For Vergennes' view of Shelburne see Spain 607: 402; Spain 608: 48–49, 127, Vergennes to Montmorin, 26 June, 13 July, and 28 July 1782; United States 22: 46–49, Vergennes to La Luzerne, 12 August 1782.

[7] Norris, *Shelburne and Reform*, 82, discusses Shelburne's belief in friendship with France and open trade with all nations as the proper foundations for British foreign policy. See also Fitzmaurice, *Shelburne*, 2: 113.

ministerial power, the streamlining of government, and the humane ideals of the Enlightenment.[8] Shelburne had little in common with Sir Robert Walpole except a love of peace, but he was able to play sublimely upon Vergennes' dreams of recreating the Europe of Fleury and Walpole, in which France and England dictated peace and stability to the continent. Vergennes' anguish at Shelburne's fall from power is readily understandable.

Vergennes' acceptance of Shelburne's role as the new Walpole is of course a measure of the extraordinary persuasiveness of both Shelburne and Rayneval. It is also a measure of how desperately Vergennes needed peace.

There were three basic reasons for France's need of a quick peace—financial, diplomatic, and military.

The financial burden of military expenditures already has been discussed, particularly the increased naval expenditures of 1782.[9] By the beginning of October 1782 Castries was begging Joly de Fleury for advances on the extraordinary appropriations for November and December in order to meet letters of exchange drawn in Saint Domingue on the navy.[10] Thus the French navy was being gradually reduced to financial circumstances resembling those of the American Congress. The Spanish situation was even more desperate. Montmorin reported that they had printed 15,000,000 piastres (75,000,000 livres) of paper money, which was already depreciating in value.[11] Montmorin believed the pres-

---

[8] The polarities of both the American and the British ways of viewing diplomacy are explored brilliantly by Felix Gilbert, *To the Farewell Address: Ideas of Early American Foreign Policy* (Princeton, N.J.: Princeton University Press, 1961).

[9] See Section 2 of this chapter.

[10] E 205: unpaged, "Précis de ce qui concerne les fonds de la marine. . . ," no date, but ca. 25 September 1782; "Castries' journal," 128–136.

[11] Spain 608: 26–27, Montmorin to Vergennes, 8 July 1782. In June the Spaniards doubled the amount of paper money in circulation. By September this paper had to be discounted by 13–14 percent. Earl J. Hamilton, *War and Prices in Spain, 1651–1800* (Cambridge, Mass.: Harvard University Press, 1947), 80–82.

ent campaign was feasible but prayed that the Bourbons would not have to make another. Vergennes at the end of May told Montmorin: "It is necessary to finish and the sooner the better when we can do it with dignity and justice. The[se] two words are the evangel I preach on all occasions to Monsieur de Grenville."[12]

To this persistent crisis were added during the summer other crises no less ominous. At the end of July Vergennes began dropping hints to Montmorin that France had to take great care with Russia.[13] Vergennes was careful not to alarm Montmorin, but in fact, the Eastern crisis had begun, the crisis of which he had warned at the end of the previous year.[14] The occasion was the revolt in June of the Tartars of the independent Crimea against their Khan, a Russian client. Catherine saw in the revolt an excuse to make use of her new alliance with the Emperor Joseph. By the end of July the depth of the crisis was apparent to Vergennes.[15] Within another month Vergennes' representative in Saint Petersburg was sending detailed reports of preparation for war against the Turks.[16] Continued war with England not only tied France's hands—an obvious reason for the imperial mediators to prolong the negotiations and for France to avoid the mediation[17]—but precluded joint steps with England to save the status quo.[18]

[12] Spain 607: 224, Vergennes to Montmorin, 31 May 1782.
[13] Spain 608: 78, 173–174, Vergennes to Montmorin, 20 July and 4 August 1782. See also Spain 608: 317–318, Vergennes to Montmorin, 7 September 1782.
[14] Spain 605: 523–524, Vergennes to Montmorin, 20 December 1781. Vergennes did not greatly fear a total dismemberment of the Ottoman Empire. Even if it were possible, it would place "two lions" (Austria and Russia) beside each other and they would not delay in seeking to devour each other. Instead he feared that Catherine would settle for seizing the Crimea and consent to Joseph taking Wallachia and Moldavia.
[15] Robert Salomon, *La politique orientale de Vergennes (1780–1784)* (Paris: Les presses modernes, 1935), 109–111.
[16] *Ibid.*, 115–116.
[17] Spain 607: 224, Vergennes to Montmorin, 31 May 1782.
[18] See succeeding section for the possibility of joint action. Russia's sudden obsession with her Crimean opportunity at least eliminated

The third element of Vergennes' haste in making peace was his gradual disillusionment with the possibility of a military solution. The surprising by Kempenfelt of de Guichen's convoy, the loss of the *Pégase* and her convoy, and de Grasse's defeat at the Saintes had already given dangerous indications that the navy was losing its capacity to sustain the initiative. At the beginning of August the council received news from the West Indies which indicated that not only the Jamaican operation but also the Windward Islands were endangered.

The news of the plans to split the forces collected at Saint Domingue had not been ill-received in France, since the plans had envisaged renewing the Jamaican operation in November.[19] Vaudreuil's sending his best ships to be repaired in North America and to bring back provisions obviously would relieve the pressure on the strained resources of Saint Domingue. It is true that the Spaniards had previously ordered their squadron to remain with the French even if they went to North America,[20] but this order had been based on the possibility of combined operations. Bellecombe raised the possibility of military operations in North America in a council of war, but the idea was rejected, since Washington was not ready for an attack on New York and since it was the wrong season to undertake anything in the south.[21] Under these circumstances the council made no mention of the Spaniards not accompanying Vaudreuil to North America. Moreover, Gálvez at least did not waste the summer season. He used three frigates and a 2,500-man expeditionary force in the manner of Bouillé to capture the Bahamas in May.[22] There was another advantage in tempo-

---

the danger that a more flexible British policy might make use of Russia's interest in protecting maritime rights. See Madariaga, *Britain, Russia, and the Armed Neutrality*, 402–405.

[19] Spain 607: 308–322, "Situation," 12 June 1782.

[20] Spain 606: 387, 440–441, Montmorin to Vergennes, 31 March and 9 April 1782; Spain 606: 409–410, orders to Gálvez, 6 April 1782.

[21] Spain 607: 312–313, "Situation," 12 June 1782.

[22] B⁴195: 101–102, 105, miscellaneous reports; Spain 608: 358–360, articles of capitulation, 8 May 1782.

rarily dispersing the Allied forces. A naval force at Boston could cover the shift of part or all of Rochambeau's expeditionary force to the West Indies. This had long been contemplated[23] and finally was ordered upon confirmation that the shift of British forces from North America to the West Indies had begun.[24]

A radical change had meanwhile occurred in the local planning for the renewal of West Indian operations. The meeting called by Gálvez on 17 June, which had decided on the immediate disposition of forces, also had decided that the squadrons should reunite at Martinique at the end of October.[25] After the meeting, however, Solano lost his nerve. He refused to sign the agreement for fear of his squadron being intercepted en route to Martinique. At a new meeting on 26 June the commanders decided to write their courts for instructions about the rendezvous. Solano and Vaudreuil continued their discussions, however, and reached agreement that their squadrons would rendezvous at Porto Cabello on the South American coast, a port safely reached from Cuba and Saint Domingue, but still to windward of both them and Jamaica.[26] The two squadrons sailed together from Saint Domingue on 4 July (13 French ships of the line, 12 Spanish)[27] and after Vaudreuil had covered

[23] Spain 606: 446, Vergennes to Montmorin, 12 April 1782; United States 21: 153–154, Vergennes to La Luzerne, 2 May 1782.

[24] United States 22: 99, Ségur to Rochambeau, 18 August 1782; Spain 608: 214–216, navy department memoir, no date but ca. 21 August 1782. See also note 8 of next section.

[25] Spain 607: 352–353, joint memoir of 17 June 1782, sent by Vaudreuil to Castries, 18 June 1782 and by Vergennes to Montmorin, 31 August 1782. See also B⁴206: 188–189, Vaudreuil to Castries, 18 June 1782.

[26] B⁴206: 191–192, Vaudreuil to Castries, 23 June and 26 June 1782; Spain 607: 408–409, council of war, 26 June 1782; Spain 608: 4, Bellecombe to Castries, 4 July 1782. The last two documents were sent by Vergennes to Montmorin, 7 September 1782. Note that Solano was senior to Vaudreuil.

[27] Spain 608: 4, Bellecombe to Castries, 4 July 1782. They left behind the *Scipion*, which was subsequently captured, the *Palmier*, which sank while returning to Europe, and a Spanish ship of the line. The *Experiment* joined the *Zélé* at Martinique.

the Spanish passage to Havana, he proceeded to Boston, where he arrived at the beginning of August.

Vergennes' first reaction to the changed dispositions was positive,[28] although he had been greatly disturbed by the reported bad condition of Solano's squadron.[29] Castries, however, quickly saw the potential for disaster in the selection of the new rendezvous.[30] Porto Cabello was to leeward of all the islands in the windward chain. There would be no way for Vaudreuil and Solano to reach these islands, where the forces from Europe would have to come in order to bring provisions. Vaudreuil and Solano would thereby grant the English an interior position from which they could attack either component of the new Allied fleet as well as the exposed Windward Islands.

The following section will deal with the council's reaction to the military crisis suddenly facing it. What seems most significant about the impending military crisis is the manner in which it coincided with the initiation of serious diplomatic negotiations with Britain. It is only in the context of the continuing financial crisis, the diplomatic crisis in East-

[28] Spain 608: 311–314, Vergennes to Montmorin, 7 September 1782.

[29] Spain 608: 178–179, Vergennes to Montmorin, 11 August 1782. Confidence in the work of the Havana dockyards can hardly have been increased by the fate of the *Palmier*, which had been recaulked at Havana. Her bottom fell out while she was returning to Europe in October with a convoy. See B⁴206: 187, Vaudreuil to Castries, 17 June 1782. It should be noted, however, that on 29 August 1782 the British *Royal George*, 100, capsized while in port. There was enormous loss of life, including the brilliant Kempenfelt.

[30] Spain 608: 405–415, "Mémoire sur les opérations de la campagne prochaine en Amérique, d'après le dernier état connu des choses aux îles," no date; Spain 608: 399–400, Vergennes to Montmorin, 18 September 1782; B⁴206: 162, Castries to Vaudreuil, 8 September 1782. The Spaniards were so disturbed with Solano (who, moreover, was not on good terms with Gálvez) that he was recalled. He was ordered to bring back with him the ships needing repair—orders which led to French fears that he would bring back his entire squadron. Spain 608: 338, Montmorin to Vergennes, 10 September 1782. Floridablanca did agree to raise the number of Spanish ships of the line to be sent from Cadiz to 25.

ern Europe, and the strategic situation that these negotiations become fully comprehensible.[31]

De Grasse's nephew had brought with him a summary of his uncle's conversation with Shelburne. Shelburne's terms and his means of conveying them were so singular that, as Vergennes told Montmorin, if it were not for the character of de Grasse, he, Vergennes, would have regarded the proposal as "a novel meant for pleasure."[32] Shelburne proposed American independence, the restitution of Saint Lucia to France, French retention of Dominica and Saint Vincent, the abandonment of British prohibitions concerning Dunkirk, a fishery for France on the Grand Bank of Newfoundland with a right to fortification of a support point, a sufficient slaving establishment in Africa, a settlement in India on the terms of 1748 or 1763, Spanish retention of her conquests in the Gulf of Mexico, a Spanish choice of Gibraltar or Minorca if an equivalent were offered, a restitution of prewar conditions with Holland, and liberty of commerce according to the principles of the League of Armed Neutrality.[33] If Vergennes could not question that Shelburne was the source of this extraordinary proposal he could not feel as confident in Shelburne's sincerity: "His [Shelburne's] character, too well-known, justifies suspicion. It is possible, nevertheless, that motives unknown to us relative to the interior condition of England and his own position inspire in him that ardent love for peace which he is pleased to manifest to the Count de Grasse."[34]

The council elected to take two steps to exploit the opening. The king ordered de Grasse, who had a royal audience

[31] As with the Anglo-American negotiations, I am spared the necessity of describing these negotiations in detail. Harlow, *Founding of the Second British Empire*, 1: 362–407, discusses them with great care and thoroughness, but, like Morris in treating of the American negotiations, in isolation from their overall strategic and diplomatic context.

[32] Spain 608: 210, Vergennes to Montmorin, 18 August 1782.

[33] England 538: 54, "Projet des preliminaires," given by de Grasse to Vergennes, 17 August 1782.

[34] Spain 608: 210–211, Vergennes to Montmorin, 18 August 1782.

on 18 August, to write Shelburne to thank him and to express Louis' interest.[35] Vergennes then began substantive discussions with Fitzherbert (despite the fact that the latter did not as yet have full powers to the satisfaction of the other Allies); Vergennes initially concentrated on the Newfoundland question, which was the least likely to cause serious difficulties.[36] Discussions with Fitzherbert had to be suspended because of a death in the British royal family,[37] but Shelburne's response to de Grasse's letter[38] was encouraging enough that the council immediately decided to send a representative to discuss the bases for settlement that Shelburne had proposed.[39]

The man chosen was Joseph-Matthias Gérard de Rayneval (1746–1812), who was not only Vergennes' chief aide but also secretary to the council of state. Rayneval's mission was to ascertain if de Grasse's points conformed to Shelburne's intentions. If they did not, Rayneval was to return immediately to France, but if Shelburne recognized them, Rayneval was to inform him they could serve as a base for negotiations. Rayneval could discuss the various points but only in a private capacity.[40]

[35] *Ibid.*; B⁸14: unpaged, sheets for August 1782. De Grasse was ordered to inform Shelburne that the bases seemed suitable for commencing negotiations, but that Louis could say nothing further without consulting with Charles.

[36] Spain 608: 235–237, Vergennes to Montmorin, 22 August 1782. Vergennes' reason for selecting this course was to have control over how rapidly the negotiations progressed. Spain 608: 173, Vergennes to Montmorin, 10 August 1782.

[37] Spain 608: 312–313, Vergennes to Montmorin, 7 September 1782.

[38] England 538: 116, Shelburne to de Grasse, 3 September 1782.

[39] This idea was first broached in Spain 608: 210–211, Vergennes to Montmorin, 18 August 1782. Spanish approval was received on 1 September. Spain 608: 266–267, Montmorin to Vergennes, 25 August 1782.

[40] England 538: 117–118, instructions for Rayneval (in Vergennes' hand), 6 September 1782; England 538: 121, 124, Vergennes to Shelburne and Grantham, 6 September 1782; Spain 608: 316, Vergennes to Montmorin, 7 September 1782. Louis had already approved a set of responses to Shelburne's proposals and this was also used by Rayneval. England 538: 104–110, untitled memoir (also in Vergennes' hand), August 1782.

Rayneval left Versailles on 7 September, the same day Vergennes informed Montmorin of Vaudreuil's and Solano's selection of Porto Cabello as their rendezvous. In another letter of the same day to Montmorin[41] Vergennes warned Montmorin of his distrust of Russia and wrote eloquently of peace. He advised Spain that no matter what happened at the siege of Gibraltar:

> prudence and our interest invite us to not refuse peace when we can make it under just and honorable conditions. A few more acquisitions will not make the fortune of the two crowns, which are strong enough. What is important for them is the reestablishment of the public consideration that the misfortunes of the last war and perhaps other causes have greatly weakened, not to say more. We have regained that consideration. Our essential interest is to conserve it. It is dependent on some events of which it would be imprudent to run the hazards if one can prevent it. England, without doubt, is very fatigued, but we are so ourselves. Our means are exhausted by dint of being diffused and it is not yet decided whether our credit or that of England will survive the other. That nation has, in its constitution and in the establishments which it has permitted her to form, resources which are lacking to us. Let us not lose the occasion if it presents itself of honorably terminating a war which has been undertaken less by ambition than in order to restore us to the equality which belongs to great powers. Europe has believed until now in our moderation. Let us not diminish that merit in their eyes.

5. The Gibraltar Disaster

As his discussions with Shelburne came to an end, Rayneval admitted in a letter to Vergennes: "My task has become as delicate as it is important and I confess to you frankly that if I had foreseen it, I should not have had the courage

[41] Spain 608: 315–318, Vergennes to Montmorin, 7 September 1782. Quotation is from f. 317.

to undertake it."[1] It is easy indeed to sympathize with Rayneval. However challenging his prior responsibilities, however encyclopedic his knowledge of Vergennes' policies, his success depended primarily on reserves of courage and wisdom which could not be tested at Versailles. His brother had been sent from Versailles to Philadelphia and had not distinguished himself. Now Rayneval was given a journey more challenging than that of his brother or even that of the young Montmorin, leaving Trier to face the rages of Floridablanca and frustrations of the Spanish court. In effect Rayneval was given responsibility for deciding between the continuation of negotiations and the indefinite continuation of war. By his instructions he had to judge Shelburne's concurrence in the proposals made to de Grasse. Moreover, while Rayneval was in England, Fitzherbert refused to restrict discussions to Newfoundland. Before Vergennes would give Fitzherbert the complete French proposals he awaited Rayneval to enlighten him on the English disposition toward peace.[2] Upon Rayneval's report would depend Vergennes' own decision on whether to continue the negotiations with Fitzherbert.

Rayneval traveled incognito to London, which as usual during the late summer had been deserted by the cabinet. Rayneval was invited to Shelburne's country estate, Bowood, where discussions began on 13 September. Although the discussions continued until Rayneval's departure on 21 September, the remaining discussions were largely an elaboration of the themes established on the first day.

Shelburne began by disavowing the de Grasse proposals as inaccurate.[3] Had Rayneval followed the letter of his in-

---

[1] England 538: 206, Rayneval to Vergennes, 18 September 1782.

[2] Spain 608: 380, Vergennes to Montmorin, 14 September 1782.

[3] For the conferences with Shelburne see Rayneval's summary, England 538: 146–192 (quotation is from ff. 160–161); the rough draft of Rayneval's summary, England, supplement 19: 268–302; Spain 609: 55–60, Vergennes to Montmorin, 6 October 1782. Whether Shelburne deceived de Grasse or de Grasse by good fortune misunderstood him is, of course, conjecture. I strongly suspect the former.

structions instead of the spirit, the negotiations would have died, bringing with their death the deaths of many young men of four or five countries and very likely the destruction of much of the Spanish colonial empire and part of the French. Rayneval, however, chose to listen to Shelburne as he spoke of his desire for a prompt and durable peace and of George's disposition to treat justly with France. Rayneval showed him the propositions that de Grasse claimed had been made and Shelburne carefully analyzed the chances for agreement on each. After a break, the two men using maps, began more detailed discussion. With some measure of confidence established Shelburne deftly produced the one key capable of unlocking Vergennes' reserve. After arguing there was no need for mediators, Shelburne spoke to Rayneval of his own diplomatic system. Rayneval described the conversation: "He thinks that when France and England are reconciled they should unite in such a manner as to remain the arbiters of public tranquility. He recalled to me on this occasion the system he had in 1768 when he left the ministry [Shelburne had been Secretary of State for the Southern Department]. He had wished to agree with France to hold a firm and decisive language with Russia and Prussia and to thereby prevent what happened in Poland."

Shelburne's main concerns as secretary of state had been the colonies rather than Eastern Europe, but his views on the problems of Europe, regardless of their origin and antiquity, offered France the immediate achievement of the goals for which she had entered the American war. In the subsequent conferences Shelburne detailed his views of a stable Europe with the other great powers rendered harmless by the lack of subsidies.[4] Rayneval provided Shelburne

---

[4] The conversation of 18 September is quoted by Fitzmaurice, *Shelburne*, 2: 180–181. Fitzmaurice traces Shelburne's interest in friendship with France to 1769, which was after his service as a secretary of state.

and Grantham (who also hosted some of the discussions) a confidential note listing France's position on the issues separating their countries. When Rayneval wrote Vergennes, "I have seen few persons of a character as resolute and decisive,"[5] it was the effect of far more than Shelburne's personality. Shelburne's winning of Rayneval ultimately hinged on his success in convincing Rayneval that England sought not only peace but reconciliation and cooperation in taming the jungle of continental diplomacy.

Ironically, on the very day Shelburne and Rayneval began at Bowood the work of peace, men at Gibraltar were being torn and burned and mutilated, as if in demonstration of the consequences of the war's continuation.

Arcon's plan for the capture of Gibraltar was centered around the use of floating gun batteries to destroy a key section of the fortress' defenses. These batteries, converted from merchant ships, were enclosed on their port sides and tops by massive timbers, and were fitted with pumps to extinguish any fires caused by heated shot. Forerunners of the converted *Virginia* of 1862, they were claimed by their inventor to possess mobility, stability, insubmersibility, incombustibility, extreme solidity, and security for the service of their artillery.[6] It is impossible to judge fairly the idea, since the Spaniards, fearing the arrival of Howe's fleet, made the attack before the batteries could be adequately tested, the crews trained, or the coordination of batteries and support vessels rehearsed. The ten floating batteries were so poorly positioned that the leading two batteries had to carry the fight. The pumps failed to work properly and the heated British shot finally ignited the batteries. Since the batteries were not given adequate naval support, the British sent out warships once they had been rendered

---

[5] England 538: 195, Rayneval to Vergennes, 15 September 1782. See also Fitzmaurice, *Shelburne*, 2: 182–183.

[6] Spain 607: 161, d'Arcon to Vergennes, 20 May 1782. Sketches of them are given by Spain 608: 58 and B⁴182: 105–107.

helpless and destroyed them before they could be towed to safety. Six months' work of 4,000–5,000 men had been destroyed in 18 hours.[7]

The failure of the attack on Gibraltar meant the French council was faced with yet another crisis. The council had only recently acted to counter another threat to the Allied war effort—the reported movement of 4,000 British troops from New York to the West Indies.[8] With great energy it not only authorized Rochambeau to embark part or all of his corps, but also ordered Vaudreuil to return to the Windward Islands, Bouillé to leave Europe immediately for Martinique, and Hector to send a regiment from Brest as reinforcements.[9] In addition, a battalion of troops was added to the supply convoy, which was still waiting at the Île d'Aix. On 10 September the *Solitaire*, *Triton*, 3 frigates, and a transport sailed from Brest for Fort Royal; they arrived there just before the *Amphion* and her long-delayed convoy from Rochefort, which finally had sailed on 2 September.

[7] Spain 608: 422–423, 445–446, Montmorin to Vergennes, 18 September and 22 September 1782. Arcon's account of the battle is given in B⁴182: 78–104, memoir of Arcon, 29 November 1782. Bessière estimated that the Allies had suffered 1,500 casualties in the attack. Spain 608: 457–458, Bessière to Vergennes, 22 September 1782. See also Spain 608: 391–396, Arcon and Bessière to Vergennes, 17 September 1782.

[8] Spain 608: 214–216, navy department memoir, no date but ca. 21 August 1782. This intelligence was false. All the British energy was presently being absorbed by the evacuation of Savannah. David Syrett, *Shipping and the American War, 1775–1783* (London: Athlone Press, 1970), 236–237. Charleston was evacuated at the end of the year.

[9] Spain 608: 214–216, navy department memoir, no date but ca. 21 August 1782; B⁴195: 278–285/B⁴217: 160–167, "Etat des choses au 20 août 1782." This precaution seems exaggerated. On 1 June 1782 there were 9,300 French troops in the Windward Islands, exclusive of 7,600 French troops at Saint Domingue, 2,300 troops embarked aboard Vaudreuil's squadron, and Gálvez' 9,200 Spanish troops. In March 1782 the British had only 8,756 troops in the West Indies, including Jamaica. Mackesy, *War for America*, 524–525. See also B⁴205: 162, Castries to Vaudreuil, 8 September 1782.

The council had also just initiated efforts to convince the Dutch to send half their fleet to winter at Brest—efforts which finally were unable to overcome Dutch caution as immovable as had been that of Charles.[10] Finally the council had sent a memoir to Spain requesting advice on how to rectify Vaudreuil and Solano's choice of Porto Cabello.[11] Both Vergennes and Castries had become disenchanted with the Jamaican expedition as a result of the Porto Cabello decision, but other than acting on the defensive there existed no clear alternative.[12] For news of successful operations in the Indian theater to reach Europe, the Allies must be prepared to fight two more campaigns, argued Vergennes; for an attack on England to be successful, sufficient forces must be found (and this necessitated Spanish agreement to a plan Charles had long opposed).

The catastrophe at Gibraltar at least ended the uncertainty as to the direction of future efforts. Spain was still afraid to attack England and still desired Gibraltar. Montmorin had to use the Jamaican operation to convince Spain to abandon hopes of taking Gibraltar directly.[13] France, needing Spanish cooperation more than ever, had little choice but to agree, even though Vergennes and Castries wished England to bear the expense of offensive operations. Vergennes quickly announced that further operational planning would be conducted by d'Estaing who would con-

[10] Holland 551: 59–61, "Obsérvations sur les circonstances actuelles relativement à la Hollande," 14 September 1782. See also Holland 551: *passim*. Note that Howe's mission left the way clear for the Dutch squadron.

[11] Spain 608: 405–415, "Mémoire sur les opérations de la campagne prochain en Amérique. . . ," no date; Spain 608: 399–400, Vergennes to Montmorin, 18 September 1782. The French asked Spain to raise her detachment from Europe from 25 ships of the line to 30 ships of the line.

[12] *Ibid.*; B⁴218: 63–64, memoir of Castries, 27 September 1782; Spain 608: 363–366, Vergennes to Castries, 13 September 1782. For further evidence of Vergennes' lack of interest in the Indian theater of operations see Spain 607: 331, Vergennes to Montmorin, 14 June 1782.

[13] Spain 608: 476–478, Montmorin to Vergennes, 26 September 1782.

sult with the Spanish court before joining the combined fleet.[14]

At the moment there was little point in strategic discussions with Spain.[15] All other activity was suspended as Spain awaited the arrival of a huge replenishment convoy for Gibraltar escorted by Howe and the British home fleet. Howe might have reached Gibraltar before Arcon's attack had the cabinet not temporarily broken up his fleet to reinforce the North Sea squadron (clearing the way for the safe passage of a Baltic convoy, but beyond that accomplishing nothing beyond further frightening the Dutch).[16] Finally on 11 September Howe sailed with his convoy and a fleet of 35 ships of the line, a force comparable to Rodney's at the Saintes.[17] The combined fleet had over a dozen more ships of the line than did Howe, but it had been damaged by a storm as it lay at Algeciras awaiting him and made only a half-hearted attempt to interfere. Howe reached Gibraltar on 16 October, quickly delivered his supplies and reinforcements, and departed; he engaged the combined fleet briefly on 20 October.[18] With his mission successfully completed, the Spanish attempt to capture Gibraltar finally ended.[19]

As the military situation worsened, Vergennes' letters to Montmorin on the Russian situation became increasingly frank. On 28 September he admitted that as yet he did not know the extent of Joseph's participation in Catherine's

[14] Spain 609: 63–66, Vergennes to Montmorin, 6 October 1782. See also Spain 608: 366, Vergennes to Castries, 13 September 1782.

[15] Spain, however, did attempt to countermand Solano's decision on Porto Cabello. Spain 608: 476–477, Montmorin to Vergennes, 26 September 1782.

[16] Mackesy, *War for America*, 479–482.

[17] Beatson, *Naval and Military Memoirs*, 6: 367.

[18] B⁴194 contains information on this operation. On 12 September the Allied fleet contained 35 Spanish and 14 French ships of the line. B⁴194: 108, journal of the campaign, entry of 12 September 1782. See also Spain 609: 101–102, Montmorin to Vergennes, 17 October 1782; Spain 609: 122–124, Córdoba to Castejon, 22 October 1782.

[19] Spain 609: 132–134, Montmorin to Vergennes, 24 October 1782.

dangerous project in the Crimea.[20] Vergennes held out a hope of blocking Catherine. If the Bourbons made peace with Britain by the end of the year the three powers could force arbitration on her. Vergennes argued, "The three powers have an equal interest that the Turks not be expelled from Europe." Within a week Vergennes wrote again to warn of the dangers in Eastern Europe and to call for combined action by the Bourbons and their present enemy.[21] Spain, however, was not receptive. Montmorin replied that Spain minimized the dangers and did not believe them sufficient reason to hasten peace with England.[22] As military crisis succeeded military crisis and the situation in Eastern Europe became more grave, the issues dividing France and Britain diminished in importance. The negotiations increasingly centered not on peace between Britain and France, but on peace between Britain and Spain, without which France would have to continue a war threatening to become catastrophic.

Vergennes received Rayneval's praise of Shelburne with some caution, particularly concerning Shelburne's European system.[23] The substance of the discussions, however,

[20] Spain 608: 489, Vergennes to Montmorin, 28 September 1782. Joseph already had informed Catherine that he was ready to follow her. By September the French representative in Saint Petersburg had learned the extent of Catherine's desires—to establish an independent state in the area Vergennes had feared would be seized by Austria. In November the courts of Austria and Russia began exerting diplomatic pressure on the Turks and a Russian army corps entered the Crimea. The French pressed the Turks to back down so as to avoid war, but at the end of the year the situation remained in doubt. Salomon, *La Politique orientale de Vergennes*, 110, 116–139, 145.

[21] Spain 609: 16, Vergennes to Montmorin, 2 October 1782. Vergennes, as before, did not scruple about exaggerating the danger. He warned of possible joint action by Austria, Prussia, and Russia (as had occurred in 1772), which hardly seems to have been an immediate danger at the time. See also Spain 609: 159, Vergennes to Montmorin, 1 November 1782.

[22] Spain 609: 72–73, Montmorin to Vergennes, 10 October 1782.

[23] Spain 609: 55–60, Vergennes to Montmorin, 6 October 1782. See also Spain 608: 490, Vergennes to Montmorin, 28 September 1782.

was encouraging and very soon after Rayneval's return the council decided to make formal peace proposals.[24]

The Anglo-French negotiations proceeded remarkably well. I believe their success was due to the strong desire of both parties for a quick settlement and to the willingness of each to concede points vital to the other. Vergennes told Montmorin that a few inches of ground more or less would affect neither the grandeur of the king nor the prosperity of his subject, but the abandonment of the German [sic] and Turkish Empires to their enemies would cause France to lose her place as the first power of Europe.[25] However exaggerated was Vergennes' statement, it does reflect Vergennes' willingness to make concessions; Shelburne, in turn, was desperately anxious to reach a settlement before having to face a hostile Parliament at its next session, scheduled to open at the end of November.[26] The final resolution of the issues was not made until the definitive peace treaty of 3 September 1783, but since no issue except India and later Dominica seriously endangered the conclusion of peace I will merely summarize the discussions:

1. *American independence.* This was the major issue of the war for France, but since Shelburne had committed himself, however reluctantly, to it and since discussions with the Americans were about to resume, Vergennes could leave the discussion to them. The nature of France's interest in the *terms* of the British-American settlement will be explained in the last section of this chapter.

[24] Spain 608: 490, Vergennes to Montmorin, 28 September 1782. See also Spain 608: 302, Aranda to Vergennes, 30 September 1782; England 538: 104–110, untitled memoir of August 1782; England 538: 125–133, response of France to Fitzherbert's note of 4 August 1782, no date. The French proposals were officially presented on 6 October; the British responded on 21 October.

[25] Spain 609: 57–58, Vergennes to Montmorin, 6 October 1782.

[26] Norris, *Shelburne and Reform*, 256. This desire also influenced the course of his American negotiations. In September he conceded enough concerning preliminary recognition of American independence to permit the beginning of substantive discussion of the remaining issues between the two countries. Morris, *The Peacemakers*, 339. These will be treated below in Section 7.

2. *The Newfoundland fishery*. France was able to obtain exclusive use of a more secure portion of Newfoundland to support her fishermen and settled for the return of Saint Pierre and Miquelon in lieu of an acceptable substitute. The British retained the best fishing grounds and sovereignty over the entire island of Newfoundland. The settlement represented a sincere attempt to eliminate the disputes which had poisoned relations between Britain and France.

3. *Africa*. Senegal was returned to France, while Britain retained Gambia.

4. *India*. This was the most dangerous of all the negotiations but since the issue was even more a threat to Shelburne than to Vergennes, the French finally accepted essentially a return to the unfavorable conditions of 1778. The British were finally forced to make some counterconcessions. The French naval campaign of 1781 had accomplished nothing and after the French squadron returned to the Mascarenes the British easily captured the Dutch ports of Negapatam on the east coast of India and Trincomalee on the east coast of Ceylon. During 1782 the French fleet, commanded by Suffren,[27] covered the landing of an expeditionary force of 3,000 troops in India, fought a series of indecisive naval battles, and recaptured Trincomalee. Though news of the recapture of Trincomalee did not reach Europe until March 1783, Vergennes had bargaining cards in the presence of French troops in India, in the impending arrival of the feared Bussy at Île de France, and at the last moment in news from Île de France indicating the probability Trincomalee would be attacked. Vergennes made clear to the English that the return of the strategically cru-

---

[27] D'Orves, the original commander, died on 9 February 1782, just after the arrival of the French squadron on the Indian coast. The best sources for Suffren's brilliant but meaningless campaign are B⁴196; B⁴197; B⁴198; and Killion, "The Suffren Expedition." Bussy met the February convoy at the Cape and arrived at the Mascarene Islands in September 1782. See also England 540: 179–180, Vergennes to Rayneval, 15 January 1782; Spain 509: 161, Vergennes to Montmorin, 1 November 1782; "Castries' journal," 148–149, 7 January 1783 and following.

cial port to Holland was vital to France, and Shelburne finally conceded the point and settled for the less-valuable port of Negapatam. France was also able for honor's sake to obtain British agreement to a conditional armistice with France's Indian allies.

5. *Dunkirk.* The abrogation of all British rights over Dunkirk was crucial to France, and Shelburne did not debate the point, although he did unsuccessfully attempt to procure a French declaration that Dunkirk would not be fortified.

6. *Commercial arrangements.* Shelburne was as anxious as Vergennes for a new commercial treaty but politically he could not risk tying it to the peace negotiations. It took a considerable effort by Vergennes to secure in the definitive peace the promise of new arrangements by the beginning of 1786; a new commercial treaty was finally signed in September 1786.

7. *West Indies.* The de Grasse proposals had envisaged the return of Saint Lucia to France and all the French conquests except Dominica and Saint Vincent to England. Although Shelburne disavowed this proposal France was able to obtain the promise of the return of Saint Lucia and French retention of Dominica. During the discussion of an Allied-held equivalent to exchange for Gibraltar this part of the settlement broke down. As we shall see, France finally accepted instead the return of Saint Lucia and retention of Tobago.

The discussion between Shelburne and Vergennes were eased by a community of interest which did not exist between Britain and Spain. Above all, Britain and Spain were divided by the issue of Gibraltar, which Shelburne had predicted to Rayneval would be a rock in the negotiations as it was in the sea.[28] Aranda's initial instructions for the peace

---

[28] England 538: 131, Rayneval's summary of the conference of 13 September 1782. Aranda authorized Rayneval some latitude in speaking of Spain's intentions. Spain 608: 316–317, Vergennes to Montmorin, 7 September 1782.

negotiations were written before the attack on Gibraltar.[29] They authorized him to offer Oran and its port of Mers el Kébir (Mazalquivir) or at best the port of Mahon on Minorca and neutralization of the island in exchange for both Gibraltar and Minorca; if Gibraltar were captured beforehand only *the use* of the port of Mahon and neutralization of the island should be offered. It was expected Spain would retain West Florida, and if Aranda ceded timber-cutting rights in Honduras and the Campeche (Yucatán) Peninsula, he was to obtain Newfoundland fishing rights for Spain. Vergennes expressed shock at the extent of the Spanish demands (to which Aranda added the retention of the Bahamas when he gave them to Fitzherbert on 6 October),[30] but he was helpless at the moment to moderate them. The failure of the Gibraltar attack at least prompted a change in Aranda's orders. He was now authorized to offer Minorca in exchange for Gibraltar if it proved necessary, but only after having obtained special authorization from the Spanish court.[31] Vergennes prophesied (correctly) that Minorca would not be considered by England an equivalent for Gibraltar.[32] By the end of October communication between France and Spain had largely broken down over the conditions Spain would accept. Montmorin believed Spain did not wish France to know these terms, so France would not press her to make peace.[33] She claimed

[29] Spain 608: 268–271, Floridablanca to Aranda, 25 August 1782. See also England 538: 100–103, memoir of Aranda, no date.

[30] Spain 608: 315–316, Vergennes to Montmorin, 7 September 1782. See also Spain 609: 47–52, Aranda to Fitzherbert, 6 October 1782. The Newfoundland fishing rights were only a matter of saving face. Aranda had the audacity to claim them on the grounds that Newfoundland had been discovered by Basque fishermen before the voyages of Columbus! Spain also wished renegotiation of the current Anglo-Spanish trade agreement.

[31] Spain 608: 437–438, Montmorin to Vergennes, 20 September 1782.

[32] Spain 609: 63, Vergennes to Montmorin, 6 October 1782.

[33] Spain 609: 135–136, Montmorin to Vergennes, 24 October 1782. Montmorin had already warned Vergennes that exerting pressure on Spain would be counterproductive. Spain 608: 185, Montmorin to Vergennes, 12 August 1782.

to have money for the next campaign, but Montmorin reported that the hard currency needed for the attack on Gibraltar had cost Spain 18–20 percent interest.

On 1 November Vergennes wrote frankly to Montmorin about the impasse the negotiations had reached.[34] Fitzherbert had explained clearly to him that Oran and Mers el Kébir would not be an acceptable compensation for Gibraltar. Fitzherbert refused to say what England would accept, and Aranda maintained a silence no less rigorous. Aranda now wished Vergennes to elicit from Fitzherbert some light on the objects Britain desired as the price for the cession of Gibraltar. Vergennes believed this strategy false since the English ministry might relinquish Gibraltar before Parliament reopened but could not run the political risk of making an offer which could compromise it. Vergennes asked that before permitting the delay to continue, Spain take into serious consideration the present state of affairs.

It was that state of affairs of which Vergennes wrote most forcefully:

> I know that it is dangerous to deliver oneself to one's presentiments but mine presage nothing very favorable for the future. Everything that has happened during this campaign announces a derangement of the moral and physical means, [of war] which makes me tremble for the next. The English have to some degree regenerated their navy while ours has been used up. Constructions have not been at all equivalent to consumptions; the body of good sailors is exhausted and the officers show a lassitude in war which contrasts in a disadvantageous manner with the energy which not only the sailors but the entire English nation eagerly manifests. Join to that the diminution of our financial means which are limited by reason of the usage which has been made of them. That inconvenience is common, no doubt, also to England, but her constitution gives her in that regard advantages which our monarchical forms do not accord us. She will pay

[34] Spain 609: 157–167, Vergennes to Montmorin, 1 November 1782. Quotation is from f. 159.

dearly for money, but she will find more easily than us all that she needs. I believe, however, that we will find what is necessary for the next campaign, but I will not respond for the one following. However, if the one of 1783 begins I fear strongly it will be followed by another and perhaps several others. I foresee with sadness that if the peace is not arranged before spring we will see a system hatch in Europe which will throw it into confusion and surely give place to ample and useless regrets. The movements of Russia on the frontier of Turkey do not have for their object solely the reestablishment in the Crimea of the deposed Khan. Probably if that power has a project as vast as many of its antecedents indicate she will have sufficient means to obtain some collaborators . . .[35]

On the same day a new and unlikely agent of peace began his journey. Vice-Admiral d'Estaing departed for Spain.[36]

6. The Search for a Gibraltar Equivalent

D'Estaing had been given by the council the most extraordinary of missions: to convince Spain that the military situation demanded peace and then, should peace fail, to command the most massive naval operation ever undertaken.[1] D'Estaing had been reluctant to undertake the responsibility of commanding the operation and it had taken

[35] The theme of a collapse of leadership and morale in the naval officer corps is echoed in Spain 609: 83, Vergennes to Montmorin, 13 October 1782, and by a biting critique of the officer corps submitted to Castries by an unidentified author, B⁴195: 292–297. The crisis of order in the navy led d'Estaing to suggest reforms, which were then adopted on a trial basis by Castries. These reforms involved giving more responsibility to auxiliary officers and were so opposed by the regular officers that a protest letter was circulated among the junior officers of the French squadron at Cadiz. See B⁴204 and B⁴217.
[36] United States 22: 411, d'Estaing to Vergennes, 1 November 1782.
[1] Montmorin had already suggested the idea of using the naval situation as a diplomatic weapon against Spain. Spain 608: 246, Montmorin to Vergennes, 22 August 1782.

most of the summer to convince him to do so. When he realized the obstacles now facing the operation (obstacles which had led even Castries to despair of its success) his desire for guidance became a near-obsession.[2] One must, however, sympathize with d'Estaing and admire him for undertaking a mission of such difficulty and of so little promise of glory. It was, in good part, his success in the first half of his mission which saved him from having to undertake the second.

D'Estaing's fleet had already begun its repairs at Cadiz by the time d'Estaing began his journey.[3] The French contingent at Cadiz ultimately reached 24 ships of the line, comprising the 14 initially present, the *Sceptre*, which unexpectedly arrived from Saint Domingue in mid-October (after a successful attack on the forts of Hudson Bay) and the nine ships of the line which brought from Brest the bulk of the troops for the Jamaican attack.[4] Initially Castries feared only about 15 of the 24 could be made ready for Jamaica. With the uncertainty about the forces actually available in the West Indies the council ordered that all vessels be sent that could possibly be repaired (expected to be at least 20).[5] Copper for doubling several ships was

[2] For d'Estaing's mission see particularly Spain 609: 107, Vergennes to Montmorin, 19 October 1782; B⁴186: 163–164, Vergennes to d'Estaing, 12 November 1782; B⁴186: 243–245, d'Estaing to Montmorin, 10 October 1782; B⁴218: 108–109, Castries to d'Estaing, ca. 5 October 1782; B⁴218: 112, Vergennes to Castries, 5 October 1782. D'Estaing was assured in advance that he would not be held responsible if the operation failed. D'Estaing, who was not only soldier and sailor, but also diplomat, naval reform advocate, and member of the Assembly of Notables, merits far more attention from historians than he has yet received.

[3] Spain 609: 168–169, Montmorin to Vergennes, 3 November 1782.

[4] The convoy left Brest on 8 December. Two more ships of the line were supposed to follow it with a convoy from Rochefort, but were delayed. Only 10 ships of the line (most of them either awaiting repairs or newly launched) were expected to remain in French ports.

[5] Eventually it was decided to arm the *Lion* as a transport and to leave behind 4 other of the 24 ships of the line. Spain 609: 304, navy department memoir sent by Vergennes to Montmorin, 7 December

found at Cadiz but work proceeded slowly.[6] D'Estaing joined the fleet on 18 December after his conferences at the Spanish court and the Brest convoy arrived just before the end of the year.[7] Over 12,000 French troops were collected at Cadiz,[8] Lafayette arrived to accompany the fleet as the future governor of Jamaica,[9] and each of the 24 Spanish ships of the line prepared to embark 200 Spanish troops.[10] The departure, already so long delayed, might not occur until the end of January[11]—not an unmitigated evil. Although the threat of the operation contributed to the momentum of the peace negotiation, the operation once launched would acquire a momentum of its own.

In early November the Spanish finally had made a serious move in their diplomatic negotiations, hitherto kept alive chiefly by English fears of making a categorical answer to the absurd Spanish proposals of 6 October.[12] The new overture was very welcome to France,[13] but the substance of the

---

1782; Spain 608: 352, 411, navy department memoirs sent by Vergennes to Montmorin, 18 September 1782; B⁴217: 112, Castries to d'Estaing, 15 January 1783.

[6] Spain 609: 168–169, Montmorin to Vergennes, 3 November 1782; Spain 609: 420, personal letter of Montmorin to Vergennes, 18 December 1782; B⁴194: 260 ff. For shortages of various matériel as a result of the earlier preparations for the attack on Gibraltar see Spain 608: 38, Montmorin to Vergennes, 9 July 1782.

[7] Spain 609: 425; Spain 610: 3, Bessière to Vergennes, 20 December 1782 and 1 January 1783.

[8] E 205: unpaged, memoir on state of forces assembled at Cadiz, no date; B⁴210: 17, 53–54, listings of troops embarked, no dates.

[9] Spain 609: 324, navy department memoir sent by Vergennes to Montmorin, 7 December 1782. See also Spain 606: 45, Montmorin to Vergennes, 11 January 1782; B⁴218: 72–73, d'Estaing to Castries, October 1782.

[10] Spain 609: 168–169, Montmorin to Vergennes, 3 November 1782. The Spanish ships are listed by B⁴203: 58.

[11] Spain 609: 425, Bessière to Vergennes, 20 December 1782. D'Estaing's initial estimate was 15 or 20 January. B⁴186: 253, d'Estaing to Montmorin, 25 December 1782.

[12] Spain 609: 143, 158, Vergennes to Montmorin, 27 October and 1 November 1782.

[13] Vergennes later defended Aranda, telling Montmorin that he, Vergennes, believed had not Aranda made the new overture the con-

proposals was less than satisfactory. Spain proposed ceding Santo Domingo (adjoining Saint Domingue) to France in exchange for France's obtaining for her all the terms she had demanded—British renunciation of timber-cutting rights in Central America, Spanish possession of Gibraltar, Minorca, West Florida and the Bahamas, Spanish participation in the Newfoundland fishery, and the abolition of existing Spanish commercial treaties with England.[14] To accomplish this, Aranda suggested to Vergennes that France cede Corsica to England. He also suggested that Vergennes send Rayneval back to England before Parliament reopened on 26 November and warned that once the Jamaican campaign began the Spanish offer would be withdrawn.

Vergennes considered the Spanish proposal to be a trap.[15] Obviously Louis could not consider providing England so strategically valuable an acquisition as Corsica (moreover, one to which France did not possess clear title), but Vergennes feared to turn down the offer. Spain might be seeking an excuse to make the offer of Santo Domingo to Britain[16] or might be attempting to transfer responsibility for finding peace terms onto Louis. France had no possessions of equal value to Santo Domingo to offer England. Rather than risk driving Spain into England's arms, the council decided to follow Aranda's suggestion of sending Rayneval to

tinuation of the war would have been certain. Spain 609: 302, Vergennes to Montmorin, 29 November 1782.

[14] Spain 609: 171–174, proposition of Aranda, 6 November 1782; Spain 609: 175–178, Aranda to Vergennes, 7 November 1782; Spain 609: 207–212, Vergennes to Montmorin, 12 November 1782.

[15] Spain 609: 181–187, Vergennes to Louis, ca. 7 November 1782; Spain 609: 207–212, 213–216, Vergennes to Montmorin, 12 November 1782.

[16] Montmorin also suspected this, but believed Britain would not be interested. Santo Domingo in British hands would naturally have posed a great danger to all the Leeward Islands, particularly to Saint Domingue. Aranda, in fact, was authorized to make the offer, but did so only indirectly. The British did not pursue the matter. Spain 609: 332, Montmorin to Vergennes, 1 December 1782; Danvila, *Reinado de Carlos III*, 5: 375–377; Conn, *Gibraltar in British Diplomacy*, 212.

England. If, against all probabilities, Rayneval found a French-held equivalent for Gibraltar, a Spanish indemnity could be discussed later; if there were none, France could give back to Floridablanca the responsibility for finding acceptable peace terms. Vergennes warned Montmorin that if England were conciliatory and Spain rejected compromise, Louis would be forced to leave Spain to provide for herself; Montmorin was left free to make use of the warning as his sagacity and prudence dictated.[17]

Fortunately, Vergennes' pessimism was not confirmed. Rayneval opened his discussions with Shelburne on the evening of 20 November.[18] For four hours Rayneval and Shelburne discussed the Spanish impasse. Shelburne pleaded for Spain to renounce Gibraltar but when he asked if Charles could be brought to desist, Rayneval had to reply no. Shelburne told Rayneval that if the cession of Gibraltar were raised in the cabinet, three ministers would resign. Finally, after ranging over the possible sources of compensation, Shelburne offered to take upon himself that George would compromise on Gibraltar if Charles offered to return the territories gained by conquest (West Florida, Minorca, the Bahamas), joined by Porto Rico, or by Guadeloupe and Dominica, or finally by Martinique and Saint Lucia. Spain could then reimburse France with Santo Domingo. Since Rayneval's courier would be too late to catch the tide to cross the Channel, Rayneval delayed sending his vital report until the following afternoon by which time Grantham and George had agreed to the compromise. The cabinet, moreover, accepted the proposals without any resignations, in spite of Shelburne's prediction.

---

[17] Vergennes also protested the idea of placing a time limit on negotiations and argued again that "peace will provide our salvation." Spain 609: 211, Vergennes to Montmorin, 12 November 1782. See also England 538: 284–289, 406–409, Vergennes to Fitzherbert, 15 November 1782; England 538: 395–399, instructions of Louis to Rayneval, 15 November 1782.

[18] England 539: 3–7; England, supplement 19: 311–315, Rayneval to Vergennes, 21 November 1782.

Shelburne and Rayneval then discussed the remaining Anglo-French difficulties, chiefly concerning India.[19] France wished enough territory to produce 10,000,000 livres annual income to offset her expenses in India; moreover, French honor demanded that her allies in India be granted a year's armistice when hostilities against Britain ended. On both issues Rayneval met great resistance.[20]

The great difficulty facing Shelburne was the impending reopening of Parliament. Unless peace were announced in the king's opening address, the public's desire to preserve Gibraltar and the navy's desire to fight another campaign[21] would overcome Shelburne's feeble resistance and drive him from office. Shelburne was able to purchase nine extra days by proroguing the opening of Parliament until 5 December on the pretext of preventing speculation on government bonds.[22] Rayneval, for his part, asked and received permission to return to Versailles to speed the deliberations.

Rayneval's courier reached Versailles on 24 November. France was willing to trade Guadeloupe and Dominica, even though Santo Domingo would require enormous expenses to cultivate and, as Vergennes sarcastically put it, would commence to be of some advantage about the middle of the coming century.[23] Aranda, however, was almost immovable, offering to give up no more than the Bahamas

[19] Another difficulty, that of the English desire to retain Dominica, was bound up in the Gibraltar equivalent question.

[20] England 539: 8–13, Rayneval to Vergennes, 22 November 1782; Harlow, *Founding of the Second British Empire*, I: 372, 374.

[21] Vergennes complained to Rayneval that the cries of English sailors (naval officers) should have no more weight at London than they did at Versailles—that in the calamities of war they found sources of advancement and sometimes of riches. England 539: 40, Vergennes to Rayneval, 25 November 1782.

[22] England 539: 14–16, 54–59, Rayneval to Vergennes, 22 November and 23 November 1782; England 539: 18, Home Secretary Townshend to the directors of the Bank of England, 22 November 1782.

[23] England 539: 36–40, Vergennes to Rayneval, 25 November 1782; Spain 609: 283–285, Vergennes to Montmorin, 26 November 1782. For Britain's supposed willingness to relent on Florida see also Spain 609: 232, Aranda to Vergennes, 15 November 1782.

(and to exchange the claims of Newfoundland fishing rights for the British settlements in Central America). Without any effect Vergennes read and re-read Rayneval's letter. Britain did not appear to attach great value to Florida, leaving Minorca as the obstacle. Vergennes argued that since Fort Saint Philip had been demolished, Minorca could be given up with minor loss to Spain. He warned of the danger that the hitherto limited war would become fanatical.

After learning that Parliament was to be prorogued until the next week, Vergennes asked Aranda to meet him again on the morning of 28 November.[24] At 8:00 that morning Rayneval entered the office of the astounded Vergennes. With his knowledge of the critical condition of Shelburne's government Rayneval was an invaluable reinforcement. From 10:00 A.M. to 5:00 P.M., with only 45 minutes for a brief snack, Rayneval and Vergennes argued the impossibility of obtaining Gibraltar by direct attack or by result of an increasingly improbable success at Jamaica. Vergennes later told Montmorin that if ever a soul had been in pain, it was assuredly Aranda's. He could not approximate the torture which Aranda suffered during the conference. Finally, Aranda's resistance collapsed. He agreed to trust the British ministry and to give Rayneval authorization to cede Minorca. Louis agreed to yield Dominica and Guadeloupe without any security from his uncle and authorized Rayneval to relent if necessary on France's territorial demands in India.

Aranda had taken an enormous risk in exceeding his instructions. On 1 December Montmorin wrote Vergennes that Floridablanca and Charles would rather leave Gibraltar in the hands of England than give up Minorca and Florida.[25] Montmorin believed any peace without all three pos-

---

[24] Spain 609: 297–302, Vergennes to Montmorin, 29 November 1782. Note that Aranda had already agreed to cede the Bahamas.

[25] Spain 609: 332–337, Montmorin to Vergennes, 1 December 1782. Both this letter and Montmorin's letter of 7 December were received on 16 December.

sessions would be regarded as humiliating. With the same astounding good fortune that Vergennes had possessed in the arrival of Rayneval, Montmorin received his own crucial reinforcement. By 7 December (and before news of Aranda's action had reached the Spanish court) Floridablanca told Montmorin that if peace depended on it, Spain would forfeit Minorca.[26] D'Estaing had been received by Charles on 24 November and Montmorin kept him at court until the Spanish decision had been made. Montmorin wrote: "I am well persuaded, sir, that we owe to him the conversion of Spain. The energy with which he has presented the picture of the decay of our navies, the impossibility of repairing a setback and finally all the consequences which could result from the events of this campaign has without doubt made a profound impression on the spirit of His Catholic Majesty [Charles] and has restored him little by little to the moderation from which he appeared so distant."

Unfortunately, the compromise settlement, forced upon Spain with such difficulty by Vergennes and Rayneval, Montmorin and d'Estaing, had already begun to disintegrate.

7. The Miraculous Peace

The first danger sign appeared late on 29 November. Vergennes learned from Franklin that the Americans and British had agreed upon preliminary articles of peace.[1] On the next day the Americans and British signed their agreement, which was conditional upon terms of peace being reached

---

[26] Spain 609: 342–345, Montmorin to Vergennes, 7 December 1782 (quotation is from f. 343). See also Spain 609: 275–281, d'Estaing to Montmorin, 25 November 1782.

[1] United States 22: 500, Franklin to Vergennes, 29 November 1782. Franklin promised to send a copy of the agreement the following day.

by Britain and France.[2] The terms were extraordinary. The Americans and British had been divided over the territorial limits to be assigned the United States, over American fishing rights in the area of Newfoundland, and over compensation for the property seized from the American colonists who had supported Britain (Loyalists). On all three issues the British made concessions which exceeded all Vergennes had believed possible;[3] Rayneval told Vergennes, "The treaty with America appears to me a dream."[4] The agreement raised urgent questions. Had Shelburne made the agreement in order to divide the Americans from France? Would the Americans continue to support France if the Bourbons' negotiations with Britain broke down because of Spain? What would be the effects of the agreement on Parliament and on British public opinion, particularly in relationship to the compromise with Spain just proposed?

It seems reasonably certain to me that Shelburne, as with his European negotiations, wished to present Parliament with a fait accompli, to put pressure on the Bourbons, and, should the European negotiations fail, to remove the Americans from the war.[5] Moreover, the cabinet had authorized the necessary concessions to the Americans before Rayneval's mission;[6] in pulling back, there would have been a great danger of raising again issues already settled.

The Americans never had to face the decision of whether to continue the war if the French negotiations failed, so that particular question is unanswerable. Congress did reaffirm on 4 October 1782 its intention to make neither separate

---

[2] The agreement is given by Bemis, *Diplomacy of the American Revolution*, 259–264.

[3] England 539: 158, Vergennes to Rayneval, 4 December 1782. This is a rough draft and was probably not sent.

[4] England 539: 221, personal letter of Rayneval to Vergennes, 12 December 1782.

[5] For Rayneval's interpretation see England 539: 222, 365–366, Rayneval to Vergennes, 12 December and 17 December 1782.

[6] Morris, *The Peacemakers*, 367–368, 372–381, 397.

peace nor separate truce,[7] but La Luzerne witnessed the unwillingness of the Americans to continue the war for the sake of Spain,[8] whose contribution to the war effort has never been understood by Americans.

Before discussing the immediate consequences of the separate agreement, it is appropriate to make a few general comments about the British-American negotiations.

The traditional American account of these negotiations resembles a kind of Yankee morality play.[9] John Jay, directing the negotiations because of Franklin's health, discovers France is secretly attempting to reach agreement on the conditions Britain should accord the United States. Jay, reinforced at a critical time by John Adams, finally convinces Franklin that the commissioners are justified in breaking Congress' orders to consult with France. With the ingenuity and energy to be expected of the representatives of a new nation, the Americans outfox the deceitful French and hostile Spaniards in order to arrange an advantageous settlement with Britain (by the barely concealed *promise* of a separate peace if the Bourbons are unreasonable). The Americans even manage to preserve their honor by making the terms of their agreement conditional upon a Franco-British peace. The Bourbons then are forced to themselves make peace (under the barely concealed *threat* of a separate peace unless they are reasonable).

This scenario may coincide with Jay's and Adams' view

[7] United States 22: 346–347, Act of Congress, 4 October 1782.

[8] United States 22: 609–610, La Luzerne to Vergennes, 30 December 1782. For Jay's hints to Britain that America would not continue the war for the sake of Spain see Morris, *The Peacemakers*, 360. See also Spain 609: 356, Vergennes to Montmorin, 9 December 1782; Holland 553: 226, Vergennes to La Vauguyon, 29 January 1783. Vergennes told La Vauguyon that he feared neither Congress nor the state legislatures, but rather feared that the American people would abandon the war.

[9] See in particular Bemis, *Diplomacy of the American Revolution* and Morris, *The Peacemakers*. One should, however, grant Bemis credit for destroying the myth of French benevolence created by Doniol.

of the events, but it badly misrepresents both the nature of the French threat to the Americans and the extent of the American accomplishment. Certainly there was not a correspondence of interest between France and the United States beyond the fact of absolute American independence itself. France did not wish the British to lose Canada, desiring instead a balance of power in North America to permit her some continued diplomatic leverage. On the other hand, none of the issues between Britain and the United States involved any significant French interest, provided France was not obstructed in her uninterrupted enjoyment of secure fishing grounds.[10] France did have an enormously compelling need for immediate peace, and her mediation between the United States and Spain, and between the United States and Britain was primarily designed to avoid any delays in the conclusion of peace.[11] If need be, she would unquestionably have sacrificed all the Americans desired beyond independence, but it would not have been to secure any peripheral territorial interests of her own.

This leads to a second point. The major American diplomatic triumph was the securing of the territory between the Appalachians, the Mississippi, the Great Lakes, and Florida. The Americans received this territory chiefly because no one else was as interested in it. France's attitude was that since none of the competing parties effectively occupied the territory, none had a compelling claim to it.[12]

[10] See the fine article of Orville T. Murphy, "The Comte de Vergennes, the Newfoundland Fisheries, and the Peace Negotiations of 1783: A Reappraisal," *Canadian Historical Review* 46 (1965): 32–46.

[11] I believe it was to avoid such delays that Rayneval was instructed on 15 November to attempt to postpone final arrangements on the borders and on the Loyalists until the definitive peace treaty. England 538: 399, instructions for Rayneval, 15 November 1782. Vergennes repeatedly urged moderation on the Americans. See for example United States 21: 336–345, Vergennes to La Luzerne, 28 June 1782.

[12] United States 22: 309–317/England 537: 389–399, "Mémoire concernant les terrains situés à l'est du Mississippi. . . ," no date; United States 22: 197–204, Rayneval to Jay, 6 September 1782; Samuel Flagg Bemis, "The Rayneval Memoranda of 1782 on Western Boundaries

Rayneval tried to arrange a common bargaining position between Spain and the United States, but the Americans refused any compromise of their territorial demands. During Rayneval's first visit to England, Shelburne suggested that Spain cede to England West Florida and an area around New Orleans. When the Spaniards proved uninterested in ceding an area around New Orleans and West Florida,[13] the area to the north, deprived of an outlet to the sea, lost its value to Britain, except as a bargaining point. Since the Spaniards already had more to demand than to offer in exchange, the obvious solution was to offer it to the Americans, who might at least offer some compensation to the Loyalists. The Americans were inflexible negotiators, but were saved by Shelburne's rush to get a settlement before Parliament reconvened to interfere with the negotiations. Luckily for them their agreement was on paper while the Spanish agreement was not. As in February 1778, the Americans' major diplomatic accomplishment was being in the right place at the right time and doing nothing to obstruct the good fortune raining on them.

What then of the question of the propriety of the Americans' conduct? Given the nature of their situation, the commissioners had little choice but to break Congress' orders to consult with France, or even to sign the agreement with its Jesuitical conditional clause (although the American action nearly caused the British cabinet to rupture negotiations with France).[14] One can even excuse the Americans'

---

and Some Comments on the French Historian Doniol," *Proceedings of the American Antiquarian Society* 47 (1937): 15–92. See also United States 22: 368–373, Vergennes to La Luzerne, 14 October 1782.

[13] England 538: 174–175, Rayneval's report of conference of 18 September 1782; Spain 609: 53–54, Vergennes to Montmorin, 6 October 1782; Spain 609: 174, proposition of Aranda, 6 November 1782; Spain 609: 103–104, 135–136, Montmorin to Vergennes, 17 October and 24 October 1782.

[14] England 539: 314–317, personal letter of Rayneval to Vergennes, 25 December 1782. Interestingly, Montmorin had earlier reported that he had let Floridablanca worry about the Americans making a

virtual abandonment of military operations after Yorktown. Few alliances are so strong that one party will accept casualties solely to put pressure on a common enemy. The Americans at least kept their army in the field and avoided making an armistice.[15] What seems least excusable to me was the self-righteousness of Jay and Adams. Jay even secretly suggested to the British an attack on West Florida and convinced his fellow-commissioners to include a secret clause giving more generous boundaries to Florida if it were captured by the British. Jay provides an illustration of the vindictiveness to which disillusioned innocence is prone; however impressive was Jay's future service to his country, he set it a bad example by his diplomacy.

The American agreement had fatal consequences for the elaborate agreement which Shelburne, Rayneval, Vergennes, and Aranda had hoped to construct. Any course Shelburne took in his desperate search for peace was full of danger; he simply did not have the political support to make concessions to both the Americans and the Bourbons. Parliament was due to reopen on 5 December. On 2 December, Rayneval, accompanied by Vergennes' 21-year-old son as secretary, brought Aranda's and Louis' concessions, and on the following day the news arrived of the American agreement. When Shelburne presented Rayneval's terms to the cabinet he met great opposition.[16] The commercial interests of the city were clamoring against the rumored transfer of Santo Domingo to rival France. In an extraordinary bargaining session Shelburne and Rayneval tried combination after combination in order to construct a new

---

separate peace so as to make Spain more tractable. Vergennes believed that the American peace commissioners did not realize the possible consequences of their action. Spain 608: 185, Montmorin to Vergennes, 12 August 1782; England 539: 380–381, Vergennes to Rayneval, 30 December 1782.

[15] It should be noted that Colonel Laurens, who had been sent to France in 1781, was killed in combat in 1782.

[16] England 539: 135–143; England, supplement 19: 327–335, Rayneval to Vergennes, 4 December 1782.

compromise. The best terms for a Gibraltar exchange that Rayneval could obtain were hardly likely to be accepted by either France or Spain. In addition to the concessions already offered (Dominica, Guadeloupe, Minorca, and the Bahamas), Shelburne asked for part of Florida plus either Trinidad or Saint Lucia.[17] Shelburne, however, offered an escape. If Spain would drop her demands for Gibraltar, Britain would give up both East and West Florida.

The opening ceremonies of Parliament would permit a few days for a response, but Rayneval warned Vergennes that if the response were not affirmative the war party in the cabinet would prevail. Rayneval had reassured Shelburne that George could, without compromising himself, tell Parliament of his best founded hopes for an approaching peace.[18]

Vergennes in reply told Rayneval: "I swear, sir, that my arms fell when I read your dispatch and after a few moments' reflection I have had to admire your sagacity in having conserved enough sang-froid not to have broken off all negotiations in view of the new demands you have been given."[19]

It was now up to Vergennes to keep the negotiations alive. If Saint Lucia were given up, Martinique would lose its value; so Vergennes asked Rayneval to attempt to find an English equivalent for it. One other desperate hope re-

[17] *Ibid.*; England 539: 151–152, "Réponse aux propositions de l'ambassadeur d'Espagne datées le 28 novembre 1782." Vergennes later admitted that even with the exchanges already agreed to, he would have been fortunate to have been considered by the public an imbecile rather than a traitor. Spain 609: 389, Vergennes to Montmorin, 17 December 1782. Note that Shelburne did make a concession concerning Florida, which he had previously demanded in total, but concerning which the Spaniards had made no offer.

[18] For the wording of George's statement see England 539: 161–162, "Copy of His Majesty's Most Gracious Speech in Both Houses of Parliament on Thursday, December 5, 1782."

[19] England 539: 168–179, Vergennes to Rayneval, 7 December 1782 (quotation is from f. 170). See also Spain 609: 353–356, Vergennes to Montmorin, 9 December 1782.

mained. Aranda had shown Vergennes a dispatch from Floridablanca authorizing Aranda to explore what advantages Spain would receive by desisting from her demand for Gibraltar. Vergennes promised Rayneval that if England would offer Minorca and West Florida, Louis would transmit the offer to Charles, while recommending its acceptance with his most active interest. He warned the English that Louis' desire for peace sprang from virtue and not from weakness and that he would continue the war if necessary.

Rayneval acted as effectively in a situation calling for firmness as he had in previous situations calling for accommodation.[20] It quickly became apparent that it would be impossible to find an equivalent for Martinique. After permitting Shelburne and Grantham time for worry, Rayneval confided the article of Floridablanca's dispatch and warned the English ministers that no other hope remained of ending the war. On 11 December, after a meeting of the cabinet, Grantham handed Rayneval an unsigned note offering Minorca and both Floridas to Spain while demanding the return of the Bahamas and the acknowledgment of British timber-cutter rights in the Campeche (Yucatán) Peninsula.[21] Vergennes was now faced with the most important meeting of his diplomatic career. He had to ask Aranda for a second time to disregard his explicit instructions. True, Floridablanca's dispatch had hinted a flexibility about Gibraltar not before seen, but once again Aranda had to be asked to commit an act of disobedience, perhaps even of treason, which might forever end his chances of serving his king as minister.[22]

---

[20] England 539: 208–216, Rayneval to Vergennes, 12 December 1782.

[21] *Ibid.*; England 539: 199; England, supplement 19: 353, unsigned note of 11 December 1782.

[22] Note, too, that Vergennes received Montmorin's dispatch of 7 December (approving Aranda's former action) during his conference with Aranda, but it is not clear at exactly what stage of the conversation. Aranda received his dispatches at the same time as did Vergennes. Spain 609: 386, Vergennes to Montmorin, 17 December 1782.

Aranda as a diplomat was proud, inflexible, and unendingly difficult; but Vergennes, who dealt with him for so many years, once wrote: "M. d'Aranda is an estimable man. He knows his duties; he is exact in filling them and it is not possible to carry any further his love and attachment for his country."[23]

At their conference on 16 December, Aranda accepted immediately the conditions offered by the British cabinet— perhaps from patriotism, perhaps from the knowledge or the assumption that Charles really desired to make the concession.[24] Aranda successfully ran the risk he accepted for his country. Not only was his action accepted (although at least outwardly with great reluctance and anger),[25] but within a decade he became the chief minister of Spain.

The solution of the Gibraltar problem was the great breakthrough of the negotiations, but a series of very dangerous obstacles had to be overcome before the preliminary agreement was signed at Versailles on 20 January 1783. The most perilous of these was the compromise on Negapatam and Trincomalee, which had to be forced upon the Dutch as well as the English. (In the end Fitzherbert and Vergennes agreed to the compromise in advance of the Dutch.)[26] Aranda sent his secretary to London to settle the details of the English logging rights, which was also a seri-

---

[23] Spain 603: 185, personal letter of Vergennes to Montmorin, 14 May 1781.

[24] England 539: 245–247, Vergennes to Rayneval, 16 December 1782; Spain 609: 368–369, Vergennes to Montmorin, 17 December 1782. It is possible that he had been given secret instructions for this eventuality by Floridablanca. Even if this were so, Aranda's action of 28 November alone would justify the great honor he merits. My guess is that although Floridablanca's instructions constituted a broad hint, Aranda was left the final responsibility. See also Spain 609: 418, Vergennes to Montmorin, 18 December 1782; Spain 609: 449–455, Montmorin to Vergennes, 28 December 1782.

[25] Spain 609: 421–422, 449–455; Spain 610: 7–10, Montmorin to Vergennes, 18 December 1782, 28 December 1782, and 2 January 1783; Spain 610: 5, Charles to Louis, 2 January 1783.

[26] Holland 553: *passim*. For the remaining negotiations see England 538; England 539; England, supplement 19: *passim*.

ous enough question to threaten the settlement.[27] The British balked at giving up Dominica, which they claimed to have believed included in the arrangements agreed upon. Finally, in exchange for obtaining Tobago and Saint Lucia, the French were forced to cede all their conquests, to abandon their last hope of significant gain in India, and to agree to only a short armistice for their allies, subject to a return to prewar boundaries. Fortunately, the final arrangements were made in time to prevent d'Estaing from sailing;[28] the agreement was signed only two days before Parliament returned from the Christmas recess which had given Shelburne his final period of grace.

Fortunate indeed it was that the Allies did not have to undertake a Jamaican campaign in 1783. Solano did not go to Porto Cabello, since the governing authorities at Havana would not permit him to leave,[29] but Vaudreuil, with Rochambeau's army embarked, sailed on 24 December for that ill-chosen destination. He had already lost one of his 13 ships of the line by shipwreck while entering Boston harbor; he lost another before his storm-damaged fleet reached South America in mid-February.[30] The British had already collected a sizeable force in the West Indies: Hood with 12 ships of the line was off Saint Domingue and a comparable

[27] See particularly Spain 609: 419, Aranda to Vergennes, 18 December 1782; Spain 609: 465, Vergennes to Montmorin, 31 December 1782.

[28] Because of bad weather d'Estaing's final preparations had been slowed. He learned on 16 January of the state of the negotiations. As a pretext for delay he had just detached eight ships of the line to meet a small incoming convoy from Havana when he learned on 2 February of the signature of preliminaries of peace. Spain 610: 185, 189, Bessière to Vergennes, 29 January and 2 February 1783; B⁴211: 137, personal letter of d'Estaing to Castries, 31 January 1783; B⁴217: 111, Castries to d'Estaing, 17 January 1783.

[29] United States 22: 527, Solano to Vaudreuil, 10 December 1782; B⁴195: 182–183, Castries to Montmorin, August 1783.

[30] B⁴267: 86–89, Vaudreuil to Castries, 19 February 1783. Vaudreuil had received only one dispatch sent after the beginning of August. B⁴216: 294–296, Vaudreuil to Castries, 17 March 1783. For Vaudreuil's squadron see B⁴266; B⁴267: *passim*.

force under Admiral Pigot was in the Windward Islands, where it was joined by eight of the line detached by Howe as he returned from Gibraltar.[31]

The long-range situation in India was hardly more promising. Both sides should have had 18 ships of the line, but Suffren had lost 3 of his through attrition and received no help from the Dutch East India Company squadron. In a brilliant campaign Suffren managed to drive off the superior English squadron, but the French expeditionary force, finally under Bussy's command,[32] was still in peril when hostilities in India finally ended in June 1783.

There, too, was little hope that naval forces could have been found for Europe. Ironically, however, as the war came to its end, the matériel shortages of Brest were much relieved as a flood of wood, masts, planks, hemp, and copper finally poured into the dockyard.[33]

Vergennes was a pragmatic man who spoke seldom in religious language even to the trusted Montmorin. Yet Vergennes ultimately could only attribute to divine intervention the final turn of the negotiations: "In reflecting, sir, upon the new turn the negotiations have taken, I humble myself before the Sovereign Being and I render Him the most lively and the most fervent thanksgiving. It is His infinite sagacity which has disposed the heart and spirit of the Catholic king [Charles] to desist from the cession of Gibraltar to which that prince appeared so strongly attached."[34]

Rayneval, too, told Vergennes he believed the peace could be regarded as a miracle.[35] It is easy to understand

[31] Another 11 of the line had orders for the West Indies. Mackesy, *War for America*, 489.

[32] Bussy finally sailed in December 1782 from Île de France with 2,000 reinforcements for the French forces in India.

[33] B³720: 328, Hector to Castries, 13 December 1782; B³723: 211 ff., Guillot to Castries, 16 November 1782 and following. The copper came from Sweden.

[34] Spain 609: 388, Vergennes to Montmorin, 17 December 1782. See also Spain 610: 223–224, Vergennes to Montmorin, 9 February 1783.

[35] England 540: 258–260, personal letter of Rayneval to Vergennes, 24 January 1783.

Rayneval's and Vergennes' awe at the difficulties that had been overcome and the dangers so narrowly escaped. Perhaps our sense of awe should be even greater since from our perspective we can better see the fragility of the institutions Rayneval and Montmorin and Vergennes served. How well had France fought and yet how close to the edge of the chasm had she come! What we can no longer share is their sense of relief. Instead, in leaving Vergennes and his representatives, my feeling is sadness. The most faithful of servants, he helped prepare the financial and political crisis during which his monarch took his first steps toward death. A man who hated war, he sent men to war for his dream of a secure France in a stable Europe, a dream of a world already dead.

CHAPTER TEN

1783–1787—Epilogue

1. The Naval Consequences of the War

THE five years between the end of the American war and the resignation of Castries resemble somewhat the last years of Louis XV's reign. Both were a period of naval retrenchment following a period of naval expansion and a period of crisis. There were, however, important differences. The mismanagement of the navy by Louis XV's last naval minister, Bourgeois de Boynes, partially endangered the navy's ability to fulfill its legitimate diplomatic role as a guarantor of the state's ability to defend itself and its vital interests. This is not to criticize Louis XV's decision to subordinate all other considerations to the resolution of the monarchy's domestic problems nor even to suggest that the decline of French naval strength was marked enough to invite attack. Nonetheless, Castries' administration (at least between 1783 and 1786) represented far better than did that of de Boynes a fair balance for his century between excessive and insufficient attention to military affairs. It is arguable that even a moderate level of naval expenditures should have been sacrificed to resolve the debt problem, but the debt problem was primarily a political problem, and Louis' failure to resolve it cannot be blamed on Castries. Given the nature of the balance of power of the 1780s, France's expenditure on naval arms was not excessive.[1] Between the end of hostilities and the beginning of 1787, 17 ships of the line were removed from the navy's rolls while 12 were launched and 7 more placed in construction. On 1 January 1787 the navy comprised 62 ships of the line,[2] of which 9 were scheduled for replacement. To maintain the

[1] See Appendix A, Note 21.
[2] This is exclusive of those in construction. See Appendix K.

navy at 60–65 ships of the line was reasonable, both in terms of the number of ships that could be manned at the commencement of a war and in terms of what would not be provocative to Britain. What differentiated the administration of Castries from the administration of Boynes was not the number of ships or even their annual replacement rate, but rather the attention and skill devoted to naval administration and to the maintenance of adequate matériel. On both of these the strength of the navy was really dependent. Castries was a superlative administrator and by his reforms he made meaningful and lasting contributions to the navy;[3] after the war the diligent search for naval matériel was continued, although under new budgetary restrictions.[4] From a diplomatic standpoint the test of arms is the impression they foster. From the correspondence of the Duke of Dorset, the English ambassador, it appears the French navy generally fostered respect but not alarm.[5]

The balance of the naval program, however, was precarious. As early as 1781 Castries had talked of his hopes for maintaining the navy at 80 ships of the line.[6] It would be comprised of eight 110s, sixty 74s and eight 64s, each type standardized so parts could be interchangeable between ships. Such a fleet could not have been manned and it was provocatively close to the effective strength of the British fleet. Such a program was contrary to Vergennes' policy of

---

[3] Lacour-Gayet, *La marine militaire sous le règne de Louis XVI*, 566–574, gives a good summary of these reforms. See also G 129 and G 130. What does Castries most credit is his attempt to make more equitable the system of naval conscription.

[4] This judgment is based on very limited study; I have had only a brief look at B¹98 through B¹101.

[5] Oscar Browning, ed., *Despatches from Paris, 1784–1790* (London: Royal Historical Society, 1909), 1: 45, 55, 98–99, 152, 209.

[6] B⁸14: unpaged, sheets for March 1781, Castries' meeting with the council of construction at Brest on 17 March 1781. Castries did succeed in standardizing ship plans for certain size ships. Lacour-Gayet, *La marine militaire sous le règne de Louis XVI*, 563. The symmetry of the numbers of ships is reminiscent of a far less ambitious proposal in 1775. See Chapter Two, Section 1, Note 11.

restraint and reconciliation, yet even before Vergennes' death, Castries had succeeded in reversing the trend toward a progressively tighter naval budget. Arms and diplomacy each wish to serve the security and advancement of the state but their alliance cannot be one of equals. Soon before Vergennes' death, there began the growth of naval arms which as in 1776 and 1777 accompanied and accelerated the decline of relations with Britain.[7] This decline would continue through the revolutions of 1789 and 1792 to the outbreak of a new war.[8]

2. The Diplomatic Consequences of the War

The negotiations for a final settlement of the American war proceeded in the shadow of the Crimean crisis, which intensified in June 1783 when Vergennes was informed both of Catherine's intention to annex the Crimea and of the Russian-Austrian alliance. Before September, when the definitive treaty of peace with Britain was signed, France had resolved on war if Austria joined the Russians in despoiling the Ottoman Empire.[1] In his struggle to save the Ottoman Empire from the fate of Poland, Vergennes received no help from Britain—Shelburne had been censured over the liberality of his peace terms and had then resigned.[2] Never-

---

[7] Between 1 January 1787 and 1 January 1792, 25 ships of the line were launched, while 12 were stricken and one was reclassified as a frigate.

[8] The interrelationship between the events of the French revolution and the traditional sources of Anglo-French tension such as naval rivalry particularly interests me. I hope to study it in another book—tentatively to be entitled, "The Naval Arms Race and the French Revolution: A Study of Arms and Diplomacy, 1787–1793."

[1] Isabel de Madariaga, "The Secret Austro-Russian Treaty of 1781," *Slavonic and East European Review* 38 (1959): 138–143; M. S. Anderson, "The Great Powers and the Russian Annexation of the Crimea," *Slavonic and East European Review* 37 (1958): 17–41.

[2] Norris, *Shelburne and Reform*, 256–270; Fitzmaurice, *Shelburne*, 2: 236–241. Shelburne resigned on 24 February 1783. For Vergennes' tribute to Shelburne see Spain 610: 280, Vergennes to Montmorin, 1 March 1783.

theless, Vergennes was able to minimize the losses of the Turks, who were pressured into recognizing the annexation, thereby saving themselves from further loss. During the four years following the end of the American war, Vergennes achieved considerable success in his program of continental peace and stability. France, of course, did not possess the power of the Germany of a century later and Vergennes consequently did not have the leverage of a Bismarck (who presided over the European status quo of the 1870s and 1880s). The maintenance of peace was a result not merely of Vergennes' efforts but rather of a combination of factors—the diplomatic conservatism of Frederick's Prussia which matched that of France, the caution of Catherine in not rushing her expansionist program, the maladroitness of Joseph, who with a more disciplined approach to diplomacy might have overturned Vergennes' system. Joseph's expansionism, unlike Catherine's, was unfocused. His various projects for expansion against the Turks, the absorption of Bavaria, and the opening of the River Scheldt (to free a trade route to Antwerp and the Austrian Netherlands) were successfully checked, in good part by the vigilance of Vergennes.[3]

Vergennes' success was partially due to the temporary removal of a demoralized England from the field of European diplomacy. Shelburne's successors, North and Fox, were themselves quickly succeeded by Shelburne's protégé, William Pitt, the Younger. During the first years of his long administration Pitt concentrated on the political and economic reform of the English state and during these years Britain practically ceased playing any part in the diplomatic movements of the continent. If she did not cooperate with France, as Vergennes once had been for a moment

---

[3] A good introduction to the diplomacy of this period is M. S. Anderson, "European Diplomatic Relations, 1763–1790," in Albert Goodwin, ed., *The New Cambridge Modern History*, vol. 8, *The American and French Revolutions, 1763–93* (Cambridge: At the University Press, 1965), 252–278.

given reason to hope, she at least did not endanger the work of peace. Britain's weakened position was most dramatically reflected by Vergennes' success in obtaining a treaty of defensive alliance with Holland, so long a virtual British client state.

The temporary removal of Britain from European diplomacy was one positive result of the American war. As a second positive result France was finally able to force Britain into the commercial negotiations promised in the definitive peace treaty. Although the terms of the commercial treaty of 26 September 1786 were generally favorable to Britain,[4] they still represented a triumph for Vergennes in his policy of forcing Britain to deal with France as an equal. Vergennes died in office on 13 February 1787 as negotiations continued for a wide-scale clarification of Franco-British commercial and colonial relations—negotiations which held the possibility of a relaxation of the mutual suspicion and hostility which precluded any rapprochement between the two countries. Vergennes had served France as foreign minister for almost 13 years. During this period there had been no general war in Europe, no substantial changes in the balance of power, and no major loss to any of France's client states. Vergennes in 1784 told Louis that the power of France should be used not to gain extra territory but rather to maintain the public order of Europe and to prevent the destruction of the different powers which form the equilibrium of Europe.[5] Vergennes' part in the maintenance of European peace and stability is the basis upon which he should be honored.

From a wider perspective, however, the administration of Vergennes was tragically unsuccessful and its lack of success was due in large part to France's participation in the American war. First of all, the American war failed to

[4] John Ehrman, *The Younger Pitt* (London: Constable and Co., 1969), 489. The most thorough account of these negotiations is Marie Martenis Donaghay, "The Anglo-French Negotiations of 1786–1787" (Ph.D. diss., University of Virginia, 1970).

[5] Memoirs and Documents, France 587: 207–225, Vergennes to Louis, 29 March 1784.

achieve France's basic objective, the permanent weakening of Britain through ending her monopoly of American trade. As the war gradually revealed to Vergennes the unreliability of the American connection with France, he was forced to admit that any hope of increased French commerce was illusory and that all France could hope was that Britain would be given no postwar commercial preference.[6] Although the British lost any official position in American trade, the persistence of former trade patterns proved that the former British monopoly was largely unnecessary. From 1784 through 1789 average British exports to her former American colonies were already 90 percent of the average from 1769 through 1774, and during the decade of the 1790s they exceeded the best prewar years.[7] As Vergennes feared, French trade with the United States could not compete with the British.[8] What was most significant in diplomatic terms was the overall level of British trade and whether the British could maintain the strength of their navy. As early as 1783 total British trade virtually equaled the record prewar figures and it increased its strength throughout the decade.[9] Pitt raised the peacetime establishment of the navy, while constructing 33 ships of the line between 1783 and 1790;[10] the British navy of the 1790s was a far stronger opponent than that faced by Sartine and Castries.

[6] United States 20: 228–229, Vergennes to La Luzerne, 3 January 1782; United States 21: 340, Vergennes to La Luzerne, 28 June 1782.

[7] Mitchell, *Abstract of British Historical Statistics*, 310–311. For a suggestion as to the reasons see Ralph Davis, "English Foreign Trade, 1700–1774," *Economic History Review* series 2, 15 (1962): 297. See also Gerald Graham, *Sea Power and British North America, 1783–1820* (Cambridge, Mass.: Harvard University Press, 1941), 58–61.

[8] B⁷460: *passim*; Romano, "Documenti," 2: 1292 (for trade during the war).

[9] Mitchell, *Abstract of British Historical Statistics*, 280–281. Mitchell's figures for years prior to 1772 do not include Scotland, so comparison is not exact.

[10] Ehrman, *Pitt*, 313. See also *Sandwich Papers*, 4: 302; B⁷473: piece 60, "Etat des vaisseaux de guerre anglais lancés à la mer depuis la fin de la guerre dernier," 1791 (which lists 38 of the line launched from 1783 through 1789). For expenditures see Mitchell, *Abstract of British Historical Statistics*, 391.

Not only was England not weakened by her loss of the American colonies, but her departure from the diplomatic scene was also temporary. Within two years of Vergennes' death his diplomatic world was shattered. England re-entered continental diplomacy and the Eastern crisis degenerated into the war which Vergennes had only postponed. Vergennes' attempt to neutralize English hostility through establishing trade relations was also unsuccessful. The commercial agreement, designed in part to serve the diplomacy of rapprochement,[11] never fully disarmed the suspicions of Pitt and the agreement was quickly sabotaged by Castries after Vergennes' death.[12]

The historian Mahan believed that the central failure of Ancien Régime France in her foreign relations was her failure to direct her efforts to destroy England as a rival. I believe, on the contrary, the central failure of Ancien Régime France in her foreign relations was her failure to secure the cooperation and friendship of England upon which French security alone could have been founded. In a century largely ruled by commercial rivalry this would have been enormously difficult but, as the brief period of Walpole and Fleury demonstrates, perhaps not impossible. To this end, which Vergennes had the genius to appreciate, the French participation in the American war finally proved disfunctional. Vergennes' English system rested on a basic contradiction. To open the possibility of Franco-British cooperation France attacked Britain at a moment of British peril and deprived her of her most treasured possession. Had Britain been an absolutist state such a contradiction would not have been fatal, but British diplomacy was ultimately

[11] The same purpose probably underlay in part the commercial agreement with Russia signed on 11 January 1787. For these negotiations see Frank Fox, "Negotiating with the Russians: Ambassador Ségur's Mission to Saint-Petersbourg, 1784–1789," *French Historical Studies* 7 (1971): 47–71. In both cases, of course, trade was also desirable in itself.

[12] Donaghay, "Anglo-French Negotiations," 138–177.

dependent on Parliament and Parliament dependent on public opinion—a ground on which the American war sowed seeds of further hatred and suspicion which future diplomacy could not uproot.

Even more important than the failure of the American war to achieve France's goals was its undermining of the internal strength of the French state upon which rested France's ability to achieve her diplomatic goals. Vergennes' death preceded by less than a month the Assembly of Notables, called by the council to resolve the crisis in royal finances which had largely resulted from the expenses incurred in the American war. France and Britain faced a roughly equal debt at the end of the war but the strength of the British economy, the resiliency of the British political system, and the ability of Pitt permitted Britain to balance her budget and to begin to reduce her debt. The French debt, in contrast, gradually absorbed the financial resources of the monarchy and threw it into the crisis in which the Assembly of Notables marked only one of the beginning stages.[13]

With the bases of French strength so eroded, France's diplomatic position at Vergennes' death was illusory, and during 1787 and 1788 her true position was made humiliatingly clear.[14] The restoration of the strength of the French

[13] Bosher, *French Finances*, 23–24; Ehrman, *Pitt*, 157–158, 239–240, 256, 274. There was also a psychological connection between the American and the French Revolution, although this point has often been greatly overstated. For a corrective view that the revolutionary mentality in France was a result of the political crisis of 1787–1788 itself see George V. Taylor, "Noncapitalist Wealth and the French Revolution," *American Historical Review* 72 (1967): 469–496. This is not to deny the educational effect (in the broadest sense) of the American Revolution.

[14] See Donaghay, "Anglo-French Negotiations," 178–206. As an ominous warning, there occurred in February 1787 the bankruptcy of Baudard de Sainte-James, treasurer-general of the navy. See Legoʹhérel, *Les trésoriers généraux de la marine*, 348–354; Denise Ozanam, *Claude Baudard de Sainte-James, Trésorier général de la marine et brasseur d'affaires (1738–1787)* (Geneva: Droz, 1969).

state and of the effectiveness of French diplomacy was achieved only at the cost of the institutions and social order to which Vergennes devoted his life.

The greatest tragedy of the American war was the way in which the war and then its resultant debt came to dominate and to blight the reign of the well-intentioned Louis XVI. Louis' failures as a king were largely a result of his character and of the social and political attitudes he inherited, so perhaps meaningful reform was foredoomed. Nonetheless, the decision of April 1776 to aid the Americans represented a rejection of Turgot's plans for reform, and the subsequent war and its debt rendered infinitely more remote any possibility of regenerating the French monarchy. The war also was a factor in the series of economic dislocations of the late 1770s and 1780s which deepened and altered the crisis facing the monarchy.[15] Perhaps the destruction of the monarchy and its social order was inevitable and even on balance beneficial.[16] Viewed, however, from the perspective of Vergennes and his associates the decision to participate in the rebellion of Britain's colonies was not only mistaken but tragic.

[15] This subject is still under study by French economic historians. The greatest of these, C. E. Labrousse, summarizes the current state of knowledge in Fernand Braudel and C. E. Labrousse, *Histoire économique et sociale de la France* (Paris: Presses Universitaires de France, 1970), 2: 529–563.

[16] See the argument of Barrington Moore Jr., *Social Origins of Dictatorship and Democracy* (London: Penguin Press, Peregrine Books, 1969), 40–110.

The Naval and Colonial Budget, 1776–1783

IT is far easier to determine the money allotted to the naval and colonial department during the War of American Independence than it is to determine how much money was actually spent. After 1776 purchases were made without appropriations on the promise of future payment, and the king was repeatedly approached to make extraordinary appropriations. The figures on expenditures given to the king were often biased; moreover, they were necessarily inexact because the naval minister himself did not know the amount of the bills outstanding. The most reliable figures for the war years were compiled only in the mid-1780s.

It is extremely important to note that not only was the yearly excess of expenditures over allotments a source of debt but that the allotments themselves were in large part based on borrowed funds.

Ordinary departmental expenses were 17,800,000 livres for the navy and 10,100,000 for colonies for an annual total of 27,900,000 livres.[1] Supplemental appropriations of 4,000,000 and 9,500,000 were made for naval expenses alone in 1775 and 1776, but the base figure was also adjusted and no mention was made of appropriations for colonies. It is likely that the allotment for 1775 was in fact 32,900,000.[2] Beginning

[1] See Chapter Two, Section 1, Notes 13–15. Hereafter all figures cited will be in livres. For purchasing power of the livre see Glossary.

[2] B⁵10: unpaged, "Mémoire sur les dépenses variables de la marine pour 1776," no date; B¹81: 273, untitled memoir, no date; B⁵10: unpaged, "Mémoire au roi," 15 July 1777. The first of these memoirs strongly suggests that ordinary funds for the navy had been raised in 1775 to 18,800,000 livres. It lists 10,424,559 for variable expenses and 400,000 for hospitals; the last component of ordinary expenses, that of fixed expenses, was generally 8,000,000. It is doubtful that any allotment above the usual 10,100,000 was made for colonies, even though part of the 7,320,000 for troop reinforcements to the Caribbean in 1775 and 1777 was contracted in 1775. See B¹84: 394–396, untitled memoir, December 1777.

in 1776 we have ministerial memoirs as sources for the allotments (hereafter called receipts) and expenditures. These memoirs give the following figures for the peacetime years of 1776 and 1777:

1776: receipts ... 42,673,000[3] expenditures ... 47,257,311[4]
1777: receipts ... 50,622,599[5] expenditures ... 58,543,000[5]

For the war years, numerous references are made to receipts:

1778: receipts ... 85,153,000[6]

[3] B⁴134: 298–301, Sartine to Necker, 17 August 1777, gives the total receipts for 1776 and 1777 as 105,726,000 livres. Subtracting 44,950,000 already received in 1777 and 8,103,000 in supplemental requests listed in advance of receipt, the total for 1776 is 42,673,000. This accords reasonably well with B⁴214: 77, untitled memoir, Fleurieu papers, July 1777, which gives naval appropriations proper at 29,300,000, leaving 13,373,000 for colonies (a quite possible figure). The figure of 29,300,-000 accords very well with other available figures—11,721,629 livres for ordinary appropriations, presumably variable expenses only (B⁵10: unpaged, "Rapport des extraits ci-joints des projets formées pour les différents ports pour l'année 1776," August 1776), plus 8,000,000 for ordinary fixed appropriations, plus 9,500,000 for extraordinary appropriations (B⁵10: unpaged, "Mémoire au roi," 15 July 1777). It is apparent that the base figure for ordinary naval appropriations was continually rising—from 17,800,000 in 1774 to 18,800,000 in 1775, to about 19,800,000 in 1776, to 20,100,000 by July 1777 (B⁴214: 77, Fleurieu papers, memoir of July 1777). By July 1777 ordinary colonial appropriations had risen to 16,600,000 (*Ibid.*).

[4] B⁵10: unpaged, "Mémoire au roi," 15 July 1777. Of this total, 28,039,078 was incurred by the navy and 19,218,233 by colonies. Cf. B⁴214: 77, Fleurieu papers, memoir of July 1777, which gives naval expenses at 29,800,000.

[5] B¹87: 260–265, untitled memoir of 1 November 1778; B¹91: 87–91, untitled memoir of 10 April 1779. B⁵10: unpaged, "Mémoire au roi," 15 July 1777, indicates that by that date 45,922,000 had been awarded, including 9,223,000 in extraordinary funds. The remaining 4,700,000 was apparently a later extraordinary appropriation.

[6] E 205: unpaged, "Etat des sommes dépensées par le département de la marine pendant les années de 1778 à 1783 . . . ," no date (hereafter cited as SD); E 205: unpaged, "Fonds remis par le trésor royal pendant les années 1778, 1779, 1780," 1 January 1781 (hereafter cited as FR 1781); E 207: unpaged, "Etat des sommes versées par le trésor royal au département de la marine dans les années de guerre de 1778 à 1782," no date (hereafter cited as SV); E 205: unpaged, "Fonds remis par le trésor royal pendant les années 1778, 1779, 1780, 1781," 1 January 1782 (hereafter cited as FR 1782).

1779: receipts . . . 131,639,380[7]
1780: receipts . . . 143,988,500[8]
1781: receipts . . . 147,500,000[9]
1782: receipts . . . 183,896,000[10] or 184,441,705[11]
1783: receipts . . . 143,000,000[12] or 146,616,985[13]
      or 147,588,938[14]

For expenditures, the initial estimates were made by adding the projected debt for the year to receipts. These figures are:[15]

1778: expenditures . . . 101,153,000
1779: expenditures . . . 156,639,840
1780: expenditures . . . 168,988,500
1781: expenditures . . . 163,500,000
1782: expenditures . . . 199,896,000
1783: expenditures . . . 158,000,000

Luckily, more precise figures are available. As the naval debt assumed greater importance, the naval minister had to account not only for meeting current expenses but for liquidating debts. From his yearly reports we can construct a table (see Table 1) giving both the years debts were contracted and the years in which these debts were paid:[16]

[7] *Ibid.*

[8] *Ibid.*; E 205: unpaged, "Fonds remis à la marine dans le cours de l'année 1780," no date. The navy also received a small sum to reimburse it for advances made to army personnel.

[9] SD; SV; FR 1782.

[10] SD; SV; E 207: unpaged, "Fonds remis par le trésor royal pendant les années 1778, 1779, 1780, 1781, 1782," no date (hereafter cited as FR 1783).

[11] E 206: unpaged, "Fonds réellement reçus du trésor royal," no date (hereafter cited as FRR). This is an inferior source and should be used with caution.

[12] SD.

[13] E 206: unpaged, untitled memoir, 1784 (hereafter cited as UM). This gives sums paid on various debts by 1 January 1784.

[14] FRR. This source indicates that another 6,000,000 were allocated to reduce debts—this, however, is indicated by no other source.

[15] SD.

[16] FR 1781; FR 1782; FR 1783; UM; E 207: unpaged, "Recettes et dépenses de la marine pendant l'année 1782," no date.

Table 1

Contracted in:	pre-1778	1778	1779	1780	1781	1782	1783	Total
Paid in:								
1778	12,003,000	73,150,000	–	–	–	–	–	85,153,000
1779	5,862,279	44,755,810	81,021,750	–	–	–	–	131,639,840
1780	497,731	3,150,562	56,392,530	83,947,676	–	–	–	143,988,500
1781	699,085	1,760,657	9,509,682	54,724,242	80,806,333	–	–	147,500,000
1782	365,159	1,915,381	2,905,363	14,026,116	60,671,130	104,012,870	–	183,896,000
1783*	–	–	–	–	10,577,382	66,742,815	69,296,788	146,616,985+
Total	19,427,254+	124,732,410+	149,829,325+	152,698,034+	152,054,845+	170,755,685	69,296,788	

*During 1783 an unspecified amount of the 3,696,350 of remaining debts contracted prior to 1781 was also paid. UM indicates only the total amount paid through 1783 on debts from 1781, 1782, and 1783. Obviously during 1783 some payments were also made on debts from earlier years. The debt remaining from 1780 and previous years was 3,696,350 as of 1 January 1783, according to E 205: unpaged, untitled memoir of 1 April 1783.

According to Castries' reports the total debt on 31 December 1783 was at least 137,178,374.[17] If this is added to the amount known to have been paid between 1 January 1776 and 1 January 1784, the total war-related expenditure is 1,062,345,772. Rounding off this figure and extrapolating from the above report, my own estimate of the *minimum* probable naval expenses for each year in livres is found in Table 2.

Table 2

Year	Appropriated	Paid by 1-1-1784	Minimum Probable Expenditures
1776	42,673,000	47,257,311+	47,000,000
1777	50,622,599	58,543,000+	59,000,000
1778	85,153,000	124,732,410+	125,000,000
1779	131,639,380	149,829,325+	150,000,000
1780	143,988,500	152,698,034+	155,000,000
1781	147,500,000	152,054,845	162,000,000
1782	183,896,000	170,755,685	200,000,000
1783	146,616,985+	69,296,788	165,000,000
Total	932,089,464+	925,167,398+	1,063,000,000+

If normal expenditures are figured at 27,900,000 per year, the navy and colonies would have cost the French crown 223,200,000 for the eight years. The probable expenditure was actually at least 840,000,000 above that. Even assuming

[17] E 205: unpaged, "Aperçu des dettes du département de la marine pour le 31 X^bre [December] 1783," no date. This figure is substantially less than a projection for the same date which had been made on 1 September 1783. This projection was of a debt of 158,922,000 (E 208: unpaged, untitled memoir of 1 September 1783). Earlier projections (B⁴217: 265–288, untitled memoir, ca. 1 April 1783; E 205: unpaged, untitled memoir of 6 June 1783) were even larger. There may have been some debt reduction by irregular means such as the transfer of goods or loan of ships. Until the payment of debts has been studied in minute detail, any conclusions about expenditures must remain tentative.

Appendix A

expenditures on the army to have been far less than naval expenses,[18] it seems likely that the cost to the French monarchy of aiding America to her independence was in excess of a billion livres,[19] exclusive of the interest on debts.[20]

[18] From 1778 through 1782 navy department appropriations were just below 692,000,000 livres, war department appropriations 531,-651,518. French national archives, M¹ᵛ663: piece 13, "Dépenses des départements de la marine et de la guerre depuis 1778 jusqu'en et compris 1782," March 1782. If the army overspent appropriations at the same rate as did the navy, expenditures would be about 800,-000,000. There is no basis for a "normal" peacetime year since the 70,000,000 livres spent both in 1774 and 1775 included funds for army expansion. Charles-Joseph Mathon de La Cour, *Collection des comptes-rendus* . . . (Lausanne: Cuchet et Gattey, 1788), 110–111, 164–167. See also Marion, *Histoire financière de la France*, 303n, for alternate figures on expenditures.

[19] E 205: unpaged, "Récapitulation de la dépense des trois départements de la marine, de l'armée et de l'artillerie depuis le 25 decembre 1775 jusqu'à 25 avril 1782," no date, gives figures for British naval expenses. Both it and Mitchell, *Abstract of British Historical Statistics*, 390–391 give figures for British naval appropriations. Converted to livres at 23:1 these figures are as follows (to the nearest 1,000):

Year	Appropriations (Mitchell)	Appropriations (E 205)	Expenses (E 205)
1775	40,595,000	38,733,000	57,420,000
1776	63,135,000	51,222,000	95,517,000
1777	81,213,000	73,837,000	105,558,000
1778	104,949,000	92,044,000	140,000,000
1779	98,233,000	105,549,000	178,741,000
1780	145,567,000	126,576,000	207,415,000
1781	151,547,000	131,934,000	227,288,000
1782	248,561,000	incomplete	incomplete

[20] As an indication of the magnitude of the problem of servicing and reducing the debt, FRR cites the following amount paid on debts and interest: 1783—6,000,000; 1784—72,000,000; 1785—52,275,000; 1786—57,074,000. For the same years the following regular appropriations were made: 1783—147,588,938; 1784—44,243,000; 1785—34,000,000; 1786—28,000,000.

Ships of the Line, August 1774[1]

Bretagne, 100 (later 110), 1766
*Ville-de-Paris, 90 (100), 1764
Couronne, 80, 1749, 1766
*Duc-de-Bourgogne, 80, 1751, 1761
Languedoc, 80, 1776
Saint-Esprit, 80, 1765
*Tonnant, 80, 1743, 1765
*Actif, 74, 1757, 1766
Bien-Aimé, 74, 1769
Bourgogne, 74, 1766
César, 74, 1768
Citoyen, 74, 1763
Conquérant, 74, 1745, 1765
Destin, 74, in construction
Diadème, 74, 1756, 1766
Diligent, 74, 1763, 1769
Fendant, 74, in construction
Glorieux, 74, 1762
*Guerrier, 74, 1753
Hector, 74, 1755
Intrépide, 74, 1747, 1757, 1768
*Magnifique, 74, 1748, 1768
Marseillais, 74, 1766
Minotaure, 74, 1757, 1766
Orient, 74, 1756, 1765
Palmier, 74, 1752, 1766
Protecteur, 74, 1760
Robuste, 74, 1758, 1768
Sceptre, 74, 1746, 1762
Six-Corps, 74, 1746, 1762
Souverain, 74, 1757
Victoire, 74, 1770
Zélé, 74, 1763

*Zodiaque, 74, 1755, 1767
*Dauphin-Royal, 70, 1739, 1750, 1768
Northumberland, 68, 1744, 1759
Actionnaire, 64, 1767
*Alexandre, 64, 1771
Artésien, 64, 1765
*Bizarre, 64, 1751, 1768
*Brillant, 64, 1774
Caton, 64, in construction
*Éveillé, 64, 1772
Fantasque, 64, 1758
*Hardi, 64, 1748, 1764
Indien, 64, 1768
*Lion, 64, 1751
*Protée, 64, 1772
*Provence, 64, 1763
Réfléchi, 64, in construction
*Roland, 64, 1771
*Solitaire, 64, 1774
Sphinx, 64, 1755
Triton, 64, 1747
Union, 64, 1763
*Vaillant, 64, 1755
Vengeur, 64, 1757, 1766
Saint-Michel, 60, 1741, 1769
*Bordelais, 56, 1763, 1771
*Flamand, 56, 1762, 1770
*Amphion, 50, 1748, 1767
*Fier, 50, 1745
Hippopotame, 50, 1749, 1768
*Sagittaire, 50, 1761

[1] Based on a list of ships in B⁵11: unpaged, folder entitled "Comparison des forces navales françaises, anglaises, et espagnoles à diverses dates," and correlated with other sources. For each ship the first number represents the number of cannon it theoretically carried, the second number its year of launching, and the third number the years it was completely reconstructed (this last listing is incomplete). Asterisk indicates that the ship was one of the 24 which were later able to go to sea without overhauls.

Ships of the Line, Changes, 1775–February 1783[1]

In Overhaul	Completed Overhaul	Construction Begun	Launched	Stricken
1775: Marseillais T[2] Intrépide B Triton R Bien-Aimé LO Victoire LO Robuste B Indien B	Intrépide B	Sphinx B[3] four others already in construction		
1776: Zélé T Languedoc T Palmier B Hector T Protecteur T César T Glorieux B Bretagne B Saint-Esprit B Actionnaire B Fantasque T Saint-Michel R Artésien T	Indien B Victoire LO Marseillais T Robuste B Palmier B César T Bien-Aimé LO Protecteur T Triton R Hector T Zélé T		Fendant R Réfléchi R Sphinx B	

1777:	Orient B Conquérant B Couronne B Flamand LO Bourgogne T Vengeur B Diadème B	Languedoc T Fantasque T Saint-Esprit B Glorieux B Bretagne B Actionnaire B Artésien R Couronne B Conquérant B Saint-Michel R Flamand LO Orient B		Caton T Destin T	Hippopotame, sold
1778:	Victoire T Bizarre B Citoyen B Protée B Souverain T Ville-de-Paris B	Neptune, 74 B Annibal, 74 B Auguste, 80 B Pluton, 74 R Scipion, 74 R Hercule, 74 R Jason, 64 T Héros, 74 T Triomphant, 80 T		Neptune B Auguste B Scipion R Sévère, 64 LO[5] Annibal B Hercule R Pluton R Héros T	
1779:	Duc-de-Bourgogne B Flamand IdF	Bourgogne T Citoyen B Ville-de-Paris B Souverain T Duc-de-Bourgogne B Flamand IdF	Magnanime, 74 R Invincible, 92 R[4] Royal-Louis, 110 B Northumberland, 74 B Terrible, 110 T Argonaute, 74 R Illustre, 74 R Brave, 74 R	Jason T Ajax, 56 LO[5] Triomphant T Ardent, 64* Magnanime R Experiment, 50*	Roland, destroyed by fire Diligent, demolished Six-Corps, demolished

Ships of the Line, 1775–1783

In Overhaul	Completed Overhaul	Construction Begun	Launched	Stricken
1780: Languedoc B Hector LO Vaillant LO	Languedoc B Hector LO Vaillant LO	Sceptre, 74 B Majesteux, 110 T	Terrible T Invincible R Royal-Louis R Northumberland B Sceptre B Majesteux T	Fantasque, converted to transport Protée, captured Union, converted to transport Minotaure, converted to transport Northumberland, re-named Atlas and converted to transport Sceptre, converted to guard ship Tonnant, demolished Fier, converted to store ship
1781: Magnifique B Amphion R Guerrier B Protecteur B	Magnifique B	Couronne, 80 B Pégase, 74 B Censeur, 74 R Alcide, 74 R Dictateur, 74 T Suffisant, 74 T Puissant, 74 LO	Illustre R Argonaute R Brave R Couronne B Pégase B	Couronne, accidentally burned Intrépide, accidentally burned

1782:				
Bretagne B	Protecteur B	Centaure, 74 T	Hannibal, 50*	Ville-de-Paris, captured
Invincible B	Amphion R	Heureux, 74 T	Dictateur T	Glorieux, captured
Victoire B	Invincible B	Téméraire, 74 B	Suffisant T	Hector, captured
Triton B	Bretagne B	Audacieux, 74 LO	Puissant LO	Ardent, captured
Provence B	Guerrier B	Superbe, 74 B	Alcide R	César, sunk
Solitaire B	Solitaire B	Deux-Frères, 80 B	Censeur R	Caton, captured
Magnanime B	Triton B	Mercure, 74 T	América[6]	Jason, captured
Vaillant R	Provence B	Séduisant, 74 T	Centaur T	Actionnaire, captured
Saint-Esprit B	Victoire B	Généreux, 74 LO	Heureux T	Pégase, captured
Languedoc B	Magnanime B	Fougueux, 74 LO	Téméraire B	Magnifique, grounded
		Borée, 74 LO		Orient, grounded
				Bizarre, grounded
				Scipion, captured
				Palmier, sunk in storm
				Solitaire, captured

1783:		
		Bourgogne, ship-wrecked
		Alexandre, destroyed as unserviceable

---

[1] Listed chronologically. Only those overhauls requiring 30 days or more are counted. T—Toulon, B—Brest, R—Rochefort, IdF—Île de France, LO—Lorient, *—captured.
[2] In overhaul since 1774.
[3] Ordered completely reconstructed, November 1774.
[4] Later 108.
[5] Purchased.
[6] At Portsmouth, New Hampshire.

Frigates[1]

Present, *1774*

Consolante, 36
  in construction[2]
Pourvoyeuse, 36, 1773
*Renommée, 30, 1767
Terpsichore, 30, 1763
*Indiscrète, 28, 1767
*Sensible, 28, 1767
*Aigrette, 26, 1756
*Alcmène, 26, 1774
*Amphritite, 26, 1769
*Atalante, 26, 1767
*Aurore, 26, 1767
*Belle-Poule, 26, 1766
Blanche, 26, 1766
Boudeuse, 26, 1766
*Chimère, 26, 1757
Danaé, 26, 1763
*Dédaigneuse, 26, 1766
*Diligente, 26, 1761

*Engageant, 26, 1765
Enjouée, 26, 1766
*Flore, 26, 1768
Folle, 26, 1759
Inconstante, 26, 1766
Infidèle, 26, 1765
Légère, 26, 1765
Licorne, 26, 1755
Malicieuse, 26, 1758
*Mignonne, 26, 1765
*Oiseau, 26, 1769
*Pléiade, 26, 1754
Sincère, 26, 1766
*Sultane, 26, 1766
*Tourterelle, 26, 1770
*Triton, 26, 1769[3]
*Zéphyr, 26, 1768
*Gracieuse, 24, 1749
Thétis, 24, 1751

Judged Unfit for Service, *1776*

Enjouée	Infidèle	Sincère
Folle	Légère	Thétis
	Malicieuse	

Additions, *1776–March 1783*

Aimable, 26 (T) 20 July 1776
Nymphe, 26 (B) 18 August 1777

Charmante, 26 (R) 20 August 1777
Sibylle, 26 (B) 30 August 1777

[1] The names of ships are followed by the number of cannon they theoretically carried, the year of their launching, and the port where they were constructed. T—Toulon, B—Brest, R—Rochefort, N—Nantes, SM—Saint-Malo, BD—Bordeaux, LO—Lorient. *—indicates those ships ready to serve without needing an overhaul.
[2] Launched, 1775.
[3] Renamed *Cybèle*, 23 July 1779.

Concorde, 26 (B) 3 September 1777

Pallas, 24 (purchased) 10 September 1777

Iphigénie, 26 (LO) 16 October 1777

Andromaque, 26 (B) 24 December 1777

Fortunée, 26 (B) 29 December 1777

Courageuse, 26 (R) 28 February 1778

Junon, 26 (R) 13 March 1778

Résolue, 26 (SM) 17 March 1778

Prudente, 26 (SM) 28 March 1778

Surveillante, 26 (LO) 28 March 1778

Amazone, 26 (SM) 11 May 1778

Gentille, 26 (SM) 10 June 1778

Gloire, 26 (SM) 9 July 1778

Lively, 22 (captured) 9 July 1778

Magicienne, 26 (T) 2 August 1778

Bellone, 26 (SM) 22 August 1778

Minerve, 26 (captured) 22 August 1778

Précieuse, 26 (T) 22 August 1778

Active, 26 (captured) 1 September 1778

Médée, 26 (SM) 20 September 1778

Fox, 22 (captured) 28 September 1778

Diane, 26 (SM) 20 January 1779

Hermione, 26 (R) 28 April 1779

Montréal, 26 (captured) 2 May 1779

Néréide, 26 (SM) 30 May 1779

Galatée, 26 (R) 20 June 1779

Fine, 26 (N) 11 August 1779

Railleuse, 26 (BD) 11 August 1779

Sérieuse, 26 (T) 28 August 1779

Lutine, 26 (T) 11 September 1779

Emeraude, 26 (T) 25 October 1779

Cérès, 26 (R) 24 November 1779

Capricieuse, 26 (LO) 23 December 1779

Vénus, 26 (B) 6 March 1780

Friponne, 26 (LO) 20 March 1780

Fée, 26 (R) 19 April 1780

Astrée, 26 (SM) 17 May 1780

Unicorn, 20 (captured) 11 September 1780

Vestale, 26 (T) 14 October 1780

Alceste, 26 (T) 28 October 1780

Romulus, 44 (captured) c. 18 February 1781

Crescent, 26 (captured) 20 June 1781

Cléopâtre, 26 (SM) 19 August 1781

Iris, 32 (captured) 11 September 1781

Richmond, 32 (captured) 11 September 1781

Guadeloupe, 28 (captured) 19 October 1781

Iris, 26 (T) 29 October 1781

Aigle, 40 (purchased) 15 March 1782

Danaé, 26 (LO) 27 May 1782
Nymphe, 26 (B) 30 May 1782
Hébé, 26 (SM) 25 June 1782
Vénus, 26 (B) 14 July 1782
Minerve, 26 (T) 31 July 1782
Junon, 26 (T) 14 August 1782

Méduse, 26 (LO) 18 November 1782
Coventry, 28 (captured) 10 January 1783
Argo, 44 (captured) 10 February 1783

Stricken, 1778–March 1783

Licorne—captured 18 June 1778

Pallas—captured 19 June 1778

Oiseau—captured 31 January 1779

Zéphyr—accidentally burned at Brest, 28 February 1779

Fox—shipwrecked 21 March 1779

Danaé—captured 13 May 1779

Prudente—captured 2 June 1779

Alcmène—captured 20 October 1779

Fortunée—captured 21 December 1779

Blanche—captured 21 December 1779

Charmante—shipwrecked 24 March 1780

Dédaigneuse—ordered converted to transport, April 1780

Indiscrète—ordered converted to transport, April 1780

Sensible—ordered converted to transport, April 1780

Diane—disappeared 17 May 1780

Capricieuse—destroyed by the enemy 5 July 1780

Belle-Poule—captured 11 July 1780

Nymphe—captured 10 August 1780

Chimère—loaned to private contractor for privateering 19 August 1780

Junon—shipwrecked 11 October 1780

Minerve—captured 4 January 1781

Gracieuse—sold 16 February 1781

Unicorn—captured 20 April 1781

Cybèle—converted to transport 1 May 1781

Inconstante—burned 26 July 1781

Lively—captured 29 July 1781

Vénus—shipwrecked 5 August 1781

Magicienne—captured 1 September 1781

Diligente—shipwrecked 5 February 1782

Aimable—captured 19 April 1782

Hébé—captured 4 September 1782

Aigle—captured 14 September 1782

Sibylle—captured 22 January 1783

Argo—recaptured 12 February 1783

Concorde—captured 2 March 1783

Order of Battle, 1 July 1778

Britain (66)

EUROPE:

Victory, 100	*Courageous*, 74	*Thunderer*, 74
Duke, 90	*Cumberland*, 74	*Valiant*, 74
Formidable, 90	*Egmont*, 74	*Vengeance*, 74
Ocean, 90	*Elizabeth*, 74	*America*, 64
Prince George, 90	*Hector*, 74	*Bienfaisant*, 64
Queen, 90	*Monarch*, 74	*Defiance*, 64
Sandwich, 90	*Ramillies*, 74	*Exeter*, 64
Foudroyant, 80	*Robust*, 74	*Stirling Castle*, 64
Berwick, 74	*Shrewsbury*, 74	*Vigilant*, 64
Centaur, 74	*Terrible*, 74	*Worcester*, 64

EN ROUTE TO AMERICA:

Princess Royal, 90	*Cornwall*, 74	*Royal Oak*, 74
Albion, 74	*Culloden*, 74	*Russell*, 74
Bedford, 74	*Fame*, 74	*Sultan*, 74
Conqueror, 74	*Grafton*, 74	*Monmouth*, 64
	Invincible, 74	

IN NORTH AMERICA:

Ardent, 64	*St. Albans*, 64	*Isis*, 50
Eagle, 64	*Somerset*, 64	*Preston*, 50
Europe, 64 (New-	*Trident*, 64	*Renown*, 50 (en
foundland)	*Centurion*, 50 (Hali-	route from West
Nonsuch, 64	fax, for New York)	Indies)
Raisonable, 64 (Hal-	*Experiment*, 50	*Romney*, 50
ifax, for New		
York)		

IN WEST INDIES:

Prince of Wales, 74 (Barbados)	*Bristol*, 50 (Jamaica)
Boyne, 70 (Barbados)	*Portland*, 50 (Antigua)

IN MEDITERRANEAN:

Panther, 60

Appendix E

CONVOY ESCORT TO ST. HELENA:
Belle-Isle, 64

INDIA:
Rippon, 60

EN ROUTE TO INDIA:
Asia, 64

EN ROUTE TO JAMAICA:
Ruby, 64

France (52)

EUROPE:

Bretagne, 110	*Glorieux*, 74	*Eveillé*, 64
Ville-de-Paris, 90	*Intrépide*, 74	*Indien*, 64
Couronne, 80	*Magnifique*, 74	*Réfléchi*, 64
Duc-de-Bourgogne,	*Orient*, 74	*Roland*, 64
80	*Palmier*, 74	*Solitaire*, 64
Saint-Esprit, 80	*Robuste*, 74	*Sphinx*, 64
Actif, 74	*Zodiaque*, 74	*Triton*, 64
Bien-Aimé, 74	*Dauphin-Royal*, 70	*Vengeur*, 64
Conquérant, 74	*Actionnaire*, 64	*Saint-Michel*, 60
Diadème, 74	*Alexandre*, 64	*Amphion*, 50
Fendant, 74	*Artésien*, 64	*Fier*, 50

EN ROUTE TO AMERICA:

Languedoc, 80	*Hector*, 74	*Fantasque*, 64
Tonnant, 80	*Marseillais*, 74	*Provence*, 64
César, 74	*Protecteur*, 74	*Vaillant*, 64
Guerrier, 74	*Zélé*, 74	*Sagittaire*, 50

IN MEDITERRANEAN:

Destin, 74	*Caton*, 64 (en route	*Hardi*, 64
Victoire, 74	to Constantinople)	*Lion*, 64

INDIAN OCEAN:

Brillant, 64	*Flamand*, 56

EN ROUTE TO EUROPE:
Protée, 64

[360]

Order of Battle, 1 July 1779

Britain (90)

EUROPE:

Brittania, 100
Royal George, 100
Victory, 100
Duke, 98
Prince George, 98
Queen, 98
London, 90
Namur, 90
Union, 90
Foudroyant, 80

Alexander, 74
Alfred, 74
Bedford, 74
Berwick, 74
Canada, 74
Centaur, 74
Courageux, 74
Cumberland, 74
Defence, 74
Egmont, 74
Hector, 74

Invincible, 74
Monarch, 74
Ramillies, 74
Shrewsbury, 74
Thunderer, 74
Triumph, 74
Valiant, 74
America, 64
Bienfaisant, 64
Intrepid, 64

FITTING:

Formidable, 90
Culloden, 74
Marlborough, 74

Resolution, 74
Terrible, 74
Ardent, 64

Prudent, 64
Buffalo, 60

WEST INDIES:

Princess Royal, 90
Albion, 74
Conqueror, 74
Cornwall, 74
Elizabeth, 74
Fame, 74
Grafton, 74
Magnificent, 74

Prince of Wales, 74
Royal Oak, 74
Suffolk, 74
Sultan, 74
Boyne, 70
Lion, 64
Monmouth, 64
Nonsuch, 64
Stirling Castle, 64

Trident, 64
Vigilant, 64
Yarmouth, 64
Medway, 60
Centurion, 50 (de-
  tached)
Preston, 50 (de-
  tached)

NORTH AMERICA:

Robust, 74[7]
Russell, 74[7]

Defiance, 64[7]
Europe, 64[7]
Raisonable, 64

Experiment, 50[7]
Renown, 50

NEWFOUNDLAND:

Portland, 50

INDIA:

Superb, 74[1]	*Burford,* 64[1]	*Worcester,* 64[1]
Asia, 64	*Eagle,* 64[1]	*Rippon,* 60
Belle-Isle, 64[1]	*Exeter,* 64[1]	

JAMAICA:

Ruby, 64	*Bristol,* 50	*Salisbury,* 50
	Leviathan, 50	

MEDITERRANEAN:

Panther, 60	*Chatham,* 50

CHANNEL ISLANDS:

Jupiter, 50	*Romney,* 50

MISCELLANEOUS:

Vengeance, 74 (en route to Jamaica)
St. Albans, 64 (en route to Europe)
Isis, 50 (en route to Europe)
Warwick, 50 (en route to St. Helena)

UNCOUNTED:

Blenheim, 90, and *Princess Amelia,* 80 (suitable for short cruises only)

France (63)

EUROPE:

Bretagne, 110	*Destin,* 74	*Alexandre,* 64
Ville-de-Paris, 100	*Glorieux,* 74	*Bizarre,* 64
Auguste, 80	*Hercule,* 74	*Caton,* 64
Couronne, 80	*Intrépide,* 74	*Eveillé,* 64
Saint-Esprit, 80	*Neptune,* 74	*Indien,* 64
Actif, 74	*Palmier,* 74	*Protée,* 64
Bien-Aimé, 74	*Pluton,* 74	*Solitaire,* 64
Citoyen, 74	*Scipion,* 74	*Triton,* 64
Conquérant, 74	*Zodiaque,* 74	*Saint-Michel,* 60
	Actionnaire, 64	

AT CORUNNA:

Bourgogne, 74	*Victoire,* 74

WEST INDIES:[2]

Languedoc, 80	*Magnifique*, 74	*Provence*, 64
Tonnant, 80	*Marseillais*, 74	*Réfléchi*, 64
Annibal, 74	*Protecteur*, 74	*Sphinx*, 64
César, 74	*Robuste*, 74	*Vaillant*, 64
Diadème, 74	*Zélé*, 74	*Vengeur*, 64
Fendant, 74	*Dauphin-Royal*, 70	*Amphion*, 50
Guerrier, 74	*Artésien*, 64	*Fier*, 50
Hector, 74	*Fantasque*, 64	*Sagittaire*, 50

INDIAN OCEAN:

Orient, 74	*Brillant*, 64	*Sévère*, 64 (en route)

MEDITERRANEAN:

Hardi, 64 (en route from Levant to Toulon)
Jason, 64, and *Lion*, 64 (en route to Straits of Gibraltar)
Triomphant, 80, *Héros*, 74, and *Souverain*, 74 (fitting out)

Spain (58)

WITH CÓRDOBA:

Santísima Trinidad, 114	*Oriente*, 70	*San Miguel*, 70
Fénix, 80[3]	*Princesa*, 70	*San Pablo*, 70
San Nicolas de Bari, 80	*San Dámaso*, 70	*San Pascual Baylón*, 70
Rayo, 80	*San Eugenio*, 70	*San Pedro Apóstol*, 70
Angel de la Guarda, 70	*San Francisco de Asís*, 70	*San Rafael*, 70
Atlante, 70	*San Francisco de Paula*, 70	*Septentrión*, 70
Diligente, 70[3]	*Santa Isabel*, 70	*Serio*, 70
Galicia, 70	*San Isidro*, 70	*Velasco*, 70
Gallardo, 70[3]	*San Joaquin*, 70	*Vencedor*, 70
Monarca, 70	*San Josef*, 70	*Astuto*, 60
	San Julián, 70[3]	*San Isidoro*, 60

CORUNNA:

San Carlos, 80	*San Vicente Ferrer*, 80	*Guerrero*, 70
San Fernando, 80[4]	*Arrogante*, 70	*España*, 60
San Luis, 80		*Miño*, 54

FERROL:

Brillante, 70[5]	*Firme*, 70[5]	*Dragón*, 60

GIBRALTAR:

Poderoso, 70	*San Jenaro*, 70[5]	*San Leandro*, 70
San Agustin, 70[5]	*San Juan Baptista*,	*San Lorenzo*, 70[5]
Santo Domingo, 70	70[5]	

HAVANA:

Dichoso, 70	*San Gabriel*, 70	*San Ramón*, 70
Magnánimo, 70	*San Juan Nepomu-*	
	ceno, 70	

LIMA:

América, 64	*Peruano*, 64	*San Pedro de Al-*
		cántara, 64

NOT COUNTED:

Africa, 70 (location and condition unknown)

[1] En route.

[2] Exclusive of *Fier Roderique*, 50, private ship in temporary service of the French navy.

[3] Later detached.

[4] Damaged early July, replaced by *Brillante*, which in turn was left behind at Cape Finisterre.

[5] Still fitting.

Order of Battle, 1 July 1780

Britain (95)

EUROPE:

Britannia, 100	Namur, 90	Courageous, 74
Royal George, 100	Ocean, 90	Cumberland, 74
Victory, 100	Union, 90	Defence, 74
Barfleur, 98	Foudroyant, 80	Dublin, 74
Duke, 98	Princess Amelia, 80	Edgar, 74
Formidable, 98	Alexander, 74	Invincible, 74
Prince George, 98	Alfred, 74	Marlborough, 74
Queen, 98	Berwick, 74	Monarch, 74
	Canada, 74	

WEST INDIES:

Princess Royal, 90	Grafton, 74	Intrepid, 64
Sandwich, 90	Magnificent, 74	Stirling Castle, 64
Ajax, 74	Montagu, 74	Trident, 64
Albion, 74	Russell, 74 (just	Vigilant, 64
Conqueror, 74	joined)	Yarmouth, 64
Cornwall, 74	Suffolk, 74	Medway, 60
Elizabeth, 74	Terrible, 74	Centurion, 50
Fame, 74	Vengeance, 74	Preston, 50
	Boyne, 70	

EN ROUTE TO WEST INDIES:

Centaur, 74	Egmont, 74	Thunderer, 74
Culloden, 74	Shrewsbury, 74	Triumph, 74

JAMAICA:

Hector, 74	Lion, 64	Bristol, 50
Sultan, 74	Ruby, 64	Salisbury, 50

NORTH AMERICA:

Robust, 74	Europe, 64	Renown, 50
	Raisonable, 64	

GIBRALTAR:

Panther, 60

Lisbon:
Rodney, 50

India:

Superb, 74	*Eagle*, 64	*Worcester*, 64
Burford, 64	*Exeter*, 64	

Newfoundland:
Portland, 50

En Route to North America:

London, 98	*Resolution*, 74	*America*, 64
Bedford, 74	*Royal Oak*, 74	*Prudent*, 64

Convoy Duty:

Chatham, 50	*Isis*, 50	*Warwick*, 50
	Jupiter, 50	

Returning from India:

Asia, 64	*Belle-Isle*, 64	*Rippon*, 60

Fitting for Europe:

Vaillant, 74	*Inflexible*, 64	*Buffalo*, 60
Bienfaisant, 64	*Nonsuch*, 64	

Fitting for West Indies:

Alcide, 74	*Ramillies*, 74

Fitting for Jamaica:
Torbay, 74

Fitting for North America:
Adamant, 50

France (69)

Atlantic Ports:

Bretagne, 110[1]	*Languedoc*, 80	*Magnanime*, 74[1]
Royal-Louis, 110[1]	*Saint-Esprit*, 80	*Northumberland*, 74
Ville-de-Paris, 100	*Bien-Aimé*, 74[1]	*Alexandre*, 64[1]
Auguste, 80	*Hector*, 74	*Vaillant*, 64

En Route to Cadiz:

Terrible, 110	*César*, 74	*Lion*, 64
Invincible, 108	*Guerrier*, 74	*Sagittaire*, 50
Actif, 74	*Hardi*, 74	

AT CADIZ:

Bourgogne, 74	*Marseillais*, 74	*Zélé*, 74
Glorieux, 74	*Protecteur*, 74	*Zodiaque*, 74
Héros, 74	*Scipion*, 74	

WEST INDIES:

Couronne, 80	*Magnifique*, 74	*Indien*, 64
Triomphant, 80	*Palmier*, 74	*Réfléchi*, 64[2]
Annibal, 74[2]	*Pluton*, 74	*Solitaire*, 64
Citoyen, 74	*Robuste*, 74	*Sphinx*, 64
Destin, 74	*Souverain*, 74	*Triton*, 64
Diadème, 74[2]	*Victoire*, 74	*Vengeur*, 64
Fendant, 74	*Dauphin-Royal*, 70	*Saint-Michel*, 60
Hercule, 74	*Actionnaire*, 64	*Amphion*, 50[2]
Intrépide, 74	*Artésien*, 64	*Experiment*, 50[3]
	Caton, 64	

EN ROUTE TO NORTH AMERICA:

Duc-de-Bourgogne, 80	*Neptune*, 74	*Jason*, 64
Conquérant, 74	*Ardent*, 64	*Provence*, 64
	Eveillé, 64	

INDIA:

Orient, 74	*Brillant*, 64	*Flamand*, 56
	Sévère, 64	

EN ROUTE TO INDIA:

Ajax, 64	*Bizarre*, 64

Spain (48)

CADIZ:

Santísima Trinidad, 114	*Angel de la Guarda*, 70	*San Justo*, 70
Purísima Concepción, 90	*Atlante*, 70	*San Leandro*, 70
Rayo, 80	*Brillante*, 70	*San Miguel*, 70
San Carlos, 80	*Firme*, 70	*San Pascual Baylón*, 70
San Fernando, 80	*Galicia*, 70	*San Rafael*, 70
San Vincent Ferrer, 80	*Oriente*, 70	*Septentrión*, 70
Terrible, 80	*San Eugenio*, 70	*Serio*, 70
	Santa Isabel, 70	*San Isidoro*, 60
	San Joaquin, 70	*Miño*, 54

FERROL:

Africa, 70	*Vencedor*, 70	*Castilla*, 60

Appendix G

HAVANA:

Dichoso, 70	San Gabriel, 70	San Ramón, 70
Magnánimo, 70	San Juan Nepomuceno, 70	

GUADELOUPE:

San Luis, 80	Guerrero, 70	San Jenaro, 70
San Nicolás de Bari, 80	San Agustin, 70	Velasco, 70
Arrogante, 70	San Francisco de Asís, 70	Astuto, 60
Gallardo, 70	San Francisco de Paula, 70	Dragón, 60

LIMA:

América, 64	Peruano, 64	San Pedro de Alcántara, 64

NOT COUNTED (Vessels in repair):

San Dámaso, 70 (Cadiz)	San Juan Baptista, 70 (Cadiz)	San Pedro Apóstol, 70 (Cadiz)
San Isidro, 70 (Cadiz)	San Lorenzo, 70 (Cadiz)	España, 60 (Ferrol)
	San Pablo, 70 (Ferrol)	

[1] Later sent to Cadiz (*Magnanime* only reached Ferrol).
[2] Squadron of La Motte-Picquet.
[3] Recently arrived with convoy.

Order of Battle, 1 April 1781

Britain (94)

EN ROUTE TO GIBRALTAR:

Britannia, 100	*Foudroyant*, 80	*Marlborough*, 74
Royal George, 100	*Alexander*, 74	*Valiant*, 74
Duke, 98	*Bellona*, 74	*Bienfaisant*, 64
Formidable, 98	*Canada*, 74	*Inflexible*, 64
Prince George, 98	*Courageous*, 74	*Lion*, 64
Queen, 98	*Cumberland*, 74	*Nonsuch*, 64
Namur, 90	*Defence*, 74	*Repulse*, 64
Ocean, 90	*Dublin*, 74	*St. Albans*, 64
Union, 90	*Edgar*, 74	*Medway*, 60
	Fortitude, 74	

CONVOY DUTY:

Leander, 50

FITTING FOR EUROPE:

Victory, 100	*Sultan*, 74[1]	*Magnanime*, 64[1]
Princess Amelia, 80	*Monarca*, 70[1]	

FITTING FOR NORTH SEA:

Berwick, 74	*Buffalo*, 60	*Preston*, 50

FITTING FOR CONVOY DUTY:

Centurion, 50	*Hannibal*, 50	*Warwick*, 50

WEST INDIES:

Barfleur, 98[2]	*Invincible*, 74[2]	*Triumph*, 74
Sandwich, 90	*Monarch*, 74[2]	*Princessa*, 70[2]
Gibraltar, 80	*Montague*, 74[2]	*Belliquez*, 64[2]
Ajax, 74[2]	*Resolution*, 74[2]	*Intrepid*, 64[2]
Alcide, 74[2]	*Russell*, 74	*Prince William*, 64
Alfred, 74[2]	*Shrewsbury*, 74[2]	*Vigilant*, 64
Centaur, 74[2]	*Terrible*, 74[2]	*Panther*, 60
	Torbay, 74	

NORTH AMERICA:

London, 98²	*Royal Oak*, 74²	*Prudent*, 64
Bedford, 74²	*America*, 64²	*Adamant*, 50²
Robust, 74	*Europe*, 64²	*Chatham*, 50

NEWFOUNDLAND:

Portland, 50

RETURNING TO EUROPE FROM WEST INDIES:

Egmont, 74	*Vengeance*, 74	*Prince Edward*, 60
Grafton, 74	*Trident*, 64	(ex-*Mars*)
Suffolk, 74		*Bristol*, 50

JAMAICA:

Princess Royal, 90	*Hector*, 74	*Ruby*, 64
Albion, 74	*Ramillies*, 74	

INDIA:

Superb, 74	*Eagle*, 64	*Worcester*, 64
Burford, 64	*Exeter*, 64	

EN ROUTE TO CAPE:

Hero, 74¹	*Isis*, 50¹	*Romney*, 50
Monmouth, 64	*Jupiter*, 50	

France (70)

ATLANTIC PORTS (FITTING):

Bretagne, 110	*Fendant*, 74	*Dauphin-Royal*, 70
Royal-Louis, 110	*Guerrier*, 74	*Alexandre*, 64
Terrible, 110	*Illustre*, 74	*Hardi*, 64
Invincible, 108	*Magnifique*, 74	*Indien*, 64
Triomphant, 80	*Protecteur*, 74	*Lion*, 64
Actif, 74	*Robuste*, 74	*Saint-Michel*, 60
Bien-Aimé, 74	*Zodiaque*, 74	

MEDITERRANEAN:

Majesteux, 110

WEST INDIES:

Victoire, 74	*Caton*, 64	*Solitaire*, 64
Actionnaire, 64	*Réfléchi*, 64	*Experiment*, 50

EN ROUTE TO WEST INDIES:

Ville-de-Paris, 100	*Diadème*, 74	*Pluton*, 74
Auguste, 80	*Glorieux*, 74	*Sceptre*, 74
Languedoc, 80	*Hector*, 74	*Scipion*, 74
Saint-Esprit, 80	*Hercule*, 74	*Souverain*, 74
Bourgogne, 74	*Magnanime*, 74	*Zélé*, 74
César, 74	*Marseillais*, 74	*Vaillant*, 64
Citoyen, 74	*Northumberland*, 74	

HAVANA:

Destin, 74	*Intrépide*, 74	*Triton*, 64
	Palmier, 64	

NORTH AMERICA:

Duc-de-Bourgogne,	*Neptune*, 74	*Jason*, 64
80	*Ardent*, 64	*Provence*, 64
Conquérant, 74	*Eveillé*, 64	

EN ROUTE TO NORTH AMERICA:

Sagittaire, 50

INDIAN OCEAN:

Orient, 74	*Bizarre*, 64	*Sévère*, 64
Ajax, 64	*Brillant*, 64	*Flamand*, 56

EN ROUTE TO CAPE AND INDIAN OCEAN:

Annibal, 74	*Artésien*, 64	*Vengeur*, 64
Héros, 74	*Sphinx*, 64	

Spain (54)

CADIZ:

Santísima Trinidad,	*Atlante*, 70	*San Miguel*, 70
114	*Brillante*, 70	*San Pascual Baylón*,
Purísima Concep-	*Firme*, 70	70
ción, 90	*Oriente*, 70	*San Pedro Apóstol*,
Rayo, 80	*San Dámaso*, 70	70[3]
San Carlos, 80	*Santa Isabel*, 70	*San Rafael*, 70
San Fernando, 80	*San Isidro*, 70	*Septentrión*, 70
San Vicente Ferrer,	*San Joaquin*, 70	*Serio*, 70
80	*San Juan Baptista*,	*Vencedor*, 70
Terrible, 80	70	*Castilla*, 60
Africa, 70	*San Justo*, 70	*Galicia*, 60
Angel de la Guarda,	*San Lorenzo*, 70	*Miño*, 54
70		

Appendix H

FERROL:

Santo Domingo, 70 San Pablo, 70   España, 60

CARTAGENA:

Glorioso, 80

HAVANA:

San Luis, 80	Magnánimo, 70	San Juan Nepomu-
San Nicolás de Bari,	San Agustín, 70	ceno, 70
80	San Francisco de	San Ramón, 70
Arrogante, 70	Asís, 70	(Pensacola)
Dichoso, 70	San Francisco de	Velasco, 70
Gallardo, 70	Paula, 70	Astuto, 60
Guerrero, 70	San Gabriel, 70	Dragón, 60
	San Jenaro, 70	

LIMA:

América, 64   Peruano, 64   San Pedro de Al-
                 cántara, 64

Holland (14)

FITTING IN DUTCH PORTS:[4]

Amiral Général, 76[5]	Amiral Piet Heyn,	Princesse Royale
Amiral Ruyter, 64[5]	54[5]	Frederique Sophie
Hollande, 64[5]	Batavier, 54[5]	Wilhelmine, 54
Zuidbeveland, 64	Erfprins (Prince	Schiedam, 54
	Heréditaire), 54[5]	

CURACAO:

Nassau, 64   Nassau-Weilbourg,
         56

MEDITERRANEAN AREA:

Amsterdam, 64 Princesse Louise, 56 Princesse Marie-
                    Louise, 56

[1] Later detached to India.
[2] Fought at the Battle of the Virginia Capes.
[3] Replacing *San Eugenio*, 70, dropped for repairs.
[4] Only those ships which were listed as ready by Holland 544: 102–104, La Vauguyon to Vergennes, 21 April 1781, were counted. One ship, the preparation of which had not actually started, was not considered. Note that 64s are frequently referred to as 68s. The French translation of Dutch ship names has been used.
[5] Sailed from Texel, 20 July 1781.

Order of Battle, 1 April 1782

Britain (94)

EUROPE:

Britannia, 100	*Foudroyant*, 80	*Edgar*, 74
Royal George, 100	*Princess Amelia*, 80	*Fortitude*, 74
Victory, 100	*Alexander*, 74	*Goliath*, 74
Queen, 98	*Bellona*, 74	*Raisonable*, 64
Ocean, 90	*Berwick*, 74	(fitting)
Union, 90	*Courageous*, 74	*Sampson*, 64
Cambridge, 80	*Dublin*, 74	*Panther*, 60
(fitting)		(fitting)

CONVOY DUTY:

Jupiter, 50	*Leander*, 50	*Romney*, 50

WEST INDIES:

Barfleur, 98	*Fame*, 74	*Agamemnon*, 64
Duke, 98	*Hercules*, 74	*America*, 64
Formidable, 98	*Magnificent*, 74	*Anson*, 64
Prince George, 98	*Marlborough*, 74	*Belliquez*, 64
Namur, 90	*Monarch*, 74	*Nonsuch*, 64
Ajax, 74	*Montague*, 74	*Prothée*, 64
Alcide, 74	*Resolution*, 74	*Prince William*, 64
Alfred, 74	*Royal Oak*, 74	*Prudent*, 64 (de-
Arrogant, 74	*Russell*, 74	tached)
Bedford, 74	*Torbay*, 74	*Repulse*, 64
Canada, 74	*Valiant*, 74	*St. Albans*, 64
Centaur, 74	*Warrior*, 74	*Yarmouth*, 64
Conqueror, 74	*Princessa*, 70	

NORTH AMERICA:

Lion, 64	*Centurion*, 50	*Rotterdam*, 50
Adamant, 50	*Chatham*, 50	*Warwick*, 50
Assistance, 50	*Renown*, 50	

FITTING FOR NEWFOUNDLAND:

Portland, 50

Appendix I

Jamaica:

London, 98   Ramillies, 74   Preston, 50
Sandwich, 98   Shrewsbury, 74   Princess Caroline, 50
Invincible, 74   Intrepid, 64

India:

Hero, 74   Burford, 64   Monmouth, 64
Sultan, 74   Eagle, 64   Worcester, 64
Superb, 74   Exeter, 64   Isis, 50
Monarca, 70   Magnanime, 64

En Route to India:

Gibraltar, 80   Defence, 74   Inflexible, 64
Cumberland, 74   Africa, 64   Sceptre, 64

France (73)

Atlantic Ports:

Actif, 74   Bien-Aimé, 74   Zodiaque, 74
    Robuste, 74

Cadiz:

Majesteux, 110   Terrible, 110   Lion, 64
Royal-Louis, 110   Indien, 64

Returning from West Indies:

Victoire, 74   Solitaire, 64   Vaillant, 64
Provence, 64   Triton, 64

West Indies:

Ville-de-Paris, 100   Conquérant, 74   Sceptre, 74
Auguste, 80   Destin, 74   Scipion, 74
Couronne, 80   Diadème, 74   Souverain, 74
Duc-de-Bourgogne,   Glorieux, 74   Zélé, 74
  80   Hector, 74   Dauphin-Royal, 70
Languedoc, 80   Hercule, 74   Ardent, 64
Saint-Esprit, 80 (in   Magnanime, 74   Caton, 64
  repair)   Magnifique, 74   Eveillé, 64
Triomphant, 80   Marseillais, 74   Jason, 64
Bourgogne, 74   Neptune, 74   Réfléchi, 64
Brave, 74   Northumberland, 74   Experiment, 50
César, 74   Palmier, 74   Sagittaire, 50
Citoyen, 74   Pluton, 74

INDIA-CEYLON:

Annibal, 74	*Artésien,* 64	*Sphinx,* 64
Héros, 74	*Bizarre,* 64	*Vengeur,* 64
Orient, 74	*Brillant,* 64	*Flamand,* 56
Ajax, 64	*Sévère,* 64	*Hannibal,* 50

EN ROUTE TO INDIA:

Argonaute, 74	*Illustre,* 74	*Hardi,* 64[1]
Fendant, 74	*Alexandre,* 64[1]	*Saint-Michel,* 60

FITTING FOR INDIA:

Pégase, 74	*Protecteur,* 74	*Actionnaire,* 64[1]

FITTING AT TOULON:

Dictateur, 74	*Suffisant,* 74

Spain (54)

CADIZ (FITTING):

Santísima Trinidad, 114	*Arrogante,* 70	*San Lorenzo,* 70
Purísima Concepción, 90	*Atlante,* 70	*San Miguel,* 70
Rayo, 80	*Brillante,* 70	*San Pablo,* 70
San Carlos, 80	*Firme,* 70	*San Rafael,* 70
San Fernando, 80	*Gallardo,* 70	*Septentrión,* 70
San Vicente Ferrer, 80	*Guerrero,* 70	*Serio,* 70
Terrible, 80	*Oriente,* 70	*Vencedor,* 70
Africa, 70	*San Dámaso,* 70	*Astutuo,* 60
Angel de la Guarda, 70	*San Eugenio,* 70	*Castilla,* 60
	Santa Isabel, 70	*España,* 60
	San Isidro, 70	*Galicia,* 60
	San Joaquin, 70	*San Isidoro,* 60
	San Juan Baptista, 70	*Miño,* 54
	San Justo, 70	

CARTAGENA:

Triufante, 60	*San Julian,* 58

SAINT DOMINGUE:

Glorioso, 80 (?)	*San Juan Nepomuceno,* 70	*San Felipe,* 70)
Santo Domingo, 70 (?)	one other (perhaps *San Fermin,* 70 or	*San Pedro Apóstol,* 70 (?)

[1] Serving temporarily as a transport.

Appendix 1

EN ROUTE FROM HAVANA TO SAINT DOMINGUE:

San Luis, 80	*Magnánimo*, 70	*San Jenaro*, 70
San Nicolás de Bari, 80	*San Francisco de Paula*, 70	*San Ramón*, 70

HAVANA:

San Agustín, 70	*San Francisco de Asís*, 70 (returned)

LIMA:

América, 64	*Peruano*, 64	*San Pedro de Alcántara*, 64

NOT COUNTED (In Repair at Havana):

Dichoso, 70	*San Gabriel*, 70	*Dragón*, 60
	Velasco, 70	

Holland (19)

FITTING IN DUTCH PORTS:

Amiral Général, 76	*Zuidbeveland*, 64	*Glindhoorst*, 54
Amiral Ruyter, 68	*Amiral Piet Heyn*, 54	*Goes*, 54
Amsterdam, 68	*Amiral Tromp*, 54	*Princesse Royale Frederique Sophie Wilhelmine*, 54
Prince Frederick, 68	*Batavier*, 54	
Union, 68	*Erfprins (Prince Hereditaire)*, 54	*Rhinland*, 54
Kortenaer, 64		*Schiedam*, 54
Zierikzee, 64		

CURACAO:

Nassau, 64	*Nassau-Weilbourg*, 56

French Troops Sent to the Western Hemisphere, 1774–1782

Location	Regiment	Battalions	When Sent
Martinique	Martinique	2	Stationed
Guadeloupe	Guadeloupe	2	Stationed
St. Domingue	Cape	2	Stationed
St. Domingue	Port-au-Prince	2	Stationed
Martinique	Navarre	1	November 1775
Martinique	Guyenne	1	November 1775
Guadeloupe	Armagnac	1	November 1775
St. Domingue	Auvergne	1	November 1775
St. Domingue	Bearn	1	November 1775
St. Domingue	Flandre	1	November 1775
Martinique	Gatinois	1	October 1777
Martinique	Viennois	1	October 1777
Guadeloupe	Armagnac	1	October 1777
St. Domingue	Agenois	1	October 1777
St. Domingue	Cambresis	1	October 1777[1]
Martinique	Champagne	1	January 1779
Martinique	Dillon	1	May 1779[2]
Martinique	Hainaut	½	July 1779
Martinique	Foix	½	July 1779[3]
Martinique	Enghien	2	February 1780
Martinique	Touraine	2	February 1780
Martinique	Royal Comtoise	1	February 1780
Martinique	Walsh	1	February 1780
North America	Soissonais	2	May 1780
North America	Bourbonnais	2	May 1780
North America	Saintonge	2	May 1780
North America	Royal-Deux-Ponts	2	May 1780
Martinique	Mixed Regiments	6	March 1781[4]
St. Domingue	Mixed Regiments	4	March 1781[5]
Martinique	Mixed Regiments	½	December 1781[6]
Martinique	Mixed Regiments	2½	February 1782[7]
St. Domingue	Mixed Regiments	4	February 1782[8]
Martinique	Berwick	1	September 1782
Martinique	Auvergne	2	September 1782

[1] Plus five companies of artillery, two companies of cavalry.
[2] Plus one legion of Lauzun's volunteers (about one-half battalion).
[3] Detached from d'Estaing's squadron.
[4] Including one battalion of Dillon. Total: 3,840 regulars (equivalent to about six battalions).
[5] Total: 2,514 regulars.
[6] Total: 298 regulars (aboard *Brave, Triomphant*).
[7] Total: 1,485 regulars.
[8] Total: 2,672 regulars.

APPENDIX K

Ships of the Line, 1 January 1787

SERVICEABLE:

Bretagne, 110
Invincible, 110
Majesteux, 110
Royal-Louis, 110
Terrible, 110
Auguste, 80
Couronne, 80
Deux-Frères, 80
    (1784)
Duc-de-Bourgogne,
    80
Languedoc, 80
Saint-Esprit, 80
Triomphant, 80
Achille (ex-An-
    nibal), 74
Alcide, 74
Argonaute, 74
Audacieux, 74
    (1784)
Borée, 74 (1785)
Brave, 74

Censeur, 74
Centaure, 74
Citoyen, 74
Commerce-de-Bor-
    deaux, 74 (1785)
Conquérant, 74
Destin, 74
Diadème, 74
Dictateur, 74
Ferme, 74 (1785)
Fougueux, 74 (1785)
Généreux, 74 (1785)
Guerrier, 74
Hercule, 74
Héros, 74
Heureux, 74
Illustre, 74
Lys, 74 (1786)
Magnanime, 74
Marseillais, 74
Mercure, 74 (1783)
Neptune, 74

Northumberland, 74
Patriote, 74 (1785)
Pluton, 74
Protecteur, 74
Puissant, 74
Sceptre, 74
Séduisant, 74 (1783)
Souverain, 74
Suffisant, 74
Superbe, 74 (1784)
Téméraire, 74
Victoire, 74
Zélé, 74
Brillant, 64[1]
Provence, 64[1]
Réfléchi, 64[1]
Sphinx, 64[1]
Triton, 64[1]
Saint-Michel, 60[1]
Amphion, 50[1]
Hannibal, 50[1]
Sagittaire, 50[1]

IN CONSTRUCTION:

Commerce-de-Mar-
    seille, 118
Etats-de-Bourgogne,
    118

Apollon, 74
Entreprenant, 74
Impétueux, 74

Léopard, 74
Orion, 74

DROPPED SINCE 1782:[2]

Actif, 74
América, 74
Bien-Aimé, 74
Fendant, 74
Robuste, 74
Zodiaque, 74

Dauphin-Royal, 70
Ajax, 64
Artésien, 64
Eveillé, 64
Hardi, 64
Indien, 64

Lion, 64
Sévère, 64
Vaillant, 64
Vengeur, 64
Flamand, 56

[1] To be replaced as new ships completed.
[2] Excluding Experiment, 50, reclassified as 44.

[378]

BIBLIOGRAPHY

1. Unpublished Material

The basic source for this work is the correspondence of the French foreign and naval ministries. The former is located in the Archives of the Ministry of Foreign Affairs; the latter has been transferred to the French National Archives. A few of the papers are in boxes, but the great majority are in bound volumes of 250–500 folio pages, written on both sides. They consist of incoming and outgoing ministerial correspondence or of rough (and occasionally final) drafts of memoirs prepared for the king. The incoming correspondence consists of the original letters, while the outgoing consists of copies written by secretaries or occasionally of summaries. In many cases the outgoing copies are rough drafts annotated by the minister himself. Listed below are: the volumes of each series utilized, a short description of the series, and the years for which these volumes have been consulted. General information as to the contents of the individual volumes will be found in the archival guides listed in the other sections of this bibliography.

National Archives: Naval Holdings[1]

Series B, General Service, contains a huge number of documents, arranged in subseries. The following subseries were used:

B[1]: Decisions. Volumes 80 through 102 (1774–1787). This subseries consists of matters brought to the naval minister or king for his decision. Although much of the matter is comparatively trivial, some of the memoirs deal

---

[1] Although housed in the National Archives, these documents may be consulted only with the permission of the Historical Service of the French Navy. I would like to thank the French Navy Department for its kindness in permitting me the use of its papers.

with strategic planning or the naval budget and are invaluable.

B²: Outgoing Correspondence. Volumes 404 through 424 (1774–1782). While very valuable for an understanding of naval administration, this collection of the minister's daily correspondence (in fact largely handled by Fleurieu), mostly with the ports, presents many drawbacks. The copies were prepared after the final draft was ready, so there are no indications of changes or corrections. More seriously, a large amount of the correspondence after 1775 is missing, particularly for the war years. This subseries does establish that much of the criticism of port commandants for extravagance is misplaced. The navy department was so centralized that decisions on even the most minor expenditures were often made at Versailles.

B³: Incoming Correspondence. Volumes 624 through 734 (1776–1782). This is the largest, most complete and most valuable group of naval documents used. A portion of the relatively unimportant Saint Malo correspondence is missing, and the Le Havre correspondence contains only copies, but the remainder consists of original letters, and is apparently complete. About 90 percent of the letters are from military and civilian port officials; the remaining 10 percent consist of miscellaneous ministerial correspondence or are copies of the transactions of the councils of the navy (the chief executive and deliberative boards of the ports).

B⁴: Campaigns. Volumes 123 through 220, 266–268, 286–288, 311–312 (1774–1782). This subseries contains letters received from ship captains and squadron and fleet commanders, plus ships' logs and various memoranda dealing with operations. (Outgoing individual correspondence is in the closed "C" series: Personnel.) It is arranged by theater of operations and by correspondent rather than chronologically. Since it is the major source for naval operations, it has been the subseries most often used by historians. Most of the volumes microfilmed by the American Library of Congress for its collection of French naval documents have come from here.

B⁵: Armaments. Volumes 9 through 29 (1774–1782). These boxes of superb documents are the quickest entrance to the study of the French navy. They contain a variety of memoirs, many prepared for the king and consisting of summaries of matériel availability or ship readiness. Also, there are yearly summaries of the operations of each ship of the navy.

B⁶: Galleys. Did not pertain to my study.

B⁷: Foreign Countries, Commerce, and Consulates. Volumes 439–445, 459–460, 473–475, 480–481 (1774–1782). These are collections of intelligence reports dealing with Spain, the United States, and England. They are valuable for understanding naval planning.

B⁸: Archives. Volumes 14 through 16 (1774–1783). Day-by-day chronologies of occurences within the ministry, etc., compiled by archivists—of some interest but not always reliable. These boxes were in disarray when used and may now be rearranged.

The following series were also used:

E: General Accounting. Volumes 204 through 209 (1774–1789). Boxes of documents pertaining to finances—requests for funds, explanations of expenditures, discussions about the naval debt. Although ill-arranged and incomplete, this is still a splendid source.

G: Memoirs and Diverse Documents. Volumes 127, 165–166, 190 (1774–1776, 1778–1779). Bound volumes of memoirs on general topics for the use of the king or the naval minister.

National Archives: Colonial Holdings

Subseries C⁹ᴬ (Saint Domingue). Volume 152 (1782). This volume has been used with limited success to supplement naval records of ship movements during the campaign of 1782.

National Archives: General Holdings

Series K (Royal Papers of Louis XVI). Volumes 161, 163 and 164. This excellent series contains memoirs presented to Louis XVI by Vergennes and other members of the council of state. Copies are often found in the foreign ministry archives (e.g., Memoirs and Documents: France 1897 contains copies of K 164:no. 3).

Series M^{iv} (Diverse Papers). Volumes 662–663. Miscellaneous papers on naval and military topics. Some are of considerable interest although the best date from the end of Louis' reign.

Foreign Ministry Archives: Political Correspondence[2]

The foreign ministry papers are divided into two groups. The Political Correspondence contains the incoming and outgoing ministerial correspondence arranged by country and filed together in chronological order. The ministerial letters to French ambassadors abroad are a particularly valuable guide to the proceedings of the king's council of state, subject, of course, to caution. The correspondence pertaining to the following countries has been consulted:

Denmark: Volume 162 (January 1779–June 1780). This source was consulted for the movement of naval supplies. It was of only slight use.

England: Volumes 506 through 534, 536–540, supplementary volumes 18 and 19 (1774–1783). This is a fine series for the period prior to the recall of the French ambassador (March 1778), although for most of the war period it contains little of interest. It is particularly disappointing for the critical period of December 1777 to March 1778 since the French ambassador was not informed until his recall of the French negotiations with the United States. Beginning with Rayneval's first trip to England it becomes indispensable. For Rayneval's missions supplement 19 (with

[2] These papers may be used only with the permission of the French Ministry of Foreign Affairs, to whom I also extend my gratitude.

[382]

the rough drafts of his correspondence) should be used in conjunction with volumes 538 through 540.

Holland: Volume 539, ambassadorial correspondence with the naval ministry (1779–1780), volumes 540 through 553 (1780–1783). This series contains material relating to the movement of naval supplies, to Dutch relations with the League of Armed Neutrality and to Dutch participation in the war.

Spain: Volumes 578 through 610, supplementary volume 17 (October 1775–1783). This magnificent set of papers is the major source not only for the American policy of the French foreign ministry but also for French and Spanish war strategy.

United States: Volumes 1 through 23, supplementary volumes 1, 3, 11–15, and 29 (1775–1780). Although a fairly useful collection, this source contains little information on the negotiations leading to the alliance. It does contain some material on French naval operations in American waters and on wartime diplomatic contacts between the two countries.

Foreign Ministry Archives: Memoirs and Documents

This section of the Foreign Ministry Archives consists of miscellaneous papers not connected directly with the day-to-day operations of the ministry. The following volumes have been used:

France: Volumes 446, 584, 586–587, 1383, and 1897. These are largely copies of memoirs available elsewhere, although many are of great interest.

Spain: Volume 146. This is a report containing information about the Spanish navy in 1776.

French National Library: Manuscript Collection

The chief collection of the Bibliothèque Nationale dealing with naval history before the French Revolution is the Magry Collection (new acquisitions, volumes 9382–9448; for the period of this book see particularly volumes 9414–9419, 9424–9435, 9491–9492). This collection contains mostly copies of papers relating to well-known naval officers and does contain some information taken from closed series of naval documents. It was, however, too narrowly biographical to be very useful. The manuscript collection also contains a written volume on the condition of the French army and navy, 1778 to 1780, which was enormously entertaining (Volume 1479 n.a.: "Etat des troupes et de la marine française"). Its ship lists, prepared by some unknown courtier, contain some ships already sunk, others still in construction, and a number apparently made up by the author. Since the king chose the name for every new ship in the French navy, one wonders how much he was impressed by his gift.

Library of the Ministry of the Navy: Manuscript Collection

Ms. 182: "Journal du Maréchal de Castries." This is a diary dictated by Castries to a female friend. It shows Castries as a simple, honest man surrounded by courtiers. Those believing this should compare the pomp of Castries' visit to Brest in 1781 to the lack of ceremony of Sartine's visit in 1775. Although the Journal is a very unreliable source for questions of motive and the character of the people it describes, it is useful as a guide to what questions were discussed in the council.

2. Selected Published Works: An Annotated Guide[3]

Acomb, Frances. *Anglophobia in France, 1763–1789.* A perceptive study of the complexities of French attitudes toward her hated, feared, and admired rival, Acomb's book is predominantly culturally rather than economically oriented.

Albion, Robert Greenhaugh. *Forests and Sea Power.* Albion deserves great respect for his challenge (only partly success-

[3] Full bibliographical data are given in Section 3.

ful) to the monopoly of naval history by conventional military historians. He somewhat overstates, however, his case for naval matériel as the key to British naval history.

Allen, Gardner. *A Naval History of the American Revolution.* Allen's history of American naval operations, for all its thoroughness, is badly dated. Allen devotes little attention to larger strategic questions in which, it must be admitted, the miniscule American navy was little involved.

Bamford, Paul Walden. *Forests and French Sea Power, 1660–1789.* Bamford has concentrated into 200 pages the history of the problems of the French navy's timber supply during one-and-a-half centuries. This succinctness, although one of this fine book's major virtues, does lead to occasional distortions. In contrast to Bamford's period at large, the French during my period were better provided with masts than with wood for construction.

Barnes, G. R. and Owen, J. H., eds. *The Private Papers of John, Earl of Sandwich, First Lord of the Admiralty, 1771–1782.* This collection is the major published source for British naval operations. It includes both the ministry's correspondence with naval captains and flag officers, and a number of memoirs presented by Sandwich to Parliament.

Barrière, Jean François and de Lescure, M., eds. *Bibliothèque des mémoires relatifs à l'histoire de France pendant le 18ᵉ siècle. Mémoires du duc de Lauzun.* Lauzun commanded at the capture of Senegal and served under Rochambeau. His reliability as a witness is in inverse proportion to the extent of his remarkable egotism.

Baugh, Daniel A. *British Naval Administration in the Age of Walpole.* Baugh has written the best book on naval administration I have ever read—wide in scope, thoroughly researched and useful even for my later period.

Bemis, Samuel Flagg. *The Diplomacy of the American Revolution.* Originally published in 1935, this remains the most useful general diplomatic history of the American war, despite its reliance on published sources and its pro-American bias.

———. *The Hussey-Cumberland Mission and American Independence.* Bemis has treated these negotiations in isolation from the strategic situation at the time, thereby rendering his study largely artificial.

Bosher, J. F. *French Finances, 1770–1795.* Bosher's brilliant, erudite and provocative work blames the failures of the Bourbon tax system on deficiencies of administration. He fails to place the ultimate blame where it belongs—on the unnecessary wars and the political rigidity of the monarchy, which created the need for the expedients Bosher justly condemns.

Bouclon, Adolphe de. *Étude historique sur la Marine de Louis XVI. Liberge de Granchain.* This biography of a naval staff officer contains a good deal of his correspondence, an unusual and valuable primary source.

Boulle, Pierre Henri. "The French Colonies and the Reform of Their Administration during and following the Seven Years' War." This is probably the best available study of Choiseul as naval and colonial minister. Particularly interesting is Part II, on the economics of the French Empire.

Bromley, J. S., ed. *The New Cambridge Modern History. The Rise of Great Britain and Russia, 1688–1725.* Although most of its articles are not pertinent to my period, this volume contains a superb introduction to European Ancien Régime navies by J. S. Bromley and A. N. Ryan.

Brougham, Henry. *An Inquiry into the Colonial Policy of the European Powers.* This book provides an explanation for the eighteenth century belief in the correspondence between a successful colonial trade and a strong navy.

Brun, Vincent-Félix. *Guerres Maritimes de la France: Port de Toulon, ses armements, son administration depuis son origine jusqu'à nos jours.* This is a year-by-year history of Toulon and its fleets. Although prolix and disjointed, it contains an enormous amount of interesting material.

Castex, Raoul-Victor-Patrice. *Les idées militaires de la marine du XVIIIe siècle.* Written at a time when the French military was obsessed with "the offensive," this is an unfair critique of the timidity of eighteenth-century French naval strategy and tactics, with no understanding of the limitations under which they were conducted. Castex, moreover, has as little understanding of diplomacy as does Mahan.

Clark, William Bell. *Lambert Wickes, Sea Raider and Diplomat.* Clark attempts to show the diplomatic context of the naval operations conducted by American privateers in 1777. This is a fine book even though Clark depends on published documents.

Clark, William Bell and Morgan, William James, eds. *Naval Documents of the American Revolution*, 6 v. to date (Washington, 1964–   ). This massive project of the navy department has not been accorded the same priority as nuclear-powered aircraft carriers or new missile submarines. The editors have had to beg the help of European historians in lieu of having their own researchers in Europe. In consequence, virtually all the documents come from American sources, making the collection virtually worthless for any but American trade historians.

Clowes, Sir William Laird. *The Royal Navy: A History from the Earliest Times to the Present*. Clowes' massive history is unparalleled in its amount of detail, an antiquarian's delight. It contains a long chapter in volume 3 by Alfred Thayer Mahan on the major fleet operations of the war.

Conn, Stetson. *Gibraltar in British Diplomacy in the Eighteenth Century*. Conn's treatment of Spanish-English diplomatic negotiations over Gibraltar during the American war is succinct and informative.

Corwin, Edward. "The French Objective in the American Revolution." My own explanation of the French interest in American independence is in large part only a footnote to Corwin's superb article. Corwin, however, has overestimated how sanguine Vergennes was about the easy achievement of his objective; Vergennes' situation was even more pressing than Corwin indicates.

———. *French Policy and the American Alliance of 1778*. Corwin's article also appeared as the first two chapters of his book. The remainder of the book is greatly disappointing since Corwin, using the faulty source collection of Doniol (see below), was betrayed by his evidence.

Creswell, John. *British Admirals of the Eighteenth Century*. This is the definitive study of the tactical problems of the age of sail.

Dakin, Douglas. *Turgot and the Ancien Régime in France*. Dakin presents a thorough exposition of the domestic French problems faced by Turgot, but makes little attempt to show their connection to French foreign policy concerns. His treatment of Turgot's great memoir on aid to America is cursory.

Danvila y Collado, Manuel. *Reinado de Carlos III*. This general history does provide the most competent history of the

Spanish diplomacy of the war period, as well as useful information on the Minorca and Gibraltar operations.

Davis, Ralph. *The Rise of the English Shipping Industry in the 17th and 18th Centuries.* Although written for a general audience, Davis' history of shipping and shipping routes is well-documented and widely informative.

Denizet, Jean. "Histoire de la marine française: essai d'orientation documentaire." This should be the researcher's first stop on the way to the naval collection of the French National Archives.

Desdevises du Dezert, G. "Les institutions de l'Espagne. Chapter VII, La Marine." This article provides an introduction to the organization and administration of the Spanish navy (which greatly resembled the organization and administration of the French navy).

Donaghay, Marie Martenis. "The Anglo-French Negotiations of 1786–1787." Donaghay's dissertation, like all others consulted (including my own), still needs polishing, but it covers immediate postwar Anglo-French relations well enough that I can recommend it in lieu of expanding my epilogue (Chapter Ten).

Doniol, Henri. *Histoire de la participation de la France à l'établissement des Etats-Unis d'Amérique.* This combination documentary collection and monograph sponsored by the French government is the major published source for the French intervention and forms the basis for most histories of the subject. Unfortunately the selection of documents is so biased to support the editor's theories (such as Vergennes' contemplation of war in the summer of 1776) that its use cannot be recommended independently of the full documentary series on which it is based.

Ehrman, John. *The Younger Pitt.* To a work of such scholarship the most appropriate reaction is awe. Among its best chapters are those on British trade and on British diplomacy during the 1780's.

Faure, Edgar. *La disgrâce de Turgot, 12 mai 1776.* Although he provides an encyclopedic account of court politics during the first two years of Louis' reign, Faure's approach often seems superficial and old-fashioned.

Faÿ, Bernard. *The Revolutionary Spirit in France and America.* Faÿ's treatment of French public opinion toward the American Revolution badly needs replacement by a study more cognizant of economic interests.

Fernández Duro, Cesáreo. *Armada Española desde la unión de los reinos de Castilla y de Aragón.* A more sophisticated and thorough treatment of Charles' navy than this brief survey is greatly overdue.

Fortescue, Sir John William, ed. *Correspondence of King George the Third from 1760 to December 1783.* This collection is a vital source for British diplomacy and war strategy, even though the documents are inadequately edited.

France. Commission des Archives Diplomatiques. *Recueil des instructions données aux ambassadeurs et ministres de France depuis les traités de Westphalie jusqu'à la Révolution Française.* These volumes of diplomatic instructions for new or returning ministers vary greatly in their usefulness. The most informative for me has been Volume I (Austria), edited by the greatest of all diplomatic historians, Albert Sorel.

Freeman, Douglas Southall. *George Washington: A Biography.* Freeman has been criticized by historiographers (e.g., David Hackett Fischer) for his approach to biography—the presentation of objective historical reality as nearly as possible as it was perceived by the subject of the biography. I believe on the contrary that Freeman, by his extraordinary thoroughness, has here presented a moving and effective biography and a superb military history.

Gottschalk, Louis. *Lafayette and the Close of the American Revolution.* Gottschalk may somewhat overestimate Lafayette's military ability, but his account of the Yorktown campaign is still absolutely first-rate.

Grouchy, Emmanuel-Henri, Vᵗᵉ de and Cottin, Paul, eds. *Journal inédit du duc de Croÿ, 1718-1784.* Croÿ was a regular dinner companion of Sartine, but he was also an insufferable egotist, a poor friend, and an unreliable reporter for posterity.

Gruber, Ira D. *The Howe Brothers and the American Revolution.* Gruber is a fine historian but the extant material for a biography of the Howes is insufficient for more than tentative answers to the searching questions Gruber has raised.

Harlow, Vincent T. *The Founding of the Second British Empire, 1763-1793*. This ponderous work deals with British colonial and trade policy, particularly after the advent of Shelburne's ministry. Harlow's account of the peace negotiations while conventional in format, does present a great deal of information, particularly on the Newfoundland and Indian issues, not readily available elsewhere. He does, however, greatly overestimate Vergennes' interest in the French colonial empire.

Harris, Robert D. "Necker's *Compte Rendu* of 1781: A Reconsideration." Harris' article is a defense of Necker's good faith rather than an examination of the political context of the *Compte Rendu*.

Heckscher, Eli F. *Mercantilism*. Heckscher's massive study is insufficiently developmental to be as useful for the latter stages of mercantilism as it is for its inception and flowering.

James, William Milburne. *The British Navy in Adversity*. This is a fine book for naval battle buffs—the diagrams are excellent—but James is not very perceptive on strategic questions.

Killion, Howard Ray. "The Suffren Expedition: French Operations in India during the War of American Independence." Killion's background chapters on French diplomacy and overall French war strategy are uninspired, but when dealing with the Indian theater of war he does an excellent job. With a few more human details his dissertation would be the nucleus of a fine biography of Suffren.

Lacour-Gayet, Georges. *La marine militaire de la France sous le règne de Louis XVI*. Lacour-Gayet's book is the best conventional naval history of the American war, although it is hardly impartial. It is also marred by early twentieth-century conceptions of strategy improper for the conducting of a limited war.

La Roncière, Charles de and Clerc-Rampal, G. *Histoire de la Marine*. This is an illustrated history of the French navy written for a general audience.

Le Conte, Pierre. *Répertoire des navires de guerre français*. Le Conte lists the years of launching and of decommissioning or loss of all French naval vessels, along with partial information as to the campaigns of each vessel. I have found his work generally both accurate and thorough.

Legg, L. G. Wickham. *British Diplomatic Instructions, 1689–1789. France. Part IV, 1745–1789.* This collection contains some 50 pages of prewar communications with Ambassador Stormont at Versailles, some dealing with American privateers.

Legohérel, Henri. *Les trésoriers généraux de la marine (1517–1788).* Because Legohérel is chiefly concerned with the navy's fund-raisers as a social group, his book is not a fully-developed history of the economic demands of the navy. Although I have challenged his statistics on the French naval budget for my period, I greatly admire his informative and imaginative book.

Loir, Maurice. *La Marine Royal en 1789.* Loir, like Baugh, deals not only with naval administration, but also with the texture of sailors' lives. Although hardly equal to its much more recent counterpart on the British navy, his work deserves a wide public.

Mackesy, Piers. *The War for America, 1775–1783.* Mackesy's book was the inspiration for my own. I still consider his book a masterpiece although he has depended on unreliable sources for French war strategy. (If I have been more fortunate it is, of course, largely a tribute to Mackesy.) My major criticism of Mackesy is his tendency to view the English political opposition from Germain's eyes, which creates some distortion.

Madariaga, Isabel de. *Britain, Russia, and the Armed Neutrality of 1780.* In its scholarship, its judgment, and its style, this is a model diplomatic history. Its point of departure is the British mission to Catherine's court, so French diplomacy is treated peripherally, although with great insight.

———. "The Secret Austro-Russian Treaty of 1781." Madariaga's article is as well-written and as indispensable to the diplomatic history of the American war as is her marvelous book.

Mahan, Alfred Thayer. *The Influence of Sea Power Upon History, 1660–1783.* Mahan's inability to understand the inherent limitations of force makes him suspect as a military historian. In addition to his defective vision of the Ancien Régime, his work is marred by a prejudice in favor of England, which he used as a model to be followed by the United States. His work is of greater value for the understanding of Mahan's own era than for the understanding of a century whose per-versions did not include Social Darwinism.

Meng, John Joseph, ed. *Conrad Alexandre Gérard: Despatches and Instructions*. Gérard's correspondence is chiefly of interest to historians of the United States. Nonetheless, this collection is extensive and well edited.

Miller, Nathan. *Sea of Glory: The Continental Navy Fights For Independence, 1775–1783*. Miller's history unfortunately is as antiquated a work as is the 60-year-old history by Allen which it seeks to replace. Even Miller's bibliography is inferior in certain respects to that of its predecessor.

Montbarey, Alexandre-Marie-Léonor de Saint-Mauris, prince de. *Mémoires autographes de M. le Prince de Montbarey*. Al-though it gives some information of Sartine's childhood, Montbarey's memoirs are a great disappointment for the war years—as shallow as Montbarey himself.

Morison, Samuel Eliot. *John Paul Jones*. This book is a repre-sentative performance of a superb biographer, but hardly of America's greatest naval historian. Morison has thoroughly researched Jones' battles, but not their relationship to the war at large.

Morris, Richard B., ed. *The Era of the American Revolution*. Among these essays is Max Sevelle's "The American Balance of Power and European Diplomacy, 1715–1778," a competent introduction to the place of rival colonies in the European balance of power.

————. *The Peacemakers: The Great Powers and American Independence*. The book's virtues of wide-ranging research and enormous labor are unfortunately overshadowed by serious historical deficiencies—a pro-American bias, repeated mistakes in detail, an old-fashioned view of diplomacy as largely the work of secret agents, a superficial knowledge of military factors, and above all an inability to distinguish the important from the trivial. It may be employed as a useful guide to sources, but only with great caution as a narrative history.

Murphy, Orville T. "Charles Gravier de Vergennes: Portrait of an Old Régime Diplomat." I am one of the many younger historians Professor Murphy has befriended, advised, and aided. Of his many fine articles this is the best. There is no introduction to Vergennes more judicious and full of insight.

Neuville, Didier. *Etat Sommaire des archives de la marine an-térieures à la Révolution.* This 700-page work is a combination history of French naval administration and guide to the naval archives, listing volume by volume the holdings of the pre-Revolutionary collection.

Nicolson, Sir Harold. *The Evolution of Diplomatic Method.* Nicolson contends that the diplomatic traditions of the Old Regime moderated the conduct of international relations. Nicolson's eloquent defense of the Old Régime should be read in conjunction with Sorel's criticism of it (see below).

Noailles, Amblard-Marie-Raymond-Amédée, Vicomte de. *Marins et soldats français en Amérique pendant la guerre de l'indépendance des Etats-Unis.* This is a competent conventional history of French military operations in the Western Hemisphere.

Pares, Richard. *Yankees and Creoles: The Trade between North America and the West Indies before the American Revolution.* The French badly overestimated the consequences of American independence on American trade patterns. Pares' splendid book suggests reasons for the persistence of trade habits despite the end of the formal British monopoly.

Patterson, A. Temple. *The Other Armada.* Patterson's very competent history of the Channel campaign of 1779 is centered around the defense of Portsmouth and Plymouth.

Perugia, Paul del. *La tentative d'invasion de l'Angleterre de 1779.* Perugia has written a diplomatic history of the Channel campaign using as a major source the Spanish correspondence. He has done a good job and I recommend his book to supplement my own brief treatment of his subject.

Potter, E. B., ed. *Sea Power.* Potter's textbook is still used for the training of all American naval midshipmen. As might be feared, it is romantic and uncritical, a mere collection of clichés pasted together by a group of amateur historians.

Renaut, Francis P. *La crépuscule d'une puissance navale.* With extraordinary deftness Renaut traces the obsolescence of the Dutch navy in all its aspects from antiquated ship construction to the professional backwardness of its officers.

Romano, Ruggiero. "Documenti e prime considerazioni intorno alla 'balance du commerce' della Francia del 1716 al 1780." Romano has here edited the most reliable and detailed general set of eighteenth-century French trade statistics available to date.

Rose, J. Holland, Newton, A. P. and Benians, E. A., eds. *The Cambridge History of the British Empire. The Old Empire from Its Beginnings to 1783.* The most pertinent of these essays is that of J. F. Rees on eighteenth-century mercantilism, "Mercantilism and the Colonies" (Chapter Ten).

Sainte-Croix, Alexandre Lambert de. *Essai sur l'administration de la marine de France, 1689–1792.* Although rather adulatory of the military, this is the most thorough administrative history of the French navy department during the last century of the Ancien Régime.

Schelle, Gustave, ed. *Oeuvres de Turgot et documents le concernant.* This is the most recent collection of Turgot's writings and includes his memoir on French intervention.

Ségur, Louis Philippe, comte de. *Mémoires; ou, souvenirs et anecdotes.* Ségur, the son of the war minister, participant in Rochambeau's campaigns and post-war ambassador to Russia, wrote one of the most evocative autobiographies of the Old Regime.

Sorel, Albert. *Europe and the French Revolution: The Political Traditions of the Old Régime.* No other work of diplomatic history approaches it. To read it should be as much a part of a liberal education as to read Burckhardt or Tocqueville.

Stevens, Benjamin Franklin, ed. *Facsimiles of Manuscripts in European Archives Relating to America, 1773–1783.* No better published source exists for the diplomacy of the American war, although the documents are very loosely organized. In addition to the documents themselves Stevens provides English translations for foreign language documents.

Stinchcombe, William C. *The American Revolution and the French Alliance.* Stinchcombe, a fine historian, has approached the alliance from an exclusively American viewpoint.

Stourzh, Gerald. *Benjamin Franklin and American Foreign Policy.* By analyzing Franklin's thought about the nature of international relations, power, economics, etc., Stourzh has enriched our understanding of Franklin's diplomacy—an enormously impressive performance by a superlative historian.

Syrett, David. *Shipping and the American War, 1775–1783.* Syrett's treatment of British shipping difficulties is most informative, although his predictions of the effects of shortages of victuallers and transports on operations in 1783, had the war continued, must be placed in the context of the disintegration of the Allied war effort.

Taillemite, Etienne. *Les archives anciennes de la Marine.* Taillemite is the best contemporary authority on the French naval archives. His essay should be read in conjunction with Denizet's essay and Neuville's book.

Tarrade, Jean. *Le commerce colonial de la France à la fin de l'Ancien Régime.* Tarrade's definitive study of French colonial commerce reflects both the virtues and the scale of values of contemporary French historiography. His chapter on the American war is less impressive than his excellent statistical chapters on French trade, although these should be read in conjunction with Romano (see above).

Taylor, George V. "The Paris Bourse on the Eve of the Revolution, 1781–1789." Taylor delivers much more than his title promises—in a major contribution to the understanding of the fiscal breakdown of the monarchy, Taylor describes the mechanism of French deficit financing.

Tramond, Joannès. *Manuel d'histoire maritime de la France des origines à 1815.* This is recommended as a single-volume history of the French navy.

Van Alstyne, Richard W. *Empire and Independence.* A tribute to the persistence of faulty theories—Van Alstyne has, in his treatment of the French intervention, repeated the untenable theory of Van Tyne.

Van Tyne, Claude H. "Influences Which Determined the French Government to Make the Treaty with America, 1778." Van Tyne maintains against Corwin and against logic that the French were motivated to aid America from fear for their own colonies.

Viner, Jacob. "Power versus Plenty as Objectives of Foreign Policy in the Seventeenth and Eighteenth Centuries." Viner persuasively argues that mercantilism viewed wealth and power as inseparably interrelated.

Wharton, Francis, ed. *The Revolutionary Diplomatic Correspondence of the United States*. Wharton's documents are of far greater value to historians of America than to historians of Europe; his editing techniques are now outdated.

Wickwire, Franklin and Wickwire, Mary. *Cornwallis: The American Adventure*. Thorough and articulate as are the authors, the questions they have posed about Cornwallis are so limited that this book seems almost quaint—a virtual hagiography of a model general with the focus of attention always on the battlefield.

Willcox, William Bradford. *Portrait of a General: Sir Henry Clinton in the War of Independence*. It is extraordinary that the British war effort should be the subject of two historical masterpieces. Willcox's book does not have the exceptional scope of Mackesy's, but he has an even finer grasp of military strategy. I know of no better military history than his treatment of the Yorktown campaign.

Witte, Jehan, baron de, ed. *Journal de l'Abbé de Véri*. In comparison to his contemporaries Véri was an admirable man, an informed witness of the highest court circles, and a fair-minded critic. Unfortunately, Witte edited his journal only to January 1781.

Yela Utrilla, Juan F. *España ante la independencia de los Estados Unidos*. Of most interest is the second volume which is a collection of 183 documents, almost all dealing with Spanish foreign policy. This collection is very imbalanced—for example, 63 pieces from 1777 and only 5 from 1779—with an undue emphasis on correspondence between Floridablanca and Aranda, who was often not informed about current negotiations.

3. Bibliography of Printed Sources[4]

Abarca, Ramon E. "Classical Diplomacy and Bourbon 'Revanche' Strategy, 1763–1770." *Review of Politics* 32 (1970): 313–337.

Aboucaya, Claude. *Les intendants de la marine sous l'Ancien Régime*. Gap: Louis Jean, 1958.

---

[4] An asterisk indicates that the entry is annotated in Section 2.

*Acomb, Frances Dorothy. *Anglophobia in France, 1763–1789.* Durham, N.C.: Duke University Press, 1950.

Affaires de l'Angleterre et de l'Amérique. 15 vols. Antwerp: 1776–1779.

*Albion, Robert Greenhaugh. *Forests and Sea Power: The Timber Problem of the Royal Navy, 1652–1862.* Cambridge, Mass.: Harvard University Press, 1926.

———. *Naval and Maritime History: An Annotated Bibliography.* 4th ed., rev. Mystic Seaport, Conn.: Munson Institute of American Maritime History, 1972.

*Allen, Gardner Weld. *A Naval History of the American Revolution.* 2 vols. Boston: Houghton Mifflin Co., 1913.

Almanach Royal. Paris: D'Houry, 1775–1784.

Alton, Arthur S. "The Diplomacy of the Louisiana Concession." *American Historical Review* 36 (1931): 701–721.

Alvord, Clarence W. *The Mississippi Valley in British Politics.* 2 vols. Cleveland: The Arthur H. Clark Co., 1917.

Aman, Jacques. "Inventaire des archives privées intéressant l'histoire maritime." *Revue d'histoire économique et sociale* 42 (1964): 220–254.

Anderson, Adam and Combe, William. *An Historical and Chronological Deduction of the Origin of Commerce From the Earliest Accounts.* Vol. 4. London: J. Walter, 1787.

Anderson, M. S. "The Great Powers and the Russian Annexation of the Crimea." *Slavonic and East European Review* 37 (1958): 17–41.

Andrews, Charles M. *The Colonial Period in American History.* Vol. 4, *England's Commercial and Colonial Policy.* New Haven: Yale University Press, 1938.

The Annual Register. London: J. Dodsley, 1774–1783.

Antier, Jean-Jacques. *L'amiral de Grasse, héros de l'indépendance américaine.* Paris: Plon, 1965.

Anthiaume, Abbé (Albert). *Un ancêtre du Borda au Havre: L'école royale de marine, 1773–1775.* Paris: Ernest Dumont, 1920.

Arneth, Alfred von and Flammermont, Jules, eds. *Correspondance secrète du Comte de Mercy-Argenteau avec l'empereur Joseph II et le prince de Kaunitz.* 2 vols. Paris: Imprimerie Nationale, 1889–1891.

Arneth, Alfred von and Geffroy, Auguste, eds. *Marie-Antoinette: Correspondance secrète entre Marie-Thérèse et le c^te de Mercy-Argenteau.* 3 vols. Paris: Firmin-Didot frères, fils et c^ie, 1874–1875.

Arnould, Ambroise. *De la balance du commerce et des relations commerciales extérieures de la France dans toutes les parties du globe, particulièrement à la fin du règne de Louis XIV, et au moment de la Révolution.* 2 vols. Paris: Buisson, 1791.

Aspinall, Arthur. *The Later Correspondence of George III.* Vol. 1, *December 1783–January 1793.* Cambridge: At the University Press, 1966.

Augur, Helen. *The Secret War of Independence.* New York: Duell, Sloan, and Pierce, 1955.

Auphan, P. "Les communications entre la France et ses colonies d'Amérique pendant la guerre de l'indépendance Américaine." *La revue maritime* 61 (1925): 331–348, 497–517.

Azéma, Georges. *Histoire de l'île de Bourbon.* Paris: Henri Plon, 1862.

Bachaumont, Louis Petit de. *Mémoires secrets pour servir à l'histoire de la république des lettres en France, depuis 1762 jusqu'à nos jours.* 36 vols. London: John Adamson, 1780–1789.

Bachelier, L. *Histoire du commerce de Bordeaux, depuis les temps le plus reculés jusqu'à nos jours.* Bordeaux: J. Delmas, 1862.

Bajot, Louis-Marie. *Catalogue général des livres composant les bibliothèques du département de la Marine et des Colonies.* 5 vols. Paris: Imprimerie Royale, 1838–1843.

————. *Repértoire de l'administrateur de la marine, ou table par ordre de dates et de matières des principales lois relatives à la marine et aux colonies, depuis leur origine jusqu'à ce jour.* Paris: Firmin-Didot, 1814.

Balch, Thomas Willing. *The French in America during the War of Independence of the United States, 1777–1783.* Philadelphia: Porter and Coates, 1891.

*Bamford, Paul Walden. *Forests and French Sea Power, 1660–1789.* Toronto: University of Toronto Press, 1956.

Banbuck, C. A. *Histoire politique, économique et sociale de la Martinique sous l'Ancien Régime (1635–1789).* Paris: Marcel Rivière, 1935.

*Barnes, G. R. and Owen, J. H., eds. *The Private Papers of John, Earl of Sandwich, First Lord of the Admiralty, 1771–1782.* 4 vols. London: Naval Records Society, 1932–1938.

Barral de Montferrat, Horace-Dominique de. *Dix ans de paix armée entre la France et l'Angleterre, 1783–1793.* Vol. 1. Paris: E. Plon, Nourrit et c^ie, 1893.

*Barrière, Jean-François and de Lescure, M. eds. *Bibliothèque des mémoires relatifs à l'histoire de France pendant le 18e siècle.* Vol. 4, *Mémoires du Baron de Besenval*; Vol. 21, *Mémoires du Marquis de Bouillé*; and Vol. 25, *Mémoires du duc de Lauzun.* Paris: Firmin-Didot frères, fils et c^ie, 1857–1862.

*Baugh, Daniel A. *British Naval Administration in the Age of Walpole.* Princeton, N. J.: Princeton University Press, 1965.

Beach, Vincent W. *Charles X of France: His Life and Times.* Boulder, Colo.: Pruett Publishing Co., 1971.

Beatson, R. *Naval and Military Memoirs of Great Britain from the Year 1727 to 1783.* Vol. 6. London: J. Strachan, 1790.

Beers, Henry Putney. *The French in North America: A Bibliographical Guide to French Archives, Reproductions and Research Missions.* Baton Rouge, La.: Louisiana State University Press, 1957.

Behrens, C. B. A. *The Ancien Régime.* London: Thames and Hudson, 1967.

Bell, Herbert C. "The West India Trade before the American Revolution." *American Historical Review* 22 (1917): 272–287.

Bemis, Samuel Flagg, ed. *The American Secretaries of State and their Diplomacy.* Vol. 1. New York: Alfred A. Knopf, 1927.

———. "British Secret Service and the French-American Alliance." *American Historical Review* 29 (1924): 474–495.

*———. *The Diplomacy of the American Revolution.* 2d ed., rev. Bloomington, Ind.: Indiana University Press, 1957.

*———. *The Hussey-Cumberland Mission and American Independence.* Princeton, N. J.: Princeton University Press, 1931.

———. "The Rayneval Memoranda of 1782 on Western Boundaries and Some Comments on the French Historian Doniol." *Proceedings of the American Antiquarian Society* 47 (1937): 15–92.

Bemis, Samuel Flagg and Griffin, Grace Gordon. *Guide to the Diplomatic History of the United States, 1775–1921.* Washington: Government Printing Office, 1935.

Bernard, Paul P. *Joseph II and Bavaria: Two Eighteenth-Century Attempts at German Unification.* The Hague: Martinus Nijhoff, 1965.

Billias, George Athon, ed. *George Washington's Opponents: British Generals and Admirals in the American Revolution.* New York: William Morrow and Co., 1969.

Blanchard, Claude-François. *Répertoire général des lois, décrets, ordonnances, règlements, et instructions sur la marine.* Vol. 1. Paris: Imprimerie Nationale, 1849.

Boatner, Mark M. *Encyclopedia of the American Revolution.* New York: David McKay, 1966.

Bonner-Smith, D., ed. *The Barrington Papers, Selected from the Letters and Papers of Admiral the Honorable Samuel Barrington.* Vol. 2. London: Naval Records Society, 1941.

Bonneville de Marsagny, Louis. *Le Chevalier de Vergennes: Son ambassade à Constantinople.* 2 vols. Paris: E. Plon, Nourrit et cⁱᵉ, 1894.

―――. *Le Comte de Vergennes: Son ambassade en Suède.* Paris: E. Plon, Nourrit et cⁱᵉ, 1898.

*Bosher, J. F. *French Finances, 1770–1795: From Business to Bureaucracy.* Cambridge: At the University Press, 1970.

*Bouclon, Adolphe de. *Etude historique sur la marine de Louis XVI: Liberge de Granchain, capitaine des vaisseaux du roi, major d'escadre, directeur général des ports et arsenaux, géographe astronome. . . .* Paris: Arthur Bertrand, 1866.

*Boulle, Pierre Henri. "The French Colonies and the Reform of Their Administration during and following the Seven Years' War." Ph.D. dissertation, University of California, Berkeley, 1968.

Braudel, Fernand and Labrousse, C. E. *Histoire économique et sociale de la France.* Vol. 2, *Des derniers temps de l'âge seigneurial aux préludes de l'âge industriel (1660–1789).* Paris: Presses Universitaires de France, 1970.

*Bromley, J. S., ed. *The New Cambridge Modern History.* Vol. 6, *The Rise of Great Britain and Russia, 1688–1725.* Cambridge: At the University Press, 1970.

*Brougham, Henry. *An Inquiry into the Colonial Policy of the European Powers.* 2 vols. Edinburgh: G. Balfour, Manners, and Miller, 1803.

Brown, Gerald Saxon. *The American Secretary: The Colonial Policy of Lord George Germain, 1775–1778.* Ann Arbor, Mich.: University of Michigan Press, 1963.

Brown, Marvin L. *American Independence through Prussian Eyes.* Durham, N.C.: Duke University Press, 1959.

Brown, Weldon A. *Empire or Independence: A Study in the Failure of Reconciliation, 1774–1783.* Baton Rouge, La.: Louisiana State University Press, 1941.

Browning, Oscar, ed. *Despatches from Paris, 1784–1790.* Vol. 1, *1784–1787.* London: Royal Historical Society, 1909.

*Brun, Vincent-Félix. *Guerres maritimes de la France: Port de Toulon, ses armements, son administration depuis son origine jusqu'à nos jours.* Paris: Henri Plon, 1861.

Buck, Philip. *The Politics of Mercantilism.* New York: Henry Holt and Co., 1942.

Buron, Edmund. "Statistics on Franco-American Trade, 1778–1806." *Journal of Economic and Business History* 4 (1932): 571–582.

Butterfield, L. H., ed. *The Adams Papers: Diary and Autobiography of John Adams.* Vols. 2 and 4. Cambridge, Mass.: Harvard University Press, Belknap Press, 1961.

Cahen, Léon. "Une nouvelle interprétation du Traité Franco-Anglaise de 1786–1787" *Revue historique* 185 (1931): 257–285.

Callender, G.A.R. *Bibliography of Naval History.* History Association Leaflets no. 58 and 61. 2 vols. London: Historical Association, 1924–1925.

Calmettes, Fernand, ed. *Mémoires du duc de Choiseul, 1719–1785.* Paris: Plon, Nourrit et cⁱᵉ, 1904.

Calmon-Maison, Jean-Joseph-Robert. *L'amiral d'Estaing.* Paris: Calmann-Lévy, 1910.

Captier, J. *Etude historique et économique sur l'inscription maritime.* Paris: Bussière, Giard, et Brière, 1908.

Castelot, André. *Queen of France: A Biography of Marie Antoinette.* Translated by Denise Folliot. New York: Harper and Brothers, 1957.

*Castex, Raoul-Victor-Patrice. *Les idées militaires de la marine du XVIIIᵉ siècle.* Paris: L. Fournier, 1911.

Castries, René de la Croix, duc de. *Le maréchal de Castries (1727–1800).* Paris: Flammarion, 1956.

Castries, René de la Croix, duc de. "La pacte de famille et la guerre de l'indépendance américaine." *Revue d'histoire diplomatique* 75 (1964): 294–306.

Caughey, John Walton. *Bernardo de Gálvez in Louisiana, 1776–1783.* Berkeley, Cal.: University of California Press, 1934.

Chadwick, French Ensor, ed. *The Graves Papers and Other Documents relating to the Naval Operations of the Yorktown Campaign, July to October 1781.* New York: Naval History Society, 1916.

Chambrun, Charles. *A l'école d'un diplomat, Vergennes.* Paris: Plon, 1944.

Charliat, P. *Trois siècles d'économie maritime française.* Paris: Marcel Rivière, 1931.

Chevalier, Louis-Edouard. *Histoire de la marine française.* Vol. 3. Paris: Hachette et c^ie, 1877.

Chinard, Gilbert, ed. *The Treaties of 1778 and Allied Documents.* Baltimore: Johns Hopkins University Press, 1928.

Clairbois, Honoré Sébastien Vial de, ed. *Encyclopédie Méthodique: Marine.* 3 vols. Paris: Panckouke, 1783–1787.

Clark, William Bell. *Ben Franklin's Privateers: A Naval Epic of the American Revolution.* Baton Rouge, La.: Louisiana State University Press, 1956.

*———. *Lambert Wickes, Sea Raider and Diplomat: The Story of a Naval Captain of the Revolution.* New Haven, Conn.: Yale University Press, 1932.

*Clark, William Bell and Morgan, William James, eds. *Naval Documents of the American Revolution.* 6 vols. to date. Washington: Government Printing Office, 1964–   .

Clavière, Etienne and Brissot de Warville, J. P. *De la France et des Etats-Unis, ou, de l'importance de la révolution de l'Amérique pour le bonheur de la France, des rapports de ce royaume & des Etats-Unis, des avantages réciproques qu'ils peuvent retirer de leurs liaisons de commerce & enfin de la situation actuelle des Etats-Unis.* London: 1787.

*Clowes, Sir William Laird. *The Royal Navy: A History from the Earliest Times to the Present.* Vols. 3 and 4. Boston: Little, Brown, and Co., 1898–1899.

Cobban, Alfred. *Ambassadors and Secret Agents: The Diplomacy of the First Earl of Malmesbury at The Hague.* London, Jonathan Cape, 1954.

Colledge, J. J. *Ships of the Royal Navy: An Historical Index.* 2 vols. London: David and Charles, 1969–1970.

Commager, Henry Steele. *Documents of American History.* New York: Appleton-Century-Crofts, 1958.

*Conn, Stetson. *Gibraltar in British Diplomacy in the Eighteenth Century.* New Haven: Yale University Press, 1942.

Coquelle, Paul. *L'alliance Franco-Hollandaise contre l'Angleterre, 1735–1788.* Paris: Plon, Nourrit et cᶦᵉ, 1902.

*Corwin, Edward. "The French Objective in the American Revolution." *American Historical Review* 21 (1915): 33–62.

*———. *French Policy and the American Alliance of 1778.* Princeton, N. J.: Princeton University Press, 1916.

Coste, Gabriel. *Les anciennes troupes de la marine (1622–1792).* Paris: L. Baudoin, 1893.

Craig, Hardin J. *A Bibliography of Encyclopedias and Dictionaries dealing with Military, Naval, and Maritime Affairs, 1577–1971.* 4th ed., rev. Houston: Rice University, History Department, 1972.

*Creswell, John. *British Admirals of the Eighteenth Century: Tactics in Battle.* Hamden, Conn.: Archon Books, 1972.

Crouzet, F. "Croissances comparées de l'Angleterre et de la France au XVIIIᵉ siècle." *Annales: Economies-Sociétés-Civilisations* 21 (1966): 254–291.

Cunat, Charles. *Histoire du bailli de Suffren.* 2 vols. Paris: Librairie commerciale et artistique, 1968.

Dagnaud, G. *L'Administration centrale de la Marine sous l'ancien régime.* Paris: M. Imhaus et R. Chapelot, 1913.

*Dakin, Douglas. *Turgot and the Ancien Régime in France.* London: Methuen and Co., 1939.

Daney, Sidney. *Histoire de la Martinique depuis la colonisation jusqu'en 1815.* Vol. 2. Fort Royal, Martinique: E. Ruelle, 1846.

*Danvila y Collado, Manuel. *Reinado de Carlos III.* Vol. 5. Madrid: El Progreso Editorial, 1896.

Dardel, Pierre. *Commerce, industrie et navigation à Rouen et au Havre au XVIIIᵉ siècle, rivalité croissante entre ces deux ports, la conjoncture.* Rouen: Société libre d'émulation de la Seine-Maritime, 1966.

———. *Navires et marchandises dans les ports de Rouen et du Havre au XVIIIᵉ siècle.* Paris: S.E.V.P.E.N., 1963.

Daubigny, E. *Choiseul et la France d'outre-mer après le traité de Paris.* Paris: Hachette et Cie, 1892.

Davis, Burke. *The Campaign that Won America: The Story of Yorktown.* New York: Dial Press, 1970.

Davis, Ralph. "English Foreign Trade, 1700–1774." *Economic History Review* series 2, 15 (1962): 285–303.

*———. *The Rise of the English Shipping Industry in the 17th and 18th Centuries.* London: Macmillan and Co., 1962.

Deane, Phyllis and Cole, W. A. *British Economic Growth, 1688–1959: Trends and Structure.* Cambridge: At the University Press, 1964.

Deane, Silas. *The Deane Papers, 1774–1790.* 5 vols. New York: Publications of the New York Historical Society, Vols. 19–23, 1886–1890.

———. *The Deane Papers: Correspondence between Silas Deane, His Brothers, and Their Business and Political Associates, 1771–1795.* Hartford, Conn.: Publications of the Connecticut Historical Society, 1930.

[Delauney]. *Histoire d'un pou français; ou L'Espion d'une nouvelle espèce, tant en France qu'en Angleterre.* Paris: 1781.

*Denizet, Jean. "Histoire de la marine française; essai d'orientation documentaire." *La revue maritime* 60 (1951): 474–510.

Derry, John W. *Charles James Fox.* London: B. T. Batsford, 1972.

Des Cars, Jean-François de Pérusse, duc. *Mémoires du duc des Cars.* Paris: E. Plon, Nourrit et Cie, 1890.

Deschamps, Léon. *Histoire de la question coloniale en France.* Paris: E. Plon, Nourrit et Cie, 1891.

Deschard, A. *Notice sur l'organisation du corps du commissariat de la marine française depuis l'origine jusqu'à nos jours.* Paris: Berger-Levrault, 1879.

———. *Organisation du corps des officiers de vaisseau de la marine française.* Paris: Berger-Levrault, 1877.

*Desdevises du Dezert, G. "Les institutions de l'Espagne. Chapter VII, La Marine." *Revue hispanique* 70 (1927): 442–540.

Dickerson, Oliver M. *The Navigation Acts and the American Revolution.* Philadelphia: University of Pennsylvania Press, 1951.

Dictionnaire de biographie française. 13 vols. to date. Paris: Letouzey et Ané, 1929– .

*Donaghay, Marie Martenis. "The Anglo-French Negotiations of 1786–1787." Ph.D. dissertation, University of Virginia, 1970.

Doneaud du Plan, Alfred. *L'Académie royale de Marine, de 1778 à 1783.* Paris: Berger-Levrault, 1878–1882.

*Doniol, Henri. *Histoire de la participation de la France à l'établissement des Etats-Unis d'Amérique.* 5 vols. Paris: Imprimerie Nationale, 1885–1892.

———. "Le Ministère des Affaires Etrangères de France sous le Comte de Vergennes." *Revue d'histoire diplomatique* 7 (1893): 528–560.

Dorn, Walter L. *Competition for Empire, 1740–1763.* New York: Harper and Brothers, 1940.

Duchêne, Albert. *La Politique Coloniale de la France: Le Ministère des colonies depuis Richelieu.* Paris: Payot, 1929.

Du Halgouet, Hervé. *Nantes, ses relations commerciales avec les îles d'Amérique au XVIIIe siècle.* Rennes: Oberthur, 1939.

Dumas, François. *Etude sur le traité de commerce de 1786 entre la France et l'Angleterre.* Toulouse: Edouard Privat, 1904.

Dumon, Francis. *Une carrière de commissaire de la marine au XVIIIe siècle, François de Magny, 1733–1800.* Lyon: Bosc et frères, 1940.

Dupont, A. *Les arsenaux de la marine de 1689 à 1910: Leur organisation administrative.* Paris: Berger-Levrault, 1913.

Durand, John. *New Materials for the History of the American Revolution.* New York: Henry Holt and Co., 1889.

Echeverria, Durand. *Mirage in the West: A History of the French Image of American Society to 1815.* Princeton, N. J.: Princeton University Press, 1957.

Echeverria, Durand and Murphy, Orville T. "The American Revolutionary Army: A French Estimate of 1777." *Military Affairs* 27 (1963): 1–7, 153–162.

Edler, Friedrich. *The Dutch Republic and the American Revolution.* Johns Hopkins University Studies in Historical and Political Science, series 29, no. 2. Baltimore: Johns Hopkins University Press, 1911.

Ehrman, John. *The British Government and Commercial Negotiations with Europe, 1783–1793.* Cambridge: At the University Press, 1962.

*———. *The Younger Pitt.* Vol. 1, *The Years of Acclaim.* London: Constable and Co., 1969.

Fagniez, G. "La Politique de Vergennes et la diplomatie de Breteuil." *Revue historique* 140 (1922): 1–25, 161–207.

Fauchille, Paul. *La Diplomatie française et la Ligue des neutres de 1780 (1776–1783)*. Paris: A. Durand et Pedone-Lauriel, 1893.

*Faure, Edgar. *La disgrâce de Turgot, 12 mai 1776*. Paris: Gallimard, 1961.

Favitski de Probobysk, A. *Répertoire bibliographique de la littérature militaire et coloniale française depuis cent ans*. Liege: G. Thone, 1935.

Faÿ, Bernard. *L'aventure coloniale*. Paris: Perrin, 1962.

————. *Bibliographie critique des ouvrages français relatifs aux Etats-Unis, 1775–1800*. Paris: E. Champion, 1925.

————. *Louis XVI, or The End of a World*. Translated by Patrick O'Brian. London: W. H. Allen, 1968.

*————. *The Revolutionary Spirit in France and America*. Translated by Ramon Guthrie. New York: Harcourt, Brace, and Co., 1927.

*Fernández Duro, Cesáreo. *Armada Española desde la unión de los reinos de Castilla y de Aragón*. Vol. 7. Madrid: Sucesores de Rivadeneyra, 1901.

Fitzmaurice, Lord Edmond. *Life of William, Earl of Shelburne*. 2 vols. London: Macmillan and Co., 1912.

Flassan, Gaëtan de Raxis de. *Histoire générale et raisonée de la diplomatie française depuis la fondation de la monarchie, jusqu'à la fin du règne de Louis XVI*. Vol. 7. Paris: Treutell et Würtz, 1811.

Flexner, James Thomas. *George Washington in the American Revolution, 1775–1783*. Boston: Little, Brown, and Co., 1967.

Fontaine de Resbecq, Hubert de. *L'Administration centrale de la marine et des colonies*. Paris: L. Boudoin, 1886.

Forster, Robert and Forster, Elbourg, eds. *European Society in the Eighteenth Century*. New York: Harper and Row, Harper Torchbooks, 1969.

*Fortescue, Sir John William, ed. *The Correspondence of King George the Third from 1760 to December 1783*. Vols. 3 to 6. London: Macmillan and Co., 1928.

Fox, Frank. "Negotiating with the Russians: Ambassador Ségur's Mission to Saint-Petersbourg, 1784–1789." *French Historical Studies* 7 (1971): 47–71.

Fraguier, Bertrand de. "Le duc d'Aiguillon et l'Angleterre (juin 1771–avril 1773)." *Revue d'histoire diplomatique* 26 (1912): 607–627.

France. Archives du Ministère des Affaires Etrangères. *Etat numérique des fonds de la correspondance politique de l'origine à 1871*. Paris: Imprimerie Nationale, 1936.

—————. *Inventaire sommaire de la correspondance politique: Etats-Unis*. Paris: Imprimerie Nationale, n.d.

—————. *Inventaire sommaire des archives du Département des Affaires Etrangères*. 7 vols. to date. Paris: Imprimerie Nationale, 1883– .

*France. Commission des Archives Diplomatiques. *Recueil des instructions données aux ambassadeurs et ministres de France depuis les traités de Westphalie jusqu'à la révolution française*. Vol. 1. *Autriche*. Ed. Albert Sorel. Paris: Germer Baillière et cie, 1884.

Vol. 2. *Suède*. Ed. A. Geffroy. Paris: Germer Baillière et cie, 1885.

Vol. 3. *Portugal*. Ed. Le Vte de Caix de Saint-Aymour. Paris: Germer Baillière et cie, 1886.

Vol. 7. *Bavière, Palatinat, Deux-Ponts*. Ed. André Lebon. Paris: Germer Baillière et cie, 1889.

Vol. 9. *Russie (II)*. Ed. Alfred Rambaud. Paris: Germer Baillière et cie, 1890.

Vol. 12, part 2. *Espagne (III)*. Ed. A. Morel-Fatio and H. Léonardon. Paris: Germer Baillière et cie, 1898.

Vol. 16. *Prusse*. Ed. Albert Waddington. Paris: Germer Baillière et cie, 1901.

Vol. 23. *Hollande (III)*. Ed. Louis André and Emile Bourgois. Paris: Fontemoing et cie, 1924.

Vol. 25, part 2. *Angleterre (III)*. Ed. Paul Vaucher. Paris: Centre Nationale de la Recherche Scientifique, 1965.

*Freeman, Douglas Southall. *George Washington: A Biography*. Vol. 5, *Victory with the Help of France*. New York: Charles Scribner's Sons, 1952.

Gershoy, Leo. *From Despotism to Revolution, 1763–1789*. New York: Harper and Brothers, 1944.

Gilbert, Felix. *To the Farewell Address: Ideas of Early American Foreign Policy*. Princeton, N. J.: Princeton University Press, 1961.

Gipson, Lawrence Henry. *The British Empire before the American Revolution.* 15 vols. New York: Alfred A. Knopf, 1939–1970.

Godechot, Jacques Léon. *France and the Atlantic Revolution of the Eighteenth Century.* Translated by Herbert H. Rowen. New York: Free Press, 1965.

Gomel, Charles. *Les causes financières de la révolution française.* Vol. 1, *Les Ministères de Turgot et de Necker.* Paris: Guillaumin et c^{ie}, 1892.

Goodwin, Albert, ed. *The New Cambridge Modern History.* Vol. 8, *The American and French Revolutions, 1763–93.* Cambridge: At the University Press, 1965.

*Gottschalk, Louis. *Lafayette and the Close of the American Revolution.* Chicago: University of Chicago Press, 1942.

———. *Lafayette Comes to America.* Chicago: University of Chicago Press, 1935.

———. *Lafayette Joins the American Army.* Chicago: University of Chicago Press, 1937.

Graham, Gerald. *Empire of the North Atlantic: The Maritime Struggle for North America.* Toronto: University of Toronto Press, 1950.

———. *Sea Power and British North America, 1783–1820: A Study in British Colonial Policy.* Cambridge, Mass.: Harvard University Press, 1941.

Grant, W. L. "Canada versus Guadeloupe, An Episode in the Seven Years' War." *American Historical Review* 17 (1912): 735–743.

Grosclaude, Pierre. *Malesherbes et son temps: Nouveaux documents inédits.* Paris: Fishbacher, 1964.

Grosjean, Georges. *La politique rhénane de Vergennes.* Paris: Société d'edition "Les belles-lettres," 1925.

*Grouchy, Emmanuel-Henri, Vte de and Cottin, Paul, eds. *Journal inédit du duc de Croÿ, 1718-1784.* 4 vols. Paris: Ernest Flammarion, 1906–1907.

*Gruber, Ira D. *The Howe Brothers and the American Revolution.* New York: Atheneum, 1972.

Guérin, Léon. *Histoire maritime de France.* Vol. 5. Paris: Dufour, Boulanger, et Legrand, 1863.

Guilhem de Clermont-Lodève, G.E.J., Baron de Saint-Croix.

Observations sur la traité de paix conclu à Paris le 10 février 1763 entre la France, l'Espagne, & l'Angleterre. Amsterdam: 1780.

Hale, Edward E. and Hale, Edward E., Jr. *Franklin in France.* 2 vols. Boston: Roberts Brothers, 1887–1888.

Hamilton, Earl J. *War and Prices in Spain, 1651–1800.* Cambridge, Mass.: Harvard University Press, 1947.

Hannay, David, ed. *Letters written by Sir Samuel Hood (Viscount Hood) in 1781-2-3.* London: Naval Records Society, 1895.

Hanotaux, Gabriel and Martineau, Alfred. *Histoire des colonies françaises et de l'expansion de la France dans le monde.* Vol. 1, *Amérique.* Paris: Plon, 1929.

*Harlow, Vincent T. *The Founding of the Second British Empire, 1763–1793.* 2 vols. London: Longmans, Green, and Co., 1952–1964.

Harper, Lawrence A. *The English Navigation Laws: A Seventeenth-Century Experiment in Social Engineering.* New York: Columbia University Press, 1939.

*Harris, Robert D. "Necker's *Compte Rendu* of 1781: A Reconsideration." *Journal of Modern History* 42 (1970): 161–183.

*Heckscher, Eli F. *Mercantilism.* Translated by Mendel Shapiro. 2 vols. London: George Allen and Unwin, 1955.

Henderson, W. O. "The Anglo-French Commercial Treaty of 1786." *Economic History Review* series 2, 10 (1957): 104–112.

Higginbotham, Don. "American Historians and the Military History of the American Revolution." *American Historical Review* 80 (1964): 18–34.

———. *The War of American Independence: Military Attitudes, Policies, and Practice, 1763–1789.* New York: Macmillan and Co., 1971.

Higham, Robin, ed. *Guide to the Sources of British Military History.* Berkeley and Los Angeles: University of California Press, 1971.

Hippeau, Célestin. *Le gouvernement de Normandie au XVIIe et au XVIIIe siècle.* Vols. 2–3. Caen: Goussiaume de Laporte, 1863–1869.

Hodges, H. W. and Hughes, E. A., eds. *Select Naval Documents.* Cambridge: At the University Press, 1922.

Hudson, Ruth. "The Strasbourg School of Law and its Role in the French Intervention in the American Revolution." Ph.D. dissertation, Western Reserve University, 1946.

Huntley, Francis. "Trade of the Thirteen Colonies with the Foreign Caribbean Area." Ph.D. dissertation, University of California, Berkeley, 1949.

Institut Français de Washington. *Correspondence of General Washington and Comte de Grasse*. Washington: Government Printing Office, 1931.

Irvine, Dallas. "The Newfoundland Fisheries: A French Objective in the War of American Independence." *Canadian Historical Review* 13 (1932): 268–285.

Isambert, François André. *Recueil général des anciennes lois françaises, depuis l'an 420 jusqu'à la révolution de 1789*. Vols. 23–26. Paris: Plon frères, 1821–1833.

Jal, A. *Glossaire nautique répertoire polyglotte de termes de marine anciens et modernes*. Paris: Firmin-Didot frères, 1846.

*James, William Milburne. *The British Navy in Adversity*. London: Longmans, Green, and Co., 1926.

Jameson, J. Franklin. "St. Eustatius in the American Revolution." *American Historical Review* 8 (1903): 683–703.

Johnston, Ruth Y. "American Privateers in French Ports." *Pennsylvania Magazine of History* 53 (1929): 352–374.

Kapp, Friedrich. *Leben des amerikanischen Generals Johann Kalb*. Stuttgart: Gottaschen Verlag, 1862.

*Killion, Howard Ray. "The Suffren Expedition: French Operations in India during the War of American Independence." Ph.D. dissertation, Duke University, 1972.

Kite, Elizabeth, *Beaumarchais and the War of American Independence*. Boston: Richard G. Badger, 1918.

Koebner, Richard. *Empire*. New York: Cambridge University Press, 1961.

Konetze, Richard. *Die Politik des Grafen Aranda*. Berlin: Emil Ebering, 1929.

Krämer, F.J.L., ed. *Archives, ou correspondance inédite de la maison d'Orange-Nassau*. 5th series, 1766–1789. 3 vols. Leyden: A. W. Sijthoff, 1910–1915.

Labrousse, C. E. *La crise de l'économie française à la fin de l'ancien régime et au debut de la révolution*. Vol. 1. Paris: Presses Universitaires de France, 1944.

Lacour, Auguste. *Histoire de la Guadeloupe.* Vol. 1, *1635–1789.* Basse-Terre, Guadeloupe: 1855.

Lacour-Gayet, Georges. *La marine militaire de la France sous le règne de Louis XV.* 2d ed., rev. Paris: H. Champion, 1910.

*———. *La marine militaire de la France sous le règne de Louis XVI.* Paris: H. Champion, 1905.

Lacour-Gayet, Jacques, ed. *Histoire du commerce.* Vol. 4, *Le commerce du XVe siècle au milieu du XIXe siècle.* Paris: Editions SPID, 1951.

Lafon, Roger. *Beaumarchais, le brillant armateur.* Paris: Société d'éditions géographiques, maritimes, et coloniales, 1928.

La Morandière, Charles de. *Histoire de la pêche française de la morue dans l'Amérique Septentrionale.* 2 vols. Paris: G. P. Maisonneuve et Larose, 1962.

Lancaster, Bruce. *The American Heritage Book of the Revolution.* New York: American Heritage Publishing Co., 1958.

La Roncière, Charles de. *Catalogue général des manuscrits des bibliothèques publiques de France. Bibliothèques de la Marine.* Paris: Plon, Nourrit et cie, 1907, with supplement in 1924.

*La Roncière, Charles de and Clerc-Rampal, G. *Histoire de la Marine.* Paris: Larousse, 1934.

Larrabee, Harold A. *Decision at the Chesapeake.* New York: Clarkson N. Potter, 1964.

Laughton, Sir John Knox, ed. *Letters and Papers of Charles, Lord Barham, Admiral of the Red Squadron, 1758–1813.* Vols. 1–2. London: Naval Records Society, 1907–1910.

Lavisse, Ernest, ed. *Histoire de France depuis les origines jusqu'à la Révolution.* Vol. 9, part 1, *Le règne de Louis XVI (1774–1789)* by H. Carré, P. Sagnac, and E. Lavisse. Paris: Hachette et cie, 1910.

Lawrence, Alexander A. *Storm over Savannah: The Story of Count d'Estaing and the Siege of the Town in 1779.* Athens, Ga.: University of Georgia Press, 1951.

Leclère, Micheline. *Les réformes de Castries, 14 octobre 1780–23 août 1787.* Blois: J. de Grandpré et cie, 1937.

*Le Conte, Pierre. *Répertoire des navires de guerre français.* Cherbourg: La Villarion, 1932.

*Legg, L. G. Wickham, ed. *British Diplomatic Instructions, 1689–1789.* Vol. 7, *France, Part IV, 1745–1789.* London: Royal Historical Society, 1934.

Bibliography

Le Goff, T.J.A. and Meyer, Jean. "Les constructions navales en France pendant la second moitie du XVIIIᵉ siècle." *Annales: Economies-Sociétés-Civilisations* 26 (1971): 173–185.

*Legohérel, Henri. *Les trésoriers généraux de la marine (1517–1788)*. Paris: Cujas, 1963.

Le Hénaff, Armand. *Etude sur l'organisation administrative de la marine sous l'ancien régime et la révolution*. Paris: L. Larose et L. Tenin, 1913.

Leland, Waldo G. *Guide to the Materials for American History in the Libraries and Archives of Paris*. Vol. 1, *Libraries*; Vol. 2, *Archives of the Ministry of Foreign Affairs*; Vol. 3, *Marine*. Washington: Carnegie Institute, 1932–1943; Unpublished manuscript (Vol. 3) in inventory room of French National Archives.

Lepotier, Adolphe-Auguste-Marie. *Brest, port océane*. Paris: Editions France-Empire, 1968.

———. *L'orient, port des Indes*. Paris: Editions France-Empire, 1970.

———. *Toulon, port du Levant*. Paris: Editions France-Empire, 1972.

Levasseur, Pierre Emile. *Histoire du commerce de la France*. Vol. 1, *Avant 1789*. Paris: Librairie nouvelle de droit et de jurisprudence, 1911.

Levot, P. *Histoire de la ville et du port de Brest*. Vol. 2, *Le port depuis 1681*. Paris: Bachelin-Deflorenne, 1866.

Lewis, W. S., ed. *Horace Walpole's Correspondence*. 36 vols. to date. New Haven, Conn.: Yale University Press, 1937–   .

*Loir, Maurice. *La Marine royale en 1789*. Paris: Armand Colin et cᶦᵉ, 1892.

Lokke, Carl Ludwig. *France and the Colonial Question: A Study of Contemporary French Opinion, 1763–1801*. Studies in History, Economics, and Public Law Edited by the Faculty of Political Science of Columbia University. New York: Columbia University Press, 1932.

Loménie, Louis de. *Beaumarchais et son temps*. 2 vols. Paris: Michel Lévy frères, 1873.

*Mackesy, Piers. *The War for America, 1775–1783*. Cambridge, Mass.: Harvard University Press, 1964.

*Madariaga, Isabel de. *Britain, Russia, and the Armed Neutrality of 1780: Sir James Harris's Mission to St. Petersburg during* *the American Revolution.* New Haven: Yale University Press, 1962.

*———. "The Secret Austro-Russian Treaty of 1781." *Slavonic and East European Review* 38 (1959): 114–145.

Magnette, F. *Joseph II et la liberté de l'Escaut: La France et l'Europe.* Brussels: Hayez, 1897.

*Mahan, Alfred Thayer. *The Influence of Sea Power upon History, 1660–1783.* 1890. Reprint. New York: Sagamore Press, 1957.

———. *Sea Power in its Relations to the War of 1812.* London: Sampson Law, Marston, and Co., 1905.

Malouet, Pierre-Victor, baron. *Collection des mémoires et correspondances officielles sur l'administration des colonies.* 5 vols. Paris: Baudouin, an X. (1802).

———. *Collection des opinions de M. Malouet, député à l'Assemblée nationale.* Paris: Valade, 1791.

———. *Mémoires et Malouet, publiés par son petit-fils, le baron Malouet,* Paris: E. Plon et c^ie, 1874.

———. *Mémoires de M. Malouet, intendant de la Marine, sur l'administration de ce département.* N.p., 1789.

Malvezin, Théophile. *Histoire du commerce de Bordeaux, depuis les origines jusqu'à nos jours.* Vol. 3. Bordeaux: A. Bellier et c^ie, 1892.

Mandrou, Robert. *La France aux XVIIe et XVIIIe siècles.* Paris: Presses Universitaires de France, 1970.

Marcus, G. J. *A Naval History of England.* Vol. 1, *The Formative Centuries.* Boston: Little, Brown, and Co., 1961.

Marion, Marcel. *Histoire financière de la France depuis 1715.* Vol. 1, *1715–1789.* Paris: Librairie nouvelle de droit et de jurisprudence, 1914.

Marsan, Jules. *Beaumarchais et les affaires d'Amérique: Lettres inédits.* Paris: Edouard Champion, 1919.

Marshall, Peter. "The First and Second British Empires: A Question of Demarcation." *History* no. 165 (1964): 13–23.

Martin, Gaston. "Commercial Relations between Nantes and the American Colonies." *Journal of Economic and Business History* 4 (1932): 812–829.

———. *Histoire de l'esclavage dans les colonies françaises.* Paris: Presses Universitaires de France, 1948.

Martin, Gaston. *Nantes au XVIIIe siècle.* Vol. 2, *L'ère des négriers (1714-1774).* Paris: Félix Alcan, 1928.

Martin-Allanic, Jean-Etienne. *Bougainville, navigateur, et les découvertes de son temps.* 2 vols. Paris: Presses Universitaires de France, 1964.

Martineau, Alfred. *Bibliographie d'histoire coloniale, 1900-1930.* Société de l'histoire des colonies françaises, 1932.

Martineau, Alfred and May, Louis-Philippe. *Trois siècles d'histoire antillaise: Martinique et Guadeloupe, de 1635 à nos jours.* Paris: Société de l'histoire des colonies françaises, 1935.

Masson, Paul. *Histoire du commerce français dans le Levant au XVIIIe siècle.* Paris: Hachette et c^ie, 1911.

Mathon de La Cour, Charles-Joseph. *Collection des comptes-rendus, pièces authentiques, états et tableaux, concernant les finances de France depuis 1758 jusqu'en 1787.* Lausanne: Cuchet et Gattey, 1788.

Maureer, M. "Coppered Bottoms for the Royal Navy: A Factor in the Maritime War of 1778-1783." *Military Affairs* 14 (1950): 57-61.

May, Louis-Philippe. *Histoire économique de la Martinique (1635-1763).* Paris: Marcel Rivière, 1930.

McCary, B. C. *The Causes of the French Intervention in the American Revolution.* Toulouse: Edouard Privat, 1928.

McGuffie, T. H. *The Siege of Gibraltar, 1779-1783.* London: B. T. Batsford, 1965.

McPherson, David. *Annals of Commerce, Manufactures, Fisheries, and Navigation, with Brief Notices of the Arts and Sciences connected with Them.* Vols. 3-4. London: Nichols and Son, etc., 1805.

Meng, John Joseph. "The Comte de Vergennes: European Phases of his American Diplomacy (1774-1780)." Ph.D. dissertation, Catholic University, 1932.

*Meng, John Joseph, ed. *Conrad Alexandre Gérard: Despatches and Instructions.* Baltimore: Johns Hopkins University Press, 1935.

Mention, Léon. *Le Comte de Saint-Germain et ses réformes.* Paris: L. Baudoin et c^ie, 1884.

Metra, Louis-François. *Correspondance secrète, politique, & littéraire, ou mémoires pour servir à l'histoire des cours, des sociétés, et de la littérature en France, depuis la mort de Louis XV.* 18 vols. London: John Adamson, 1787.

Miller, Daniel A. *Sir Joseph Yorke and Anglo-Dutch Relations, 1774–1780.* The Hague: Mouton, 1970.

*Miller, Nathan. *Sea of Glory: The Continental Navy Fights For Independence, 1775–1783.* New York: David McKay, 1974.

Mitchell, B. R. *Abstract of British Historical Statistics.* Cambridge: At the University Press, 1962.

*Montbarey, Alexandre-Marie-Léonor de Saint-Mauris, prince de. *Mémoires autographes de M. le prince de Montbarey.* 3 vols. Paris: Alexis Eymery, 1826–1827.

Morales Padron, Francisco. *Spanish Help in American Independence.* Madrid: Publicaciones Españolas, 1952.

*Morison, Samuel Eliot. *John Paul Jones: A Sailor's Biography.* Boston: Little, Brown, and Co., 1959.

Morris, Richard B. *The American Revolution Reconsidered.* New York: Harper and Row, Harper Torchbooks, 1967.

*Morris, Richard B., ed. *The Era of the American Revolution.* New York: Columbia University Press, 1939.

*Morris, Richard B. *The Peacemakers: The Great Powers and American Independence.* New York: Harper and Row, Harper Torchbooks, 1965.

Morton, Brian N. *Beaumarchais Correspondance.* 3 vols. to date. Paris: A. G. Nizet, 1969– .

Murphy, Orville T. "The Battle of Germantown and the Franco-American Alliance of 1778." *The Pennsylvania Magazine of History* 82 (1958): 55–64.

*———. "Charles Gravier de Vergennes: Portrait of an Old Régime Diplomat." *Political Science Quarterly* 83 (1968): 400–418.

———. "The Comte de Vergennes, the Newfoundland Fisheries, and the Peace Negotiations of 1783: A Reappraisal." *Canadian Historical Review* 46 (1965): 32–46.

———. "Dupont de Nemours and the Anglo-French Commercial Treaty of 1786." *Economic History Review* series 2, 19 (1966): 569–580.

———. "The French Professional Soldier's Opinion of the American Militia in the War of the Revolution." *Military Affairs* 32 (1969): 191–198.

Namier, Sir Lewis. *England in the Age of the American Revolution.* London: Macmillan and Co., 1961.

Nebenzahl, Kenneth, ed. *Atlas of the American Revolution.* Chicago: Rand McNally & Co., 1974.

Necker, Jacques. *Compte rendu au roi par M. Necker, directeur général des finances, au mois de Janvier 1781.* Lausanne: J. P. Haubach, 1786.

———. *De l'administration des finances de la France.* Vol. 2. Paris: 1784.

Neeser, Robert Walden, ed. *Letters and Papers Relating to the Cruises of Gustavus Conyngham, a Captain of the Continental Navy, 1777–1779.* New York: Naval History Society, 1915.

Nemours, Alfred. *Haiti et la guerre de l'indépendance américaine.* Port-au-Prince, Haiti: Henry Deschamps, 1950.

*Neuville, Didier. *Etat sommaire des archives de la Marine antérieures à la Révolution.* Paris: L. Baudoin, 1898.

Neuville, Didier; Buche, Henri; and Mallon, Jean, eds. *Inventaire des archives de la Marine. Série B. Service général.* 8 vols. to date. Paris: L. Baudoin, Imprimerie Nationale, 1885– .

*Nicolson, Sir Harold. *The Evolution of Diplomatic Method.* London: Constable and Co., 1954.

*Noailles, Amblard-Marie-Raymond-Amédée, vicomte de. *Marins et soldats français en Amérique pendant la guerre de l'indépendance des Etats-Unis (1778–1783).* Paris: Perrin et cⁱᵉ, 1903.

Norris, John M. *Shelburne and Reform.* London: Macmillan and Co., 1963.

Nouvelle biographie générale, depuis les temps les plus reculés jusqu'à nos jours. 46 vols. Paris: Firmin-Didot frères, 1862–1877.

O'Donnell, William Emmett. *The Chevalier de la Luzerne, French Minister to the United States, 1779–1784.* Louvain: Bibliothèque de l'Université, 1938.

Ogg, David. *Europe of the Ancien Régime, 1715–1783.* New York: Harper and Row, 1965.

Oursel, Paul. *La diplomatie de la France sous Louis XVI: Succession de Bavière et Paix de Teschen.* Paris: Plon, Nourrit et cⁱᵉ, 1921.

Ozanam, Denise. *Claude Baudard de Sainte-James, Trésorier général de la marine et brasseur d'affaires (1738–1787).* Geneva: Droz, 1969.

Padover, Saul K. *The Life and Death of Louis XVI.* New York: D. Appleton-Century Co., 1939.

Pares, Richard. *War and Trade in the West Indies, 1739-1763.* New York: Barnes and Noble, 1936.

*————. *Yankees and Creoles: The Trade between North America and the West Indies before the American Revolution.* Cambridge, Mass.: Harvard University Press, 1956.

Pariset, François-George, ed. *Bordeaux au XVIIIe siècle.* Bordeaux: Fédération historique du Sud-Ouest, 1968.

*Patterson, A. Temple. *The Other Armada: The Franco-Spanish Attempt to Invade Britain in 1779.* Manchester: Manchester University Press, 1960.

Paullin, Charles Oscar. *Diplomatic Negotiations of American Naval Officers.* Baltimore: Johns Hopkins University Press, 1912.

————. *The Navy of the American Revolution: Its Administration, its Policy, and its Achievements.* Chicago: The Burrows Brothers, 1906.

Paullin, Charles Oscar, ed. *Outletters of the Continental Marine Committee and Board of Admiralty, August 1776–September 1780.* 2 vols. New York: Naval History Society, 1914.

Perkins, James Breck. *France in the American Revolution.* Boston: Houghton Mifflin Co., 1911.

Pernoud, Régine. *La campagne des Indes: Lettres inédits du Bailli de Suffren.* Mantes: Imprimerie du "Petit Mantais," 1941.

*Perugia, Paul del. *La tentative d'invasion de l'Angleterre de 1779.* Paris: Félix Alcan, Presses Universitaires de France, 1939.

Petrie, Sir Charles. *King Charles III of Spain: An Enlightened Despot.* London: Constable and Co., 1971.

Pitman, Frank Wesley. *The Development of the British West Indies, 1700–1763.* New Haven, Conn.: Yale University Press, 1917.

Pohler, Johann. *Bibliotheca historico-militaris.* Vol. 3. Cassel: F. Kessler, 1895.

Postlethwayt, Malachy, *The Universal Dictionary of Trade and Commerce.* 2 vols. London: S. Strahan, 1774.

*Potter, E. B., ed. *Sea Power: A Naval History.* Englewood Cliffs, N.J.: Prentice-Hall, 1960.

Préclin, Edmond and Tapié, Victor L. *Le XVIIIe siècle.* 2 vols. Paris: Presses Universitaires de France, 1952.

Priestly, Herbert Ingram. *France Overseas through the Old Régime: A Study of European Expansion.* New York: D. Appleton-Century Co., 1939.

Rambert, Gaston, ed. *Histoire du commerce du Marseille.* Vols. 4–7. Paris: Plon, 1954–1966.

Ramsay, G. D. *English Overseas Trade during the Centuries of Emergence: Studies in Some Modern Origins of the English-Speaking World.* London: Macmillan and Co., 1957.

Ramsey, J. F. "Anglo-French Relations, 1763–1770: A Study of Choiseul's Foreign Policy." Ph.D. dissertation, University of California, Berkeley, 1935.

Rashed, Zenab Esmat. *The Peace of Paris, 1763.* Liverpool: At the University Press, 1951.

Raynal, Guillaume-Thomas-François, abbé. *A Philosophical and Political History of the Settlements and Trade of the Europeans in the East and West Indies.* Translated by J. O. Justamond. 8 vols. London: A. Strahan and T. Cadell, 1788.

*Renaut, Francis P. *Le crépuscule d'une puissance navale: La marine hollandaise de 1776 à 1783.* Paris: Graouli, 1932.

———. *L'espionnage naval au XVIIIe siècle: Le "secret service" de l'Amirauté brittanique au temps de la guerre d'Amérique.* Paris: Graouli, 1936.

———. *Le pacte de famille et l'Amérique: La politique coloniale franco-espagnole de 1760 à 1792.* Paris: Leroux, 1922.

———. *Les Provinces-Unies et la guerre d'Amérique (1775–1784): De la neutralité à la belligérance (1775–1780).* Paris: Graouli, 1936.

Reussner, André. *L'Hygiène navale à la fin du XVIIIe siècle.* Paris: Leroux, 1931.

Reynolds, Clark G. *Command of the Sea: The History and Strategies of Maritime Empires.* New York: William Morrow & Co., 1974.

Rice, Howard C. and Brown, Anne S. K., eds. *The American Campaigns of Rochambeau's Army, 1780, 1781, 1782, 1783.* 2 vols. Princeton, N.J. and Providence, R.I.: Princeton University Press and Brown University Press, 1972.

Richmond, Sir Herbert W. *The Navy in India, 1763–1783.* London: Ernest Benn, 1931.

———. *Statesmen and Seapower.* Oxford: Clarendon Press, 1947.

Robson, Eric. *The American Revolution in its Political and Military Aspects, 1763–1783.* London: Batchworth Press, 1955.

Rochambeau, Jean-Baptiste-Donatien de Vimeur, comte de. *Mémoires militaires, historiques, et politiques de Rochambeau, ancien maréchal de France.* Vol. 1. Paris: Fain, 1809.

Rodney, George. *Letter-books and Order-book of George, Lord Rodney, Admiral of the White Squadron, 1780–1782.* 2 vols. New York: Naval History Society, 1932.

*Romano, Ruggiero. "Documenti e prime considerazioni intorno alla 'balance du commerce' della Francia dal 1716 al 1780." *Studi in onore di Armando Sapori,* vol. 2, pp. 1266–1300. Milan: Instituto Editoriale Cisalpino, 1957.

*Rose, J. Holland; Newton, A. P.; and Benians, E. A., ed. *The Cambridge History of the British Empire.* Vol. 1, *The Old Empire from Its Beginnings to 1783.* Cambridge: At the University Press, 1929.

Rousseau, François. *Règne de Charles III d'Espagne (1759–1788).* Vol. 2. Paris: Plon, Nourrit et cie, 1907.

Roux, J. S. *Le Bailli de Suffren dans l'Inde.* Marseille: Barlatier-Feissat et Demonchy, 1862.

Rouzeau, L. "Aperçu du rôle de Nantes dans la guerre d'indépendance d'Amérique." *Annales de Bretagne* 74 (1967): 227–278.

Rush, N. Orwin. *Spain's Final Triumph over Great Britain in the Gulf of Mexico: The Battle of Pensacola, March 9 to May 8, 1781.* Tallahassee, Fla.: Florida State University Press, 1966.

Russell, Jack. *Gibraltar Besieged, 1779–1783.* London: William Heinemann, 1965.

Sagnac, Philippe. *La fin de l'ancien régime et la révolution américaine.* 3d edition, rev. Paris: Presses Universitaires de France, 1952.

*Sainte-Croix, Alexandre Lambert de. *Essai sur l'administration de la marine de France, 1689–1792.* Paris: Calmann-Lévy, 1892.

Saintoyant, J. *La colonisation française sous l'ancien régime.* Vol. 2, *Du traité d'Utrecht à 1789.* Paris: La renaissance du livre, 1929.

Salomon, Robert. *La politique orientale de Vergennes (1780–1784).* Paris: Les presses modernes, 1935.

Satineau, Maurice. *Histoire de la Guadeloupe sous l'ancien régime, 1635–1789.* Paris: Payot, 1928.

*Schelle, Gustave, ed. *Oeuvres de Turgot et documents le concernant*. Vol. 5. Paris: Félix Alcan, 1923.

Schöne, Lucien. *La politique coloniale de Louis XV et de Louis XVI*. Paris: Augustin Challamel, 1907.

Schumpeter, Elizabeth Boody. *English Overseas Trade Statistics, 1697–1808*. Oxford: Clarendon Press, 1960.

Scott, James Brown, ed. *The Armed Neutralities of 1780 and 1800: A Collection of Official Documents, preceded by the Views of Representative Publicists*. New York: Oxford University Press, 1918.

*Ségur, Louis-Philippe, comte de. *Mémoires; ou, Souvenirs et anecdotes*. 3 vols. Paris: A. Eymery, 1824–1826.

———. *Politique des tous les cabinets de l'Europe pendant les règnes de Louis XV et de Louis XVI*. Paris: F. Buisson, an IX (1801).

Ségur, Pierre-Marie-Maurice-Henri, marquis de. *Au couchant de la monarchie: Louis XVI et Turgot, 1774–1776*. 2 vols. Paris: Calmann-Lévy, 1910–1914.

———. *Le Maréchal de Ségur (1724–1801), ministre de la guerre sous Louis XVI*. Paris: E. Plon, Nourrit et cie, 1895.

Sen, S. P. *The French in India, 1763–1816*. Calcutta: K. L. Mukhopadhyay, 1958.

Sheffield, John Baker Holroyd, Lord. *Observations on the Commerce of the American States*. London: J. Debrett, 1784.

Sheldon, Laura. *France and the American Revolution, 1763–1778*. Ithaca, N.Y.: Andrus and Church, 1900.

Sherburne, John Henry. *The Life and Character of John Paul Jones, A Captain in the United States Navy during the Revolutionary War*. New York: Adriance, Sherman, and Co., 1851.

Smith, Adam. *An Inquiry into the Nature and Causes of the Wealth of Nations*. 1776. Reprint. New York: Modern Library, 1937.

Smith, Myron J. *Navies in the American Revolution: A Bibliography*. Metuchen, N.J.: Scarecrow Press, 1973.

Smyth, Albert Henry, ed. *The Writings of Benjamin Franklin*. Vols. 7–10. New York: The Macmillan Co., 1907.

*Sorel, Albert. *Europe and the French Revolution: The Political Traditions of the Old Régime*. Translated by Alfred Cobban and J. W. Hunt. Garden City, N.Y.: Doubleday and Co., Anchor Books, 1971.

Spinney, David. *Rodney*. London: George Allen and Unwin, 1969.

Steuart, A. Francis, ed. *The Last Journals of Horace Walpole during the Reign of George III from 1771 to 1783.* 2 vols. London: The Bodley Head, 1910.

*Stevens, Benjamin Franklin, ed. *Facsimiles of Manuscripts in European Archives relating to America, 1775–1783.* 25 vols. London: privately printed, 1889–1898.

*Stinchcombe, William C. *The American Revolution and the French Alliance.* Syracuse, N.Y.: Syracuse University Press, 1969.

Stourm, René. *Les finances de l'ancien régime et de la révolution.* 2 vols. Paris: Guillaumin et c^ie, 1885.

*Stourzh, Gerald. *Benjamin Franklin and American Foreign Policy.* Chicago: University of Chicago Press, 1954.

Surrey, N. M. (Miller), ed. *Calendar of Manuscripts in Paris Archives and Libraries Relating to the History of the Mississippi Valley to 1803.* 2 vols. Washington: Carnegie Institute, 1926–1928.

*Syrett, David. *Shipping and the American War, 1775–1783: A Study of British Transport Organization.* London: Athlone Press, 1970.

*Taillemite, Etienne. *Les archives anciennes de la Marine.* Paris: Académie de la Marine, 1961.

―――. *Dictionnaire de la Marine.* Paris: Seghers, 1962.

*Tarrade, Jean. *Le commerce colonial de la France à la fin de l'Ancien Régime: L'évolution du régime de "l'Exclusif" de 1763 à 1789.* 2 vols. Publications de l'Université de Poitiers, Faculté des Lettres et Sciences Humaines, no. 12. Paris: Presses Universitaires de France, 1972.

Taylor, George V. "Noncapitalist Wealth and the French Revolution." *American Historical Review* 72 (1967): 469–496.

*―――. "The Paris Bourse on the Eve of the Revolution, 1781–1789." *American Historical Review* 67 (1962): 951–977.

Temperly, Harold H. V. *Frederick the Great and Kaiser Joseph: An Episode of War & Diplomacy in the Eighteenth Century.* 1915. Reprint. London: Frank Cass and Co., 1968.

Thomas, Daniel H. and Case, Lynn M. *Guide to the Diplomatic Archives of Western Europe.* Philadelphia: University of Pennsylvania Press, 1959.

[Tickell, Richard.] *La cassette verte de Monsieur de Sartine, trouvée chez Mademoiselle du Thé.* The Hague: 1779.

Tocqueville, Alexis de. *The Old Régime and the French Revolution.* Translated by Stuart Gilbert. Garden City, N.Y.: Doubleday and Co., Anchor Books, 1955.

*Tramond, Joannès. *Manuel d'histoire maritime de la France des origines à 1815.* 2d edition. Paris: Société d'editions géographiques, maritimes, et coloniales, 1929.

————. "Les reformes de M. de Boynes." *La revue maritime* 61 (1925): 152–180.

Troude, O. *Batailles navales de la France.* Vol. 2. Paris: Challamel ainé, 1867.

Trudel, Marcel. *Louis XVI, le Congrès américaine, et le Canada, 1774–1789.* Quebec: Editions du Quartier Latin, 1949.

United States. Library of Congress. Division of Bibliography. *List of Works relating to the French Alliance in the American Revolution.* Compiled by Appleton Prentiss Clark Griffin. Washington: Government Printing Office, 1907.

United States. Library of Congress. Division of Manuscripts. *A Calendar of John Paul Jones Manuscripts in the Library of Congress.* Compiled by Charles Henry Lincoln. Washington: Government Printing Office, 1903.

————. *Naval Records of the American Revolution, 1775–1788.* Prepared by Charles Henry Lincoln. Washington: Government Printing Office, 1906.

United States. National Parks Service. Historical Division. *A Bibliography of the Virginia Campaign and Siege of Yorktown, 1781.* Yorktown: Colonial National Historical Park, 1941.

Usher, Roland G. "Royal Navy Impressment during the American Revolution." *Mississippi Valley Historical Review* 37 (1951): 673–688.

Valentine, Alan. *Lord George Germain.* Oxford: Clarendon Press, 1962.

*Van Alstyne, Richard W. *Empire and Independence: The International History of the American Revolution.* New York: John Wiley and Sons, 1965.

Van Powell, Nowland, painter. *The American Navies of the Revolutionary War.* New York: G. P. Putnam's Sons, 1974.

Van Tyne, Claude H. "French Aid before the Alliance of 1778." *American Historical Review* 31 (1925): 20–40.

*———. "Influences Which Determined the French Government to Make the Treaty with America, 1778." *American Historical Review* 21 (1916): 528–542.

Vicq-D'Azyr, Félix. *Eloge de M. le Comte de Vergennes, lu le 12 fevrier 1788, dans la séance publique de la Société royale de médicine.* Paris: Clousier, 1788.

*Viner, Jacob. "Power versus Plenty as Objectives of Foreign Policy in the Seventeenth and Eighteenth Centuries." *World Politics* 1 (1948): 1–30.

Viollet, Paul. *Le Roi et ses ministres pendant les trois derniers siècles de la monarchie.* Paris: L. Larose et L. Tenin, 1912.

Ward, Sir A. W. and Gooch, G. P., eds. *The Cambridge History of British Foreign Policy, 1783–1919.* Vol. 1, *1783–1815.* Cambridge: At the University Press, 1939.

Weber, Henry. *La compagnie française des Indes (1604–1875).* Paris: A. Rousseau, 1904.

*Wharton, Francis, ed. *The Revolutionary Diplomatic Correspondence of the United States.* 6 vols. Washington: Government Printing Office, 1889.

Whitridge, Arnold. *Rochambeau.* New York: Macmillan Co., 1965.

*Wickwire, Franklin and Wickwire, Mary. *Cornwallis: The American Adventure.* Boston: Houghton Mifflin Co., 1970.

*Willcox, William Bradford. *Portrait of a General: Sir Henry Clinton in the War of Independence.* New York: Alfred A. Knopf, 1964.

Witt, Cornélius-Henri de. *Thomas Jefferson and American Democracy.* Translated by R.S.H. Church. London: Longman, Green, Longman, Roberts, and Green, 1862.

Witte, Jehan, baron de. "L'abbé de Véri et son journal." *Revue d'histoire diplomatique* 39 (1925): 131–167, 263–301.

*———, ed. *Journal de l'Abbé de Véri.* 2 vols. Paris: Jules Tallandier, 1928–1930.

*Yela Utrilla, Juan F. *España ante la independencia de los Estados Unidos.* 2 vols. Lérida: Graficos Academia Mariana, 1925.

Zeller, Gaston. *Histoire des relations internationales.* Vol. 3, *Les temps modernes (Deuxième partie): Louis XIV à 1789.* Paris: Hachette, 1955.

INDEX

Adams, John, 274, 277n, 326–329

Africa, 19, 143, 302, 313; military operations in, 125, 159

Aiguillon, Duke d', 7

Almodóvar, Marquis de, 114, 127–128, 141–142, 147–148, 150

American independence: as article of Convention of Aranjuez, 142–143; commercial effects of, 341; French interest in, 11, 44, 93, 114, 118, 327; as peace condition, 93; as part of peace negotiations, 312, 325–329; recognition by Britain, 289–290

American trade: British dependence on, 37–44; French interest in, 37–38; place in British Empire, 40

American trade with Britain, volume of, 39, 341

American war, cost to France of, 350

Aranda, Count de, 34, 61, 70, 94, 100, 263; character, 332; relations with Floridablanca, 396; proposes invasion of Ireland, 34n; proposes expansion of British expeditionary force, 150; proposes expedition be shifted to Cornwall, 156; and Rodney's relief of Gibraltar, 171–174; proposes renewing attack on Britain, 203–204; and relief of Gibraltar in 1781, 223; comments on visit of Artois, 281; and peace negotiations, 292, 294, 314–316, 319–320, 322–324, 331–332;

becomes chief minister of Spain, 332

Aranjuez, Convention of, 142–143

Arbuthnot, Admiral, 191, 244

Arcon, Chevalier d', 269–270, 278, 307–308

Army, American, 41, 90, 106, 191, 239–248, 329n

Army, British, 16–17, 56–57, 89–90, 106–107, 109, 189, 191, 246, 308

Army, Dutch, 231n

Army, French, 16, 148n, 152, 279–280, 350, 377

Artois, Count d', 280–281

Assembly of Notables, 343

Austria: alliance with France, 8–9, 165; and Bavarian succession, 96, 113, 126, 133, 141, 152; secret alliance with Russia, 215–216, 338; and Crimean crisis, 298–299, 310–312, 338

Austrian Netherlands, 8, 208

Bahamas: capture of, 299; in peace negotiations, 320, 322, 330–331

Balance of power, 8–10, 37, 152, 165

Barbados, attempts to capture, 188, 249

Barbary, Company of, 24

Barras, Count de, 222, 239–248

Barrington, Admiral, 278

Barrington, Lord, 129

Bavarian succession, 96, 113, 126, 133, 141, 152

Beaumarchais, Caron de, 31, 48, 65, 72, 88, 274

Beausset, Commodore, 182

Bellecombe, Major-General, 252

Library of Congress Cataloging in Publication Data

Dull, Jonathan R   1942-
  The French Navy and American independence.

  Bibliography: p.
  Includes index.
    1. United States—History—Revolution, 1775-1783—
French participation. 2. United States—History—Revolu-
tion, 1775-1783—Naval operations. 3. France—Foreign rela-
tions—1774-1793. I. Title.
E265.D8   973.3'2'4   75-2987
ISBN 0-691-06920-4

DATE			
FEB 2 8 1992			
DEC 1 3 1994			